CANADIAN CONTENT:
CULTURE AND THE QUEST FOR NATIONHOOD

'A national image must be created that will have such appeal as to make any image of a separatist group unattractive. Resources must be directed into such things as national flags, anthems, education, arts councils, broadcasting corporations, film boards.' Pierre Trudeau, making this declaration during the upswing of Québécois separatism in the mid-1960s, knew that nationhood is shaped by the desires, designs, and activities of people who have influence over systems of culture and communication. He was not the first person to justify state involvement for the sake of the nation, nor would he be the last. For over a century, nationalists have turned to the arts and mass media as a means of vesting a political construct with an inclusive and familial essence or, in other words, of turning a federation into a nation. Yet, whereas the intent to articulate and imprint a national sense of self has been constant, the essence of that vision has radically changed over time.

Canadian Content explores the ways in which nationhood has been defined and pursued through culture during the past century. As a framework for the study, Ryan Edwardson distinguishes between three moments of Canadianization: an Anglophilic nationalism supporting the arts and nationally mandated mass media in order to ensure that the colony-to-nation transition remained rooted within the British Empire; the 'new nationalist' idea of Canada as a sovereign Peaceable Kingdom to be achieved through a leftist, often grassroots, multi-brow culture in the mid-1960s and early 1970s; and, as of the late 1960s and continuing today, the government's effort to promote federal unity through direct investment in cultural activities and industries, resulting in the massive cultural bureaucracy now operating under the aegis of the Department of Canadian Heritage. Examining each phase in its turn, *Canadian Content* looks at Canada as a post-colonial process of not one but a series of nationhoods, each with its own valued but selective and tentative set of cultural criteria for orchestrating and implementing a national experience.

Exploring the relationship between culture and national identity, this study offers an idea of what it means to be Canadian and explains just how ongoing, adaptable, and problematic the pursuit of nationhood can be.

RYAN EDWARDSON holds a PhD from Queen's University.

Canadian Content

Culture and the Quest for Nationhood

RYAN EDWARDSON

UNIVERSITY OF TORONTO PRESS
Toronto Buffalo London

© University of Toronto Press Incorporated 2008
Toronto Buffalo London
www.utppublishing.com
Printed in Canada

ISBN 978-08020-9759-0 (cloth)
ISBN 978-08020-9519-0 (paper)

Printed on acid-free paper

Library and Archives Canada Cataloguing in Publication

Edwardson, Ryan, 1974–
    Canadian content: culture and the quest for nationhood / Ryan Edwardson.

Includes bibliographical references and index.
ISBN 978-0-8020-9759-0 (bound)
ISBN 978-0-8020-9519-0 (pbk.)

1. Canada – Cultural policy – History – 20th century.   2. Nationalism –
Canada – History – 20th century.   3. Cultural industries – Government policy –
Canada – History – 20th century.   4. Cultural industries – Canada – History –
20th century.   I. Title.

FC97.E9 2008   971.064   C2007-904638-X

University of Toronto Press acknowledges the financial assistance to its publishing program of the Canada Council for the Arts and the Ontario Arts Council.

University of Toronto Press acknowledges the financial support for its publishing activities of the Government of Canada through the Book Publishing
Industry Development Program (BPIDP).

This book has been published with the help of a grant from the Canadian Federation for the Humanities and Social Sciences, through the Aid to Scholarly Publications Programme, using funds provided by the Social Sciences and
Humanities Research Council of Canada.

Contents

Illustrations follow page 184

Acknowledgments

Thanks are owed to many people. First and foremost, I want to thank Ian McKay, whose tremendous insight as doctoral adviser, mentor, and friend made this project possible. Words are not available to express the depth of my appreciation. I also wish to thank Tim Smith, Harold Mah, Geoff Smith, Jeff McNairn, Elsbeth Heaman, and Yvonne Place for the guidance and insight they offered during my time in the Department of History at Queen's University. Further, much is owed to Mary Vipond of Concordia University for her support during my doctoral and postdoctoral endeavours.

Researching this book would have been impossible without the friendly assistance provided by archivists at Library and Archives Canada and the National Film Board of Canada. Jean Matheson at LAC helped arrange for the reproduction of a number of the photos published in this book. Robin Mathews was kind enough to provide access to his personal papers. Margaret Atwood gave a photo from her personal collection.

A tremendous debt of gratitude is owed to the University of Toronto Press. Len Husband showed unwavering support for the project from the first time we met. One could not ask for a better editor. I wish to thank the two anonymous readers who took the time to offer tremendously constructive feedback and suggestions. This book is better because of their efforts. Frances Mundy at UTP has helped bring this project to fruition. Elizabeth Hulse deftly copy-edited the text, and I thank her on the behalf of myself and the readers.

I gratefully acknowledge the economic support of Queen's University, Concordia University, and the Social Sciences and Humanities Research Council of Canada for doctoral and postdoctoral support.

The publishing of this book has been made possible in part by funding from the Aid to Scholarly Publications Programme.

On a personal note, I wish to extend tremendous thanks to the people who made my life enjoyable during my time at Queen's University: Ross Cameron, Will and Keely Speechley, Steve Noakes, Erin-Marie Legacey, Vivian Lee, Christian Leuprecht, Andrea Javor, Maren Larson, Gord Dueck, Stephen Cole, Neel Jethwa, Adrian Elliot, Keren Bromberg, and many others. Much is also owed to Jeff and Heather Wilson, Scott Wilson, Christina Dabrowski, Andre Dupuis, Mark Sampson, Sarah Morrison, Michelle Fleming, and Tanuki Speechley for love and laughter. I thank the Sleepless Goat Cafe for years of office space. Finally, thanks go to my family, especially my mother, Jenny Strachan, for her decades of unwavering support and constant encouragement. Thank you all.

CANADIAN CONTENT:
CULTURE AND THE QUEST FOR NATIONHOOD

Introduction: A Guide to Canadianization

If anyone came up to me and asked me for advice, I'd tell them to stay away
from the Canadian music business. It's full of politics and bureaucracy. It's
trouble. Don't sign to a Canadian company. Don't sign to a Canadian publisher. Go south of the border. You'll get a better deal ... I think it's a disgrace
and I think it's a shame that we have to deal with this kind of stupidity all the
time ... Fuck you! That's all I've got to say to those guys. Fuck you man!

Bryan Adams, musician[1]

Bryan Adams was pretty sure of his Canadianness. For the Canadian
Radio-television and Telecommunications Commission (CRTC) to tell
him otherwise, then, was a personal outrage. Technically, the CRTC
bureaucrats did no such thing; they only informed him that his 1991
album *Waking Up the Neighbours* – his biggest ever in a string of international hits – did not qualify under the regulation that required stations to broadcast a minimum 30 per cent Canadian content. With
credit for the lyrics, music, and production shared with British producer
Robert 'Mutt' Lange (who three years later married Shania Twain,
another of Canada's international music stars) and with much of it
recorded, mixed, and mastered in London and New York City, the
album used very little in the way of Canadian resources. Unfortunately
for the CRTC, Adams was one of the most well known and outspoken
figures in the Canadian music industry. He was an icon of Americana
rock, his hits including 'Summer of '69' and 'Cuts like a Knife.' As such,
Adams did not accept the commission's verdict without inciting a media
uproar, one that, not coincidently, acted as a wonderful publicity event
for the new album.

Spin doctors operated overtime as Adams and his supporters twisted the industry-based Canadian content assessment into a declaration of personal non-Canadianness. Regulatory issues were easily equated with those of identity by people who cared little about the difference. 'If you go to America or England, or almost any other country in the world, they don't have those kinds of stipulations on their artists,' Adams fumed. 'They're rewarded on the basis of their music, not government regulation. You would never hear Elton John declared un-British. You just wouldn't. It's a disgrace. The Canadian government should get out of the music business entirely.'[2] It was an easy attack which worked the media into a frenzy. The government had apparently abused its governance of culture.

Adams did not go unchallenged. An internationally famous musician critiquing a system that had aided him and many other struggling artists earlier in their careers? As Canadian Independent Record Production Association president Brian Chater plainly put it, 'Piss off, Bryan, obviously [the Canadian content regulation] has helped you.'[3] Adams had bit the hand that had fed him as a pup and sought to begrudge others the same assistance. *Billboard*'s Canadian correspondent and bureau chief Larry LeBlanc insightfully noted that stars such as Adams received the bulk of airplay at the expense of the smaller Canadian acts the regulations were designed to aid. In letting Adams's album count for the Canadian content quota, many other acts, including those without the weight of international stardom, would not have got airtime.[4] Even without *Waking Up the Neighbours*' hit track '(Everything I Do) I Do It For You' being declared Canadian content, the song could still be played nineteen times a week per station – almost three times a day, every day. Adams did not need inclusion under the Canadian content regulations in order to receive plenty of airplay.

In the end, the unleashed media flood proved too much for the CRTC, and in an act heavy with significance, the regulator acceded to Adams's complaints.[5] An additional 'point' in the Canadian content tabulation was awarded if both the lyrics and the music were by a Canadian in conjunction with a non-Canadian, a new rule made just retroactive enough to include the release date for *Waking Up the Neighbours*. Academics Bart Testa and Jim Shedden have argued that 'the episode revealed both that the protective scaffolding of Cancon had done its job and had become irrelevant. The musicians it had enabled were now stronger than the rules themselves.'[6] Yet, if anything, the opposite was true. Adams's outcry and the regulatory response revealed that Canadian musicians struggled not only against American music on the airwaves but also against the well-established – and often foreign-residing – Canadian acts no longer in need of the regulatory assistance. The reason for this situation was simple: state intervention into the music industry helped to ensure airplay for Canadian artists, an action taken in the name of nationhood, but market dynamics determined which musicians would dominate.

Canadianization and the Nationalist Imperative

Canadian Content: Culture and the Quest for Nationhood explores the changing ways in which Canadian nationhood has been defined and pursued through cultural means during the twentieth century. Significantly different and even ideologically opposed generations of intelligentsia, operating upon conceptions of national direction and culture prevalent at the time, identified and mobilized cultural outlets – the arts, publishing, broadcasting, film, and academia – for the sake of vesting a political construct with the feel of an inclusive familial entity or, in other words, of turning a federation into a nation. This process of Canadianization not only contributed to the imprinting of a sense of place but was essential to adapting the national project to challenges and changes, particularly the rise of mass media, shifts in ethnic demographics, the threat of American imperialism, an increasingly politicized Québécois nationalism, and an escalation in transnational economic and trade engagements. Out of it emerges a striking picture of how the Canadian 'imagined community' has been underwritten and shaped by select figures capable of influencing the cultural circumstances through which the imagining has taken place, reinventing (or reimagining) nationhood in accordance with the times, yet portraying it as axiomatic.[7]

Offered herein is a reconnaissance of the changing construction, constitution, and character of the Canadian national project, an exploration undertaken by conceptualizing Canadianization as a paradigm in which nation-builders tried to use culture to imprint a sense of nationhood.[8] The analysis reveals three predominant moments or phases in which nation-building intertwined with cultural activities in the minds, desires, and designs of individuals capable of shaping the tone and temper of nationhood: the 'Masseyism' that saw support for the arts and cultured mass-media content as a means of negotiating the colony-to-nation transition amidst the upheavals of modernity experienced in the first half of the century; the 'new nationalism' that sought to empower multi-brow cultural outlets and employ quotas, subsidies, and ownership regulations in the struggle against imperialism (mid-1960s to mid-1970s); and the 'cultural industrialism' advanced by Pierre Trudeau's Liberal government in 1968 (and continuing today under the leadership of the Department of Canadian Heritage), which radicalized the relationship between the state and culture for the sake of federalism. Looked at individually, these moments reveal how nation-builders identified and mobilized cultural devices in hopes of imprinting a sense of nationhood during periods of insecurity. Seen together, they expose changing conceptions of nation, culture, state involvement, and an ongoing post-colonial process of not one but a series of radically different nationhoods, each held fast in the minds and imaginations of its advocates only to give way to a new model tenuously tailored to the realities of maintaining a national project in a changing world.

Narratives tell of Canada coming of age and finding its true self, a fragile youth coming into adulthood among trials and tribulations (born at Confederation, coming of age at Vimy Ridge, establishing its independence from the 'mother' country during the Second World War, etc.), yet this simplification and even fictionalization says little about the country as a post-colonial national project, one that took shape with the confederation of four British North American colonies in 1867 and gradually integrated the others.[9] A global decline of empires spanning the nineteen and twentieth centuries and a desire among some to offload colonial expenses ushered in not only a new age of federations and states (which are political entities) but, and quite crucially, ideas of nationhood. As empires and colonies were restructured into countries and subjects were converted into citizens, populations became organized upon the idea that, as theorist Elie Kedourie describes it, 'humanity is naturally divided into nations, that nations are known by certain characteristics which can be ascertained, and that the only legitimate type of government is national self-government.'[10] Ernest Gellner, one of the most influential of modern theorists on topics of nationalism and national identity, has popularly argued that the process of 'inventing' nations offered opportunities for a select part of the population to consolidate positions of leadership and control by centralizing and streamlining political, economic, and social systems in accordance with its own interests.[11]

This colony-to-nation phenomenon was furthered in the early decades of the twentieth century by the First World War and by the formation of the League of Nations in 1919 as the 'custodian of a new world order' (an idea advanced with the creation of the United Nations in 1945).[12] Mobilizing the population for the war effort, maintaining resoluteness, and justifying the casualties all entailed an active employment of myths, symbols, and other identifiers valued for reifying a sense of nationhood. The power of national identifiers is evidenced in their ability to galvanize otherwise diverse and disparate people, from the willingness to sacrifice life in battle against citizens aligned with other nations to the collective rejoicing at something as immaterial as the victorious final seconds of an international hockey series. Identifiers are key to placing the citizenry within an ideological communalism in which class, capital, and social standing are overshadowed by compatriotism. That soldiers shedding blood on the battlefield come disproportionately from the lower economic strata while industrialists and others of the privileged class remain safe on the home front (and get to pocket wartime production monies) testifies to the strength of the familial bond of nationhood, even in the face of glaring class inequalities.

Identifiers are essential to the quest for nationhood, but in order to be effective, they must be adapted and updated over time in order to keep the national project in line with shifting demographics. As the 'two races' Dominion of Canada evolved into a multicultural Peaceable Kingdom and ethnic nationalism gave way to a civic equivalent, one finds the northern climate, once used to identify Canadians as 'racially' hardy members of the British Empire – and often used as an excuse for rejecting dark-skinned immigrants supposedly too fragile for the environment – being reworked into a signifier of the 'canoeable Canada,' a nation of camping, cottage country, and outdoors essentialized within all Canadians, no matter their ethnic lineage or urban lifestyle.[13]

The production and dissemination of identifiers, particularly as sought by nationalistic intelligentsia, has not been possible without state intervention because the systems of communication essential to Canadianization have also offered much to industrialists and profiteers. One has to look no further than the work of revered political economist Harold Innis to see how the same 'space-binding' media that allows for the formation of empires and states also opens up new opportunities for commercial interests seeking large audiences for the sale of goods.[14] And with the dynamics of the North American marketplace ensuring that domestic distributors had no need for domestic cultural content and the identifiers contained within, an inherent barrier was established between producer and consumer. Distributors in effect created profit-based blockades. The result, as historian Mary Vipond noted in *The Mass Media in Canada*, was an infrastructure 'largely Canadian-owned but filled with American content.'[15]

Two points need to be clarified before we proceed. First, there is a popular tendency, both within and outside academia, to speak of 'English-Canadian nationalism' and 'French-Canadian nationalism.' This book attempts to avoid the habit of linking nationalism with linguistic identifiers and lumping different nationalist movements together along these lines because this habit tends to prevent a more nuanced appreciation of the different character, content, and goals of nationalist movements and activities. Although moments of so-called English-Canadian nationalism have been articulated largely by English-speaking intellectuals, there have been significantly different ideas of nationhood (Vincent Massey and Maude Barlow present dissimilar and even opposing conceptions of the Canadian nation). As well, support has come from people of many linguistic groups, detractors have often involved fellow English-speakers, and the term 'English-Canadian nationalism' canceals the breadth of what have historically been attempts to imprint a pan-national project. Similarly, there have been different veins of French-Canadian nationalism, including variations of the Québécois separatism that arose to prominence in the early 1960s, and thus to place all the models under the same moniker disadvantageously blurs distinctions and ignores the fact that many self-identified French Canadians and Québécois disagreed with nationalist ideologies and activities labelled with their name.

Second, one commonly finds 'national identity' used interchangeably with 'national culture.' For the sake of clarity, this book uses 'national identity' to refer to the constructed and contested embodiment, repository, and/or representation of national essence. 'Identity' is an inclusive way of dealing with the complexities of character and personality assigned to the national construct. 'Culture,' on the other hand, is an evolving concept with changing definitions. Raymond Williams has famously noted that culture is 'one of the two or three most complicated words in the English language,' its meaning ranging from the process of tending to agriculture to the refinement of a class to both a synonym and an antonym for civilization.[16] In post-Confederation Canada, culture went from being associated with spiritualism and mental enlightenment to, by the end of the twentieth century, including almost any form of experience or interaction. 'National culture,' for the sake of clarity, will thus refer to activities and forms popularly identified as cultural within their time and place and, in addition, linked to the national construct and/or the citizens within it.

Masseyism

The first moment of Canadianization, one named after Vincent Massey, the high-profile cultural philanthropist, diplomat, and first Canadian-born governor general, had its roots during the first half of the twentieth century among discourses of post-colonialism and changes wrought by modernity. The colony-to-nation transition facilitated the emergence of an up-and-coming 'intelligentsia' of educated elites who possessed economic, political, and cultural capital. These figures were capable, in terms laid forth by Antonio Gramsci, of forming a tentative hegemonic class by combining 'the popular and democratic aspirations and struggles of people,' including the desire for nationhood, with 'its own class-interests so as to achieve national leadership.'[17] Competition was fierce, particularly between those who envisioned Canadian nationhood as resting within the British Empire and others who believed it to be situated within a North American continentalism, a conflict played out on a political level between the Conservative and Liberal parties.[18] Rival ideologies and positions of power meant that post-colonialism ended up taking shape as a 'third space,' as Homi Bhabha theorizes, one of overlap, compromise, and a functionality made feasible by a shared desire to turn a collection of former colonies into an essentialized nation.[19]

Nation-builders had a rough project with which to work. The Dominion of Canada, confederated in 1867 but taking years to include all the British North American colonies, was made up of an ideologically, ethnically, and geographically diverse population of multiple founding peoples, ethnic enclaves, and disparate regional identities. The peoples of Ontario and Quebec had very different origins and ideas about nationhood. Maritime populations were divided on joining Confederation, with many colonialists viewing their interests as lying to the east with Britain, not to the west in a federation likely to be dominated by the centre. British Columbia joined in 1871 only after bankruptcy and fears of American annexation left little choice. Manitoba was created out of disputed land (and over Louis Riel's dead body). Alberta and Saskatchewan did not even exist until 1905, at which time the federal government parcelled these two provinces out of sparsely populated territory purchased from the Hudson's Bay Company back in 1868. And Newfoundland did not enter Confederation until 1949, with many residents feeling betrayed at Joey Smallwood's success in achieving this union.

Canadian post-colonialism was all the more complex because it coincided with modernity, a rapid series of technological, scientific, and social changes occurring in the decades surrounding the turn of the twentieth century. New systems of mass communication, fuelled in large part by advertisers seeking markets for the goods of expanding manufacturing industries, provided Canadians with an abundance of advertising-funded entertainment drawn largely from (or inspired by) American producers. The consumerism that satisfied some Canadians, however, left others feeling concerned about the impact of the new entertainments and goods upon national life. Commercialization and commodification seemed to be eroding the liberal humanism, spiritual values, and public virtues deemed essential to national development.

The first few decades of the twentieth century were awash in calls from nationalistic culturists seeking highbrow Canadian content as a counterweight to the abundance of socially corrosive entertainments. Mass life led to barbarous homogenization; refinement led to social cohesion and prosperity. Under such cultural precepts, the nation was pledged to seek the summit, not abase itself in the gutter.[20] The colony-to-nation transition, particularly one in line with Canada's British inheritance, necessitated not only greater state patronage for the arts but, and quite crucially, checks and balances on the mass entertainments unleashed by modernity. Too much of Canadian society seemed under the influence of American pulp periodicals such as *True Confessions* and *Detective Stories Magazine*, radio programs of inferior quality (and layered with advertisements), and escapist Hollywood feature films promoting American lifestyles. Such threats to public – and thus national – morality could not be allowed in a time of sensitive colony-to-nation transition. Upon the shoulders of the learned and enlightened citizens fell the responsibility for ensuring that the masses were elevated above their instincts and to prevent their exploitation by savvy profiteers and money-makers, a task that in turn necessitated petitioning and pressuring the state to intervene in systems of communication. Canadian stability required no less than restrictions on pulp periodicals, a national broadcasting system capable of regulating the actions of the private sector and offering cultured Canadian content, and limitations on the availability of escapist Hollywood films, which, if the federal government was unwilling to counter, then it should at least encourage the start of a cultured national cinematic alternative.

The calls for intervention placed great demands upon a very apprehensive federal government. Outside a few concessions to the arts community, most notably the creation of the National Gallery of Canada, little had been done to involve the state – and taxpayer dollars – in areas of culture and mass entertainments. Greater patronage for the arts threatened to entangle bureaucrats in issues of censorship and criticism for their allocation of monetary resources. How would the public react to federal dollars going to the ballets and orchestras enjoyed by the elites while the common person struggled for his or her daily wage?

Nationalists were more successful in convincing the government that national stability required intervention in mass media. There was a general acceptance of the need to keep an eye on the broadcasting sector because airwaves are limited in quantity and the content has a tremendous ability to sway audiences, something the state witnessed (and participated in) first-hand in 1927 upon linking privately owned radio stations together to broadcast the Diamond Jubilee of Confederation celebrations. And with the Royal Commission on Radio Broadcasting (established in 1928) putting its weight behind the idea of a national broadcasting system, there was sufficient support for the federal government to establish the Canadian Radio Broadcasting Commission in 1932, followed by the Canadian Broadcasting Corporation in 1936. The request for restrictions on pulp periodicals was a bit trickier. The Liberal Party, viewing the periodical sector as aligned with Conservative Party interests, had no interest in supporting its critics, but following the success of R.B. Bennett in the 1930 election, a periodical tariff was introduced which served the interests of nationalists and some of the party's supporters in the publishing industry. This tariff, testifying to the tone and temper of the times, was based upon levels of advertising content as a means of restricting advertising-dense pulp magazines while leaving highbrow periodicals, a type that usually contained little in the way of advertisements, largely unaffected. Finally, although the federal government was unwilling (and jurisdictionally unable) to restrict the importation of American feature films, it did establish the National Film Board of Canada in 1939 to produce educational, industrial, informational, and documentary films, thereby offering nationalists an opportunity to canonize a cultured alternative to the films coming from Hollywood.

Bringing federal bureaucrats onside with greater funding for the arts took much longer to accomplish. Patrons, audiences, and the artists themselves continued to bear the expense of cultural activities, but as the talent increasingly became skilled and professionalized in the 1920s and 1930s, one finds the development of a culture economy that aided in the ability to turn a craft into an income. In fact, by mid-century the professionalized class of cultural workers had secured so much influence over the arts community that one finds their interests overshadowing and replacing earlier precepts that had identified the arts as an ennobling form of refinement to be enjoyed through recreation, leisure, and amateurism.

Yet even with an increasing number of artists and craftspeople organized within representative bodies capable of petitioning the state for greater patronage, the federal government proved resolute in holding onto its position. What culturists needed was an opportunity to convince federal bureaucrats of the importance of culture to national life and its worthiness of significant financial support. The timing seemed right in the immediate wake of the Second World War as bureaucrats began allocating funding for areas of reconstruction and planning, but the attempts to cast a spotlight upon the cultural agenda failed to capture sufficient attention. More and more it became clear that the path to arts funding rested in convincing the government to establish a commission dedicated to surveying the nation's learned and mass-media activities.

A combination of support for the cultural community among some influential civil servants, the growing popularity of the Co-operative Commonwealth Federation among the electorate, and the need to account for the state's ad hoc intervention in mass media helped to sway a very apprehensive Liberal government into forming a 'culture commission.' The Royal Commission on National Development in the Arts, Letters and Sciences of 1949 – the so-called Massey Commission, after its chairman, Vincent Massey – was a monumental opportunity for nationalistic culturists and intellectuals to articulate a national cultural blueprint. Herein lay an opportunity for the cultural community to come together in a commission of its own design, one empowered by an Anglophilic nationalism, a desire to replicate international cultural achievements within the Canadian context (other countries paradoxically offering a shovel for uncovering the distinct identity buried in the Canadian soil), and an upholding of the Dominion of Canada (with some continental concessions) as the national design.[21] The very nature of the commission allowed nationalists to entrench their cultural interests by aligning themselves with the like-minded Canadian Broadcasting Corporation and National Film Board of Canada while, in addition, substantiating the need for a federally funded yet arm's-length arts council (a goal eventually achieved in 1957 with the formation of the Canada

Council for the Arts). These nationally mandated bodies offered a tremendously important means of guiding the nation along cultured lines, serving the very ideological and economic interests of the cultural community to which they owed much of their existence.

The Masseyites managed to achieve a commission in line with their national design and cultural weltanschauung, but even with the use of mass outlets to provide a cultured middle ground, the paradigm was inherently limited by its attempt to popularize a non-populist ideology through content unpalatable to many audiences. At most, an elitist cultural nationalism could present cultured content alongside mass options and hope that Canadians would naturally gravitate towards the refined alternatives. This was not to be, particularly as a 1950s continental economic boon made mass entertainments more available and acceptable, if not normative, than ever before. Canadians were embracing what historian Paul Rutherford has called a 'mass affluence' of 'money, security, leisure, and freedom sufficient to enjoy North American abundance.'[22] Many Canadians, particularly those who were part of the new 'teenager' phenomenon, were for the most part quite happy to consume the television shows, popular novels, blockbuster films, and modern music offered in great quantity by the distributors, exhibitors, and retailers.

The copious amounts of mass entertainment in the 1950s, much of it American in origin, satisfied consumers but left many people in the domestic entertainment industries frustrated at the flow of dollars to their competition. This situation was not new, as for decades the industries had fought for access to audiences. Now, however, with the economic worth of the industries reaching new highs, the private sector seemed to stand a good chance of convincing the government that the benefits of a strong commercial sector far outweighed any drawbacks to intervention. What followed was an amazing change in the entertainment sector, one that radically curtailed the influence of the Masseyites and helped to lay the foundation for a second wave of Canadianization in reaction to the abundance of foreign cultural content. Between 1959 and 1966, a period that began only two years after the Masseyites finally succeeded in pressuring the government to create the Canada Council for the Arts, several mass-media industries successfully pressured the state into altering the marketplace. Privately owned television broadcasters, led by the Canadian Association of Broadcasters, received freedom from CBC governance as of 1959 and opportunities to compete directly against both the CBC and over-the-border American broadcasting signals in major city markets (areas that had previously been held exclusively by the CBC). The federal government agreed that there was something to be said for allowing audiences to receive more American programming from Canadian stations as a means of keeping advertising dollars in Canada (and in the pockets of broadcasters) instead of losing them to American stations within signal range of Canadian television sets. In exchange for the creation of these new 'second stations' operating outside the CBC's national network, however, all broadcasters as of 1961 would have to abide by Canadian content regulations and a quota system requiring a minimum amount of domestic programming, to be determined by the use of industrial resources.

It was also in 1959 that the Association of Motion Picture Producers and Laboratories of Canada, representing the interests of many people in the film industry, petitioned the federal government for a quota system in Canadian theatres and an end to the National Film Board's monopoly on government contracts. Opportunities for the feature-film industry, the association argued, would increase the contribution it made to the economy. Although the federal government rejected the demands put forth by the AMPPLC, the petition helped to prompt a greater look at the economic potential of the industry and led a few years later to the creation of the Canadian Film Development Corporation as a means of investing in the production side of the industry.

Finally, the third successful push for intervention came from the periodical sector which, backed by the report of the Royal Commission on Publications in 1961, asked the government to change the income tax act so that advertisers could claim a deduction for domestically focused advertising only if the space was purchased in a Canadian magazine. That way, as in the television sector, advertisers would be encouraged to use domestic periodicals instead of the popular American alternatives. Prime Minister Lester B. Pearson agreed that the idea offered significant economic gains to Canada, but his government, in introducing the Paperback and Periodical Distributors Act in 1964 in order to bring about this alteration, exempted *Time* and *Reader's Digest*, the two dominant foreign periodicals, as a result of pressure from the United States.[23] The contribution of periodicals did not, in the view of the Pearson administration, outweigh that of cross-border trade (particularly on the eve of the ratification of the Auto Pact) and the need to improve relations with the United States after tense years between John Diefenbaker and John F. Kennedy.

What the Masseyites had offered in terms of national cultivation, money-makers topped by promising the state a windfall of tangible economic gains. The new initiatives did not satisfy everyone in the private sector, however, including producers who continued to be shut out by distributors and exhibitors more interested in imports than domestic goods. Many people felt that their goods made an important contribution to domestic expression and that, despite the advertisements which often came in tow, the content was essential to the development of a national project. To have distributors and exhibitors fail to offer opportunities for producers to engage with audiences, then, frustrated those Canadians who were increasingly distressed the lack of domestic discourse. Looking around, one could not help but feel inundated with a profusion of not only foreign entertainments but undue influence on daily life and even a sense of subjugation. Canada was on the brink of a new nationalist movement, one with strong ideological ties to the new age of popular culture and attuned to the middle-class, middlebrow, middle-of-the-road interests and ideas of its protagonists, both the cultural assumptions of the Masseyites and the recent inroads made by profiteers were about to be challenged by a wave of intelligentsia articulating a new national design, proposing new ways of conceptualizing culture, and offering a plan for reclaiming national sovereignty.

The New Nationalism

The abundance of new homes, modern technologies, and leisure time enjoyed by Canadians during the 1950s owed much to American investment. Although revelling in the economic benefits of continentalism as the 1950s folded into the 1960s, some Canadians began to feel that the massive influx of foreign monies might have brought with it unforeseen problems. Prosperity had come about in large part by allowing the business sector, backed by a continentalist-minded federal government seeking foreign investment, to open key industries and natural resources to American corporations. This economic dominance interwove with the profusion of foreign cultural and entertainment goods in pressing upon many Canadians a sense of vulnerability to the United States, one made all the more worrisome given the crumbling of John F. Kennedy's Camelot among internal civil protests and external militarism.

In the mid-1960s one finds a bevy of economists, political scientists, authors, filmmakers, artists, publishers, and academics, to name merely a few of the professions, taking a leading role in warning Canadians that continentalism had led the nation into a position of vulnerability. The short list includes Walter Gordon, Melville Watkins, Abraham Rotstein, James Laxer, Jack McClelland, Mel Hurtig, Peter C. Newman, Margaret Atwood, and Robin Mathews, but this is only a small sample. The new nationalist intelligentsia did not have to work hard for an audience in the years leading up to and in the wake of the 1967 Centennial celebrations and Expo 67; this was a period of national reification as state-funded events helped Canadians to celebrate their existence and the international community placed Canada in the spotlight on the world stage. There was no shortage of people willing to engage in issues of identity and nationhood, including a university-age baby-boom generation that contributed much to the passions and many going so far as to mobilize grassroots movements, rallies, and political events in the face of American imperialism at home and abroad.

Canadians were reimagining the 'imagined community' into a Peaceable Kingdom, a socialist-leaning nation of equality, multiculturalism, peacekeeping, and a social-welfare safety net directed to ensuring that all Canadians could benefit from the nation's wealth. This was not only nation-building but nation-reclaiming; turning inwards offered a means of consolidating nationhood in a time of American imperialism. There was popular support for rolling back foreign investment in favour of domestic ownership and Crown corporations, particularly in areas linked to national stability, and the placing of public interests above those of capital gains, even if doing so meant a decline in the standard of living. The Peaceable Kingdom was a project that spoke loudly not only of the leftist leanings of these intelligentsia and the influence held by the expanding middle class but also of new immigration patterns that required facilitating a shift in national design from ethnic to civic nationalism. Pre-existing models for nationhood were incompatible with the needs and interests of this new intelligentsia. Obsolete was the Masseyites' view of Canada as a 'two races' nation built upon its British inheritance; of great threat was the continentalism that the Liberal Party seemingly had in store for the nation. An alternative project was being articulated and orchestrated by those in a position to do so.

Canadians had to act immediately, in the nationalist parlance of the time, to reverse the slide into the American empire. Political devices – particularly the New Democratic Party and, for the more socialist of its members, a 'Waffle' splinter wing – were deemed essential to reclaiming national sovereignty, of course, but it was in cultural expression that nationalists identified the means of ideologically liberating a nation indoctrinated by foreign content. As influential nationalists Abraham

Rotstein and Gary Lax warned in the introduction to *Getting It Back: A Program for Canadian Independence,* 'the issue of an independent and creative cultural life in this country may be the ultimate determinant of our prospect of survival.'[24] Culture needed to be freed from elite domination and ostracizing paternalism in order to encourage a national project with a wider social base. Refinement mattered less than opportunities for domestic discourse, particularly if the content involved national identifiers – references to the nation conveyed through stories, figures, events, and other elements – capable of situating the Canadian experience and identity. Within this paradigm a comic book such as *Captain Canuck* would thus be worth more to nationhood than any Shakespearean play offered by the Stratford Festival.[25]

Securing distribution for Canadian content was no easy task in a marketplace where many exhibitors, particularly those in the broadcasting and film sectors, had long benefited from the ensured profitability that came with imports. The new nationalist intelligentsia, many of whom were involved in the production industries, knew that opening outlets for domestic expression would require a range of alterations to the marketplace, including the use of quotas. 'A quota requirement,' as the nationalistic Committee for an Independent Canada argued in a 1972 position paper, 'is simply a device to cause some segment of society to do some currently unpopular or unfashionable thing which has been deemed to be in the best interests of society in general.'[26] Quotas were, however, but one of many ways in which nationalists envisioned broadening domestic discourse as a means of reifying their Peaceable Kingdom. Calls went out for extending Canadian content regulations to radio broadcasting; quotas to ensure screen time for domestic films; minimum levels of indigenous works in government-funded playhouses, theatres, galleries, and orchestras and even requirements that positions in arts institutions be limited to Canadian citizens; subsidies for book and periodical publishers; the removal of the *Time* and *Reader's Digest* exemption; and faculty and Canadian course quotas in universities and colleges. Existing quotas and economic incentives were important precedents which, if the state was willing, could be expanded to open the door for all sorts of Canadian content. That much of it would fall in line with the world view of the nationalist intelligentsia was certainly not coincidental; these were not patrons but participants, members of a thriving cultural economy who found both their ideological and economic interests to be fundamentally connected to opening outlets of domestic discourse to greater indigenous expression. Success in bringing about a radical overhaul of the systems of culture and communication, however, required convincing a federal government that had done much to lead the nation down the road of continentalism in the first place.

Cultural Industrialism

Pierre Trudeau found much of interest in the call for intervention. His administration, coming to power in 1968, needed to not only tap into the rise of nationalist sentiments among the public but, and much more crucially, confront and offset a Québécois separatism threatening to unravel federalism. The so-called Quiet Revolution – the less quiet moments leaving the echo of mailbox bombings in the streets of Montreal – was a radical overhauling of Quebec that set loose new forces of modernization, secularism, and politicization in many areas where traditionalism and Catholicism had previously reigned. The transition was one in which many residents saw themselves as evolving from 'French Canadian' to 'Québécois.' Although the Quiet Revolution is generally identified with the 1960–6 period of Jean Lesage's premiership, these years provided germination for an up-and-coming middle class of Quebecers to begin overhauling areas of society long dominated by English-speaking residents, while some of the more far-reaching of participants – empowering the idea of 'Maîtres chez nous' – even identified Quebec's future as entailing a separation from the federalist project.

This latter sentiment was a fundamental threat to the political structure that Trudeau revered as essential to the functionality of a Canadian state. Combating this menace required no less than a willingness to cast aside concerns about censorship and jurisdiction and to involve the state directly in cultural activities. 'One way of offsetting the appeal of separatism is by investing tremendous amounts of time, energy, and money in nationalism, at the federal level,' as Trudeau had told a joint meeting of the Canadian Political Science Association and the Association of Law Teachers back in 1964. 'A national image must be created that will have such appeal as to make any image of a separatist group unattractive. Resources must be directed into such things as national flags, anthems, education, arts councils, broadcasting corporations, film boards.'[27] Having won the prime ministership, Trudeau had the ability to implement this agenda. Over the course of the next decade, his administration oversaw a change from tenuous support to a proactive structuring of cultural activity, underwriting a third model of Canadianization, which posited nationhood upon the success of cultural industries.

Out of this policy emerged the current situation in which federal
bureaucrats have become guardians of Canadian cultural life, overseeing vast economies in which the production of industrially quantified
Canadian content – with little concern for the qualitative elements – has
become an end in and of itself.

Fortunately for the Trudeau administration, there was already in
place a bureaucratic foundation upon which to form the federal government's first comprehensive cultural policy. The Canadian Broadcasting
Corporation (1936), the National Film Board of Canada (1939), and
several national arts institutions had been joined by the Canada Council
for the Arts (1957), television content regulations (1961), assistance to
periodical publishers (1964), and the Canadian Film Development Corporation (1968). Administrative steps had been taken back in 1963,
under the prime ministership of Lester B. Pearson, to begin consolidating the government's cultural bodies under the umbrella of the secretary of state, a position successively held in the early to late 1960s by Jack
Pickersgill, Maurice Lamontagne, and Judy LaMarsh. This centralization of cultural power included the creation of the Standing Committee
on Broadcasting, Film, and Assistance to the Arts in 1965 as a forum for
engaging the representatives of the increasingly numerous cultural bodies and programs.

It is worth noting that such an accumulation of cultural bodies was
internationally commonplace by the 1960s. The Arts Council of Great
Britain had been created back in 1945 as the first of the major national
arm's-length funding bodies. Under Charles de Gaulle, France introduced a ministry of culture in 1959. Even the United States, with abundant private-sector patronage, established the National Foundation on
the Arts and the Humanities in 1965. National development in the arts
was, according to the foundation, 'primarily a matter for private and
local initiative,' yet the government acknowledged that it had an obligation to aid culture because of its contribution to the nation. 'An
advanced civilization must not limit its efforts to science and technology
alone, but must give full value and support to the other great branches
of scholarly and cultural activity in order to achieve a better understanding of the past, a better analysis of the present, and a better view of the
future.'[28] It was a declaration fit for the Canada Council.

Trudeau took federal cultural activities up a notch via the simply
titled Arts and Cultural Policy of 1968. Step by step, area by area, the
prime minister and his cultural lieutenants – particularly, successive secretaries of state Gérard Pelletier, Hugh Faulkner, and John Roberts and

Canadian Radio and Television Commission head Pierre Juneau –
began supporting the production and dissemination of Canadian content in hope that opening systems of discourse would lead to support for
federalism. The intervention distilled down to a system of quotas where
possible and, in areas where quotas were too controversial or outside
federal jurisdiction, the creation of bodies and programs to subsidize
production. A quick overview reveals an impressive breadth of cultural
mobilization: earmarked funds for artistic events promoting national
unity; increasing Canadian content regulations for television and, as of
1970, instituting them for radio; the creation of the Federal Book Publishing Policy (1972) and later the Canadian Book Publishing Development Program (1979) to subsidize the book industry; a removal of the
Time and *Reader's Digest* exemption (1975); a voluntary quota agreement
with several film exhibitors (1976); an increase to the Capital Cost
Allowance as a means of encouraging private-sector investment in the
film industry (1976); changes to immigration laws to ensure Canadian
academics preferential treatment in university and college job hiring
(1977/82); and substantial amounts of money for Canadian Studies programs through the Department of External Affairs (1974) and the
Department of the Secretary of State (1979).

Bringing cultural activities under federal guardianship came surprisingly easily. Governmental initiatives satisfied many 'soft' nationalists
and cultural workers seeking opportunities and monies; Canadian content levels increased across the board and the cultural economy
boomed. Federal initiatives seemed to be a success or, at the very least,
an improvement over the status quo. As the tone and temper of contestation eased and the new nationalism declined during the 1970s, federal
bureaucrats found themselves relatively unchallenged in orchestrating
the relationship between culture and nationhood.

Federal successes did not come without costs for qualitative goals,
however. The Trudeau administration was able to accomplish much of
its intervention by entering into cultural life through an industrial back
door, but doing so in turn entailed treating culture as a commodity. Economic incentives and industrial point systems all placed Canadian content within the dynamics of profitability and cultural commodification,
which encouraged industries to strip it of national identifiers – or, more
commonly, replace Canadian ones with American equivalents – in order
to attract the interest of distributors at home and abroad. The commercialism that had once been anathema to cultural nationalists now was
identified as the means of ensuring cultural vitality; advertising, marketing,

co-productions, and the tailoring of Canadian content to the interests of foreign markets were all treated as key to the success of Canadianization. The end result was that any sense of intrinsic value was replaced by an economic one. Culture, in terms put forth by theorist Jean Baudrillard, was now treated on par with Levi jeans and washing machines.[29] One finds, for example, American film and television producers being lured to Canada with the offer of 'Canadian content subsidies' for merely employing a sufficient number of citizens in set crews, as lighting and sound technicians, and so on. That treating Canadian content as a commodity helped the cultural industries to come in on the ground floor of a transition from internationalism to globalization merely made these activities all the more innocuous if not legitimate in the eyes of cultural bureaucrats.

By the early 1980s one finds a stark reversal of Trudeau's desire to open systems of communication and culture to Canadians, yet at the same time, cultural industrialism continued to prove itself in economic terms and ease of administration. So much so, in fact, that over the next two decades federal bureaucrats successfully engaged in a neo-conservative clawing back of the public sector in favour of private-sector growth, all the while continuing to emphasize the importance of culture to nationhood. One finds a massive wave of cutbacks to the public sector in 1984, accompanied by an industrially minded reworking of the Canadian Film Development Corporation into Telefilm Canada (1984) – its roster then including the Canadian Broadcast Program Development Fund, the Feature Film Fund, the Canadian Production Marketing Assistance Fund, and the Festival Bureau – a repositioning of the National Film Board towards aiding private-sector production under the National Film and Video Policy (1984), and more emphasis on aiding industrial production through initiatives such as the Book Publishing Industry Development Program (1986), the Sound Recording Development Program (1986), the Cultural Industries Development Fund (1990), the Publications Assistance Program (1993), and the Canadian Film or Video Tax Credit (1994), to name but a few.

Cultural industrialism did not continue without crises, yet the federal government did well in maintaining and validating this model of Canadianization. The Free Trade Agreement negotiations of the 1980s, for example, brought to light the problem of placing cultural success within industrial activity, yet bureaucrats succeeded in convincing many Canadians that culture had been kept 'off the table' (despite all the evidence to the contrary). A decade later, in a moment testifying to the fact that seeking foreign markets in turn entails opening one's own, the World Trade Organization negated Canadian legislation designed to ward off foreign split-run magazines. Despite clear evidence of sovereignty over cultural policy having been surrendered, many critics were placated by watered-down legislation and the assurances of bureaucrats.

The Department of Canadian Heritage is the current administrator of cultural industrialism, its bureaucrats diverting public attention from the problems inherent in the system by pointing out the high levels of employment, large sales figures, and foreign investment. Tallies and statistics are presented as evidence of national cultural vibrancy when, from a more critical point of view, industrial activity cannot be equated with culture, a national sense of self, or even opportunities for domestic expression; sales merely signify achievements in producing, marketing, and exporting goods.[30] Subsidizing the production of Hollywood films may attract American production dollars, but it does not offer an outlet for indigenous discourse in the same way as the National Film Board or screen time for domestic filmmakers. That subsidized private-sector industries offer economic returns as evidence of successful federal cultural guardianship merely allows bureaucrats to further shift from funding public bodies such as the NFB and the CBC – which often offer more in terms of social than economic gains – to those in line with monetary interests. Out of this trend emerges a stark picture as to how the federal government has bought into the profit-minded approach that intervention had initially been designed to overcome and, in doing so, bureaucrats have undermined the ability to use systems of communication in favour of discourse valued for something other than economic worth.

The Trials and Tribulations of Canadianization

Canadianizers, from Vincent Massey to Sheila Copps, have not had an easy time trying to imprint a sense of Canadian nationhood through culture. Division and conflict have characterized the entire process as cultural patrons, participants, producers, distributors, intellectuals, the state, and the public as a whole fought over issues of nationhood, culture, and intervention. A vast melange of politicized, empowered, orchestrated, and conflicting notions have taken place as competitors sought to use culture and systems of communication for their own gains. Ideological and economic interests blurred and convoluted the line between actions taken on the behalf of the nation and those that merely served the advocates. Art for nation's sake posed a challenge to ideas of art for art's sake. 'Freedom of choice' became a means for industrialists to guise the pursuit of profitability. Earlier ideas of arm's-length state patronage were infringed upon by a federal mobilization of arts for political and economic gain, a shift which, in turn, butted against the fact that, as cultural bureaucrat Bernard Ostry has noted, 'culture in the larger perspective does create a sense of community, forming common views of reality with which citizens can identify; but in detail, the commitment of art and artists may be to disrupt the existing order.'[31]

That vested interests and genuine concerns look so much alike and have been, in fact, often intimately intertwined has meant that nation-builders could not escape the slings and barbs of critics and cultural antagonists. One of the more colourful – if not sardonic – disparagements of Canadianization has been put forth by novelist Mordecai Richler via his character Barney Panofsky in *Barney's Version*. Although the following passage was intended to be a swipe at cultural nationalism and protectionism, if looked at in light of the shift from public- to private-sector investment, it also offers a powerful statement about the problem of relying upon profiteers and industrialists to be the facilitators of domestic discourse.

> When it was required of me, I could rumba as a latter-day patriot, sheltering in the Great Cham's last refuge of the scoundrel. Whenever a government minister, a free-marketeer responding to American pressure, threatened to dump the law that insisted on (and bankrolled to a yummy degree) so much Canadian-manufactured pollution on our airwaves, I did a quick change in the hypocrite's phone booth, slipping into my Captain Canada mode, and appeared before the committee. 'We are defining Canada to Canadians,' I told them. 'We are this country's memory, its soul, its hypostasis, the last defense against our being overwhelmed by the egregious cultural imperialists to the south of us.'[32]

Or, more telling of the work undertaken by some scholars over the past few decades, one can look at the writings of Ramsay Cook, a historian and public intellectual who has done much to deconstruct this topic.[33] In *Canada, Quebec, and the Uses of Nationalism*, Cook argues that

> Canadian cultural nationalists are rarely concerned with simple or specific questions such as the percentage of foreign art gallery curators in Canada, the amount of advertising revenue scooped up by the Canadian edition of Reader's Digest, or the volume of American-produced cable TV that is beamed into Canada. These things are symbols of what is more basic – the

challenge of Americanization. Or in a more positive sense, Canadian cultural nationalists want to preserve, or develop, a set of Canadian social or cultural values that will guarantee our distinctiveness from the United States. Once that is understood, it is not difficult to comprehend the cultural nationalist's conviction that state intervention, direction, and even ownership must be seen as fundamental to the whole process of differentiating Canada from the United States.[34]

Cook denies nationalists their use of an anti-imperialist discourse. Cultural nationalism has not been a case of 'fending off the threat of assimilation by a conqueror' so much as one of distinguishing the country from its peers on the international stage.[35] Not one to give nationalists any more due than they deserve, he reminds readers that 'nationalism is about ethnic survival and growth. It is also about self-interest and power.'[36] In other words, as Cook stated in his 1970 article 'Nationalism in Canada or *Portnoy's Complaint* Revisited,' a piece written during the heyday of the new nationalism, 'what nationalists in Canada have wanted is power to alter the face of the country, to shape its spirit, to make it over in their own image.'[37]

There is certainly truth in such assessments. Nationalism brings Canadians into an entire set of social, economic, and political structures that may not actually serve their interests. 'National good' is equated with 'public good' when in fact it often entrenches class and economic interests benefiting a minority. Further, mobilizing culture in the quest for nationhood is a means of maintaining this hegemony by striking, in Martyn Lee's words, 'a resonant chord within the popular consciousness, of winning the hearts and minds of ordinary people.'[38]

Yet for all the artificiality of nationalism and the ideological and economic advantages provided to its advocates, Canada exists within a world of nation-states, a relatively recent phenomenon not likely to dissolve any time soon. For most people, the issue is not whether constructing a national identity is good or bad, or even possible or impossible, but choosing which national project to support. No amount of learned discussion will convince Canadians to shed an emotional tie that offers such important social cohesion in an age in which the rural gemeinschaft has largely given way to an urban gesellschaft. Acknowledging that Canada is a construct designed to organize populations and resources is little more than pointing out that there is a forest hidden by the trees. Of more pragmatic good is to give credit to the process by which ethnic privilege is replaced by civic rights, progressive values, social diversity, and ethnic and religious tolerance, all of which are at odds with traditional – and exclusionary – nationalisms. Activists in the 1960s and early 1970s showed how mobilizing the state in the name of a Peaceable Kingdom led to significant gains in confronting environmental exploitation, altering capital accumulation with a goal of wider social prosperity, and ensuring opportunities for expression that offered little or no profit to the distributor but much to the public in terms of social good.

That federal bureaucrats are able to continue to offer a semblance of the Peaceable Kingdom within a neo-conservative prioritization of the private over the public sector – one functional for both the Liberals and the Conservatives – makes it likely that the current model of Canadianization will not dissolve any time soon. At the very least, one finds little in the way of challenge or alternative. Globalization does more to entrench than erode cultural industrialism, while younger Canadians, among whom nationalism has traditionally thrived, have been largely disenfranchised from the national project they stand to inherit.[39] The Anglophilic enthusiasm and opportunities for positions of national prominence in the first few decades of the twentieth century, the grassroots energies and prospect of reifying an idealized Canada in the 1960s, the youthful romanticism and subsidized inclusiveness offered during the Trudeau era – none of these have an equivalent in the early twenty-first century. Is there little surprise, then, that Molson, Roots, and Tim Hortons, among other corporations, are finding it easy to profit from this void? It is a testament to the lack of social cohesiveness that occurs when money-making becomes the foundation for cultural activity and domestic expression.

Despite the instability of positing the nationhood upon cultural industrialism, the federal government is not about to let go of a Canadianization that contributes so much to the economy and, in avoiding qualitative hang-ups, eases the handling of a civic nationhood wrought with ethnic tensions. Now it is a matter of seeing how well the state and the cultural industries benefiting from the monies maintain this hold in the face of a public increasingly confused, if not concerned, about what it means to be Canadian. Federal success in maintaining the status quo of Canadianization will at the very least require continuing an unabashed equating of economic gains with cultural vitality, a diverting of attention from problems arising from globalization, an undermining of areas in which alternative paradigms can be developed, and some success in convincing Canadians that, despite the anemic condition of the public sector, they are still in possession of a Peaceable Kingdom.

Canada provides a fascinating case study in which to explore how nationhood has been defined and pursued through culture. Moments of Canadianization reveal the evolving tone of nationalist movements, conceptions of nationhood, and ways in which culture has been identified and operationalized. By no means does this book offer a definitive answer to the question of Canadian identity, but it does attempt to provide a glimpse into the period between modernity and globalization in which several generations of privileged and influential citizens of a political federation tried to construct a nation in northern North America, the ideas explored herein speaking loudly of dissimilar orchestrations and reifications of culture and nationhood. In understanding how culture and nationhood have been brought together in different ways, one comes closer to comprehending what it means to be Canadian and, in a wider sense, a citizen in a world of nation-states.

Before we conclude, it is important to note that the lack of material on newspapers and sports is not accidental: these two areas are not directly addressed simply because they did not make significant appearances within the paradigms of Canadianization modelled in this book. Newspapers were widely available, actively consumed, and high in domestic information; thus they did not attract much attention from nationalists seeking to increase levels of Canadian content. Likewise, although many people in contemporary Canada view sports to be a form of cultural activity, this has not always been the case. Sports did not show up on the high-cultural radar of the Masseyites, for example, and although federal cultural policies came to include elements of sport, as in the linking of the nation and physical activity seen in Participaction, these activities occurred largely outside the paradigm of cultural industrialism.[40] What follows is not a survey or synthesis but a series of models offering a glimpse into how nationhood and culture were brought together within the minds of the protagonists themselves. If all areas of cultural activity had been as omnipresent in the Canadian cultural complex as hockey or as readily available as newspapers, Canadianization would have been a much easier task.[41]

1 Colony to Nation: Morality, Modernity, and the Nationalist Use of Culture

The editors of the *Canadian Forum* showed little reservation in pontificating on the importance of their inaugural, October 1920, issue to Canadian nationhood.

> Real independence is not the product of tariffs and treaties. It is a spiritual thing. No country has reached its full stature, which makes its goods at home, but not its faith and its philosophy ... The creation of a permanent monthly journal of opinion is a thing not to be undertaken lightly; but the need which it tries to meet is a real one. Too often our convictions are borrowed from London, Paris, or New York ... The *Canadian Forum* had its origins in a desire to secure a freer and more informed discussion of public questions and, behind the strife of parties, to trace and value those developments of art and letters which are distinctively Canadian.[1]

Therein lay a statement that could sound just as strikingly true if uttered by nationalists of later generations -- the overwhelming presence of foreign ideologies; the need for outlets aiding in domestic discourse; and the essential role of culture, or 'art and letters' at that time, in national life. Canadianization was underway. In launching the *Canadian Forum*, its editors, advocates, and supporters-at-large established a venue in which learned voices could articulate national goals and mobilize cultural life, a cog in a nation-building machine being assembled in the nationalist wake of the First World War.

Nationalism came easily to up-and-coming intellectuals of significant education and to all those Canadians who saw themselves as enlightened citizens responsible for public morality and for protecting the masses from gutter instincts. Upon the shoulders of the learned and privileged rested the responsibility for guiding the population along a path to nationhood that travelled the moral high ground. Colonies, after all, can be confederated, but a national sense of place cannot be legislated; it requires extensive work in mediating and consolidating the correct myths, symbols, values, and other identifiers of a supposedly essentialized national design but which, in fact, reflect the interests and imaginings of its architects. Never before, at least in the eyes of these Canadians, had the nation faced such challenges to its spiritual consolidation. The turn of the century had brought with it radical alternations to everyday life, from the discovery of X-rays and electrons to the invention of automobiles and air travel to the building of industrial factories and skyscrapers, a so-called modernity shaking the foundation upon which the colony-to-nation process rested. In some areas the changes were merely baffling; in others they threatened to plummet the population into a melting pot of soulless consumerism and debauchery. New technologies required one to come to terms with abrupt changes in interacting with the world – mass printing replicated and disseminated content on a large scale, film projection challenged one's sense of place, and broadcasting sent programming over vast distances with no regard for physical barriers – but the real threat seemed to be situated in how advertisers and the suppliers of tasteless, titillating entertainment were using the media to facilitate the sale of material goods.[2]

A provocative mobilization of cultural activity offered much to people who sought a national design vested with moral rectitude, yet the arts and letters alone were not enough to reclaim a population inclined towards all-things-mass. The realities of nation-building in a mass-media society required implementing limitations to the founts of commercial debauchery where possible and, conversely, establishing public institutions capable of offering the masses a cultured alternative to mass content. Canadians would not give up their radios and cinemas; so why not use those outlets to convey content which, in refining tastes, would naturally lead to even more demand for more for such material? Accomplishing such a feat of cultural nationalism, however, required calling upon the state to alter systems of communication and create publicly owned institutions capable of offering opportunities for cultural engagement that were otherwise unlikely to be made available in a marketplace which operated in the interests of profiteers. It was a difficult proposition in an age in which the federal government actively avoided entangling itself in cultural activities and, as critics were more than eager to argue, the desire to link culture to national identity inherently infringed upon the idea of art for art's sake. What nationalists would defend as a means of encouraging domestic cultural expression, others would decry as a twisting of arts in favour of nationalist agendas. Canadianization, however, required that advocates be adamant and unapologetic about making use of culture whenever and wherever possible; nation-building required that sort of fortitude.

The Masseyites

> He would be a bold man who would deny in Canada the existence of a distinctive national feeling. Canada's war effort was distinctly a national effort ... and the direct result of this effort has been that Canada has been assigned, not only a place in the Assembly of the League of Nations, but has been pronounced eligible for election to the Council of the League. This means, if it means anything, that Canada has now not only achieved a national consciousness, but has won from the rest of the world – not even excepting the United States – the recognition of this national consciousness.[3]

W. Stewart Wallace, a librarian at the University of Toronto, was not saying anything out of the ordinary in making that statement in a 1920 issue of the *Canadian Historical Review,* a periodical founded that year. It was an idea, and use of media, increasingly common at the time. Emerging from a period awash with nationalistic symbols and banners, tales of heroic victories and sacrificial defeats, and the construction of myths and monuments of commemoration, nationally minded, if not nationalistic, thinkers found periodicals to offer an advantageous means for geographically dispersed intellectuals to discuss ways in which Canadian nationhood could be established. Learned journals were a great supplement to private correspondence and in-person meetings, opening the discourse to a range of participants able to share ideas about what lay ahead for the nation and how they, as intellectuals, had a responsibility to guide the former colonies into nationhood. In doing so, these thinkers were building upon the earlier contributions to learned life made by the *Canadian Monthly and National Review* (1872–8), *Queen's Quarterly* (1893–), and the *University Magazine* (1907–20), periodicals that set the stage for an explosion of successors, including the *Canadian Bookman* (1919–39), the *Canadian Forum* (1920–2000), the *Dalhousie Review* (1921–), the *McGill Fortnightly* (1925–7), and the *University of Toronto Quarterly* (1931–).[4]

One needs to be concerned not only with '*what* was said,' as historian Mary Vipond points out, but '*who* said it and *how*.'[5] Among the intellectuals at the forefront of nationalist discourse were Vincent Massey, Graham Spry, Brooke Claxton, J.W. Dafoe, O.D. Skelton, and Lorne Pierce, figures who, along with their contemporaries, formed what Vipond describes as a tentative 'nationalist network,'

> an integral part of a broader English-Canadian élite, formed by both birth and merit, but still an élite of education and position, almost entirely British-Canadian and resident in the major urban centres. The intelligentsia was not radical, then; its members were not so much social critics as aspiring social leaders and moulders of public opinion. Few of them advocated fundamental social change; they all, however, felt that more rapid change than they had ever known before was enveloping them and other Canadians, and believed it to be their duty both to form responses to the new situation and to develop institutions which could cope with it.[6]

Theirs was an informal yet exclusive network, one with an Anglophilic ethnic nationalist underwriting, which served the interests of the privileged few. 'That [they] … devoted more time to the Masseys than to the masses was not accidental; it derived from class and leadership assumptions which gave ordinary Canadians little role to play except as consumers of nationalist propaganda,' Vipond notes.[7]

Culture and the outlets through which it was defined and mobilized offered much to those who were interested in fostering a sense of nationhood. It is important to keep in mind, of course, that at this time culture was conceptualized quite differently from the way it is perceived in contemporary Canada. Recreational activities, from sports to tavern life, offered much enjoyment and pleasure in the lead-up to modernity, but such pastimes were not cultural per se. Nor did ethnic folk life, or 'cultural heritage,' as it is currently construed, fall into this category. Culture, defined by the elites possessing this form of capital, was intimately linked to experiences of refinement and enlightenment as expressed through fine art, poetry, literature, plays, choral and orchestral music, and other such 'cultured' activities. In the discourse of the time, culture was 'high' above the 'low' elements of life, with the former offering social enhancement and the latter leading to social debasement. Or, as Maria Tippett puts it in *Making Culture: English-Canadian Institutions and the Arts before the Massey Commission,* 'cultural activity belonged to leisure time, to the amateur. It existed on Mount Olympus far away from the masses, from commerce, from the music, folk dances, and plays of New-Canadian cultural groups, and from the American forms of popular culture.'[8] Culture was not something the common person could possess, so much as experience, often within parameters connecting spiritual development to ideas of citizenship and social morality. This concept is significantly different from contemporary notions of culture in which, historian Ian McKay notes, 'culture is reduced to … a buzz-word for any general phenomenon or situation which happens to engage our interest,' from 'automobile culture' to the 'culture of narcissism.'[9]

Culturists and the intelligentsia were inherently served by this earlier conceptualization of culture, yet significant effort was necessary in order to ensure that the masses consumed content that was both refined and linked to the national project. It was not enough to enlighten the population: the masses needed to be elevated through content rooted in the Canadian context, the myths and symbols and stories and various identifiers that could evoke a spatial sense of self. Lorne Pierce, for example, used his position at Ryerson Press to support Canadian authors and the publication of works ranging from history books to children's readers to the monographs of Harold Innis.[10] The British-owned Macmillan Company of Canada had its own advocate of Canadian books, company president Hugh Eayrs, who added Canadian authors – including Frederick Philip Grove, Stephen Leacock, and E.J. Pratt – to the roster of British and American works the press reprinted for the domestic audience.[11] Ryerson and Macmillan even ventured into co-producing Canadian educational books as alternatives to the American and British texts making up much of the market. Of course, it is important to note that although Canadian books held a special place within the publishing sector, the international character of cultural activity meant that culturists paid attention to the vibrant writing emerging from other countries. E.K. Brown, F.R. Scott, and Morley Callaghan all eagerly embraced American works as part of a shared continental experience.[12] Audiences clamored to get their hands on 'best-seller' fiction imported or reprinted in Canada by publishers who relied on foreign book opportunities for the bulk of their income.[13] Canadian books were thus made available thanks in part to the foreign works competing against them in the marketplace.

For the more wealthy of cultural nationalists, patronage offered a means of exchanging economic capital for its cultural equivalent and, in doing so, of influencing the tone and temper of culture's contribution to nationhood. Patrons were certainly genuine in their concern for artists

and appreciation of their work, but philanthropy also reflected well on
its patrons while at the same time allowing them to selectively aid those
artists who were most attuned to the moral mission they had in mind.
Grants were not determined by a panel assessing artistic merit, as was
later the case with the Canada Council for the Arts, but upon donor
interest, and thus privileged figures were able to transform their cultural precepts into normative values. Patrons had the ability to decide
what was and what was not cultural and, in turn, what was or was not
Canadian content.

Lord Strathcona, Sir Edmund Walker, J.S. McLean of Canada Packers,
and the Masseys were a few of the more prominent cultural patrons purchasing art, funding facilities, and sitting on the boards and administrations of cultural groups and institutions.[14] Certainly, no figure stands
out more than Vincent Massey, a prolific patron who came from a family
of philanthropists; their legacy still resonates in buildings such as Hart
House and Massey Hall in Toronto. Among Vincent's most notable cultural contributions during the first half of the century was the founding
of the Dominion Drama Festival in 1932, for which he contributed to
the formation, operation, and budget. Tellingly of his nationalism,
Massey encouraged festival performers to use original domestic material, although there was little willingness among performers to try
untested and unknown Canadian works against competitors presenting
renditions of established international material.[15]

Nationalistic patrons knew that designating the work of domestic artists – at least those who shared the same vision – as manifestations of the
national essence offered much to the quest for nationhood. A preference among many collectors and critics for aesthetically placid, foreign
visual arts, including the popular Dutch and Barbizon school styles, as
emulated by Canadian-born artists Horatio Walker and Homer Watson,
offered nationalists a great opportunity to carve out a dichotomy of the
'national' and the 'foreign.' Therein lies a prime example as to how this
Anglophilic nationalist paradigm sought not merely to culturally elevate
Canada via international examples but, and much more crucially, to
selectively foster essentialistic, yet artistically tangible, expressions of the
'national spirit' with an eye to paradoxically defining Canada as both a
unique dominion and a nation unto itself. That a Toronto-based artistic
collective calling itself the Group of Seven was actively blending art and
nationalism made the dichotomy of national and foreign all the more
feasible. These artists, famous in the Canadian canon for combining
brash aesthetics with an interest in promoting a national sense of place,

had learned much from C.W. Jefferys, George Reid, Dave Thomson, and others who spent time at the Arts and Letters Club of Toronto (formed in 1908). Group of Seven member J.E.H. MacDonald has reminisced about

> the arts league and its annual publication, the Graphic Arts Club with its Canadian evenings, (fellows all singing Sid Howard's canoe songs ...), the visiting evenings we used to have at different artists' studios to make half-hour compositions on Canadian subject ... there was a ... stirring of *Canadian Ideals*. Old Cruikshank, for instance, with his 'Breaking the Road' was a more direct Canadian influence among us than *any* Kreighoff. And Reid's City Hall decorations means much to us ... Dave Thomson's drawings in the art league calendars, and his water colours of Algonquin Park and Scarboro Bluffs were landmarks to us.[16]

Conflicts often arose between artists rooted in more traditional aesthetic approaches and those who drew upon the new European impressionist and expressionist techniques, but these did not diminish the shared interest in landscape art as a means of communing with the essence of Canada and channelling the national spirit. Arts and Letters Club founding member Wyly Grier encapsulated this sense of purpose in the club's 1913 *Year Book*: 'our art will never hold a commanding position ... until we are stirred by our climate; and held to patient and persistent endeavor by the great pioneer spirit which animated the explorers and soldiers of early Canada.'[17] Artistic representations of land and environment had the power not only to evoke a shared sense of experience but also to offer the population a sense of historical lineage in which the present was clearly tied to the past.

By the 1920s the artists comprising the Group of Seven were contributing to the national project by modifying the European modernist fusion of aesthetics and ideology into one in which the techniques – breaking sharply from the comfortable and placid – were applied not in a European art for art's sake but in a Canadian art for nation's sake, which rejected European ideologies in favour of what the artists saw as being spiritually positive.[18] While many foreign-focused patrons, audiences, and critics were quick to reject the works because of their aesthetic similarities with European modernist art – techniques and ideologies considered to be disruptive and debased – nationalistic patrons and art collectors understood and appreciated how the Group members were using the techniques as tools for unveiling and exploring components of Canadianness. The aesthetic tools of the European avant-garde provided exactly what nationalistic artists on this side of the ocean needed to contribute to the quest for nationhood. In fact, the conflicts over their work even offered a means for nationalists to spin controversy into martyrdom and portray the Canadian artists as patriots fighting an uphill struggle for a distinctly national art.[19] The Group of Seven contributed much, then, to a nationalistic intelligentsia eager to identify and praise, as in the following passage from the November 1920 issue of the *Canadian Forum*, the great strides being made in cultivating nationhood: 'Those who realize that art needs immediate support as well as belated approval, and who in this age of dead-leveling have not forgotten where the true aristocracy of the human race has so often been found to lie, will watch this adventure of the "Group of Seven," its effect abroad and then its effect at home, with keen interest and perhaps with a certain confidence. The outcome of it all might be that the active interest and support which Canadian artists are beginning to find in Kingston, Sarnia, and Saskatoon might cease to be sporadic and become a characteristic of national tradition.'[20]

Canonization served the interests of nationally minded culturists but raised concerns among others who decried the usurping of art for nation's sake. As one critic argued in a letter to the editors of the *Canadian Forum* (March 1922), 'art, generally speaking, can be encouraged by organization; and the result of that encouragement will in the process of time become, naturally, the "national art." But to presume there is such a thing as "the national art" which the Canadian writer can achieve by "trying," or by using Canadian "settings," is to betray ignorance of the real nature of art.'[21] The criticism was just as relevant in terms of brashly painted landscapes being canonized as a national school of painting. A nationalistic rebuttal would, of course, root itself in the argument that artists were merely channelling the national essence in which they live, acting as mediums for a national art that was neglected by patrons and critics who kowtowed to the opinions of foreign authorities.

Canadianizers saw no harm in canonization; what they feared was the reduction of culture to a commodity, a situation increasingly commonplace in the early 1920s among theatres that sought to attract ticket revenues. With cultural activity growing from gatherings of amateurs to groups of trained artists and performers, the interest in making a craft into an economy attracted the support of many entrepreneurs; that doing so undermined the ability of patrons to keep cultural activity in line with their precepts and interests mattered little to professionals seeking a steady income. This was a moment of challenge in which proponents of the arts differed over the role that art was to play in society. On one side of the conflict was the 'Little Theatre' movement, what the *Canadian Forum* praised as 'the non-commercial, non-professional attempts which are being made here and there in the great world to make the theatre a vital and ennobling thing.' Hart House Theatre, the Community Players of Montreal, and the Winnipeg Community Players all operated, at least relatively, along non-commercial lines and did so while offering a combination of Canadian works and international classics. Such theatres carried a tremendous weight upon their shoulders in providing an experience 'of Canada's own, something rugged and terse and ineloquent.'[22] On the other side stood playhouses that chose works capable of drawing large audiences, theatres operated by 'exploiters who care nothing for art and everything for money,' in the words of the *Canadian Forum*. 'These in the time-honoured phrase profess to "give the people what they want," whereas it is nearer the truth to say that the people want what they get and can be made to like almost anything, good or bad, if they are handled properly ... If anything national is to come out of it, that characteristic must not be allowed to harden.'[23] It was a conflict between nationalists and the providers of cultural commodities which would soon be joined by similar battles within mass media.

Although far from securing complete influence over the cultural sector, patrons did manage to wield significant authority because artists had few other sources of income and support. Poetry readings, local displays of art, theatrical productions in community halls – signs of cultural activity are everywhere in early-twentieth-century Canada, yet almost nowhere do we find the state. Federal involvement was sporadic and uneven, and it was certainly not driven by an overpowering desire to intervene in cultural activities. The state wanted little to do with the arts at this time; it had created the National Gallery of Canada (established in 1880, incorporated in 1913), but there was no national library, ballet, theatre, orchestra, or advanced training facilities, let alone grants and funding to the cultural community. Prime Minister William Lyon Mackenzie King apparently even ignored an offer by Vincent Massey to finance a new facility for the National Gallery if the government would donate the land.[24] Cultural entanglements threatened to pull the state into controversial areas of censorship and artistic dictatorship, and thus they offered much more in the way of problems than gains. Much safer were activities linked to celebratory events and memorials, episodes in which state participation was not only acceptable but expected. The Diamond Jubilee of Confederation in 1927 stands out as among the most important of such events at this time. Speeches by major figures, including Mackenzie King and Governor General Lord Willingdon, along with appearances by musical groups, choirs, and folk performers, allowed the state to entrench its interests safely within a communal celebration of nationhood. Historian Robert Cupido has called the Diamond Jubilee 'the most ambitious attempt, during this critical period of transition to modernity, to stimulate a new, pan-Canadian sense of national community and private social and political cohesion by exploiting the power of public spectacle and appealing to a mythologized common history.'[25] The national identity being espoused, of course, was one modelled upon ideas of Canada's British heritage and 'two races'; immigrants of non-traditional ethnicity were encouraged to adopt established ethnic norms, with assimilation a gift bestowed upon them.

Political nation-building was much more linked to the jurisdiction of the federal government – almost exclusively under the Liberals – during the 1920s, particularly in regards to securing control over dominion affairs. In 1922 the Liberals did not automatically follow Britain into military conflict in Chanak, Turkey. A year later Canada signed its first treaty with the United States, in regards to fishing rights, without having a British co-signature. Then, at the Imperial Conference of 1926, the Balfour Declaration recognized Canada and the other dominions as equals within the empire. This acknowledgment allowed Canada to create foreign embassies and legions, and in 1927 it sent its first representative to Washington, followed the next year by representatives to Paris and Tokyo. A snowball effect culminated in the Statute of Westminster in 1931, endowing the Canadian parliament with full power over its constitution. Only the British North America Act remained under Britain's power, staying that way for another half-century until Pierre Trudeau decided to make its patriation part of his legacy.

Interestingly, even American philanthropists did more to fund the arts in Canada than did the federal government. The Carnegie and Rockefeller foundations, in particular, aided many artists and universities in the name of international intellectual progress.[26] Of course, in this age of modernity, the United States also provided the continent – if not the world – with plenty of mass entertainments, something Canadian elites had to contend with as part of instituting their cultured postcolonial project. What culture was helping to build, modernity threatened to take away.

The Impact of Modernity

'I feel more and more that perfect relaxation and quietness is absolutely necessary for one who is in the modern battle,' wrote Frederick Varley, artist and future founding member of the Group of Seven, in a letter to his wife in the autumn of 1913. 'There is no doubt about it, Maud. Today is warfare unceasing. The world never lived so quickly and vividly as the present time and one must have silence for a few moments in order to keep strong.'[27] Varley was reflecting on his experience with modernity, a massive yet loosely defined moment that Marshall Berman describes in the seminal *All That Is Solid Melts into Air: The Experience of Modernity* as a

> maelstrom of modern life ... fed by many sources: great discoveries in the physical sciences, changing our images of the universe and our place in it; the industrialization of production, which transforms scientific knowledge into technology, creates new human environments and destroys old ones, speeds up the whole tempo of life, generates new forms of corporate power and class struggle; immense demographic upheavals, severing millions of people from their ancestral habitats, hurtling them half-way across the world into new lives; rapid and often cataclysmic urban growth; systems of mass communication, dynamic in their development, enveloping and binding together the most diverse people and societies; increasingly powerful national states, bureaucratically structured and operated, constantly striving to expand their powers; mass social movements of people, and peoples, challenging their political and economic rulers, striving to gain some control over their lives; finally, bearing and driving all these people and institutions along, an ever-expanding, drastically fluctuating capitalist world markets. In the twentieth century, the social processes that bring this maelstrom into being, and keep it in a state of perpetual becoming, have come to be called 'modernization.'[28]

Entrepreneurs and investors found much to like in the mass communications unleashed by modernity. Therein lay opportunities for the production and dissemination of profitable entertainments, many of which could not only be sold for their own value but also be piggybacked with advertisements offering numerous consumer goods.

No medium made clearer the presence of a consumer age than the periodical press. The very technology that contributed to nationalist discourse through learned periodicals also allowed for consumer magazines offering exciting stories about national news and events, celebrities, home and personal lifestyles, and plenty of advice, tips, and opinions, all wedged in between advertisements for a range of items such as Kodak cameras and Victrola record players, Ford automobiles and Goodyear tires, and Palmolive soap and Player's cigarettes. Canadians eagerly picked up copies of *Saturday Night* (1888–2005), *Maclean's* (originally titled *Busy Man's Magazine*, 1905–), and *Canadian Home Journal* (1905–59), along with their later counterparts *Canadian Homes and Gardens* (1924–62), *Mayfair* (1927–61), *Chatelaine* (1928–), and *Liberty* (1932–64). American periodicals were also substantially represented, as *Ladies Home Journal* (1883–), *Reader's Digest* (1922–), and *Time* (1923–) did not cease their distribution at the border, and Canadians engaged in the same stories, news, and concerns as their foreign counterparts. The vibrancy of American magazines, their content funded by a large domestic market and thriving advertising budgets, proved to be very alluring to Canadian audiences. On 3 March 1923, in the same week *Maclean's* presented a story called 'When Fielding Came Back,' Stephen Leacock's reflections on drama in 'The Drama as I See It,' a complete novelette entitled 'The Horror at Stavely Grange,' and other such pieces, most of them illustrated with simple sketches and paintings, *Time* made its dramatic debut. American news stories, including sections dedicated to the 'Supreme Court,' 'Women,' 'Prohibition,' 'Labour,' and 'Negroes,' were accompanied by international reports ranging from parts of the British Empire to Korea and Bolivia. American offerings conveyed a sense of sophistication, with international news reports accompanied by sections on books, the arts, religion, medicine, sport, finance, and even aeronautics.

The levels of periodical excitement were taken up a notch a decade later with the release of *Life* by *Time*'s co-founder Henry Luce. On 23 November 1936 *Life* ushered in a new age of visual entertainment through a photo-rich layouts of celebrities, cities, art, and technology. The first issue alone profiled actress Helen Hayes, peaked into an 'exotic' Chinatown school, celebrated NBC radio personalities, revealed Franklin Roosevelt's personal social scene, and laid out photo-spreads of life in England, Russia, Italy, France, Spain, and Brazil.[29] Mixing the domestic with the international, the familiar with the striking, *Life*'s tidal wave of photos visually engaged audiences in a world they could not imagine through words and sketches alone. What did *Maclean's* offer on the day *Life* hit the stands? Stories on 'Backstage at Ottawa,' 'B.C.'s Session Talk,' and 'Gas Buggies,' along with some fiction, recipes, and jokes.[30] The contrast was telling of an American periodical penchant for high-budget glam and visual stimulation or, at the very least, the Canadian inability to afford to do the same.

Visual entertainment was also claiming new ground during these decades thanks to technologies capable of flickering a sequential series of still images to give a sense of movement and change. In the late 1880s the famous American inventor Thomas Edison and his assistant, William Kennedy Laurie Dickson, attracted attention for their work on a self-contained kinetoscope machine capable of showing a short series of moving images. A few years later Ottawa-born Andrew and George C. Holland were among the first entrepreneurs to draw public attention to the kinetoscope, one of the more renowned exhibitions occurring in New York City on 14 April 1894.[31] Exhibitions began in Canada as of 1896, including showings by the Holland brothers that summer in Ottawa and Toronto, often as part of travelling revues, burlesques, and cabarets. Advances in celluloid film and projection technology soon allowed the images to escape their confined boxes and be cast upon large screens, a step forward in developing a cinematic entertainment industry.

Feature-film production and exhibition as it currently operates emerged in the second decade of the twentieth century, with the first Canadian feature film, *Evangeline,* screened in 1913.[32] Based on a 1847 poem by American Henry Wadsworth Longfellow, *Evangeline* told a romantic tale about a young woman searching for her lost beloved in the wake of the expulsion of the Acadians in 1755. This film was but one piece in a thriving decade of film production and exhibition. Ernest Shipman, popularly identified as the 'grandfather' of domestic film production, created twelve feature films between 1919 and 1922 based on the works of Canadian authors. Among these was the first Mountie feature, *Cameron of the Royal Mounted* (1921). Filmed in the Banff area, it drew upon stereotypes and clichés by bringing together a Mountie, a damsel in distress, roaming Natives, and plenty of wilderness backdrops. Shipman's films were viewed by audiences in Canada, the United States, and Europe.[33]

Domestic successes did not last, however, as filmmakers faced off against Hollywood interests backed by the U.S. State Department. The Motion Picture Producers and Distributors of America's Foreign Department (1922) and the Motion Picture Division of the Bureau of Foreign and Domestic Commerce (1926) took an early lead in organizing foreign distribution and exhibition as part of strengthening Hollywood's hold on external markets.[34] These entrepreneurs, and the government that supported them, understood that film production was in many ways secondary to securing the systems of distribution and screening. No company was more effective at doing so in the Canadian marketplace than the Famous Players Canadian Corporation, which, despite its name, was American-controlled and dedicated to the purpose of eliminating its Canadian competition. Some activities were out in the open, as in the vertical integration of film production, distribution, and exhibition, which gave American-owned and aligned theatres exclusive access to many of the top Hollywood films. Other actions were more covert and devious. Famous Players pushed many independent theatres out of the marketplace through the use of an infamous 'wrecking crew,' which employed backhanded techniques ranging from pressuring land-owners to evict the cinematic rivals to, on at least one occasion, releasing a stink bomb in a packed theatre.[35] Financed by tremendous capital and possessing exclusive access to some of the most desired films, Famous Players did much to deny domestic filmmakers and theatres a chance at providing a viable alternative.

Experiences with periodical publishing and film projection set the stage for radio broadcasting, a technology not stopped by border crossings, restricted to subscriptions or in-person purchases, or confined to theatres. Signals literally permeated the air, travelling through walls and into living rooms. The earliest form of radio and telegraph transmission was administrated by the Department of Marine and Fisheries, and in 1919 the first broadcasting licence was awarded to the Marconi Wireless Telegraph Company to transmit in Montreal (the station XWA, now CFCF). The potential of turning 'money into air' led to a boom in station construction and licence applications, with entrepreneurs and investors establishing relationships with advertisers keen to develop audiences for their wares. As profit-based ventures, stations relied heavily upon a combination of inexpensive domestic and cheaply obtained American content designed to attract the largest possible listenership. Telling of the times, the programming included orchestral music, dramatized stories (often of the adventure or mystery type), news, religious services, and livestock reports. The new industry was so lucrative that station owners formed the Canadian Association of Radio Broadcasters in 1926 to protect their interests from possible state encroachment. Competition, the association argued, should be the only form of regulation, as anything else was undemocratic – or, more truthfully, unprofitable.[36] By the end of the decade over sixty stations provided a combination of informational and entertainment programming to a broad audience of listeners.[37]

The Struggle for a Moral Nation

Mass entertainments pleased many people, but there were plenty of others, including culturists and a bevy of social critics, who viewed the content as symptomatic of a mass society plagued by visceral instinct. A cultured nation could not be formed among the dregs of the base, and upon the enlightened citizenry fell the responsibility and burden of guiding the common person away from mass influences. For these Canadianizers, there was little choice but to tackle pulp magazines, radio broadcasting, and film projection as sites of ideological contestation needing to be brought in line with their vision of nationhood. In some instances doing so entailed an attempt to restrict the availability of mass entertainments, especially violent and sexualized pulp periodicals. Nationalists saw nothing good to be had from magazines that seemed to be contributing to social ills and moral degradation. Radio broadcasting and film exhibition, on the other hand, although they disseminated 'mindless' American content, offered outlets for increasing the level of domestic expression and discourse. Simply put, if left unrestrained, mass media polluted the body politic, but if brought in accordance with nationalist interests, they could be used to disseminate cultured Canadian content that would contribute to the nation's moral and spiritual constitution. Such grand ambitions, however, required an authority over systems of communication which nationalists lacked; they needed the support of federal bureaucrats if the lofty goals of Canadianization were to be achieved.

Pulp magazines – with alluring covers of women in torn dresses, police with guns ablaze, and serial murderers lurking in shadows – offered one of the best sources of titillating entertainment in this pre-television era. These were also the qualities which, as of the early 1920s, drew the critical attention of newspaperman and politician Horatio Clarence Hocken, the Toronto Women's Liberal Association, the Imperial Order Daughters of the Empire, and the Association of Canadian Clubs, among other moral activists. Lowbrow magazines, these voices warned, contributed to social ills and, given that many of them came from the United States, inundated vulnerable and susceptible audiences with American values and characteristics. It was in Canada's best interest, these nationalists warned the government, that legislation ban the importation of these debased offerings.[38] These objections and calls for intervention found a receptive audience among members of the Canadian National Newspapers and Periodicals Association

(formed in 1919), who appreciated the economic merits of protectionism. It made great sense, then, to join in the desire for tariffs and taxation on American imports as a means of guising industrial interests
within social concerns.[39]

Racy pulp periodicals were easy for nationalists to target because the
content was often very blatant. Radio programming, on the other hand,
in bringing audiences both information and entertainment, posed a
much more subtle and thus greater threat to cultural goals. The
medium itself also presented a tremendous opportunity for something
more than mere commercialism to those who recognized and wished to
activate its nation-building potential. Not only did nationalists have to
convince the state of the need to more thoroughly regulate station owners, then, but they also had to convince federal bureaucrats of the
importance of a public broadcasting system, one modelled on the British Broadcasting Corporation and capable of facilitating domestic
expression and a national sense of self. The movement culminated in
the formation of the Canadian Radio League and the question, as
Graham Spry famously put it, 'The state or the United States?'

American cinematic offerings were not desired any more than their
radio program counterparts. The reels tended to present titillating and
escapist content and, in some ways even more threatening in the eyes of
nationalists, disseminated what were seen as American values, lifestyles,
and norms; that Hollywood's offerings were far from representative of
the United States as a whole mattered little in a time of moral and
national dichotomization. The abundance of foreign indoctrination
prompted many Canadians into calling upon the government to invoke
a legislated quota system similar to the one instituted in Britain in
1927.[40] Although the British legislation was problematic because the
lack of a quality clause led to cheap 'quota quickies,' it did provide filmmakers and crews with an opportunity to develop their skills and
strengthen the industry.[41] Similar legislation for Canada offered a
chance to increase the presence of domestic content on the silver
screen. If Britain had a quota, was Canada not justified in doing the
same – was Canada not a dominion?

Requests for state intervention into periodical publishing, radio
broadcasting, and film exhibition certainly seemed reasonable to
nationalists. After all, Canada was increasingly having its way of life
unduly shaped by outlets of mass media that operated in the interests of
profiteers. Ensuring that audiences had access to content valued for its
social importance instead of its mere economic worth seemed to be a

sufficient justification for state intervention. Although the bedlam of modernity added to the credibility of nationalist cultural arguments, federal bureaucrats were wary of intervention that could turn into political pitfalls. Yet at the same time, there was an appreciation of how careful and strategic involvement in the mass media offered an opportunity to guise federal interests within actions popularly promoted as necessary for the nation as a whole.

The federal response to nationalist calls for intervention during the 1920s were shaped not only by these concerns and interests but, it is important to note, by political priorities and jurisdictional realities. Prime Minister Mackenzie King and the Liberal Party had no interest in altering the periodical situation, as placing limitations upon freedom of thought stood out as a dangerous area for a liberal state to venture into. Besides, King and his peers viewed the periodical sector as critical of the government and tied to Conservative Party interests; so this factor alone was enough to ensure an unsympathetic response.[42] Broadcasting, on the other hand, was something the Liberals strongly valued for its ability to affirm federal, if not Liberal, leadership. After all, this was a government which, as part of the Diamond Jubilee in 1927, had linked twenty-two privately owned radio stations to create a coast-to-coast network to broadcast the festivities.[43] The state was well aware of the gains to be had through the broadcasting system.

In 1928 the Liberal government took a step towards forming a national broadcasting system by establishing the Royal Commission on Radio Broadcasting, popularly referred to as the Aird Commission after its chairman, Sir John Aird. The commission's report was a mere twenty-nine-page booklet containing only nine pages of discussion before appendices, a size that testified to the newness of the medium. In line with nationalist arguments and federal interests, the commission found that a public broadcasting system offered the best way of regulating the limited natural resource of airwaves and providing opportunities for discourse that would contribute to a sense of nationhood. 'Broadcasting will undoubtedly become a great force in fostering a national spirit and interpreting national citizenship,' the commission powerfully declared.[44] And as the Canadian Radio League had pointed out, a public system was becoming the norm in many nations, including Britain and Germany; so Canada seemed justified in following suit.

The Liberal Party's electoral loss to R.B. Bennett's Conservatives in 1930 meant that the call for a periodical tariff now fell upon an administration interested in protecting its interests in that sector. A year after its victory, the Conservatives instituted a periodical tariff based upon levels of advertising and thus designed to hinder commercially dense magazines more than higher-end periodicals such as the *Saturday Evening Post.* Positing intervention upon levels of commercialism speaks volumes as to just what was valued as cultural and as needing to be kept free from censorship at this time in Canadian life.[45] Fascinatingly, the measure in some ways backfired, as a number of American periodical publishers, following an industrial pattern that went back to the 1880s, opened branch plants in Canada to avoid the tariff.[46] Consequently, the 'trashy' American products became even more a part of the Canadian experience, if not ideologically then at least now in terms of not only consumption but also location of production.

As for radio broadcasting, a jurisdictional challenge by the provinces meant that the issue was dragged through the courts, but by early 1932 Bennett could confidently call broadcasting a 'natural resource over which we have complete jurisdiction.'[47] Like their Liberal counterparts, the Conservatives appreciated the importance of regulating such a valuable system of communication. Yet at the same time, broadcasting across Canada's vast geography cost much more than the government was willing, if not able, to ante up, and a desire to offer the private sector an opportunity to turn 'air into money' meant that the nationalist desire for a public broadcasting system similar to the British Broadcasting Corporation fell by the wayside in favour of a hybrid of the British and American templates.

In 1932 the Canadian Radio Broadcasting Act created the Canadian Radio Broadcasting Commission (CRBC), and four years later the commission was restructured into the Canadian Broadcasting Corporation (CBC). The new body was both regulator of and competitor against privately owned affiliate stations. All broadcasters, whether publicly owned or private-sector affiliates, were required to air CRBC programming, as no independent networks were allowed. This is not to say that station owners did not make profits; stations would have closed up if money was not being made. Along with attracting audiences, affiliate stations, by using CRBC programming, had the freedom to broadcast plenty of other material, including low-cost American content that attracted significant advertising dollars. According to broadcasting historian Robert Babe, 'while the CRBC ruled that no more than 40 per cent of the daily schedule could be comprised of imported "programs," and such regulation was (apparently) adapted by the CBC, stations had the flexibility of filling out the program schedule with recorded music or other "non-program" material.'[48] The new national system commenced broadcasting in May 1933, and by 1935 there were fifty-four stations across Canada, seven publicly owned and operated and forty-seven privately owned affiliate stations.[49] Ironically, and quite antithetically to nationalist interests, the formation of a hybrid network meant that American commercial programming would now be extended into previously untouched communities.[50]

Conservative governance came to an end in 1935 with Bennett's loss to Mackenzie King. With this change of power returned a government that had supported intervention into broadcasting but rejected restrictions on periodical imports. Canada would not put a tax on the free flow of ideas, King argued, particularly given that the United States lacked an equivalent tariff on Canadian periodicals.[51] That there were few domestic magazines poised to enter the American market did not enter the equation. Removing the periodical tariff resulted in a mass exodus of branch plants since it was cheaper to produce the periodicals in the United States and then ship them to Canada.[52] The situation would remain unchanged until 1941, and even then the alteration was brief, as a wartime trade deficit with the Americans prompted the Liberal government to introduce the War Exchange Conservation Act to restrict the import of certain goods, including American fiction periodicals. Domestic publishers benefited from the protected market, but when the war ended, so too did the act. This time, however, not all of the branch plants that had been set up to avoid the tariff shut down their operations in favour of recentralizing production in the United States. Reader's Digest, one of the more popular of magazines in Canada, decided to keep publishing from its Canadian facilities. Time Magazine Inc., which published one of the few periodicals rivalling Reader's Digest in popularity, had not set up a branch plant but instead achieved strong sales by printing a split-run version – a re-edited American edition in which a few pages of Canadian material were added – out of Chicago.[53] These two strategies seemed to be the best way for the publishers to target Canadian consumers and advertisers, and both had secured a grasp on the marketplace that they would spend the next few decades expanding, to the detriment of their Canadian competition.

Finally, unlike concessions in other areas of mass media, cultural nationalists were unable to convince either Liberal or Conservative administrations to establish quotas for the feature-film sector. Film distribution did not use a limited natural resource as in radio, and the focus on petitioning at a federal level overlooked the fact that film fell under provincial jurisdiction. A glimmer of hope was offered by the British

Columbia and Ontario provincial governments, as both began investigating the possibility of a quota in 1929 and 1931 respectively, but this inquiry did not progress too far because the Motion Picture Exhibitors and Distributors of Canada (a part of the Motion Picture Producers and Distributors of America) convinced the governments not to take action.[54]

Advocates of a Canadian cinematic alternative to Hollywood had little success in altering the status quo, yet in some ways an even better solution was about to come along, one more in line with their cultural ideology than that offered by the feature-film format. The Canadian Government Motion Picture Bureau, established in 1917 to create films promoting Canadian exports, tourism, immigration, and industrial endeavours, seemed outdated and in need of replacement by the 1930s. Federal bureaucrats were dealing with massively expanding industries, bureaucracies, and schools all requiring something similar yet on a much larger scale. In 1938 the federal government invited Scottish-born documentary film maker and bureaucrat John Grierson to survey the national film situation and make recommendations for improvements.[55] The result was the National Film Commission (soon the National Film Board of Canada, or NFB), formed the following year to coordinate state film production and, quite significantly, to produce films of national merit.[56]

Cultural nationalists could not have asked for a more like-minded civil servant than Grierson, who not only helped to create the board but also became its first commissioner. Fusing documentary techniques with a strong sense of community awareness and a nation-building agenda, Grierson laid the foundation for a cinematographic style steeped in high-cultural identifiers and capable of distinguishing the national from the non-national.[57] Peter Morris, an authority on the history of Canadian film, recounts that during the years 1939–45 the NFB's 'achievements were remarkable: the release of over 500 films in five years; two propaganda series (*The World in Action* and *Canada Carries On*) released monthly to theatres in Canada and abroad; the establishment of non-theatrical distribution circuits that were international models; and, not least, the training of a group of young Canadian filmmakers.'[58] The state even managed to reach isolated villages of immigrants by using over seventy mobile film units, a task driven in large part by the desire to assimilate newcomers into the national hegemony.[59]

The National Film Board established a strong reputation as a producer and distributor of top-quality Canadian content, getting its works into schools, industries, community centres, church basements, and even as shorts between American feature films, all of which contributed to drawing audiences into a cinematic discourse of nationhood. Success in this area conversely meant that the state could continue to relish the economic contribution made by American films to the Canadian theatrical industry, even if much of that money was returned to the non-Canadian producers. In fact, the tax monies were so significant that the government gave American films an advantage over other foreign films. A 5 per cent general tax instituted in 1936 on non-Canadian film remittances required Americans to pay only 2 per cent. When the general tax was increased to 15 per cent in 1941, Americans had to pay only 10 per cent.[60] And even though the U.S. Supreme Court outlawed vertical integration in 1948 as part of opening the American marketplace to greater competition, Canada remarkably did not do the same, instead allowing Hollywood production companies to continue owning theatres and maintaining monopolies over film exhibition for the sake of the tax revenues they provided.[61]

Not everyone was happy with the cinematic status quo, of course, particularly domestic feature filmmakers, who continued to be overlooked by nationalists, the state, and American-aligned theatres. As long as nationalists and the federal government could rely on the NFB to produce Canadian content and theatre owners had access to Hollywood gems, these filmmakers would be largely shut out of the marketplace. Quite interestingly, this situation almost changed in the wake of the Second World War as Canada's dollar reserves dropped from $1.5 billion in 1946 to $500 million in 1948 and the government decided to target hundreds of American items for import restrictions, including textiles, machinery, produce, and feature films. According to government estimates, American film distributors removed approximately $12 million a year, an amount later revised downward to between $5 and 8 million.[62] Legislation offered domestic filmmakers a chance to gain from a need for their goods, as periodical producers had occasionally done over the years.

Unfortunately for the feature-film production industry, a lobby group led by Famous Players president J.J. Fitzgibbon and Motion Picture Association of America vice-president Francis Harmon convinced the federal government – in particular, the American-born 'Minister of Everything,' C.D. Howe – of an alternative solution to Canada's monetary woes: the Canadian Co-operation Project.[63] In exchange for no new restrictions on the Canadian film market, the Motion Picture Association of America promised 'films on Canada's trade-dollar problem; more complete

newsreel coverage of Canada; short films about Canada to be both produced and distributed; consideration of NFB releases for theatrical distribution in the U.S.; use of Canadian sequences in feature pictures; radio
recordings presenting Canada's problems by Hollywood stars; [and]
more careful selection of films shown in Canada.'[64] Given that Howe and
the federal government wanted to expand the tourism industry – the
Canadian Government Travel Bureau had just begun a cinematic campaign with this goal in mind – the Americans offered a timely option.[65]

The decision distilled down to a matter of money. Howe viewed feature films as an industrial product similar to any other and thought that
the possible increase in tourism dollars promised greater economic
rewards than those from keeping film monies in Canada. The Canadian
Co-operation Project, he explained to the House of Commons on 12 February 1948, offered 'a substantial quid pro quo to offset the drain of
dollars caused to the industry ... I think I can say Canada will get good
value from the industry in return for permitting the industry to take
Canadian dollars across the line.'[66] Quota systems in other countries
were dismissed – with no evidence – as being ineffective. Instead, as
Howe told his peers, 'the financial facts of the movie industry in Canada,
the tastes and habits of the Canadian movie-going public, and the har-
monious relations we have enjoyed with the United States producers, in
short, the special status of the industry in Canada, called for a more
imaginative and constructive approach than quota restrictions.'[67] Howe's
use of the phrase 'special status of the industry' to describe American
interests certainly rings very differently from its use a few decades later,
when it was invoked in defence of the Canadian cultural industries.

Maintaining Hollywood's monopoly only cost the Americans a few
cinematic tokens. A passing reference to Chicago, for example, was
changed to Toronto, as if occasional name-dropping would encourage
Americans to venture northward for vacations. Canada became a product placement, much like soda pop and the other consumer goods that
companies pay filmmakers to include as props. Perhaps the most notori-
ous moment came when James Stewart in *Bend of the River* identified a
group of birds as 'red-wing orioles from Canada' when, in fact, there was
and is no such bird.[68] It is ironic that the government sponsored a plan
in which Americans were being Canadianized, albeit very minimally,
through the injection of Canadian references.

The Canadian Co-operation Project dwindled off in the mid to late
1950s after negligible success. What the Motion Picture Association of
America called 'a most happy [agreement] for both Canada and for the

[American] industry,' a not surprising assessment given that the project had been its idea, *Kinematography Weekly* described as 'a crafty scheme ... which has brought satisfaction to no one but the MPAA and to the supporters of the idea inside Canada who have no desire to see Hollywood's monopoly in the Dominion weakened in any way.'[69] For its part, the NFB concluded that the project contributed nothing to the feature-film production industry because the few American film companies that came to Canada tended to bring their own crew members.[70] Once again members of the domestic production industry – actors, technicians, labs, and studio facilities – were left out in the cold, caught between government apathy, Hollywood monopoly, and a nationalist disregard for the feature-film format.

It is worth noting that many other countries were not as reluctant as Canada to stand up to Hollywood. The Motion Picture Association of America's 1949 *Annual Report* happily notes that the Canadian government did not follow the international trend of establishing restrictions and quotas following the Second World War.[71] The protectionism instituted by many governments, including those of Britain, France, and Germany, gave way over the next few years, however, as Hollywood teamed up with a U.S. State Department eager to spread American ideology throughout war-torn Europe. In *Not Like Us: How Europeans Have Loved, Hated, and Transformed American Culture since World War II*, Richard Pells shows how accepting desperately needed reconstruction funds meant reducing quotas and opening markets to American imports. Despite the language difference in some of the countries, American films quickly secured a large share of the marketplace: 'By 1951, 61 per cent of the movies playing on any given day in Western Europe were American. The figures in industrial countries were even more striking: American film occupied 85 per cent of screen time in Ireland; 75 per cent in Belgium, Denmark and Luxembourg; 70 per cent in Britain, Finland, Greece, and the Netherlands; 65 per cent in Italy and Portugal; 63 per cent in Norway; 60 per cent in Sweden; and 50 per cent in France and Switzerland. By 1958, nearly 50 per cent of Hollywood's profits came from abroad (compared to 40 per cent in 1937), and European ticket sales accounted for a major portion of these earnings.'[72] The European need for American reconstruction funds meant succumbing to Hollywood's cinematic – and the American government's ideological – expansionism. Canada, which on the other hand, emerged from the Second World War with a booming economy, surrendered its feature-film sector in exchange for a token gesture of tourism dollars.

Conclusion

Confederation brought British North American colonies together into a federal state, but it was the Canadianization undertaken by Anglocentric ethnic nationalists in the early decades of the twentieth century, particularly through a network loosely comprising educated elites, well-to-do patrons, artists, and social critics, which set the post-colonial tone. Seeking to imprint a cultured national design of British inheritance upon the Canadian community, these nation-builders corresponded through learned periodicals, gathered in organizations and clubs, offered patronage to like-minded artists, and generally did their best to popularize the idea that post-colonial development required what culture could provide – enlightenment, moral direction, and the elevating of public tastes. As modernity and new mass media introduced titillating pulp magazines, commercialized radio shows, and escapist Hollywood films, many people became even more concerned about the need to increase levels of cultured Canadian content as a counterweight to undesirable elements. Modernity threatened to reduce the post-colonial project to little more than a foreign-influenced society of all-things-mass. Yet operating according to cultural dogma did not mean opposing modernity. Learned cultural figures understood the realities of nation-building in an age of mass media and that along with fighting off offensive lowbrow material, they needed to mobilize systems of communication as a means of disseminating cultured alternatives. Post-colonial development required adapting high-cultural precepts to mass-media devices. Fortunately for Canadianizers, the federal government appreciated the contribution of broadcasting and film to the state, and the Canadian Broadcasting Corporation and the National Film Board became significant components of an emerging cultural strategy.

The results were certainly spectacular. By the 1940s one finds an educated elite and intelligentsia, a strong colony-to-nation sentiment, nationally minded cultural patronage and artistic expression, institutions and outlets for national discourse, and state involvement in the arts and mass media, tenuous and uneven, but sufficient by mid-century to give the cultural community the impression that Ottawa might be convinced to sanction – and fund – a thorough post-colonial cultural blueprint. Canadianization required no less than the attention and support of federal bureaucrats.

2 Culturing Canada: The Massey Commission and the Broadcasting, Film, and Arts Triumvirate

A nation is an association of reasonable beings united in a peaceful sharing of the things they cherish; therefore, to determine the quality of a nation, you must consider what those things are.

St Augustine,
quoted in the Massey Commission's report[1]

Culture must be understood as the expansion of the intelligence in its search after truth and beauty. Indeed, culture must be defined by the qualities which enrich the intelligence in the order of knowing; that is to say, the knowledge of the speculative sciences, of the liberal arts, and in general of all the imitative arts, as well as the moral sciences in so far as they remain in the field of speculation and thus add to the enlightenment and splendour of the intelligence.

Ferdinand Vandry,
rector of Laval University, 1951[2]

Many of us have long understood that the Canada Council is the cultural counterpart to Meals on Wheels.

Literary critic John Metcalf[3]

Vincent Massey had no doubt as to the importance of culture in society or the role to be played by the federal government. 'No state today can escape some responsibility in the field to which belong the things of the mind,' he professed in *On Being Canadian*, his 1948 treatise about Canadian nationhood. 'Our peoples need to understand the way of life which they are defending in the war of ideas of today so that they can defend it better. The state indeed has very serious obligations in this field. But Canada cannot be said to have accepted this principle. We seem to trail far behind most civilized states in our *governmental* recognition of the arts and letters and the intellectual life of the community.'[4] Yet Massey was adamant about maintaining distance between the state and the arts: 'We need public money for the encouragement of our cultural life, but we want it without official control or political interference. That is why a Ministry of Fine Arts or a federal Department of National Culture would be regrettable. The very phrases are chilling. The arts can thrive only in the air of freedom.'[5] This view is certainly in striking contrast to the present day; the Department of Canadian Heritage represents exactly what Massey feared.

Artists, intelligentsia, and cultural commentators of all sorts rallied behind the influential voice of Vincent Massey. Grandson of farm machinery tycoon and cultural philanthropist Hart Massey, he held positions as Canada's first diplomatic minister to the United States (1926–30), high commissioner to the United Kingdom (1935–46), and chancellor of the University of Toronto (1947–53). His work in the arts was just as prolific, from acting and directing at Hart House Theatre in Toronto to chairing London's National Gallery (1943–6) and the National Gallery of Canada (1948–52). Massey's decade as high commissioner in Britain refined and amplified his Anglophilism and his belief that Canadian nationhood laid within the empire. Further, having seen the British state do much to aid its artists, he returned to Canada in 1946 with a desire to convince his own government to follow in its footsteps. Thus with restrained passion, as was characteristic of Massey, he called for arm's-length funding for the arts as a necessary part of ennobling the post-colonial project in the face of an increasingly mass life.

Such a request was nothing new and certainly not something the state had shown any fondness towards. Even from someone as highly regarded as Vincent Massey, the call for an arts council to fund cultural activity would carry little weight among politicians too wary to venture into areas of culture. No, securing monies would take more than mere petitioning; the state would have to be pushed, poked, and prodded down a road paved and smoothed by the cultural community. To do so, they needed an occasion with public stature and political influence, an opportunity to convince the national audience of the importance of the arts. Cultural nationalists needed a commission, a state-sanctioned forum in which they could assess the straits the arts and learned communities were in, assemble appropriate recommendations, and justify intervention to both the state and the general public. Fortunately for culturists, postwar reconstruction and federal planning made such a commission more feasible than ever before. At the very least, decades of ad hoc state intervention into the mass media required bureaucratic addressing. Still, it took a strong dose of political influence and good timing for culturists to succeed in pressuring the government into establishing the Royal Commission on the National Development in the Arts, Letters and Sciences in 1949.

Herein lay a monumental opportunity for the social elites, artists, cultural critics, and moral watchdogs to consolidate and protect a cultured vision of nationhood against the spectre of all-things-mass, while incorporating both the arts and the mass media as tools for defining what did and what did not constitute Canadian content and identity. Assembled from and empowered by the same cultural community that had issued the request, the commission was able to bring artists and mass-media participants, public- and private-system advocates, together to argue and jockey for position, yet by its very configuration the forum ensured that nationalists maintained a strong lock on the outcome. Canadianizers were given an opportunity to increase their hold on culture and systems of communication by ingraining their interests in a report that extolled the importance of the Canadian Broadcasting Corporation and the National Film Board, two important public bodies guided by nation-building mandates and offering cultured alternatives to commercialism, and by recommending that the federal government create an arm's-length arts council that would encourage international high-cultural standards in the Canadian context. Operationalizing Canadian content within public institutions offered a substantial means of further consolidating a highbrow national design, one serving the supposed best interests of the masses yet one not coincidentally in line with the needs of patrons, artists, and other culturists.

This act of Canadianization did not come without a cost to cultural precepts, however. Over the past few decades, ideas of cultural constitution had been adapted to the interests of organizations, institutions, and bureaucracies increasingly characterized by an involvement with professionalization, commerce, and mass communication. Artistic activity was ordered and arranged through representative bodies that included the Canadian Handicrafts Guild (1906), the Canadian Authors Association (1921), the Canadian Society of Painters in Water Colour (1925), the Sculptors' Society of Canada (1932), the Canadian Society of Graphic Art (1933), the Canadian Writers' Foundation (1945), and the recently founded Federation of Canadian Artists (1941), all of which attempted to secure greater positions within the emerging cultural economy. Learned figures had also been organizing and arranging their interests through the Canadian Historical Association (1922), the Royal Canadian Geographical Society (1929), the Canadian Political Science Association (1929), and the Canadian Psychological Association (1939), to name but a few organizations. The ideological underwriting of this first wave of Canadianization had also been compromised for the sake of pragmatism with the turn towards an institutional triumvirate composed of the Canadian Broadcasting Corporation, the National Film Board, and the proposed arts council, bodies that by their very nature contained elements that deviated from, if not opposed, what had made culture so attractive in the first place. The CBC aired mass entertainment and relied upon sponsorship dollars; the NFB screened its shorts in between sensationalized Hollywood features in mainstream theatres; and a federal arts council stood to further distance culture from leisure and amateur pursuits by serving professionalized artists who were selling their goods and performing for ticket revenues.

As the mortar of nation-building, culture was getting dirty. But for elites who sought to imprint their image of the nationhood, cultural workers needing a steady income for their endeavours, social commentators concerned about public morality and the proliferation of titillating escapism, and all the citizens of a political federation who wanted to increase opportunities for domestic expression and facilitate a sense of nationhood, the cost to cultural precepts was worth the price. After all, a nation was at stake.

Creating a Cultured Commission

In order to understand the formation of the Royal Commission on National Development in the Arts, Letters and Sciences – or, more simply, the Massey Commission – one must look few years earlier at a meeting held in June 1941 at Queen's University in Kingston, Ontario. The Conference of Canadian Artists was a landmark assembling of artists and culturists who came from across the country to discuss artistic techniques, trends, and the need for arm's-length state patronage. They brought with them ideas shaped by the activities of foreign governments, as it had only been two years earlier that the British government had formed the Council for the Encouragement of Music and the Arts, and one year previous to meeting in Kingston, many of the artists had viewed a tour of murals produced as part of the United States' Federal Art Project (an initiative of Franklin Roosevelt's 'New Deal'). Americans did more than merely offer an example of state intervention, however; the Carnegie Corporation, which along with the Rockefellers had done much to aid Canadian cultural life over the years, helped to fund the gathering and, in turn for doing so, pressured the organizers into including sessions on the need to establish federal aid for the arts.[6] For a long time Canadians had relied upon American monies, and by mid-century these foreign philanthropists were insisting that more be done to make the Canadian government pull some of its own national cultural weight.

The idea was certainly popular among many of the participants, as it was hard to resist the lure of funds to help make a living out of something that for many people existed as only a leisure activity or handicraft. Some of the participants, including André Bieler, Arthur Lismer, Walter Abell, John Alford, A.Y. Jackson, and Frances Loring, went so far as to rally support at the conference for the start of a new group, the Federation of Canadian Artists, to petition the state for economic aid.[7] The new organization emerged from the Kingston conference with a strong sense of purpose but needed to find an appropriate opportunity to slip the interests of artists into the government's line of sight. The Special Committee on Reconstruction and Re-establishment of 1944 seemed to offer such an occasion, and it was here that the federation made its first major push by joining with fifteen other cultural groups in presenting a 'Brief Concerning the Cultural Aspects of Canadian Reconstruction.' The gist of the brief, which argued that a vibrant, thriving cultural life was essential to postwar reconstruction, was simple but direct and weighty: a nation needed creative elements just as much as material ones, and without support for culture, Canada would be a nation in name only. Although the committee members could not do much more than pass the ideas on to a government with a clear disinterest in intervention, at the very least the brief helped to facilitate communication between cultural groups and to articulate their interests within bureaucratically friendly discourse.

What the arts community needed was a commission of its own, a forum in which ideas could not only be expressed but consolidated. Prime Minister Mackenzie King and the National Liberal Foundation rejected the idea of a commission to look into the nation's artistic and learned sectors. The cultural initiatives of the British and the United

States governments that had inspired Canadian artists left King decrying the 'mad desire to bring about state control and interference beyond all bounds.'[8] The mere existence of a 'culture commission' threatened to entangle the government in issues of which it wanted no part.

Not all political parties felt this way, however. The Co-operative Commonwealth Federation (CCF) was making a significant impact on the political scene, putting Tommy Douglas and six other members into the House of Commons in 1935; a decade later Douglas led the party to victory in the Saskatchewan provincial election, and at the federal level the party secured twenty-eight seats in the House of Commons. Cultural intervention was not feared by these politicians; in fact, the CCF identified it as a crucial part of encouraging social development. *Make This Your Canada: A Review of CCF History and Policy*, a booklet co-written in 1943 by future New Democratic Party leader David Lewis and F.R. Scott, explained that if the CCF achieved federal leadership, then

> the arts and the cultural life of Canada [will not] be neglected. We need a National Library at Ottawa, branch libraries in all strategic centres and traveling libraries for the rural communities. The new use of micro-film reproduction makes every book in the world available if we want to have it. A National Theatre also is needed, with local theatre groups and traveling companies of players. The National Film Board at Ottawa has already shown how a film industry can be publicly developed and its products sent into every corner of the country. The National Art Gallery will be lifted out of its present stultifying penury. Democratic people's organizations will be assisted and encouraged to stimulate popular interest and activity in the arts and handicrafts. Music can be stimulated on a nation-wide scale with trained conductors living in local communities and working with local orchestras and choirs.[9]

Culture not only elevated public tastes; it offered a chance to structure nationhood within socialist designs.

The increasing electoral support for the Co-operative Commonwealth Federation and its socialist policies placed the Liberal and Conservative parties on the defensive. Remember, the welfare state that Canadians currently tie so passionately to their national sense of self did not exist at this time. Unemployment insurance had been instituted on a basic level only as of 1940, and it was in part a response to the CCF's rise in popularity that the government introduced a family allowance in 1944. Over the next decade and a half the ruling Liberal Party would continue to respond to the shift to the political left by introducing the National Health Program (1948), the Unemployment Assistance Act (1956), and the Hospital Insurance and Diagnosis Services Act (1957). For its part, the Conservatives adopted a new name – Progressive Conservatives – in hopes of tapping into this electoral uprising.

The popularity of the CCF, support for the arts among some Liberal voices – particularly Minister of Defence Brooke Claxton and the Canadian University Liberal Federation – and the need to account for decades of ad hoc state involvement in the arts and mass media meant that Mackenzie King and, as of November 1948, his like-minded successor, Louis St Laurent, could not continue to dodge the request for a 'culture commission.'[10] It was not with grand pomp but with significant reluctance, then, that St Laurent announced the commission as part of the 26 January 1949 throne speech.

Often romanticized as a cornerstone of state support for the arts community, the Royal Commission on National Development in the Arts, Letters and Sciences needs to be understood more as a moment of cultural consolidation, one in which nationalists and social critics justified decades of ad hoc intervention while laying out measures to further imprint a cultured national design. A state-sanctioned, bureaucratically friendly forum offered an opportunity for cultural nationalists to consolidate earlier gains in the arts, broadcasting, and film sectors while, as a crucial next step, recommending that the state institute a council to fund the arts.

A learned commission required no less than learned commissioners. Vincent Massey was the obvious choice for the position of chair, given his civil service and cultural community experience at home and abroad. Having recently returned from Britain, he was both qualified and available to take up the position. Other commission members were carefully selected in order to represent English- and French-speaking Canada. Massey was joined by Hilda Neatby, head of the history department at the University of Saskatchewan; Norman A.M. MacKenzie, president of the University of British Columbia; Georges-Henri Lévesque, a Dominican priest and dean of the Faculty of Social Sciences at Laval University; and Arthur Surveyer, a Montreal engineer whose support for the business sector would ultimately became troublesome for the commission.

A carnival of excitement followed the commission as it travelled across Canada charting cultural, learned, and mass-media activity. From religious associations to community groups, university professors to housewives, theatre troops to filmmakers, a chorus of briefs and appearances made public opinions heard, and much of it shared a concern about the toll taken by modernity upon Canadian social and moral health. These 'concerned onlookers,' as historian L.B. Kuffert has described them, 'warned that renewed prosperity and blind faith in progress might make Canadians a dangerously passive lot.'[11] The result was that the commission operated within an atmosphere conducive to articulating and bureaucratizing, with novel thoroughness, the idea that Canada was to be a learned nation and that this goal could only be achieved through the implementation of Canadian content of high standards – what the commission would go on to describe as experience 'which enriches the mind and refines the taste,' a 'cultural life' producing a 'cultured community.'[12] As in the earlier attempts to alter systems of cultural and mass-media communication, this ideological positioning offered an efficient dichotomy in which culture could continue to be set apart from commercial entertainments and commodities that debased social norms.[13] Crime comic books, for example, were singled out by the Canadian Federation of Home and School as entertainments that corrupted an entire generation of Canadians. 'It is significant that the growth of this trade has paralleled the growth in juvenile delinquency,' argued the federation.[14] Or, as the commission reported about private-sector broadcasting, 'many of the radio programmes have in fact no particular application to Canada or to Canadian conditions and ... some of them, including certain children's programmes of the "crime" and "horror" type, are positively harmful.'[15] Soap operas, the adult equivalent, met with similar condemnation for being 'guilty of melodramatic exaggeration, unreality, and an excessive use of commonplace and stereotyped form.'[16] These were neither cultural nor positive contributions to the nation.

That being said, although the commission is easily characterized as a highbrow event with contempt for all-things-mass – and a lot of its rhetoric certainly went in that direction, despite the commission's attempt to propagate an image of itself as a populist event – one has to pay attention to how it continued the phenomenon of pragmatic cultural negotiation, coordinating the ideological and economic needs of culturists and social critics with the realities of a mass-media society. Herein lay not just a critique of modernity but a compromise in which mass media became essential to disseminating cultured alternatives to commercialism. Replace some of the commercial radio, film, and periodical material with superior goods, and the population would in turn crave better content; broadcast a radio program on literature or the arts, and Canadians would be more likely to read a book or paint. Culturists were not unlike the advertising sector in trying to foster and mould desire for specific products.

It should come as no surprise that the commission attracted the support of the Canadian Broadcasting Corporation and the National Film Board of Canada. These two nationally mandated alternatives to the private sector found the commission a timely opportunity to redeem themselves in the face of government criticism and private-sector profit-hounding. Here was a venue in which a nationalistic pro-cultural agenda served a variety of ideologically similar, if not collaborative, groups and individuals. A carefully guided commission promised to ensure that the CBC and the NFB emerged as meriting an increase in state monies and, in turn, could act on the behalf of the cultural community, with which it shared a nation-building weltanschauung.

The CBC and Canadian Content

Almost twenty years of pan-national radio broadcasting had done much to supply the coast-to-coast audience with information, entertainment, and a sense of community. But broadcasting was a double-edged sword, a powerful medium the commission saw as possessing 'enormous powers to debase and to elevate public understanding and public taste.'[17] Fortunately for cultural nationalists, the Canadian Broadcasting Corporation was a like-minded nation-builder and provider of cultured programming – what the CBC's brief to the commission described as material 'of real quality' designed to 'naturally' enrich the public palate.[18] This was Canadian content defined not upon public desire but upon public good. Ratings were 'a dangerous guide for true valuation of a program or program schedule,' the corporation explained to the commission, as they 'may be fairly high yet the real value to the public may well be relatively low.'[19] None of the network's nationalist peers could have said it any better.

Operating a broadcasting network, particularly one offering a large quantity of indigenous content, took a lot of money, and that was something the CBC lacked. Cultural goals were inherently limited by a federal unwillingness to sufficiently fund production costs, and the national broadcaster found itself left with no choice but to supplement Canadian content with commercially appealing American programming. Whether defending its use of such content or simply stating the facts of the matter, the CBC explained to the commission that this material secured revenue, provided variety, and maintained audiences tempted by over-the-border American signals.[20] One thus finds Canadian shows such as *Happy Gang, Wayne and Shuster,* and *NHL Hockey* – programs contributing names and events to the national myth-symbol roster – supplemented by the American-made *The Aldrich Family, Amos 'n' Andy, Father Knows Best,* and *The Roy Rogers Show.*[21] Whatever the danger, the CBC could not escape an economic need to use imports. Its own vision of Canadianization was limited by this constraint. Nonetheless, despite concessions in programming, the CBC did much to bring about its mandate: over 80 per cent of its broadcast hours were Canadian, and approximately 80 per cent of total hours were non-commercial, at least by its own calculations.[22]

Appearing in front of a like-minded commission offered the CBC an important opportunity to defend its position as both regulator of and competitor against privately owned affiliate stations. These affiliates, regulated as part of the national network but free to program other material during non-CBC broadcasting hours, had been attracting significant support, particularly among Conservative Party politicians, for the idea of opening the broadcasting market to networks outside CBC regulation. The bind of having to provide CBC programming during peak hours, something the CBC saw as reasonable given that station owners and investors were profiting from their use of a limited natural resource, frustrated those who wanted to maximize the airing of economically lucrative American shows. It was paramount, then, for the national broadcaster to make good use of its time in front of the commission by affirming its privileged position in the broadcasting sector. In its own defence, the CBC told of how it acted with complete impartiality and 'devotion to public interest' and warned that any changes to the regulatory status quo would have grave repercussions for national stability by eroding its ability to protect Canadians from the 'swamping' and 'submerging' of national life by the private sector.[23] Affiliates had devalued the contribution of broadcasting to the nation by airing an excess of American 'records and transcribed programs' and in using its money to lobby for regulatory changes instead of putting it towards indigenous talent.[24] If the CBC's regulatory powers were brought to an end, then the national broadcasting experience would become little more than a way of filling the pocketbooks of stations owners at the expense of other Canadians.[25]

The CBC did not lack support from its economic beneficiaries. 'If it were not for the Canadian Broadcasting Corporation, it would be … impossible for the artist to make a living in radio,' reported the Vancouver

Branch of the Association of Canadian Radio Artists.[26] Such a testament was telling of the degree to which the cultural community relied upon the CBC in the face of private-sector disinterest. Conversely, it is not surprising to find criticism levelled at stations owners who did little to support the domestic industry. The American Federation of Musicians of the United States and Canada, for example, complained that the Canadian Association of Broadcasters had ignored its request for a 5 per cent levy on private-station gross revenue to be put towards developing domestic talent. 'This commission may be informed by some independent radio station operators of the services which they have given the community, and of the encouragement and employment given to some Canadian actors, artists and musicians,' commented the federation. 'If such representations are made to this commission, may we suggest that the operators be asked to supply supporting data, showing the monies paid to native actors, artists and musicians.'[27]

Performers and other such broadcasting talent believed that, in using a limited natural resource, stations owners had an obligation to provide Canadian content. The Canadian Association of Broadcasters made no secret of its disagreement with such a notion. Public-trust obligations, retorted the association throughout the 1930s and 1940s and now in front of the commission, entailed no more than offering programming popular with audiences and promoting community awareness through local news reports and airing public events.[28] Complaints by the CBC and artists about the quality of programming were dismissed as subjective criticisms flying in the face of program ratings – who were these cultural critics to tell Canadians what was and was not good for them? The only solution to such a parochial system, the association repeatedly professed both at the commission and elsewhere, was for the CBC's regulatory powers to be removed so that the market could supposedly be more competitive. That doing so promised economic advantages for stations owners seemed, and certainly not coincidentally, to escape being noted by the association.

'Giving the public what it wants,' as the Canadian Writers' Committee's brief described this common defence from distributors and exhibitors, carried little weight among many producers. The idea that audiences were getting to choose their material was a falsehood, retorted the committee, as 'the public did not want *Hamlet* until Shakespeare created it. The Canadian public did not know it wanted *Marie de Chapdelaine* until it read it.'[29] Or, as the Vancouver Branch of the Association of Canadian Radio Artists argued to the commission,

'you cannot blame the Canadian public too much for failing to appreci-
ate and support Canadian talent if they are never informed that it
exists.'[30] Only by opening outlets for Canadian content could the material actually attract an audience. Despite claims to the contrary, distributors and exhibitors were not serving the interests of audiences so much
as providing a selection of content chosen for its profitability, and when
it was limited to material already proven to be lucrative in the American
marketplace, there was actually a denial of options.

It should come as no surprise that the Massey Commission sided with
the CBC over the private sector; after all, the national broadcaster was
preaching to the converted. Broadcasting was not a business but a natural resource of tremendous social and cultural importance, the commission argued in its report, one needing to be kept in line with public
interests.[31] Altering the CBC's regulatory powers would impair the
national system by replacing its ability to 'encourage Canadian content
and the use of Canadian talent' with the private sector's 'excessive commercialism.'[32] The private sector had shown its true nature by doing little other than maximizing profits through the use of 'inferior cultural
standards' that debased 'public taste.'[33]

With television technology currently under development, the commission concluded that it was more important than ever that the CBC
be able to regulate broadcasting on the behalf of the population. This
'new and unpredictable force in our society,' one for which Americans
had established broadcasting stations yet Canadian entrepreneurs had
yet to do the same, needed to be treated similarly to radio, as the commercial tendencies already plaguing the broadcasting sector were likely
to be increased.[34] 'Like radio,' the commission argued, 'it is a valuable
instrument of national unity, of education, and of entertainment,' while
at the same time 'the pressure on uncontrolled private television operators to become mere channels for American commercial material will
be almost irresistible.'[35] Harnessing television for nationalist designs
meant recommending 'that the Canadian Broadcasting Corporation
exercise a strict control over all television stations in Canada in order to
avoid excessive commercialism and to encourage Canadian content and
the use of Canadian talent.'[36]

Rhetoric aside, the commission was quite right in noting that the CBC
placed an interest in indigenous discourse, even if often defined in narrow cultural terms, above the lure of money-making. In doing so, the
national broadcaster was in the best position to balance opportunities
for the private sector with the need to air programming that was not

profitable but did offer much in terms of domestic discourse. Just as the private sector was given opportunities to make money off the airwaves, so the population seemingly had a right to access content that otherwise may not have been made available. That Canadianization placed so much of it within cultured precepts did not detract from this idea so much as it cast Canadian content in a particular colour.

The NFB and 'Truly' Canadian Films

A decade of prolific film production, following its creation in 1939, had secured the National Film Board of Canada a position of reverence among nationalists and general audiences alike. This did not mean that the board had escaped criticism from all fronts, however. Possible links to a Russian spy ring, as revealed by Soviet legation cipher clerk Igor Gouzenko in 1946, brought NFB filmmakers under investigation by the Royal Canadian Mounted Police.[37] And that was not all. From the very start of the film board there were complaints that it wasted taxpayer funds and that its existence and operations undermined the development of the private sector because of its exclusive access to federal film monies.[38] Only a decade after the NFB had been established, then, it found itself facing accusations, scrutiny, political complaints, and profit-hounding. In the Massey Commission lay a timely opportunity to reaffirm the board's importance in national life while at the same time supporting the shared interest in offering a cultured alternative to the commercial sector.

The NFB did not have to worry about the commission members appreciating its contribution to the nation. Audiences watched its reels in schools, in workplaces, and as shorts in local theatres. The two main news series, *Canada Carries On* and the corresponding French-language version, *En avant Canada*, reflected the board's desire to increase 'Canadian content in newsreels shown in theatres in Canada and abroad, and to inform Canadians and others about Canada.'[39] A sampling of the footage reveals coverage of 'the British Empire and Commonwealth Games, the St. Lawrence Seaway, Canadian troops in the Arctic, the geological structure of Canada, the Canadian garment industry and the town of Sorel, Quebec.'[40] In addition, dramas and documentaries combined entertainment and education as a middle way of engaging audiences in socially important elements of national life. Canadians learned – in a dramatized form – about how the Mounties catch criminals in *R.C.M.P. File 1365: The Connors Case*, the connection between mental illness and society in the *Mental Mechanisms* series; and family conflict issues in *The Son*.[41] Although flawed and scarred, the film board offered more to cultural nationalists than anything found in the private sector. There was no lack of an educated evoking of a national sense of place in the content offered by the film board.

Along with the commission's provision to the NFB of a chance to redeem itself, independent filmmakers were given an opportunity to air their thoughts on the industry and, quite significantly, argue that their goods made a significant contribution to national life. If the private sector could garner support from the commission, then there was a chance that the government could be persuaded to intervene and break Hollywood's monopoly. Script writers, represented by the Canadian Writers' Committee, pointed out to the commissioners that it was 'unfortunate that Canadians see almost no feature films expressing the Canadian point of view.' Given that Canadians would continue to watch feature films, should not they at least see Canadian ones? All the industry needed, the committee explained, was a quota system to help to bring in funds and get domestic reels into the marketplace.[42]

Yet this was not to be. 'Nearly all Canadians go to the movies; and most movies come from Hollywood,' the commissioners noted in their report. They even agreed with the private sector that the abundance of American films was problematic, as – telling of the view of high culture as being international – financial support from the American Carnegie and Rockefeller foundations helped Canadians 'to be ourselves' while Hollywood instead 'refashions us in its own image.'[43] But sympathy for the industry and concern about the impact of American films was not enough to convince the commission to recommend that the federal government implement a film quota. Unlike airwaves, movie houses were not a limited natural resource and public trust justifying a strong degree of nationalization.[44] Even the Association of Motion Picture Producers and Laboratories of Canada (AMPPLC), formed in 1948 as a voice for the production and processing side of the film industry, questioned the success of quotas in other countries and expressed concerns about the possibility of an audience backlash if such regulation was instituted.[45] Feature-film makers had little chance of bringing the commission onside when they could not even present a united front.

Perhaps the biggest reason that the private sector did not attract the support of the commission, however, was that its offerings were not needed by the culturists. As long as the National Film Board produced a domestic cinematic experience safely within cultured designs, independent filmmakers would be left to sit out in the cold. Historian and social commentator Frank Underhill certainly expressed a common belief when, in a 1951 *Canadian Forum* article, he noted that 'if we produced Canadian movies for our own mass consumption they would be as sentimental and vulgar and escapist as are the Hollywood variety; and they would be sentimental, vulgar, and escapist in the American way.'[46] It was a position shared by the commission and its view that the nation had the NFB to produce 'the truly and typically Canadian films.'[47] The tragedy was not that Canada lacked a feature-film industry but that NFB films made up such a small share of the content watched by Canadians.[48] Feature filmmakers had little claim to Canadianness within this paradigm of Canadianization.

The Arts and the Desire for a Council

Surveying the mass media and entrenching ideas of what constituted socially positive cultural content was part of the class-based sense of public responsibility carried by many of these culturists and social critics: it was their duty, as the learned and enlightened members of society, to protect the 'common man' from being exploited by profiteers and to make sure that the masses consumed content in their best interests. Having taken care of that task, the cultural community could now focus on an issue closer to the hearts – and wallets – of those who had petitioned for the creation of the commission and whose ideas shaped its activities – an arm's-length, state-funded arts council. For too long artists had had to rely upon patrons while the federal government did little more than offer the occasional token. Now, with the cultural community able to implant its arguments and interests in the report of a royal commission, there was a chance to change all that. Making this effort a success, then, meant that advocates had to survey the cultural straits they already knew existed, assemble a shopping list of needs, and put forth a platform capable of convincing the government to act.

There was no difficulty in tallying a list of cultural deficiencies. Too many authors and artists were forced to leave Canada to find work in nations with cultural facilities, both the Canadian Writers' Committee and the National Conference of Canadian Universities reported to the commission.[49] Existing buildings, facilities, and premises were small, out of date, and required extensive overhauling. In many cases they did not exist at all, especially outside metropolitan areas. 'The Royal Ontario Museum and the Toronto Art Gallery are a long way from Kapuskasing and Kirkland Lake and Timmins,' the Northern Ontario Art Association complained.[50] University resources were deemed to be just as poor, particularly when measured on an international scale. The National Conference of Canadian Universities called the size of libraries 'humiliatingly inferior to that of the wealthiest American Universities.'[51] The list went on and on as briefs, surveys, statistics, and reports were assembled in support of the idea that funding for the arts and learned areas of life was not merely an aid to 'a luxury,' as the Federation of Canadian Artists put it, 'but an essential prerequisite to the development of a stable national culture.' The government was faced not with a choice but with a responsibility.[52]

Artists, patrons, social critics, and culturists at large could not have hoped for a more supportive report than the one presented by the commission. Articulate and inspiring, the ideas and arguments made by the cultural community were given a substantial flair and authoritative voice. If the dramatic arts were traditionally 'the most striking symbol of a nation's culture' and 'the central structure enshrining much that is finest in a nation's spiritual and artistic greatness,' Canada was in tremendous need of help.[53] Likewise, the concert stage 'is almost entirely dominated by artists with no particular interest in Canadian music who come to Canada from the well-organized and powerful concert agencies of the United States.'[54] According to the report,

> for the young artist at the beginning of his concert career, to whom frequent public appearances are an essential part of his training, the problem in Canada is particularly acute. He is entering into a highly competitive field largely controlled by agencies outside Canada which have at their disposal great resources in talent, finance and promotional skill. If, by some means, he can arrange a concert tour of Canada, he will barely meet his expenses … It is not surprising if he renounces sooner or later the unequal struggle and joins in the exodus to the South, where he has probably received much of his advanced training in one of the highly endowed and well equipped schools of music … It seems to us unfortunate that so many of our best people should be compelled to go and remain out of the country for lack of opportunity at home.[55]

The same was said for Canadian authors, as the lack of domestic publishing opportunities forced them to write with an eye to the foreign market if not actually to relocate abroad.[56] Here one finds a parallel to the talent drain that would come to plague the popular music, film, and television sectors for the rest of the century. With nationalistic culturists defining Canadian content within a high-cultural paradigm at this time, however, it was the loss of vital contributors in the arts and learned areas that was the crisis needing to be addressed.

Identifying the problems was the easy part; selling the need for change would be more difficult because to have culture, the report acknowledged, 'we must pay for it.'[57] Culturists were not naive in regards to how some Canadians viewed those who made a living in the arts. The report could not seem to be yet another call for taxpayer dollars to be given over to the privileged painter or playwright who could not bother to get a 'real job.' The arts council proposal had to be not about the artists but about the nation and its stability and health in a time of commercial and ideological threats. It would, to say the least, be a very hard sell, but the commission put forth a report that struck a number of chords connecting culture to the needs of the nation. For readers concerned about the wellness of the population, the report argued that 'vast sums of money are spent on health; but moral and spiritual well-being, equally important, is forgotten.'[58] For those interested in ensuring national sovereignty, there was a testament to 'cultural defenses' as essential components of national security to ward off the encroachment of foreign values and ideologies.[59] Anti-modernists were told that cultural funding would provide 'firmer bulwarks' against 'the tidal wave of technology.'[60] For those of a pragmatic nature, the commission argued that without state support for culture, the other funds spent on national development would result in 'nothing but an empty shell.'[61] And if the federal government could not be swayed by these arguments, the commission linked the creation of an arts council to the gains offered in terms of political appearance and respectability. How could Canada's international peers look upon it as a strong nation when it depended on American foundations for cultural funding?[62] Canada was a beggar relying on the kindness of others. State patronage would be a sign of national maturity, placing Canada 'in step with most modern nations,' as it had 'long been a reality in most countries in the world.'[63] If federal bureaucrats would not provide it for the sake of artists and the cultural needs of the nation, perhaps they would do it for themselves.

No matter how convincing the arguments, one had to expect a mixed public response. The *Canadian Forum* not surprisingly welcomed the Massey Commission's recommendation that broadcasting be kept within a public system, and the periodical was particularly happy that funding for the arts was to take place through an arm's-length arrangement. 'To turn culture over to a ministry is a possibility but not an acceptable one,' argued the editorial board. 'It is full of too many dangers for the demo-cratic spirit, and for the freedom of the creative people who are the advance scouts, the trail-breakers of individual liberty.'[64] Conversely, it was noted that the commission's report was 'cried down in some sections of the press as long hair, pro-British, and unrelated to the interests of the man on the street. The report flies in the face of commercial interests in the mass media: the broadcaster, the would-be televiser, the film peo-ple.'[65] The latter criticism even came from among the commissioners, as Arthur Surveyer, the token representative of business interests, insisted on including a personal statement in the report. Surveyer reiterated his sup-port for the private broadcasting sector, including an independent broad-casting regulatory body, and the idea that the government should split its film contracts between the NFB and the private sector.[66] A blemish on a report that otherwise exalts the interests of culturists, his statement cer-tainly had little impact on the thrust of the report.

Among the readership emerged critics who identified other problems with the report. Robert Legget, engineer, professor, and future compan-ion of the Order of Canada, complained that the Royal Commission on National Development in the Arts, Letters and Sciences was too much about the arts and letters and not enough about the sciences. In a talk given to a joint meeting of the Kingston branches of the Engineering and Chemical Institutes of Canada (and reprinted in the *Dalhousie Review*), Legget complained that 'of the four hundred pages, no more than twenty-five are devoted to a discussion of the place of the sciences in Canada today, and of the hundred and thirty pages of Part Two (the con-clusions) precisely half a page is enough to contain the recommendations on science.'[67] Technophobia ran throughout the report, he claimed, when one should worry not about technology but about 'the perils arising from undisciplined minds and of loose and distorted thinking.'[68]

The nationalistic tone of the report also attracted its share of atten-tion. Frank Underhill, for example, thought that the effort taken to draw lines between Canadians and Americans overlooked how 'we are very like the Americans both in our good qualities and in our bad qualities ... These so-called "alien" American influences are not alien at all; they are just the natural forces that operate in the conditions of twentieth-century civilization.'[69] Instead of dichotomizing Canadians and Americans, Underhill argued, one had to realize that there were masses and intellectuals of all national affiliation; nationalism should not be allowed to derail the development of a transnational intellectual community rising above the transnational masses.[70]

All these were legitimate complaints, but despite the commission's deficiencies, the report was generally well received, as many people agreed that culture contributed to social morality and nationhood.[71] Of course, appreciating the merits of the arts was quite different from supporting the establishment of a council to fund them. How would the public react if the federal government actually set about diverting taxpayer dollars towards something seen by many as primarily benefiting a small group of artists and their audiences? This question was what worried federal bureaucrats. Not only was the government being asked to ante up taxpayer dollars, but doing so required that it venture into an ideological minefield filled with issues of censorship, jurisdiction, and state control. All of these concerns ensured that there would be little change to the status quo, and it soon became clear that the commission had recommended the formation of an arts council to a government much too cautious to act. 'Throughout the early 1950s the Liberal government tossed the council proposal around like a hot potato, but could never bring itself to serve it up to the public,' historian Paul Litt has colourfully noted.[72] Advocates could not even turn to the Conservative Party, sitting in opposition to the Liberals, to pressure the government since it was even less keen to support the arts. Conservative Party leader John Diefenbaker baulked at accepting the report and affirmed his support for the interests of radio station owners seeking an end to the regulatory powers of the CBC.[73] Nationalist designs had been well served by the commission and many of the Canadians who sent in briefs and made appearances, but now the ball was in the government's court with little movement in sight. It would take more than the recommendations of a commission to make it venture into such a turbulent area.

The Coming of Television

Unlike the federal government's response to the recommendation for an arts council, television broadcasting was one issue that could not be put to the side for later consideration. This new technology brought the thrill of the movie theatre into the comfort of one's living room, amplifying the dynamics – and appeal among advertisers – of radio broadcasting. American television signals had begun crossing the border in 1948, a year before the Massey Commission launched its inquiry and four years before Canadians started broadcasting their own signals. An estimated 100,000 Canadians residing in border communities were receiving American programming by the time that the CBC got around to sending its own signals.[74] It would take a few years before a national tele-vision system was up and running, but right from the start the CBC was sure to push for a public service as the best way to approach the new technology, given that television shared with radio the same natural resource of airwaves. Letting the private sector operate outside CBC reg-ulation, chairman A. Davidson Dunton warned the government in early 1950, meant allowing an abundance of American programming. Market dynamics and 'commercial arithmetic' ensured this result.[75] Under CBC supervision, commercialism could be selective, minimal, and in line with national interest, serving audience interests while bringing in essential monies to the national network. That the television service should include American programming was not surprising, and the gov-ernment itself had stated the need for 'a core of Canadian television broadcasting' supplemented by 'some good programmes from other countries.'[76] According to the CBC, the level of Canadian content could probably be pegged at about 50 per cent.[77] As for what constituted Canadian content, this was initially to be defined quite simply until the system was up and running. In Dunton's words, it constituted 'anything that was done by Canadians in Canada,' the list of examples including hockey games, newscasts, plays, and charity auctions.[78]

Black and white television broadcasting commenced in 1952, one year after the Massey Commission released its report extolling the CBC as a pillar of nationhood and emphasizing the importance of keeping television within the regulation of the national broadcasting system. Now it was a matter of seeing if the CBC was capable of matching its radio success with cultured television content. On 8 September the CBC's first two stations, CBLT Toronto and French-language CBFT Montreal, greeted a limited viewing audience with their first television feed: the CBC symbol, upside down and inverted. That soon corrected, it was followed by Canada's first show, *Let's See*, which brought puppets Uncle Chichimus and his niece Hollycock together with weatherman Percy Saltzman in introducing the programs for that evening and pro-viding a weather forecast. Of course, there was little to introduce, as the broadcaster was only to be on for three hours a day.

Culture and commerce had made for strange bedfellows in radio broadcasting, and television proved to be no different. The need to attract audiences and advertisers meant giving the arts an entertaining spin with programs such as *The Big Revue*, a Westinghouse-sponsored variety show (which included the talents of Mavor Moore and Norman Jewison behind the scenes) offering segments of sketch comedy, jugglers, singers, instrumental music, ballet and dance numbers, and a twenty-five-piece house orchestra. There was also *The C.G.E. Show* (later *C.G.E. Showtime* and then just *Showtime*), named after its sponsor, Canadian General Electric, which was a radio program carried over onto the television screen. Similar in many respects to *The Big Revue*, *The C.G.E. Show* offered much in the way of high-quality musical performances thanks to a house choir and orchestra.

Many Canadians would not tolerate, or at the very least be interested in, a strict diet of drama, ballet, dance, and theatre, and with the national broadcaster unable to afford the cost of producing all its own programming, it made sense to turn to readily available and inexpensive American shows. Given that Americans were very adept at producing mass entertainment, the national broadcaster could continue to place its own productions – and conceptions of Canadian content – within the cultured side while also getting to reap the commercial revenues attracted by the imports. During the very first year of broadcasting, then, the CBC established a microwave network between Toronto and Buffalo in order to pipe in American programming, thereby making the national television experience slightly American from the very beginning.[79] It was not even all that national in terms of audience either. Only Toronto and Montreal had stations in 1952, and the addition of an English-language station in Ottawa (CBOT) in 1953 merely reinforced the national network as a central Canadian phenomenon. Together the three stations reached approximately one-third of the population.[80]

Rapidly expanding the range of television dissemination meant, given that the federal government was not willing to fully fund the task, taking on private-sector affiliates. CBC owned-and-operated stations were set up in the larger cities, and the private sector was allowed to have affiliate stations licensed by the CBC to broadcast in the smaller ones. Station owners were required to provide CBC programming but, as in radio, had the freedom to air highly profitable yet inexpensive American programming during non-CBC hours. By 1955 one finds this combination of stations covering much of the national audience. There were five more CBC stations in place – Vancouver (CBUT), Winnipeg (CBWT) – French-language Ottawa (CBOFT), English-language Montreal (CBMT), and Halifax (CBHT) – with both English- and French-language broadcasting in Ottawa and Montreal, and a whopping thirty affiliate stations either broadcasting or under construction.[81] Three years later there was over fifty stations in total, along with five satellites, transmitting programs from coast to coast.[82]

Station owners were happy to have broadcasting licences but were far from content with their status within the system. It was not enough to merely make money; maximizing profitability meant bringing an end to their secondary status and the requirement that they air CBC programming. The Canadian Association of Broadcasters, which had long provided a voice for the grievances of station owners, criticized CBC regulation as a restriction on freedom of expression despite the fact that, as stations owners continued to ignore, airwaves were a limited natural resource and public trust. Besides, as was abundantly clear to any viewer of private-station offerings, there already seemed to be little in the way of barriers to turning air into money. So striking was the presence of American shows that, as one member of the Special Committee on Broadcasting only half joked in 1955, 'it is unfortunate we cannot import Canadian programs.'[83]

Conversely, station owners seemed – as predicted by many a critic – to be offering little in the way of domestic programming outside that provided to them by the CBC. The Canadian Association of Broadcasters told the Special Committee on Broadcasting in 1955 that the total amount of Canadian programming offered was typically 50 per cent, although there was no established criteria for its measurement.[84] In fact, with the association trying to portray station owners as good community citizens, putting the amount at only 50 per cent speaks volumes as to how low Canadian content, even liberally defined, really may have been.

Despite apparently roughhousing the public trust, station owners did not have to worry too much about a regulatory backlash. These early years of television broadcasting were still highly laissez-faire, and the suggestion at the Special Committee on Broadcasting of a possible 50 per cent Canadian programming quota provoked rebukes from the allies of the private sector. Quotas were for those 'afraid of competition,' one committee member retorted, falling back on the popular argument that quality programs would attract an audience no matter what their origin.[85] Even the CBC conceded that a quota might make a significant dent in the profitability of the private sector, an acknowledgment that surely deflated nationalist hopes for a more substantial return on using the airwaves.[86]

The situation was questionable enough, at the very least, to merit an investigation. It was an idea also in line with the Massey Commission's recommendation that 'not later than three years after the commencement of regular television broadcasting,' such an inquiry be held.[87] In 1955 Canadian Pulp and Paper Association president Robert Fowler was invited by the federal government to chair the Royal Commission on Broadcasting, the first of two broadcasting reviews headed by Fowler (the second being the Advisory Committee on Broadcasting a decade later). The findings were not all that surprising. As a provider of cultured programming, the CBC was treated with acclaim, its 'high standards' doing much to elevate public tastes, while at the same time offering a substantial level of Canadian content.[88] These achievements allowed Fowler to excuse the CBC's reliance upon commercially based foreign programming – including shows featuring Ed Sullivan, Sid Caesar, Milton Berle, and Jackie Gleason – as a necessity of budget restraints and a federal government unwilling to sufficiently cover production expenses.[89]

It is no surprise that the public sector fared less well. Station owners were criticized by the commission for ignoring local talent, spending production funds on inexpensive, action-packed American programs of the 'lowest common denominator,' and inundating audiences with 'as many advertising messages as the operator thinks he can "get away with."'[90] The request by the Canadian Association of Broadcasters for an end to the CBC's regulatory powers and the establishment of a separate network carried no weight with the Fowler commission. Given the fact that stations already abused the public trust during the hours outside CBC programming, what would happen if they were given complete freedom? Fowler did not want to see that question answered.[91]

Pointing out private-sector deficiencies was certainly easier than devising a means by which to correct them. A tariff on imported programs, one of the simpler options, was rejected by the commission as a restriction on the transmission of ideas.[92] A more acceptable method was to leave access to American programming unhindered but conversely require stations to broadcast a measured and minimum amount of domestic content. Where would the programs come from, though? Either the CBC had to produce and offer them to the affiliates or, as a second option and one truer to the need for stations to make a return on the public trust, station owners could be required to create more programs or purchase them from private-sector producers.[93]

Suggesting an increase in program offerings was only part of the answer. Just how was Canadian content to be identified and measured? Tabulating the percentage of production funds spent on Canadian talent was rejected because it equated capital expense with cultural value.[94] Another option was to assess the amount of domestic talent – writers, actors, set workers, post-production, and so on – involved in a program, but this too presented problems because of the vast number of people involved in a show and the belief that employment alone provided a poor measure of nationality.[95] If the commission could not even settle on a way of counting the citizenship components of a program, how could one begin to integrate qualitative elements such as Canadian themes and identifiers? Such questions plagued the attempt to address the issue of Canadian content, but one point stood out: something had to be done because the system was only going to get bigger, more complex, and much more alluring to money-makers and profiteers.

There was no doubt about it: Canadian content was becoming an increasingly heated issue, and now was the time to get fundamentals legislated. The Royal Commission on Broadcasting put its weight behind the importance of ensuring that broadcasting was not reduced to the whims of station owners and that profitability was not a fine way of measuring the private-sector return on using a public trust. Requiring a minimum level of Canadian content seemed to be the best option for ensuring that audiences had access to a broader selection of shows than would otherwise be offered by the affiliate stations. Doing so, however, meant that Canadian content might have to be treated in quantitative terms – a numbers game holding questionable results for Canadianizers. Yet ironically enough, with cultural nationalists relying more and more upon institutions and bureaucracies to articulate and implemente their national design, such a situation seemed to be inevitable.

The Canada Council for the Arts and Money for 'Longhairs'

A nationalist design for broadcasting withstood the scrutiny of a federal commission, leaving only a state-funded arts council as the unresolved part of the cultural triad. Change did come, but hesitant, if not downright resistant, federal bureaucrats did not so much alter their positions as concede to a combination of internal pressure and a rather timely monetary windfall. The deaths of millionaires Izaak Walton Killam and Sir James Hamet Dunn in 1956 supplied over $100 million in tax revenue to the state, a boon that offered a way of aiding the arts while avoiding the contentiousness of taking tax money from the 'workingman' and giving it to the 'artsy longhair.' It took the persistence of some cultural sympathizers within the Liberal Party, however, particularly Secretary of the Treasury Board John Deutsch, Minister for Citizenship and Immigration Jack Pickersgill, and Privy Council Office economist Maurice Lamontagne, to press the uniqueness of the opportunity upon the resistant Prime Minister Louis St Laurent. It was thus in 1957 that years of nationalist effort, from early patronage to recent organized petitioning, culminated in the launch of the Canada Council for the Arts, a body which, according to its legislation, would 'foster and promote the study and enjoyment of, and the production of works in, the arts, humanities and social sciences.'[96] To these ends, the initial $100 million was divided into half for an Endowment Fund (only the interest was to be used) and half for a University Capital Grants Fund (with both initial capital and interest to be used). Placing the money in an endowment ensured council autonomy by freeing it from annual federal grants, a situation that in turn worked well for the wary government. Bernard Ostry has correctly noted that 'no doubt the habit of establishing art institutions as independent Crown corporations owed at least as much to the politicians' fear of having to answer for the high-jinks of artists as it did to the need to keep the arts free from political interference.'[97]

The Canada Council for the Arts was the latest institutional component of a cultural nationalist design that had taken half a century to build. Yet this grand success also showed how much cultural life had changed over the course of those years. In mobilizing culture for nation's sake, the essentialized values and characteristics that had made it so attractive in the first place, particularly within an amateur experience away from commerce, had been overshadowed by a professionalized class of cultural workers. Making an occupation out of the arts meant sacrificing some of culture's autonomy – or, in a more sympathetic view, emphasizing the national components of cultural activity – in order to secure state monies. Success in doing so also meant that, despite the idealization of 'arm's-length' funding, there was now a bureaucratic filter that determined what was and what was not cultural operating upon the interests of the reigning cultural elite who would go on to comprise the council's leadership. What patrons had done out of their own pocket, it seemed, could now be bankrolled by the government.

One finds Brooke Claxton, the Liberal Party bureaucrat who decades earlier had fought to bring broadcasting under federal jurisdiction and whose advocacy on the behalf of culture contributed to the founding of both the Massey Commission and the Canada Council, taking on the position of chair. At the council's opening proceedings, Claxton made clear his dedication to what he called this new 'great and honoured trust' to help Canadians 'contribute to the artistic treasure-house of all mankind.'[98] The position of Council vice-chair went to Massey Commission member Georges-Henri Lévesque. Together they upheld a vision of empowering the council as a counterweight to modernity, vesting cultural activity with the role of guiding the nation in an increasingly complex world. For this task, Canada needed not merely domestic culture but the best of culture. Canadians, the *First Annual Report* explained, 'must have world-class standards. There is no place for what may be called "the little Canadian" either in the sense of glorifying what Canadians do because they are Canadian or belittling anything done for the same reason.'[99] The arts community was now set to engage in a new era of activity, offering its cultured content to a population steeped in all-things-mass. But did Canadians want to put down their magazines and turn off their televisions in order to take in a play, ballet, or orchestra? Was the cultural nationalism of decades past, so very concerned about securing an elevated national sense of self in the face of commercialization, attuned to audiences seeming quite content with their mass entertainments?

Conclusion

All in all, the Royal Commission on National Development in the Arts, Letters and Sciences was a spectacular moment of cultural articulation and planning, a bureaucratic orchestration offering nationalists a chance to secure state backing in the task of using culture in the quest for nationhood. Key to this task were the ways in which the commission opened its doors to public concerns about social ills and the desire for an increase in Canadian content. Although responding in part to modernity and mass entertainments, the choir of voices did not seek a turning back of the clocks to a pre-mass-media period. Instead, tremendous support was given to using nationally mandated broadcasting and film bodies to disseminate cultured alternatives to the commercial sectors. The Canadian Broadcasting Corporation, the National Film Board, and the proposed state-funded arts council offered a safe, state-sanctioned, nationally mandated, and culturally conscious institutional triumvirate through which to posit, define, and disseminate Canadian content. In turn, the CBC and the NFB used the commission as a timely opportunity to re-entrench their privileged positions over the private sector, while cultural community participants rallied support for a funding body that could help many to make a living – if only at a subsistence level – out of something that had earlier been a leisure activity.

Culturists now seemed set to take their task of civilizing the masses to a new level. Yet timing, whether on the theatrical stage or in culturing a nation, is everything. The high-cultural triad key to the first wave of Canadianization was finalized just in time for a wave of postwar prosperity that encouraged consumerism at an unprecedented level, and one finds Canadians having few qualms about engaging in the abundance of big-budget, finely polished, and very exciting mass-media content. That so much of it came from the United States rankled those in the domestic mass-media industries almost as much, and in some ways even more so, than it did the cultural intelligentsia. For industrialists to access a bigger share of the mass-media market, however, required breaking down the strong hold that the broadcasting and film monopolies had on much of the capital. Over the next decade the cultural intervention celebrated by nation-builders would be countered by mass-media industries making a strong case for the economic benefits to be had by further opening the market to the private sector. In their success lay a great setback to the Canada dreamt of by the Masseyites.

3 From Institution to Industry: Mass Media and State Intervention, 1958–1966

Growing up in Winnipeg, I didn't go to the movies expecting a reflection of life in Winnipeg. The movies were a compensation for living in a backwater; they put us in touch with another world.

Martin Knelman, film critic[1]

For many Canadians, particularly by the late 1950s, the Massey Commission's cultural ideology was as little a part of daily life as the likelihood of encountering Massey himself. From early patronage to the Canada Council, restrictions on pulp periodicals to nationally mandated broadcasting and film bodies, nationalists had done much to mobilize culture on the behalf of a nation struggling with the upheavals caused by modernity and a population concerned about social morality and the deadening of Canadian life. But in the end, social anxieties could not make up for the fact that this nationalism articulated a grand cultural blueprint which largely ostracized the very audience it sought to guide into a cultured nationhood. The Canadianization undertaken by the Masseyites could do little more than offer cultured alternatives to the mass entertainments made so readily available by the private sector, and when given a choice, many Canadians were quite content with the mass options. An abundance of economic wealth to thoroughly enjoy the selection of entertainment, including among so-called teenagers with plenty of pocket money and leisure time, certainly helped to foster an impression that middle-of-the-road consumption was not all that harmful and in many ways was an acceptable way of easing the tensions of daily life. The Canada envisioned by the Masseyites was giving way to an increasingly continentalist country, and the previously vilified mass entertainments, more and more normalized through availability, consumption, and new learned insights into their place in society, were being accepted by many people as a form of 'popular culture.'

Canadianization had done much to imprint a sense of nationhood upon the collection of former colonies during the first half of the century, but there seemed to be little need for this paradigm, at least as articulated by the Anglophilic artsy longhairs, in the 1950s. The arts and all-things-cultural were fine and dandy, yet consumers showed that their love for mass-media content had not waned. Television signals, from both the CBC network and American stations along the border, supplied audiences with plenty of exciting programming. Music permeated homes, automobiles, and portable radio sets. Movie theatres dotted cityscape and landscape, from downtown cinemas to countryside drive-in venues. Periodicals racks overlapped glossy covers that enticed readers into stories of the familiar and the exotic. Elvis Presley appeared on the *Ed Sullivan Show* in 1956. *Ben-Hur* hit theatres three years later. While the Canada Council prepared to fund orchestras, guitar-stringed rock and roll evoked the unrestrained screams of doe-eyed girls and gyrated the hips of testosterone-charged boys. Mass-media threats to social morality were so common that they were becoming commonplace. Such was the cost, it appeared, of prosperity.

That much of the exciting mass content came from the United States mattered little to consumers immersed in a continentalism that shared much with their southern counterparts. To Canadian producers and disseminators, however, the situation was economically devastating. Television and radio station owners, relegated to the status of CBC affiliates and prevented from forming their own networks, wanted the system overhauled in their favour. Filmmakers, shut out of the domestic market by Hollywood's monopoly and unable to access federal film contracts, saw their survival as hinging upon measures that would open the marketplace to greater competition. And periodical publishers, struggling against foreign imports – particularly *Time* and *Reader's Digest* – that attracted the bulk of domestic advertising dollars through 'Canadian versions,' showed great determination in trying to bring an end to what they saw as an uneven marketplace. These three mass-media sectors not only shared a desire for new opportunities but, and quite crucially, understood that overhauling the system required persuading the state to act on their behalf.

For decades, nationalists had done well in convincing the federal government to alter the marketplace for the sake of cultural gains, and now mass-media representatives would try to do the same by wooing bureaucrats with talk of dollars and cents. The possibility of bringing the state on their side was not all that far-fetched. Culture did not lend itself to bureaucratic ledgers; its benefits did not fill federal coffers. Whereas the public sector was an expense borne by the federal government, the private sector promised to boost the Canadian economy by competing against American imports and keeping monies, particularly advertising dollars, at home. The requests made by the private sector even had the convenience of largely avoiding the contentious pitfalls plaguing cultural intervention, as any movement of the state into the mass media could be easily spun as being about industrial development.

All signs pointed forward, and between 1958 and 1966, a period starting only one year after the Canada Council for the Arts began its task of national cultivation, the federal government, under John Diefenbaker's Progressive Conservative leadership as of 1957, followed by Lester B. Pearson's Liberals half a decade later, began altering the marketplace in favour of private-sector interests. Broadcasters were released from the CBC's regulatory control, the income tax act was changed to encourage advertisers to use domestic periodicals, and an investment corporation was established to develop the economic potential of feature-film making. The industrial did not operate separate from the ideological, of course, and these tenuous steps signified a state interest in exploring the fiscal benefits to be had by teaming up with industries often at odds with the public sector. Seeds were being sown that would later be nurtured during a third moment of Canadianization: a cultural industrialism in which the federal government mobilized cultural devices for the sake of stabilizing federalism in the face of Québécois separatism. But for now, with bureaucrats selectively responding to industrial requests more than proactively structuring cultural activity via a comprehensive cultural program, one finds this to be a transitionary period in which the entertainment industries challenged the first paradigm of Canadianization and helped to set the stage for a second – a new nationalism seeking to reclaim Canadian sovereignty – by wooing the state with talk of economic revenues and, in some cases, praise for the middle-of-the-road expression that might ride on its coattails.

Canadian Content Regulations and the Obligations that Come with Freedom

Hamstringing the Canadian Broadcasting Corporation was certainly not a new idea. The Canadian Association of Broadcasters had spent the past two decades calling for an end to CBC regulatory powers and the national network's exclusive access to the major cities. And in the 1950s, with the television market rapidly expanding, the mouthpiece for station owners showed no signs of backing down. Plenty of advertising money was being spent on American over-the-border stations with signals that penetrated the major cities – and attracted audiences – where the CBC operated without domestic competition. If the private sector could be freed from CBC regulation and compete head to head in these markets, the stations stood a good chance of latching onto monies otherwise lost to Americans. Was it not better for Canadians to get their American programming from domestic stations rather than foreign ones? Advertising revenues would be kept in Canada – or, more accurately, in the pocket-books of station owners – without any infringement on the ability to offer audiences a 50 per cent level of Canadian content. If anything, advocates claimed, these new monies could be used to increase the quality and availability of domestic programming.[2] That this assertion reeked of balderdash did not put off those Conservative Party members who publicly supported station owners and the argument that changing the broadcasting system would benefit audiences and station owners alike. Having spent decades facing commissions, committees, and hearings that favoured culturists over commercialists, the Canadian Association of Broadcasters was happy to have ingratiated itself with the Conservatives. All station owners had to do was wait until the Conservatives switched seats with the Liberals in the House of Commons

That day came soon after the election of 10 June 1957, when John Diefenbaker led the Progressive Conservative Party to victory over Louis St Laurent and the Liberals. A lawyer with plenty of political experience as leader of the Saskatchewan Conservative Party, Diefenbaker was a hit on the federal stage thanks to his powerful theatrical style and strong appeal to the 'common man,' especially rural interests feeling ostracized from the powerful central Canadian core; here stood a tremendous contrast to the aged, stale, and privileged 'Uncle Louis' St Laurent. Diefenbaker put forth a 'Northern Vision' in which the nation would not only harvest its natural resources but process them at home; sought to reorient continentalism towards a more economically self-sufficient Canada; employed a Red Toryism to attract voters concerned about developing Canada's social programs; and offered a solid dose of an Anglo-oriented nationalism that managed to combine a reverence for the British inheritance with the idea of a multi-ethnic 'unhyphenated' Canada. These elements, among others, aided him in securing a minority government which, with a return to the ballot box less than a year later, was followed by the largest majority in Canadian history.

The first time the Conservatives had come to power since R.B. Bennett's government in 1930–5, this victory marked not only a change in government but also a significantly different approach to the broadcasting sector from that held by both the Liberals and earlier Conservatives. Bennett had been an advocate of a national broadcasting system, his administration creating the Canadian Radio Broadcasting Commission, out of which evolved the Canadian Broadcasting Corporation. But over the past couple decades the Conservatives had gradually formed a tentative alliance with the private sector and expressed a clear and lingering distaste for the CBC. Whereas the Royal Commission on Broadcasting of 1955 had left the CBC feeling assured of its position in the broadcasting industry, the change in federal leadership promised to alter the status quo in favour of the private sector. The Broadcasting Act of 1958, then, brought to a partial end a cornerstone of the first wave of Canadianization, a nation-building achievement dating back to 1932. The Diefenbaker administration saw fit to strip the national broadcaster of its regulatory powers and vest them in a new body, the Board of Broadcast Governors (BBG), which would now be responsible for regulating both the CBC and the private sector. As legendary CBC figure Knowlton Nash put it in *Swashbucklers: The Story of Canada's Battling Broadcasters*, Diefenbaker felt that 'the CBC had become a propaganda mouthpiece for the Liberals,' and the new Tory-influenced regulatory body was a way of keeping the national broadcaster in check.[3] Diefenbaker first chose Conservative Party national director Allister Grosart to lead the board, only to end up with the more neutral Andrew Stewart, president of the University of Alberta.[4] An academic, economist, and civil servant, Stewart lacked broadcasting experience but proved eager to learn all he could and took his new position to heart.

Along with being released from CBC regulation, the private sector benefited from 'second station' television licences created for eight major cities – Halifax, Montreal, Ottawa, Toronto, Winnipeg, Calgary, Edmonton, and Vancouver – where the CBC had been operating without domestic competition (over-the-border American signals were a different matter). Now instead of being relegated to the smaller markets, the private sector could compete against the CBC for big city audiences and big advertising dollars. Business interests lunged at the new station opportunities, notably 'Big' John Bassett, a boisterous and charming Tory loyalist who won the prized Toronto second-station licence for his CFTO-TV.[5]

Bassett envisioned dominating the Toronto market and even winning a 'Battle for Buffalo' in which Americans tuned into his station's signal.[6] These new second stations, existing outside the CBC network, were allowed to form their own network in order to exchange programs. After initially taking shape as the Independent Television Organization, an informal co-op designed to organize the shipping of material between stations, it was reworked a year later into the Canadian Television Network, a microwave-signal network allowing a much quicker transmission of programming, and soon after evolved into CTV. By the end of the 1970s this network would come to be a dominant force from coast to coast, expanding to include 20 affiliates and 216 rebroadcast transmitters reaching 95 per cent of English-speaking Canadians.[7]

Diefenbaker had struck a significant blow against the CBC, let alone the desire of Masseyites for a pillar of cultured Canadian content, in the name of increasing the competitiveness of the marketplace. What the administration either failed or chose not to recognize, however, was that exclusive access to sponsorship dollars had previously allowed the CBC to air programming which otherwise might go unaired, and now, with the private sector active in the same markets and able to attract advertisers with shows of more mass interest, the CBC would be pressured to abandon its unprofitable offerings and shift its focus from audiences to advertisers. Was this a shocking development? Certainly in part, yet it was not completely incomprehensible. Television in the late 1950s occupied a different ideological position from that of radio in the 1930s; the unease that many Canadians felt towards broadcasting in the time of modernity was giving way to an acceptance of its entertainment value. American programming was becoming less a moral threat and more a competitive one.

The Conservative Party's radical reconfiguration of the broadcasting sector necessitated new checks and balances to ensure that the second stations, operating free from the CBC and thus not having to provide its programming, offered some degree of Canadian content. Throughout the 1950s the Canadian Association of Broadcasters had told various governmental broadcasting committees and commissions that approximately half of program offerings were Canadian in content, yet now it was necessary for the state to actually establish a means of identification and measurement. In a way that worked well for bureaucracies and echoing the ideas of the Royal Commission on Broadcasting of a few years earlier, the BBG cast qualitative elements aside in favour of a simpler quantitative method. This approach allowed the board to tally

Canadian content levels while keeping a safe distance from appearing to impose its ideas of Canadianness upon broadcasters; measurements of quality were not allowed to enter this paradigm, as any state-based evaluation of substance and worth threatened to drag the board into controversies it was unwilling to face.

On 1 June 1959 the board proposed a 55 per cent Canadian content regulation to ensure that broadcasting was 'basically Canadian in content and character' as required by the Broadcasting Act of 1958.[8] Given the difficulties of bringing stations in line with the new system, they were given an adjustment period in which the quota, measured over four-week periods, would begin on 1 April 1961 at 45 per cent and be increased to 55 per cent on 1 April 1962. Private broadcasters thus had a couple of years from the date of the announcement to establish a base of Canadian content programming and achieve the target level. It should not have been a difficult task – the level was in line with what the Canadian Association of Broadcasters had long been claiming to provide, and the CBC, asked by the BBG to suggest a workable figure, found that 55 per cent was appropriate, given existing program offerings, production facilities, and talent.[9] The new regulation, although created in response to the new second-station licences, was to be a blanket one applied to all television stations, meaning that even the CBC and its affiliates had to measure their output upon what would be an industry-based checklist. The board defined Canadian content as follows:

(a)   any program produced by a licensee,
    (i)   in his studio, or using his remote facilities, and
    (ii)   to be broadcast initially by the licensee;
(aa) any program produced by a network operator,
    (i)   in the studios of that network operator,
    (ii)   in the studios of an affiliated station, or
    (iii) by using the remote facilities of either network
        operator or the affiliated stations of the network operator;
(b)   news broadcasts;
(c)   news commentaries;
(d)   broadcasts of events occurring outside Canada in which
    Canadians are participating;
(e)   broadcasts of programs featuring special events outside
    Canada and of general interest to Canadians;
(f)   subject to subsection (5), programs produced outside Canada,
    (i)   in Commonwealth countries, or
    (ii)   in French language countries; and

(g) programs of films or other reproductions which have been made in
     Canada, if
     (i)   the maker is a Canadian citizen, ordinarily resident in Canada or a
           company incorporated under the laws of Canada or of a province
           and a majority of its directors are Canadian citizens,
     (ii) an application in a form prescribed by the Board has been submit-
           ted to the Board presenting evidence of Canadian and non
           Canadian content, and
     (iii) the Board, after considering the evidence contained in the applica-
           tion, has approved the production as one of Canadian content and
           character.[10]

While serving the BBG's bureaucratic nature, this approach to Canadian content posed a significant challenge to the highbrow qualitative
identification of Canadianness upheld by the Masseyites and ingrained
in the CBC, the NFB, and the Canada Council. The national sense of
self became reduced – if only in terms of television broadcasting – to a
numeric value.

Attracting both tremendous praise and heated condemnation, the
Canadian content regulations were anything but uncontroversial. For its
part, and certainly not surprisingly, the Canadian Broadcasting Corporation supported the content requirements and even hoped to increase
its own level of Canadian content to 75 per cent on the English-
language service – the French-language service had little problem
achieving such an amount.[11] Supporting the regulations placed the
CBC in an awkward position, however, as the broadcaster risked offending the privately owned stations that were still network affiliates: remember, only eight 'second station' licences free of the CBC network had
been established at this point, although more were to come. These affiliates now had to continue airing CBC programming while also going
through the bureaucratic task of tabulating their levels of Canadian content.[12] Despite the difficult situation, the CBC's Board of Directors
thought it had managed to successfully make its support clear without
drawing too much hostility from the affiliates.[13]

Given that the content regulations measured Canadianness in terms
of industrial usage, the Association of Radio and Television Employees
of Canada was highly supportive of the move – one could not ask for a
much better 'make-work' program. Extending the regulations to
include commercials would further aid the industry, the association
argued, but the BBG rejected the suggestion as complicating an already
difficult process.[14] As for the association's request that similar regulations

be instated for radio broadcasting, the board similarly decided that any expansion would have to wait until the television situation had been sorted out.[15] Instituting Canadian content regulations for television was enough for the BBG handle at this time.

For television station owners, the new regulations meant bureaucratic effort – and, in turn, expense – to keep track of Canadian content levels, not to mention actually having to pay for enough material to fill quota hours. In rejecting the proposed regulations, the Canadian Association of Broadcasters claimed that its members were already 'doing everything possible to strengthen the Canadian identity.'[16] Evidence of their effort was to be seen in how they offered viewers a selection of Canadian 'news, comment, their effort and information'[17] – four ways of saying exactly the same thing! Within the association's own defence was an inadvertent confession of how they offered nothing but the most inexpensive of programming. It cost little to assemble a news broadcast and even less to set up a camera for a 'question period' type show or to place a 'man on the street' to ask passersby their opinion on topics. Creating a quality dramatic or entertainment series with a talented cast and crew and based upon the work of a Canadian was a much more expensive proposition. Given that the Canadian Association of Broadcasters had long professed to the government that its member stations used approximately half their airtime for Canadian programming, why did it show such a fear of the Canadian content regulations? A glimpse of the truth is evident in the CAB warning to the BBG that the new regulations would require stations to repeat their programs in order to fill the required airtime.[18] Stations were perhaps not offering as much Canadian content as they had been claiming, and now that the amount was to be quantified – even in very liberal ways – the actuality of the situation would be exposed.

Contesting the proposed Canadian content regulations required that the CAB take old arguments and spin them anew. Regulations were a form of censorship and thus inherently negative, the association argued.[19] Ratings alone should determine program offerings; airing shows of interest was a sufficient return on using the airwaves to make money. 'Why is it that head counting is considered a proper way to determine the value of an election but an improper way to determine the value of ... programming?'[20] Such weighted arguments allowed station owners to guise profitability within democracy, ignoring how ratings served not the breadth of audience interests but those of advertisers and station coffers. True to the matter is the fact that, as communications theorist Sut Jhally has noted, 'if the market is like a voting machine then it will most reflect the "choices" of those who have the most to spend.'[21]

The advertising industry, represented by the Association of Canadian Advertisers and the Canadian Association of Advertising Agencies, made clear its objection to the idea of Canadian content regulations. A veiled threat was even levelled in which advertisers warned that they might bypass television altogether and take their dollars elsewhere – there were more attractive venues than Canadian television programs.[22] It turned out to be rather accurate calculation, given that even after a decade and a half into Canadian content regulations, CTV found it necessary to sell thirty-second slots during Canadian programs at a 22 per cent lower price than during non-Canadian shows. A greater discount was had with the purchase of fifty-two or more spots, and a further discount if the purchaser bought spots for a combination of Canadian and non-Canadian programs.[23] Cheaply made Canadian content necessitated rock-bottom prices.

The Liberals, now sitting in opposition and quite angered by the changes to the broadcasting system, let loose with a salvo of complaints. Canadian content had been reduced to an industry of numbers, noted Liberal broadcasting critic Jack Pickersgill, a highly respected civil servant who had helped bring about the Canada Council, at the 20 February 1961 meeting of the Special Committee on Broadcasting. Eagerly facing off with the BBG's Andrew Stewart, Pickersgill rejected flat out Stewart's declaration that there was a 'perfectly clear' means of measuring Canadian content. The numeric approach meant an item had 'to be Canadian but it does not have to be talent.'[24] Pickersgill had raised a valid point, one of many that committee members joined in on by putting forward possibilities for Stewart to address. 'If a show were produced in New York for Wayne and Shuster, with Canadian talent, would that be "Canadian content" even though it is being imported from the United States?' 'If the [British] royal ballet were performing, say in Massey Hall, and was televised?' 'If a Stratford play was televised, even though it was made up of outside talent, would that still be Canadian content?'[25] Measurements were made all the more complex by bureaucratic ambiguities such as accepting non-citizens as Canadian if there was evidence that they intended to stay in Canada.[26] Quantitative regulations offered a means of tabulating domestic program production, but as the committee members were correct in noting, doing so confounded the importance of ensuring that the time put aside for Canadian content actually served to open a discourse between Canadians.

Despite coming at the Canadian content regulations from opposite sides, the Canadian Association of Broadcasters and the Canadian Broadcasting Corporation both asked the Board of Broadcast Governors for flexibility and to take into consideration the newness of the task at hand. A degree of openness was sought or, in a less generous word, a loophole. The CAB thought that there would be leeway in the regulation's desire for 'varied and comprehensive' programming and the idea of 'Canadian in character.'[27] For its part, the CBC inquired about the board's acceptance of 'international events of national interest in Canada as a form of "grey area,"' an option listed in the regulations but largely undefined, and hoped it would include events such as Khrushchev's visit to the United States and baseball's World Series.[28] Instead of closing up the loopholes, the national broadcaster wanted to stretch one of them wide open. Yet as a 'very special events' exception, this loophole, it turned out, only included programming of international note that could not be produced in Canada, and even then stations had to contact the Board of Broadcast Governors to find out if a proposed program would qualify. Murray Chercover, president and managing director of the CTV network, recounted in 1970 that 'once, not quite facetiously, I contacted Dr. Stewart of the BBG and advised that there was a tremendous excitement about Northern Dancer, a Canadian horse bred by E.P. Taylor up at Windfields Farms in Toronto, that this horse was running in a pre-derby spring race in Florida and that we would like to bring it in. We thought that was an event in which Canadians were participating outside the country – certainly the excitement was there – and we got a very amusing wire back saying that they could not apply Canadian content to any part of the horse.'[29]

A more accessible loophole was found in the acceptance of foreign content of any sort if it came from the Commonwealth or France, with Commonwealth content counting as a Canadian content half-credit (i.e., a one-hour show would be worth half an hour Canadian content) and material from France a quarter-credit. The BBG allowed the inclusion in order to help stations to fill quotas, to offset the dominant presence of American programming, and because Britain's Independent Television Authority accepted Canadian programs as a full credit as part of its quota system.[30] The lack of a reciprocal full credit from Canada, however, soon drew complaints from the Independent Television Authority, and in 1962 the BBG raised it to an equal level. Of course, as the Canadian Council of Artists and Authors reminded the BBG,

Canadian producers were competing against a variety of international sources, not only the United States; so this inclusion operated contrary to the interests of domestic producers.[31]

Audiences expressed mixed feelings about the proposed Canadian content regulations. For a long time many people had shown a general apathy towards the national broadcasting system, defending it ideologically but not always being very keen to tune into its offerings. It was almost as if just knowing that the CBC existed, that it was out there doing its mandated task, was all that some people needed to feel secure in the nationalness of the television sector. Andrew Stewart, giving a talk to the Hamilton Association for the Advancement of Literature, Science and Art in January 1961, told of how

> the Canadian content regulations are a matter of controversy. In this debate we have a clear illustration of a conflict of objectives; a situation in which we cannot have our cake and eat it. From my contacts and experience with the public it seems quite evident that the vast majority of Canadians support the intention that broadcasting in this country should be basically Canadian in content and character. They believe that broadcasting is important to the life of the nation, and with the broadcasting service to contribute to the national purposes of Canadian identity, Canadian unity, and the self-expression of Canadians through active participation in broadcasting. However, as listeners and viewers, when they turn on their radio and television sets, and a choice of program is open to them, they will frequently select the one which is not Canadian in preference to the Canadian program. While there are conflicts of interest, the differences which give rise to controversy are not so much between people as within the same people. At times, as members of the public, Canadian lend their support to Canadian content; at other times, as audience, they cast their votes against it.[32]

It was no easy situation for the BBG to navigate and certainly one that infuriated station owners. Audiences, the Canadian Association of Broadcasters complained, 'say they want and insist upon a Canadian content; yet, where they have an opportunity to do so, they turn in rather large numbers to outside stations.'[33] That so much of the domestic programming being offered was of pitiful quality, thus prompting audiences to turn elsewhere, went unacknowledged. It was much easier to blame viewers than for broadcasters to account for their own role in the situation.

As of February 1961, with the start of Canadian content regulations only two months away, the system seemed to be in place. There were bureaucratic guidelines, regulatory flexibility, and a review panel in place to assess programs for possible inclusion as Canadian content. The Board of Broadcast Governors thought that quotas would be filled with little, if any, programming quality deterioration.[34] For its part, the Canadian Association of Broadcasters conceded that 55 per cent was not 'unworkable' and that audiences should not expect 'much change in the quantity or the type of television programming available.'[35] In other words, audiences could expect the same mixture of low-budget news, sports, and live local reports already making up much of broadcasters' self-made offerings.

Television station owners were not alone in wanting to change the broadcasting status quo; radio station owners, many of whom understood the economic potential of the new 'teenager' phenomenon and the desire for the jangly guitar sounds of rock and roll, had begun to make things difficult for the Canadian Broadcasting Corporation. Even with rock and roll an undeniable part of Canadian life by the late 1950s and early 1960s, the CBC continued to show a disinterest in offering such entertainment, which meant that privately owned affiliate stations were limited in their ability to air the latest 'hit' American rock-and-roll records. In a 1962 self-authored history, the corporation explained that 'all listeners do not like the same things, and there are minority groups whose tastes must be taken into account. But whether the listener likes jazz or classical music, light opera or chamber music, discussion programs, daytime serials or book reviews, CBC feels he should have programs to meet his particular taste somewhere in its schedules.'[36] Jazz, classical, opera, and chamber music served a variety of tastes? Rock and roll and its related immoral musical forms, epitomized by the pelvis-shaking threat of Elvis Presley, did not make the list. Given popular dynamics, it is not surprising to find affiliate stations wanting out of the national network, and the CBC, unwilling to adapt itself to the demands of a modern audience, decided to let many of them go. As of 1 October 1962, the radio sector was reshuffled: the CBC kept all twenty-four owned-and-operated stations and fifty-four of the affiliates, which were to broadcast a minimum twenty-six hours and seven minutes of CBC programming each week, while the other privately owned stations were free to use their airtime as they saw fit.[37]

Unlike the television sector, radio stations were not held accountable through a similar system of Canadian content regulation. The

Board of Broadcast Governors looked fondly upon the idea of extending the regulations to radio but wanted to make sure it first had a handle on instituting them in the television sector. The closest that the BBG came to Canadian content regulations at this time was in handling the growing interest in multilingual broadcasting. In 1962 the BBG introduced the Foreign Language Broadcasting policy to help assimilate the 'great influx of immigrants in the years since 1945.' Stations requesting to broadcast in a 'third' language – that is, not English or French – could do so if they also provided listeners with programming on Canadian history, politics, society, and English and/or French language instruction. The only significant attempt at Canadianizing radio, then, was as part of assimilating non-English- and French-speaking immigrants. The policy was in tune with the well-worn idea of Canada as a nation of 'two races' still very present in the early 1960s, but over the next couple decades, as the national project increasingly adapted to changes in demographics, it would scrape up against steps toward multiculturalism.[38]

All in all, Conservative Party rule marked a significant turn from the public to the private sector, and its activities in the television sector not only took a toll upon the CBC but set a precedent for quantifying Canadian content counter to the goals of those who had done much to place nationhood within qualified parameters. The significant inroads to be had by allowing the CBC to regulate the television sector, offering Canadian content of national weight, were replaced by a numbers game in which stations needed to only air something involving domestic industrial resources. The newly formed Board of Broadcast Governors, trying to get a grasp on a television sector under flux, probably had no idea that stations such as CHCH-TV Hamilton would go so far as to claim Canadian content points for the 'test pattern' played during off-air hours.[39] Although funding and tabulating Canadian content required effort by stations, the cost clearly did not outweigh the gains offered by freedom from the CBC network. The only losers in the reshuffling of the broadcasting system were the CBC and the people who enjoyed its programming, as the national broadcaster now had to go toe to toe with privately owned stations for limited advertising dollars in the big city markets. And that was not all. What had started out as a means of identifying and measuring levels of domestic television programming established important precedents and techniques for anyone seeking to quantify the elusive essence of national self and ensure its availability through a quota system.

The Feature-Film Industry and the Call for Assistance

Federal intervention into the film sector was not a new idea among those people who relied upon the industry for employment; back in 1949 the Massey Commission had offered an important opportunity to air grievances and put forth requests for change. Little resulted from the time spent in front of the cultural commission, however. The National Film Board, having found an ally among the cultural intelligentsia, emerged from the Massey Commission quite confident of its place in national life. Independent filmmakers and their colleagues, on the other hand, garnered little more than sympathy and a refusal to support requests for a theatrical quota and access to government film contracts. Theatres did not employ a limited natural resource as did broadcasting, and, given that Canadians had the NFB to make 'truly' national films, culturists required nothing from the offerings of the private sector. The theatrical circuit also had little use for their goods, given that Hollywood ensured the Canadian market had an ample supply of the latest American big-name films. With the NFB taking care of governmental film production and Hollywood having a lock on the theatrical circuit, feature filmmakers found that they could not even attract investment dollars to help produce their works. Money men had little regard for an industry that rarely returned initial funds, let alone profit, and even the federal government's Industrial Development Bank was not willing to take a chance on filmmakers.[40] It should come as no surprise, then, that filmmakers produced only a dozen or so full-length feature films between 1950 and 1957.[41]

That being said, not all was rosy at the National Film Board either, as an increase in theatrical use of full-length feature films during the early 1950s meant a declining need for NFB 'shorts' as fillers. By 1954 the NFB was concerned enough about the drop in demand that it began reminding its distribution agent at Columbia Pictures that audiences were interested in NFB films. A decision was also made to launch an advertising campaign in order to promote the idea that NFB films filled a unique cinematic niche.[42] A possibility not discussed by the film board at this time, however, was a quota system to secure screen time for its films. In fact, no discussion of a quota appears in the archived minutes of its meetings until 27 January 1958, a year and a half before the Board of Broadcast Governors proposed quotas for television broadcasting, and even then it was little more than an idea made in passing. The NFB members acknowledged that other countries, including Britain, used quotas to aid domestic production, but such a measure was not in line with the values of the board. Its place in national life and its cinematic style should not have to be imposed upon the public; having NFB films 'forced' upon audiences was antithetical to its underlying ideology. A better option seemed to be surveying the international film community to see how other governments handled the cinematic situation and then using these examples to argue for greater federal funding.[43]

The reports that rolled in throughout 1959 were not exactly what the National Film Board had envisioned. More and more, it became clear that while other governments were active in supporting their film sectors, much of the support went to feature films produced by the private sector. Not only that but the techniques used to aid the industry stood in direct opposition to the ideas espoused by cultural nationalists: it was often the case that direct funding was combined with theatrical quotas and box-office levies that turned over some of the revenues to domestic filmmakers. A few examples, taken that from the reports discussed by NFB personnel, are sufficient to provide an impression of the variety of approaches being used at this time.

Britain is, first and foremost, the obvious example to look at, given that much of Canadian cultural life had been modelled on its achievements. Back in 1949 the British government had formed the National Film Finance Corporation with an approximately $5-million budget and a legislated box-office levy to support filmmakers. In addition, an annual quota, although varying, ensured approximately 26 per cent of screen time for domestic films (with a minimum of 75 per cent of total production expenses to be spent on Commonwealth citizens in order for a film to quantify as British). Tellingly of the relationship between Canada and Britain at that time, Canadian films were included in the British quota and levy, although an upcoming legislative change to take place as of 1 January 1960 would maintain the inclusion in the quota but not the levy. The National Film Board did not qualify for the levy anyway, because it received state funds: the levy was only for the private sector.[44] Even Britain, then, was doing more for Canadian feature-film makers than their own government. Survey results from Sweden showed how the large number of imported American films was being offset through a tax-incentive program – similar to the Canadian Capital Cost Allowance used in the 1970s to questionable ends – which helped its industry to produce approximately forty feature films a year, a massive number compared to the one or two features being made in Canada at that time.[45] In a final example, and one that the film board certainly found to be much too controversial to implement in Canada, the government of India had instituted a blend of import quotas and restrictions on the export of theatre remittances. American films could have 75 per cent of the screen time, but no more than 12.5 per cent of the net collection would be returned to the production companies.[46] Apparently, India did not see the ideological infringement as being as important as the loss of revenues.

In hoping to find international examples that could be parlayed into a funding increase for itself, the National Film Board came into receipt of precedents making a strong case for state intervention to aid the private sector. This situation coincided with two other events further marking 1959 as a year of quota contention: the Board of Broadcast Governors implemented the quota system in television broadcasting, and, of great relevance to the film sector, in October of that year the Association of Motion Picture Producers and Laboratories of Canada delivered to the federal government and the NFB a petition seeking theatrical quotas and access to federal film monies. Soon after its creation back in 1948, the AMPPLC had told the Massey Commission that insufficient film production made a quota unfeasible, but a decade later it had reversed its position completely. Now the AMPPLC called for guaranteed screen time as part of the Board of Broadcast Governors' television quota system, 'a modest quota' in theatres, tariffs to support domestic production, and an end to the NFB's exclusive access to government film contracts.[47] A domestic feature-film industry offered economic and social benefits to the nation, the association argued, but these could only be achieved if the government ended the NFB's privileged position and the unfair control exercised by American theatrical interests. Unlike in Britain, where cheaply made 'quota quickies' had given the industry a poor reputation, the AMPPLC thought that Canadians could avoid such a problem by requiring that a minimum amount be spent on production.[48] That way audiences not only benefited from 'seeing themselves' on the silver screen but could also be assured of a quality experience.

As the government's adviser on cinematic issues, it fell to the National Film Board to address the petition and make recommendations on how to respond. The answer was not surprising. For no reason would the private sector be allowed access to government film contracts because the NFB relied upon the monies to keep itself afloat, particularly in a time in which the theatrical exhibition circuit was finding less need for its products. Infringing upon the NFB was equivalent to infringing upon the nation itself – or, more accurately, its ability to offer a cultured national alternative to the feature-film sector and to maintain its canonized position among culturists.

That the National Film Board would seek to protect its exclusive access to federal film monies is predictable, yet it is interesting to note that the request for a theatrical quota, something that did not seem to infringe upon the NFB, was also rejected. Several reasons stand out as to why the board took this position. Most obvious is the fact that the NFB had already dismissed the quota possibility for its own films and thus doing the same for the private sector made sense. In fact, the NFB had even turned down an offer from the Board of Broadcast Governors to require television stations to show its films; the board was 'reluctant to see its product imposed by decree,' as one member put it during a meeting of the board of directors.[49] In its report to the government, however, the board argued that the quota request should be rejected not because of such an ideological reason but because of the lack of available films to fill a quota. Simply put, the idea was 'premature.'[50] It is interesting to note that a copy of the AMPPLC's petition in the NFB archives is covered with pencilled comments apparently from the time of submission, and while the author is unknown, it is worth mentioning that the scribbles include the following: 'BBG has established Can. Content – let producers take advantage of that' and 'Not until there is enough production to warrant.'[51] These two points would become cornerstones of the federal response to the AMPPLC petition.

Evidence in the NFB archives also points to a looming sense that supporting the call for quotas, or 'any measure affecting the interests of the U.S. film industry in Canada,' as it was phrased by the board, would result in a backlash from the Motion Picture Export Association (MPEA; a branch of the Motion Picture Association of America), thereby harming an important export market for NFB films.[52] Such trepidation was not unwarranted: the MPEA had long fought for international film dominance. A section in its 1954 *Annual Report*, one quoted in the NFB's report to the government, described the task of using 'vigilance and constant surveillance ... to keep open the foreign markets which are vital to industry [and using] constant negotiation with foreign governments to overcome the strong pressures for protection of domestic film industries and imposition of restrictions on imports.' The MPEA identified exhibition quotas, limitations on film rental prices, and remittance levies as problems to be overcome. Trouble spots included thirty-one countries and regions, from Argentina to France to Israel to the United Kingdom, with many countries making the list several times for having multiple restrictions on American films.[53] Given the docility of the Canadian government towards film regulations and the legacy of the Canadian Co-operation Project, it is not surprising that Canada was not listed even once.

In defending its exclusive access to government contracts and being careful not to upset the theatrical status quo, the National Film Board made a remarkable suggestion that would come to colour Canadian cinematic life. Instead of pushing for the proposed changes, the AMPPLC and the rest of the feature-film industry could ask the federal government to look into providing direct investment monies.[54] And as will be examined later in this chapter, the film sector pushed this idea forward to such a degree that in only a few years time the government formed the Interdepartmental Committee on the Possible Development of Feature Film Production in Canada and, in 1966, the Canadian Film Development Corporation. No doubt the NFB thought this suggestion made sense in a self-preservation sort of way – feature-film investment monies would keep the private sector away from the board's bread and butter – but the ideological consequences of promoting a feature-film industry, including a weakening of the NFB's hold on defining the national cinematic experience within a cultured paradigm and with it the board's privileged position in Canadian life, seem to have been unforeseen or at the very least unconsidered. The suggestion of feature-film investment, then, marks an early moment in what would become a shift from a federal interest in the cultured offerings of the NFB to one favouring investment in the private sector, a change which, by the early 1980s, even involved the film board being restructured into a training facility for the very private sector to which it had long stood as an alternative. But that development was still to come.

The Association of Motion Picture Producers and Laboratories of Canada received the federal rejection of its petition on 2 November 1960, in a face-to-face meeting with Minister of Citizenship and Immigration Ellen Fairclough and National Film Commissioner Guy Roberge. The official response was. that government film contracts were crucial to the NFB's income and that the sensitivity of their content required the careful handling provided by the film board. As for theatrical quotas, the government agreed with the NFB that Canada lacked sufficient films to make a quota feasible. In some ways even more problematic, as Fairclough pointed out to the disheartened AMPPLC, was the fact that film exhibition came under provincial jurisdiction and thus the effort should be put towards petitioning the provinces, if not for a quota, then perhaps for access to monies through a tax at the box office.[55] In the meantime, the federal bureaucrats noted, the AMPPLC and like-minded filmmakers might be able to benefit from the BBG's Canadian content regulations by selling their work to broadcasters in need of domestic material.[56]

Television, it seemed, offered the most immediate solution to private industry woes. Two days after the disappointing meeting with representatives of the federal government, the AMPPLC met with the National Film Board, the Canadian Broadcasting Corporation, and the Board of Broadcast Governors to discuss the possibility of securing special consideration for its films.[57] Although sympathetic to the plight of the private sector, the NFB and the CBC possessed in-house facilities and thus had little need for external resources. The Board of Broadcast Governors, on the other hand, thought it might be able to help out the film industry by including some allowances in the regulations. For example, films produced by Canadians but shot elsewhere could be counted as 100 per cent Canadian content as long as two-thirds of the crew consisted of Canadians. Foreign footage was acceptable so long as it made up no more than 50 per cent of a film; anymore than that and the film would have to be assessed on an individual basis. Foreign investment was also allowed without any detrimental impact on Canadian content assessments. And to help filmmakers grab the attention of broadcasters, a new coding system could be applied to a film's tin and leader to inform stations that the footage was Canadian content – not unlike the MAPL emblem later used by the record industry to draw the attention of radio stations.[58] While the AMPPLC joined the Association of Radio and Television Employees of Canada in hoping that the BBG would consider television commercials under the quota system, as such production often involved film-industry resources, the board reiterated its earlier decision that commercials had to wait until the existing system was running smoothly.[59] At the very least, the Canadian content regulations offered the possibility of helping filmmakers to tap into the television market and, if successful, maybe even spark demand for their films in theatres.[60] The *Canadian Film Weekly Year Book* thought the regulations would be 'a considerable boost for Canadian production,'[61] while the *Year Book of the Canadian Motion Picture Industry* noted how they were 'hailed generally and pleased Canadian film producers, who saw it as a business booster.'[62] There was no lack of optimism, and now it was a matter of seeing if the opportunity would bear fruit.

The distribution and exhibition section of the feature-film industry, with something to lose if a theatrical quota were instituted, curiously did not make a public spectacle over the AMPPLC's demands. There were no grand gestures about how quotas were censorship and limited public access to goods. Yet it made little sense for theatre owners to complain until the threat seemed real. Film historian Ted Magder convincingly argues that 'undoubtedly, they would be heard from if the state decided to use measures that would disrupt their normal market operations, but any complaints in advance of such measures might backfire and serve the interests of those who sought a more radical solution to the problem.'[63] There was little to worry about, it seemed, as long as quotas remained a distant possibility.

With the cinematic status quo proceeding largely unchanged, Canadians could at most hope for a few domestic feature films mixed in with plentiful Hollywood escapism. Over the next few years filmmakers offered up such B-movies as *The Ivy League Killers* (1959), *The Samaritans* (1960), and the 3–D film *The Mask* (1961).[64] For its part, the National Film Board managed to hold onto its place in the cinematic canon through its highly praised documentaries *City of Gold* (1957; based on Pierre Berton's tale about the Klondike gold rush), *Circle of the Sun* (1961; documenting a Blood sun dance), and *Lonely Boy* (1961; a look at the rising career of Paul Anka). The film board even released its first feature film in 1963 with *Drylanders,* a docudrama set in the early twentieth century about a family leaving Montreal for life in rural Saskatchewan – a step pointing to a growing appreciation for the feature-film format among some of the board's filmmakers. Of course, these domestic works were up against such outstanding Hollywood creations as *Ben-Hur* (1959), *Spartacus* (1960), *The Magnificent Seven* (1960), *To Kill a Mockingbird* (1962), and *The Manchurian Candidate* (1962). Without similar budgets it seemed as if Canadian films stood little chance of luring the attention of exhibitors away from their supply of Hollywood films. But as some filmmakers began to hope, if the federal government could not institute a quota for a theatrical sector outside its jurisdiction and was unwilling to venture into a controversial area by trying to convince the provinces to institute a quota system, perhaps it could at the very least treat the film sector as an industry in need of assistance. This was, after all, a suggestion made even by the National Film Board itself. At least with state investment, feature films would have American-style budgets and filmmakers could challenge one of the core prejudices – and excuses for not screening Canadian films – held by distributors and exhibitors.

The Periodical Industry and the *Time* and *Reader's Digest* Controversy

Vincent Massey and his fellow commissioners had not seen much importance in talking about the contribution of middle-of-the-road consumer
magazines; the industry was mentioned only briefly in the commission's
report and even then with self-admitted 'diffidence.'[65] The commission's
attention had been reserved for the two styles of publication seen as most
threatening and as serving the interests of the cultural intelligentsia and
their model of Canadianization. The first sort were the lowbrow pulp
periodicals, particularly those of the lurid detective-story type, with their
brazen covers of women in torn clothing, police with guns drawn, and
criminals lurking in the darkness, which moralists fought to suppress.
The other kind were the highbrow periodicals that cultural nationalists
employed in the service of their national design, the small and often
non-profit literary and artistic magazines revered by the commission for
being 'a most important part in the cultural life of our country; their precarious life, their premature extinction and their courageous reappear-
ance are no doubt all essential to our slow growth as a cultivated
community.'[66] Middle-brow magazines such as *Maclean's* and *Chatelaine*
fell between the profane and the sacred, meriting neither condemnation
nor great praise, and as such, they were given little attention or support.
The biggest point of interest, it seemed, was in noting the commissioners' 'pleasant recollection of the session' with the Periodical Press Association and how its representatives 'presented their problems to us with
skill and good humour.'[67] To this end the report did little more than reit-
erate what the commission had been told with none of the emotion and
grand rhetoric reserved for areas of importance to culturists. 'We are
informed that the important Canadian magazines have a Canadian content of seventy or eighty per cent,' the report noted, 'that they do
attempt to interpret Canada as a whole to all Canadians, that they comment vigorously upon national issues in a non-partisan spirit, and that
they manage to survive and even to flourish although American periodicals outsell them by more than two to one in their Canadian market.'
Their industrial character was well served by the fact that 'Canadian magazines, unlike Canadian textiles or Canadian potatoes, are sheltered by
no protective tariff.'[68] Consumer periodicals, then, were little more than
any other industry, at best a way of keeping Canadians up to date on
national news and issues and at worst another cog in the machinery of
commercialism and social standardization.

Authors Isaiah Litvak and Christopher Maule have given a more quantitative, and quite bleaker, description of what the Massey Commission

called a 'flourishing' industry. In their assessment American magazines not only had a solid lock on the marketplace but increased it from 67 per cent in 1948 to 80 per cent in 1954, the publishers of *Time* and *Reader's Digest* in particular doubling their take of the market's advertising dollars from 18 per cent in 1948 to 37 per cent in 1955.[69] Problems were pronounced enough, in fact, that the Liberal Party, half a year away from losing to the Conservatives, introduced a 20 per cent advertising tax on Canadian editions of foreign publications to come into effect as of 1 January 1957. Now the Canadian versions of *Time* and *Reader's Digest*, both of which reused material from the American editions while attracting a fresh set of advertising dollars from the Canadian marketplace, faced extra taxation for doing so (although this measure actually seemed to aid the government's coffers more than it did the struggling domestic industry). The advertising tax did not end up mattering all that much, however, because it was in effect for less than a year before the Conservative Party won the election and brought it to an end. Diefenbaker called the tax a restriction on the free flow of ideas and even claimed that it weakened the contribution of foreign magazines to the Canadian economy.[70] Besides, Reader's Digest Association (Canada) had not paid the tax and was taking the federal government to court over it; so the Conservatives could relieve themselves of a headache by just dropping the legislation.

Such a controversial move was offset in part by establishing a commission to report on the health of the periodical industry, a sector important not only to periodical contributors and staffers but also to the pulp, press, and advertising industries. The Royal Commission on Publications (1960), chaired by *Ottawa Journal* president Michael Grattan O'Leary, had the task of investigating the complaints of unfair competition with an eye to foreign overflow publications and split-run 'Canadian editions.'[71] Hearings, held across Canada from November 1960 to January 1961, offered periodical publishers and various industry participants an opportunity to air their grievances and put forth suggestions for increasing the strength of domestic publications. Lloyd M. Hodgkins, president of the Magazine Publishers Association of Canada, told the commission of how approximately 125 periodicals had been launched since the 1920s, only to result in 81 failures. In the 1950s alone there had been 10 new magazines but 9 failures.[72] A major reason for this pattern, Hodgkins explained, was that advertisers could often purchase space in American overflow magazines and split-runs targeting the Canadian marketplace at a cost less than that of domestic equivalents.[73] As long as advertising dollars flowed to American magazines recycling themselves for the Canadian market, and thus letting their lower overhead expenses be translated into cheaper costs for advertising space, Canadian periodicals would continue to be at a disadvantage. Advertising dollars were, after all, the lifeblood of the industry. *Chatelaine*, for example, relied on advertising for 77 per cent of its total revenue in the late 1950s.[74]

Representatives from Time Inc. and Reader's Digest Association (Canada) certainly did not look forward to appearing in front of the commission. After all, they were identified by many people as the biggest problem with the industry. These two publishers managed to attract over 40 per cent of the domestic periodical advertising monies by, in the case of Time, publishing a split-run edition out of New York using regular material with an added Canadian section, while Reader's Digest thrived in the Canadian market by using a domestic branch plant to republish its magazine with minor editorial changes.[75] The unfair position they held was deemed so corrosive to the development of a domestic industry that, in the summer leading up to the commission, Liberal Party broadcasting critic Jack Pickersgill had used it as a warning as to what was in store for television with the opening of the market to the private sector: 'stuff on which the main earnings have been made in another country will be brought out here cheaply and more or less dumped and used to attract advertising which would otherwise go into things produced in Canada by Canadians for Canadians.'[76]

Although not Canadian-owned, the two periodical publishers defended themselves as being important components of the Canadian magazine sector. Time's split-run Canadian edition included several pages of national news and events slipped into its otherwise American version and thus performed a role in helping keep Canadians up to date on national events. The periodical did not, however, have an actual staff office in Canada, and only two of the eleven or twelve people working on the Canadian section at its New York facilities were Canadian citizens.[77] Conversely, Reader's Digest Association (Canada) made 'no pretense of being a magazine to inform Canadians about Canada,' explained E. Paul Zimmerman, president of the Canadian division.[78] Audiences received the same content as other nations but with domestic advertisements. Reader's Digest did, however, re-edit its Canadian issues, including a French-language version, *Sélection du Reader's Digest*, in Canada and employed more than four hundred Canadians; in fact, all the employees at the branch plant were citizens, right up to the senior management and president.[79] Reader's Digest Association (Canada) may have been proud of this claim to Canadianness, but it mattered little to commissioner J. George Johnston, who dismissed the company as a 'branch-plant ... that is all.'[80]

Canadian publishers had much to gain economically in revealing the unfair economics of the marketplace, yet there was even more to be had by identifying consumer periodicals as important contributors to Canadian nationhood. Within their pages rested more than merely advertisements and other forms of commercialism; the discussion of Canadian ideas, trends, issues, and values in these middle-brow venues made them just as important as their highbrow and learned periodical peers. Consumer periodicals engaged readers in a range of content, offering a national take on everyday life, whether it was politics and social affairs in *Maclean's* and *Mayfair,* the voice of Canadian women in *Chatelaine,* or the residential aesthetic explorations of *Canadian Homes and Gardens.* It was an idea in line with the broader shift from a highbrow qualification of culture to one incorporating elements of daily life as a type of 'popular' culture. Lloyd M. Hodgkins of the Magazine Publishers Association of Canada impressed upon the commission the idea that, 'as publishers in Canada, we respect the right for Canadian people to purchase magazines or periodicals of their choice regardless of the country of origin of these publications. We also believe that it is vitally important to Canada as a nation, desirous of its own identity and character that Canada has a strong national magazine press which reflects the Canadian point-of-view.'[81] By their very nature these periodicals might not best serve the interests of culturists in the same way as small literary and poetry magazines or learned periodicals such as the *Canadian Forum* and *Dalhousie Review,* and there was no denying that consumer magazines had plenty of advertising and promoted consumerism, but that being said, Masseyite culturists were increasingly losing their hold on the tone and temper of cultural nationalism; a new wave of intellectual thought was starting to conceptualize cultural devices in a different way. For Hodgkins and others in the publishing industry, the fact that their goods were middle-brow did not prevent the medium from offering a positive and important outlet through which Canadians could achieve a sense of nationhood.

The Royal Commission on Publications agreed. 'Canada's particular responsibilities, her government, her constitutional structure, her ideals and aspirations, her memories and milestones, even her discords, are facts in her existence which cannot be approached understandably or usefully by communications media owned or controlled in another country, even though that country may be friendly,' explained the commission in its report to the government.[82] The Canadian periodical sector had finally found commissioners – and, it was hoped, a pipeline to federal policy-making – receptive to the idea that magazines offered more than merely a mixture of entertainment and advertisements. Periodical publishers were not like their private-sector broadcasting and film-distribution peers in acting as outlets for American content; these struggling presses often engaged in questions of nationhood and identity or, at the very least, covered the activities of Canadians, if only in terms of home decoration or the consumer goods being purchased that season. A significant outlet of pan-Canadian communication had gone unappreciated by the cultural elite because the content served largely middle-brow audiences and came wedged between advertisements. The fact that the industry struggled in its contribution to national life, the commission noted, needed to be changed. 'It is indeed a sorry state of affairs which permits *Time* magazine to say of its "Canadian" edition that "no other journal provides as much information about Canada to as many readers throughout the world,"' the report declared.[83] Here was not so much a hostile declaration against the United States as a note of concern about separate national interests and the importance of periodicals as a medium for national communication. Could Canada not produce a periodical offering national news coverage and perhaps even catch the attention of some international readers? *Maclean's* came close, but economic anemia prevented it from going toe to toe with *Time*'s Canadian edition.

Identifying systemic problems within the periodical industry proved to be much easier than devising a way of correcting them. The commissioners needed to keep in mind the Conservative administration's recent decision to end the almost as recent tax on split-run American magazines. Diefenbaker had called the tax a form of censorship, yet, the commission noted, intervention was an internationally accepted idea and Canada had 'less restriction and regulation of expression, less assistance, and less protection of domestic publishing than nearly all the [other countries surveyed].'[84] Now was the time for Canada to follow suit, and fortunately for the commissioners, there were a number of domestic precedents of intervention that might be replicable in the periodical sector. Along with tariffs and customs for traditional industries, there was now the Canada Council for the Arts and Canadian content regulations for television broadcasting. The council and the content regulations did not end up offering a sufficient solution, however. In the end, Canada Council–style subsidies were rejected as being 'alien' to the periodical press, and unlike broadcasting, magazine racks were not a limited natural resource.[85] A new measure needed to be devised, one tailored to the periodical sector and the problems of passing legislation in an area rife with issues of censorship.

'There is no threat to the free flow of ideas in the insistence that any economic disabilities now suffered by Canadian periodicals with respect to their American contemporaries should be removed,' Claude Bissell, president of the University of Toronto and chair of the Canada Council, had pointed out to the commission during the hearings.[86] Bissell hit on a key point: levelling the playing field was not akin to engaging in censorship; quite the opposite, it was a means of reducing the censorship that existed when foreign content possessed an unfair position in the marketplace. That American companies were recycling content paid for in other markets yet getting to attract a fresh set of advertising dollars from the Canadian one lay at the root of the disadvantage. The best solution for bringing about change, then, seemed to be in encouraging advertisers to use Canadian magazines instead of their foreign competition. There was already legislation in place giving advertisers a tax deduction for space purchased in magazines, but this was applicable not only to Canadian but to all magazines. This situation, as marvellously described in the nationalistic rhetoric of publisher H.T. Mitchell during the hearings, led to 'the weird spectacle of financing indoctrination with a foreign viewpoint using Canadian dollars withdrawn from economic support of truly Canadian media expression.'[87] A clear and seemingly justifiable solution to periodical woes lay in altering the income tax act to allow such deductions only if the advertising took place in domestic periodicals – why should advertisers get a tax incentive on something that ran counter to the encouragement of national discourse? This approach not only made ideological sense, but it was also a measure that fell within the federal government's ability to implement. As the commission argued in its report, changing the legislation 'involves no "tax on ideas or information," no actual interference with readership preference, and, with no tax or customs duty, would have the merit of administrative simplicity.'[88] Representatives of the advertising industry had claimed during the hearings that any restrictions on taking out space in foreign periodicals would deprive them of 'a fundamental right.'[89] That might be true, but receiving an income tax deduction for doing so was not a right but an incentive.

The commission had struck upon an amazing way for federal bureaucrats to encourage one industry – in this case, advertisers – to aid a fellow industry instead of its foreign competition. It was an industrial backdoor through which the government could be active yet not overly obtrusive; it was a method that could be invoked not only in the periodical sector but also in a number of other advertising-reliant domestic media. And when faced by critics of intervention, defenders of the periodical advertising tax incentive could point out that the deduction was nothing new but merely a fine tuning of existing legislation. This seemed to be a fair decision.

Henry Luce, the person behind the success of *Time*, *Life*, and *Fortune*, was not about to stand by and watch the Canadian government make tax changes affecting the privileged position held by his periodical enterprise. With great economic capital came political influence, and Luce found it easy enough to mobilize the U.S. Department of State to act on his behalf and exert pressure upon the Canadian government. On 5 September 1961 the *Toronto Star* reported that an official complaint about the recommendations had already been issued, even though Ottawa had not yet given its endorsement.[90] A week later it was reported that Diefenbaker had shown signs of bowing to American pressure by establishing a subcommittee to dilute the recommendations, although the prime minister claimed that the reason for doing so was not because of U.S. influence but because the report was 'too harsh.'[91] Still, Diefenbaker showed great skill at handling a difficult situation and – certainly in part as a result of the vein of anti-Americanism running throughout his administration – rebounded that winter, telling the press that 'we in Canada believe we have the right to assert the preservation of those things which are Canada's,' and that he would not bow to American pressure or else 'we shall in the days ahead be dependent entirely or almost entirely on the viewpoint of another nation.'[92] The commission's report continued to go unimplemented, however, and electoral loss to the Liberals two years later saved the sitting government from having to handle the hot topic.

It had been an interesting six years of Conservative Party leadership, a period marked by a pronounced private-sector challenge to public-sector privilege. Business owners, investors, and profiteers in general were trying to court the government with economic returns of greater tangibility than the cultural contributions offered by nationalists, socially concerned citizens, and the benefactors of public-sector opportunities. Diefenbaker was happy to side with television station owners in hamstringing the CBC, since doing so offered both political gains and a means of diverting advertising dollars away from American stations along the border. That doing so in turn meant quantifying Canadian content and requiring the CBC to give a new weight to advertisers over audiences meant little to the Conservatives. Independent film producers were less successful in positing their challenge to the public sector because the National Film Board, as the federal government's consultant on cinematic activities, defended its exclusive access to state contracts and protected the theatrical status quo. Instead, the board argued, the private sector should try to fill the needs of television stations for Canadian content and promote the possibility of federal investment. Finally, electoral defeat let Diefenbaker escape entangling his government in a periodical controversy with the United States, but the issue was not about to fade away with the changing of federal administrations. The O'Leary commission had given consumer magazine publishers the credit they had been denied by the Masseyites, a credit that seemed to make sense amid the growing perception that 'mass culture' might be mass but was also perhaps more cultural than some elites would care to admit.

Federal Assistance for Periodical Publishers and Feature Filmmakers

A mixture of anxious filmmakers, frustrated periodical publishers, defensive advertisers, and hostile Americans provided a rough welcome for the newly elected Liberal government and its leader, Lester B. Pearson, a distinguished civil servant and diplomat who had won a Nobel Peace Prize during his time as Minister of External Affairs. Although more inclined towards intervention than the Conservatives, the Liberals had to keep in mind that Canadian-American relations had become antagonistic as a result of what was no less than sheer antipathy between Diefenbaker and John F. Kennedy. Repairing the relationship with Canada's top trading partner was all the more a priority because the governments were on the brink of signing the Auto Pact, an automotive parts trading agreement promising tremendous economic benefits. It should come as no surprise, given the masterful ways in which the American government had long been successful in protecting the interests of its entertainment industries, that the U.S. Department of State should imply that the Auto Pact might not be ratified if the Canadian government altered the income tax act in favour of domestic periodicals. Pearson found himself having to take into account not only all of the economic and political considerations but also, and quite tellingly of the status of the periodical industry, the fact that things had worsened in recent years – *Canadian Home Journal* (1905–59), *Mayfair* (1927–61), and *Canadian Homes and Gardens* (1924–62) had recently ceased publication, and *Liberty* (1932–64) was on the brink of following suit. Important contributors to national periodical activity and readership stretching back to the early part of the century had come to an end.

The solution that Pearson thought was a compromise, other people would label a betrayal. The Paperback and Periodical Distributors Act (1964) removed the ability to deduct advertising space purchased in a non-Canadian periodical targeted at the Canadian market, but in accordance with American demands, the legislation exempted *Time* and *Reader's Digest*. It was an amazingly short-sighted decision: advertisers could now focus their expenditures on *Time* and *Reader's Digest* and thereby make these two periodicals even more powerful. The publishers of *Time* and *Reader's Digest* could not have dreamt up a better situation for themselves. They stood to reap a windfall from having their American competition purged from the tax deduction. There were even ideological gains since, as Isaiah Litvak and Christopher Maule have noted, the measure reified their claims of Canadianness: 'legislatively defined, *Time* and *Reader's Digest* were as Canadian as the maple leaf and beaver.'[93] American mass-media interests had once again proven that they were quite skilled at rallying their government to protect their interests abroad. Conversely, the Canadian government did its best to avoid upsetting the Americans, and another media monopoly was allowed to continue unabated. *Time* and *Reader's Digest* joined Hollywood in sitting comfortably beyond nationalist reproach.

Filmmakers hoped to do better than their periodical industry compatriots when it came to ending their marginalized position. In the years immediately following the Association of Motion Picture Producers and Laboratories of Canada's unsuccessful petitioning of the federal government for access to government contracts and a theatrical quota, several film organizations – the Association Professionnelle des Cinéastes, the Directors Guild of Canada, and the Society of Film Makers – took their case directly to the press. During the first half of 1964 one finds significant newspaper coverage of the plight of filmmakers and the idea that a feature-film industry could make significant contributions to the economy while offering an outlet for domestic expression.[94] By that August the support seemed to have built up to such a level that, in conjunction with celebrating the twenty-fifth anniversary of the National Film Board,

Secretary of State Maurice Lamontagne launched the Interdepartmental Committee on the Possible Development of Feature Film Production in Canada, chaired by Guy Roberge of the NFB.

In May 1965, after nine months of gestation, the committee recommended that the federal government introduce a combination of funding (loans, grants and awards, subsidies, tax concessions, and production advances) and bureaucratic aids (a film registry office, a film industry advisory committee, and a film development corporation).[95] Quotas did not make the list, however. 'If the philosophy of the Government's assistance programme is one of encouragement, inducement and persuasion, then a quota system represents a means of last resort,' the committee concluded.[96] This decision was made in the face of briefs arguing that quotas were a necessary measure. The Directors Guild of Canada, for example, explained to the committee that 'the fact that most of Canada's theatres are controlled by foreign interests, the same that control distribution, the same that produce films in their own country for Canadian consumption, fairly well denies the action of the marketplace to Canadian film-makers.'[97]

The May report turned into an October presentation, and then finally, in the summer of 1966, two years after the secretary of state had started the ball rolling, the House of Commons tabled the idea as Bill C-204, to establish the Canadian Film Development Corporation (CFDC). Modelled in part on the Industrial Development Bank and taking some leads from the National Film Finance Corporation in Britain, the CFDC was given a ten-million-dollar budget for loans, awards, and its administrative expenses.[98] Like the Canada Council, the corporation was to aid domestic production, but it differed in expecting a return on its money. This was investment in industry, not patronage for culture; the focus was first and foremost on dollars and cents. It was a telling sign of federal bureaucrats buying into the idea that the private sector could provide economic gains not offered by the National Film Board. 'Good commercial films can make a positive contribution to employment and income to our balance of payments,' as Secretary of State Maurice Lamontagne told *Time* (Canada) in October 1965.[99] A few months later he was replaced by Judy LaMarsh, a civil servant known for her outspokenness and willingness to tackle issues as she saw fit. And like Lamontagne, LaMarsh appreciated the economic possibilities of a feature-film industry. In an interview with *Take One* magazine that autumn, LaMarsh explained that the corporation had a threefold purpose: to contribute to the economy through employment and tourism, to aid filmmakers in the production of their craft, and to promote Canada at home and abroad. (It is interesting to note that the first and third points overlap in regard to the contributions the films were to make to the tourism industry, a purpose that had characterized federal film activity from the very start – the Canadian Government Motion Picture Bureau, the Canadian Co-operation Project, and even to some degree the National Film Board.)[100]

Treating film as an industry meant that federal funds needed to be used for films most likely to make a profit; this endeavour was not about the quality or worthiness of expression but about sheer money-making potential. 'There's no point in producing some great artistic success which is a commercial flop,' Judy LaMarsh told the *Globe and Mail* in September 1966. 'We won't be able to distribute it.'[101] Canadians could now make their own versions of 'go-go stories,' the phrase LaMarsh used to described the dance- and music-based films popular among teenagers at the time, but she did not see the investment dollars going towards 'cheap, trashy Canadian movies.'[102] What LaMarsh did not understand, or at least did not publicly acknowledge, was that subsidies are as attractive to the makers of smut as they are the makers of mainstream works, and there is little concession for morality or any other qualitative assessments in a bureaucratic body concerned about the economic bottom line. The corporation would go on to provide significant funding to films involving 'the commercial exploitation of sex' because, as the CFDC explained to the *Toronto Star*, such films were 'a worldwide phenomenon and Canada cannot possibly be an exception.'[103]

Unwilling to let the corporation – and, by extension, the government – face criticism for making subjective assessments about the qualitative value of proposed film grants to national discourse, federal bureaucrats created something that would be nothing more than a tool for industrial activity in and of itself. It is amazing that Judy LaMarsh could reassuringly tell the House of Commons that the films would have to 'be of a Canadian nature or of Canadian content' yet in the same breath talk of determining these qualities by using a quantified system adapted from the television sector.[104] Such grand rhetoric about offering Canadians domestically relevant content failed to match up to the reality of the situation, one in which, as film historian Ted Magder has noted, Canadian content meant merely having citizens for 'at least two of a film's three principal creators (producer, director, and screenwriter) ..., [while] a maximum of two of the other major creative contributors (cinematographer, designer, editor, composer) could be non-Canadians.'[105] Australia would learn from the Canadian mistake and ensure that the Australian

Film Commission, created in 1975 with the same general purpose as the CFDC, not only used citizenship and employment criteria but also gave significant consideration to a film's contribution to national life.[106] In doing so, the Australian government showed an understanding of the difference between having a film industry in Australia and promoting an Australian film industry.

Another problem was that the state did not back Canadian Film Development Corporation investment with a theatrical quota for its films. The Interdepartmental Committee on the Possible Development of Feature Film Production in Canada had suggested that quotas be left as 'a last resort,' it is true, but the decision fell upon the federal government, even if it only meant trying to convince the provinces, which had jurisdiction for film exhibition, to establish a quota or for the feds to search for a jurisdictional loophole. Yet the government chose to do nothing. In fact, Secretary of State Maurice Lamontagne dismissed quotas as 'restriction and control,' and his successor, Judy LaMarsh, called them 'negative' and 'harmful.'[107] These were not assessments of quota effectiveness but value judgments, ones showing either an unbelievable naïveté about how the film sector operated or simply a desire to escape controversial jurisdictional issues. LaMarsh went so far as to try to avoid the quota issue by declaring that the government had 'heard nothing to suggest that we will not get co-operation from the distributors.'[108] Somehow, and very improbably, the secretary of state avoided seeing all of the evidence to the contrary: the decades of theatrical disregard for domestic films; the exhibitor alliances with Hollywood; the gambles entailed in showing Canadian films instead of the American ones already successful abroad; and the simple fact that theatre owners were not about to speak out against screening Canadian films or else risk the government instituting a quota system. Even non-English-speaking countries found it necessary to use quotas to guarantee audiences access to films created outside the United States' cinematic hegemony. Weak-kneed politicians pretty much ensured that the corporation would have some difficult years ahead of it.

The sheer prospect of federal monies for film production – failure to distribute the films was still some distance off – was enough to excite filmmakers about what lay ahead. The *Globe and Mail* was not off the mark in telling its readers that 'although the period of gestation has been somewhat prolonged, optimists are caroling that Canada is on the verge of a feature film industry.' Of course, as the newspaper noted, this development was due in large part to filmmakers now having money when previously they had had very little.[109] The optimism reflected the hope that films with large budgets would be able to attract the interests of exhibitors; the strength of the opposition against Canadian films had yet to be fully encountered. Soon the government would see, and be forced to acknowledge, that film distributors and exhibitors had continuously rejected Canadian films not just because, as theatre owners had long claimed, the budgets had been low and the quality lacking. No, the roots of the disinterest stretched all the way to Hollywood, and as filmmakers began to stand around with movie tins in their hands and nowhere to screen the contents, many would come to see that this was a problem that could not be solved by investment dollars alone.

Conclusion

Over the course of less than a decade, members of the entertainment industries wooed federal bureaucrats with promises of economic returns more alluring and much more tangible than the cultural gains spoken of by the Masscyites and their public-sector compatriots. The positing of Canadian nationhood upon cultural devices undertaken during the first moment of Canadianization had clearly become out of date in an age of continentalism and popular culture; politicians and profiteers found the gains of private-sector growth to be too lucrative to oppose in the name of high-cultural refinement. Canada needed not to be saved from mass media but to engage in it with the same tenacity as its American competition. Broadcasters benefited from a Progressive Conservative government happy to reduce the role of the CBC for the sake of program variety and reducing the loss of Canadian advertising dollars to stations south of the border. The Board of Broadcast Governors' creation of Canadian content regulations to ensure a private-sector return on using the airwaves – measuring nationalness by industrial activity and with no minimum monetary expenditure required – would prove to be little more than a requirement that stations lose out on getting to offer a schedule of only American programming, rather than having to spend money on domestic shows of actual interest to Canadians.

Periodical publishers, for their part, managed to rally support from the Royal Commission on Publications and in turn a recommendation that the income tax deduction for periodical advertising be narrowed to cover only domestic magazines. The returning Liberal government responded by passing the Paperback and Periodical Distributors Act but, in weighing the benefits of the periodical sector against those of an

Auto Pact that might not be ratified without concessions to the United States, chose to exempt *Time* and *Reader's Digest* from the legislation.

Lastly, the Association of Motion Picture Producers and Laboratories of Canada was initially unsuccessful in petitioning for access to government film contracts and an exhibition quota, but a mere few years later, and in line with a suggestion from the NFB, the industry was rewarded with the Canadian Film Development Corporation. The National Film Board might still be holding onto a privileged position among cultural nationalists, yet the federal government, from which its received its funding, was beginning to explore a better investment for film monies. A new fiscal rationale and appreciation of middle-of-the-road content seemed to be creeping, slowly but surely, into the inner workings of national cultural activity. The three institutional pillars upholding the Masseyites' Canadianization – the Canadian Broadcasting Corporation, the National Film Board, and the Canada Council – were up against the eroding impact of changes benefiting television station owners, periodical publishers, and feature filmmakers; identifying Canadian content in terms of high-cultural experience, something quite hard to measure, was being overshadowed by a bureaucratic preference for quantitative assessments of Canadianness. At the same time, the federal government was finding out that it could avoid any discomfort over funding artsy longhairs by focusing its efforts on industrial development and, in doing so, actually get an economic return on its investment. Quotas, tax incentives, and investment monies seemed a way of aiding opportunities for domestic entertainment, if not expression, while returning revenues to the state coffers.

Here one finds the state opening systems of communication to greater private-sector participation in exchange for economic gains and Canadian content becoming identified with industrial criteria. The high-cultural model of Canadianization was increasingly surrendering its influence over the tone and temper of nationhood to industrial measures and a middle-of-the-road popular culture differentiated from the American alternative. Whether the new federal initiatives would make a positive contribution to the quest for nationhood or merely further frustrate members of the cultural community remained to be seen.

4 Canadian Content Woes: Cultural Imbalance and Undercurrents in the 1960s

Peter C. Newman was furious about the federal government's decision to exempt *Time* and *Reader's Digest* from the Paperback and Periodical Distributors Act of 1964. The situation had been made all the worse because Walter Gordon, the Liberal Party's finance minister, had shown an interest in limiting American influence over the Canadian economy. As Newman roared in a letter to his friend Abraham Rotstein in the summer of 1965,

> you are reading the letter of an *EX*-Walter Gordon disciple. His militant sponsorship of legislation forever garroting Canadian periodicals and awarding Time and Digest a monopoly over the Canadian magazine industry is a step that has disillusioned me, more than I can admit (in print). Aside from the fact that magazines are my livelihood (and newspapers merely a temporary madness) surely the most important aspect of nationalism is to build up a purely Canadian cultural barrier to preserve this society against American cultural intrusion, which is the more dangerous form of imperialism. With no national newspapers (or any chance of such a venture) Gordon has now handed over to two American magazine empires the monopoly over the printed word for national distribution in Canada. I think he's inconsistent and stupid.[1]

According to Newman, Gordon had told him that the proposed legislation had angered the Americans so much that 'nothing, not even if we'd sent tanks armed with nuclear warheads to Castro, could have got the Americans madder. And, significantly, the Canadian government backed down before the power of Time Inc.!'[2] Once again, it seemed, Canada was vulnerable to American industries capable of using the U.S. Department of State to exert their interests.

Newman's anger was shared by many other Canadians, who expected the recent changes in the arts and entertainment sectors to provide more opportunities for domestic expression and discourse. The Canada Council for the Arts (1957) marked a new age of Canadian high-cultural activity; Canadian content regulations (1961) in the television sector offered new employment opportunities for both on-screen and behind-the-scenes talent; the Canadian Film Development Corporation (1968) was heralded as a step forward for the production industry; and of course, the Paperback and Periodical Distributors Act (1964) was passed, exemption and all, by federal bureaucrats promising to help the struggling magazine industry bring readers content of domestic origin.

Yet despite all this intervention and assistance for Canadian content, distributors and exhibitors continued to stick with material acquired from other marketplaces, whether the plays of William Shakespeare or the acting of William Shatner on *Star Trek* (the irony being that the Canadian-born Shatner left the anemic domestic industry only to be imported as part of a foreign program). Theatres, orchestras, and ballets overlooked Canadian performers and compositions in favour of foreigners and established international works; television station owners skirted Canadian content requirements by making use of numerous loopholes or, at best, filling time slots with content as inexpensive as putting a pianist in front of a camera for a few hours; radio stations did not even have to fill such quota hours, resulting in no need for Canadian recordings; movie-theatre owners showed little interest in the new crop of films because Hollywood offered consistently profitable alternatives and, in many cases, exerted control over distribution and exhibition through vertical integration and block booking; and lastly, there was no periodical revolution, no triumph of the Canadian magazine, because advertisers continued to get a tax deduction for purchasing space in *Time* and *Reader's Digest*.

It should not be surprising, then, to find disappointment and frustration among playwrights, actors, filmmakers, periodical publishers, and other producers taking on tones of nationalism and anti-Americanism during the 1960s. The issue of domestic expression was becoming interwoven in ideas of national sovereignty and the need to ensure discourse otherwise prevented by profiteers and imperialistic American industries. International artistic achievements had gone from being learning aids to becoming barriers to the exhibition of Canadian cultural works, while the entertainment industries, increasingly becoming valued for their contribution to 'popular culture,' were being ignored, despite vast steps forward in the quality of goods. With distinctions between cultural brows coming to mean less than the origin of the content, indigenous high and popular culture were both being vested with an important role in the quest for nationhood. The result was a growing nationalistic undercurrent, cautious yet increasingly present, determined to rectify the situation. A new moment of Canadianization, one that was casting aside the Anglophilic ethnic nationalism of the Masseyites and the continentalism of the Liberal Party in favour of a civic nationalism defining and empowering Canada as a Peaceable Kingdom, would take root within the imbalance.

The Arts and the Costs of Internationalism

The Canada Council for the Arts supported the establishment of cultural branch plants from the get-go because the Masseyites, as was common during their time, identified European cultural achievements as templates for elevating Canada to international standards. Foreign experts were thus seen as a prerequisite to replicating artistic triumphs with a Canadian flair. In the March 1982 issue of *Saturday Night*, dedicated to the council's twenty-fifth anniversary, columnist and long-time social commentator Robert Fulford recounted how Canadian culture had been nurtured by British nannies, immigrants who

> brought with them the British rules, and then improvised as they went along. John Grierson at the National Film board, Celia Franca at the National Ballet and the National Ballet School, Tyrone Guthrie and Michael Langham and Tanya Moiseiwitsch at the Stratford Festival, Gweneth Lloyd at the Royal Winnipeg Ballet – the list is long and impressive. Even those native Canadians who played central roles in this period – Alan Jarvis, who directed the National Gallery with flair and imagination from 1955–1959; George Woodcock, who founded *Canadian Literature* magazine in 1959 and provided the basis for academic study of fiction and poetry in this country; and Massey himself – were educated in England and formed by British models.[3]

Major sites of cultural construction were handed over to foreign cultural figures for the sake of bringing Canada culturally up to par with its peers. Doing so served earlier ideas of cultural design and purpose, but what would happen when arts institutions outgrew the need for foreign talent?

The early years of the Canada Council passed without much of a hitch. Funding activities were plentiful, increasing from $749,000 in the first year to $4,297,000 by 1966–7, and were eagerly received by cultural groups from coast to coast: the Halifax Symphony Orchestra to the Vancouver Symphony Orchestra, the nearly bankrupt National Ballet to the growing Royal Winnipeg Ballet to the recently created Les Grands Ballets Canadiens.[4] Money even went towards bringing youths to the Stratford Festival Theatre and to shows by the Canadian Players, as upon the next generation of Canadians rested the nation's cultivated future. In its 1960–1 *Annual Report* the council explained that its objectives 'in spending these large sums of money are to foster ability among those who have it; to find ways in which it can maintain active organizations by helping them to continue and enrich the work they are doing; to provide for the people of Canada a more attractive and more varied mental and spiritual fare through theatres, opera, ballet, festivals and other "cultural" enterprises.'[5] These objectives also meant that the arts were more accessible than ever before. 'No longer must audiences politely ignore the ubiquitous reminders of last night's basketball game,' the Canadian Conference of the Arts happily noted in the summer of 1965. 'In many cities they can now enjoy fine performances in comfortable air conditioned theatres and auditoria.'[6] And for their part, the Humanities Research Council and the Social Sciences Research Council (later the Social Sciences and Humanities Research Council) distributed funds to universities and academics in order to support a growing infrastructure and aid in research projects, something that benefited many in the academy.

The activities of the Canada Council were joined in the mid-1960s by federal bureaucrats allocating funds towards the building of cultural institutions and venues in preparation for the 1967 Centennial celebrations. How could Canadians engage in nation-building events without theatres, stages, galleries, and orchestral pits? The traditional federal wariness towards cultural intervention was offset by its enthusiasm for nation-building spectacles. One hundred years of national life merited one hundred million dollars of federal money, and a new body, the Centennial Commission, was created in 1965 to administrate it all. For many people, the highlight was the Centennial Train, which travelled across the country and stopped along the way to let audiences visit its boxcars of Canadiana. Also of great popularity were the communal singalongs to Bobby Gimby's 'Canada!' – 'One little two little three Canadians,' as the lyrics famously began.

Orchestrating pan-national celebrations was only a part of the commission's task. Events rallied people together, but cultural institutions literally cemented national existence and gave nation-building narratives the sort of presence that came with stone and steel. That so many of the institutions were vested with a high-cultural tone was not accidental. 'Centennial year was a civilizing year,' proudly recalled Peter Ackroyd, the Centennial Commission's director of public relations.[7] Canada was moved 'up a notch on the "civilized" scale' thanks to the '67 museums and art galleries; 428 community centres; 520 recreational structures ... The 100 million of public funds expended on this program was well spent.'[8] Each province was given money for a major project, among the most ambitious being the Confederation Centre of the Arts in Charlottetown ($2.8 million), Le Grand Théâtre du Québec in Quebec City ($2.8 million), and the crown jewel, the National Arts Centre in Ottawa ($4.5 million of a projected $36 million project that in the end cost $46.5 million).[9] Here, enthusiasts could exclaim, was evidence of Canada as a modern and progressive nation. And it did not hurt that the new institutions made cultural activities more welcoming – and tourist-friendly – to people who otherwise might not be interested in attending an artistic event.

No project said more about the desire to link the arts and tourism than the National Arts Centre in Ottawa, a large-scale venue combining the celebratory character of the Centennial year with the federal desire to draw more tourist dollars towards the national capital. G. Hamilton Southam, an influential newspaper publishing heir and civil servant, was given the position of NAC project coordinator and, once it was built, became its first director. Here was someone more than capable of pontificating on what he called the 'civilizing influence' of cultural activities.[10] By its very nature, the National Arts Centre meant an affirmation of Masseyesque high-cultural designs, but it is important to note that under Southam this site of cultural construction was different, in fact, from the goals of the Canadianizers. Massey and his contemporaries had done much to draw attention to the importance of Canadian producers – authors, playwrights, composers, choreographers – within the national cultural paradigm. It quickly became clear that Southam, on the other hand, approached the NAC more as an international than a national arts centre. He showed little interest in providing special opportunities for Canadians and made clear his disapproval of cultural nationalism – he was a culturist, not a nationalist. In taking this stance, he not surprisingly faced significant opposition. 'I would hate like hell to have millions and millions of dollars spent on this cultural centre for the arts and not have 55 per cent Canadian content,' a member of the

House of Commons explained to Southam during the 13 June 1966 meeting of the Standing Committee on Broadcasting, Film, and Assistance to the Arts. 'If this Canadian content rule is a good thing for the broadcasting and television world, would it not be a good thing for the performance arts too? It cannot be wrong for one and right for the other?'[11] Southam took offence at this idea, however, and rejected it as 'a narrowly nationalist view of what constitutes artistic activity.' The National Arts Centre, he retorted, was to showcase arts of excellence and quality without consideration for nationality.[12] He even went so far as to tell the *Ottawa Citizen* that attracting foreign performing companies to Canada was crucial to garnering respect on the international scene.[13] External acknowledgment was, after all, a seal of approval sought by many culturists of his generation.

This institutional cornerstone for Canadian cultural activity, a testament to one hundred years of nationhood and a supposed boon to actors, directors, dancers, choreographers, and other such talent, increasingly seemed to be little more than a venue for bringing foreign performers and tourist dollars to the nation's capital. Why else would the NAC not list any Canadian music in the program for its opening celebrations, scheduled to take place in June of 1969, complained the Canada Music Council to the Ottawa Citizen.[14] Mavor Moore, one of the best-known figures in Canadian theatre, exclaimed to the newspaper press that the government had apparently spent taxpayer money on 'pride and tourism.'[15] Former Theatre Passe Muraille director Jim Gerrard likewise used an interview in the *Globe and Mail* to characterize the centre as being little more than millions of dollars spent on 'mortar and bricks' at the arts community's expense.[16] Newspaper publishers were happy to give coverage to such complaints; after all, the arts centre was a great story of ballooning budgets sucking at the taxpayer teat, its initial projection of $36 million having expanded to a whopping $46.5 million by the time of its completion. The fact that influential people in the arts community were criticizing the centre made it all the more worthy of coverage. It is interesting to note that Ken Glass, artistic director of the Factory Theatre Lab, opted not only to talk to the press but also to write to the secretary of state and demand an explanation as to why the government cared more about theatres with tourist potential than those putting on Canadian works.[17]

The National Arts Centre was not alone in becoming a target for culturists who were concerned that internationalism had begun to suffocate indigenous artistic expression. The Stratford Shakespearean

Festival of Canada, incorporated in 1952 in the small Ontario town from which it took its name, had once been a jewel in the crown of the Canadian cultural scene. A decade and a half later, however, the festival theatre was increasingly decried as a testament to a Canadian obsession with antiquated foreign templates and the government's interest in serving tourists more than the needs of an evolving cultural community. Stratford had been created in line with a Masseyesque Anglophilic nationalism which, by the 1960s, was viewed by many Canadians as being an echo of days past.[18] Martin Kinch, artistic director of Theatre Passe Muraille, for example, used an interview in the *Globe and Mail* to call Stratford the pinnacle of 'primarily middle class tourist events.'[19] *Toronto Telegram* columnist Ron Evans described the theatre as the embodiment of a Canadian reliance upon 'simpering English plays' that had 'gone ungrieved from the London theatre,' their cast 'loaded with expatriate British actors who long for a return to the dear, dead days of the plumy tones, well-groomed profile, natty dressing gown and ascot.'[20] Even Irving Wardle, a British drama critic who wrote for *Time*, criticized Stratford for having 'not produced any major Canadian director, playwright, or heroic actor apart from the absentee Christopher Plummer.' The theatre had failed to 'shake off its dependence on Britain and develop a specifically Canadian identity.'[21]

The administrators of artistic venues might have avoided a sizable chunk of the criticism if they had given more opportunities to Canadian playwrights, composers, and choreographers. The reliance upon international big-name works guaranteed to draw crowds had meant employment for some actors, musicians, and dancers yet little support for the creators of original pieces. The Canada Council had been doing a good job in aiding many areas of the arts, but this did not mean that culture was immune from the interests of profit-minded venue owners. The fact that the council was giving so much of its funds to venues that failed to support the efforts of Canadians made the situation all the worse. Canada, some critics were beginning to argue, would be little more than a cultural branch plant until more was done to support the production and exhibition of domestic works. The situation was ripe for reconsideration.

Television and the Conundrum of Canadian Content

For many Canadians, the complaints of a small part of the population, one popularly characterized as elitist and as looking down on the common person, were not of much concern. The arts had once been an important part of community activities, intertwined with leisure and social gatherings, but by the 1960s these pastimes were sharing their position – and often holding onto only a sliver of the national audience – with the content being offered by the mass media. Material that had once been criticized for its connection to commercialization and commodification was increasingly becoming normative through its presence in daily life and a growing appreciation of its middle-of-the-road attributes. Mass entertainment, at least some of it, was becoming popular culture.

Television programming was of particular interest among audiences and, with the recent start of Canadian content regulations, carried with it great expectations for shows of domestic relevance. Audiences and industry participants alike soon noticed, however, that stations had no intention of living up to anything other than the promise of helping to keep advertising revenues in Canada (and in their pockets). Station owners operated on the simple equation of weighing production costs against projected advertising dollars, and it made most sense to produce low-cost Canadian content just to fill regulatory hours, rather than risk spending a lot of money on something that might not attract advertisers. Of the five programs initially shared by CTV network members, three were cheap game shows (*Showdown, 20 Questions*, and *Take a Chance*) and two were musical variety programs (*Cross-Canada Barn Dance* and *Westcoast*).[22] Offerings during the rest of the 1960s were much the same, including the game show *Mr. & Mrs.*, musical varieties *Country Music Hall* and *Pig & Whistle*, and the informational *Bright and Early*, *Question Period*, and *Canada: 101*.[23] Non-network Canadian content could be had even more cheaply, often entailing little more than setting up a camera and turning it on. As Secretary of State Judy LaMarsh complained to members of the House of Commons, stations were airing footage of 'some individual playing an organ in an empty studio and this has been able to qualify as a Canadian program.'[24] But why would it not be the case? There was no requirement that a minimum amount of money be spent on a program. A member of the House of Commons noted the obvious in arguing that 'if you want Canadian content you had better get some kind of incentive formula in your policy to distinguish between the fact that it costs a great deal more money and takes more talent to put on a live drama production than it takes to put on a bunch of western singers, and so on.'[25]

With shows made more to fill Canadian content requirements than to attract advertisers, stations had no qualms over relegating them to the least profitable of broadcasting slots, often early in the day when many people were at work, or late at night after many had gone to bed. CKLW-TV Windsor went so far as to run *World of Wonder,* a children's program, between 1:00 and 1:30 a.m.[26] The absence of Canadian content during prime-time hours, typically 7:00 to 11:00 p.m., was so striking that in 1962 the Board of Broadcaster Governors began requiring a minimum of 40 per cent Canadian content between 6 o'clock in the evening and midnight. This proved to be not much of a problem for broadcasters, however, as they could easily place news and other Canadian content at the margins while reserving the 'true' prime time of 7:00 to 11:00 p.m. for American programs.[27]

A selective use of time slots was but one way for station owners to skirt the requirement of providing Canadian content. Many stations replayed existing programs instead of spending money on new ones because the regulations did not prevent them from doing so. CHCH-TV Hamilton, for example, ran Pierre Berton's talk show twice during the evening schedule, and CFPL-TV London broadcast the one-hour *Under Attack* twice a day.[28] Stations also engaged in co-productions, usually with American companies, to cut down on the cost of Canadian content. This loophole was particularly popular when it came to creating children's programming. *The New Adventures of Pinocchio, The Mighty Hercules, Rocket Robin Hood,* and *Spiderman,* all of which contained little more than flip-book animation, were made in conjunction with American companies but quantified as Canadian content.[29] Live-taped children's shows were not much, if any, better. *Romper Room,* owned by a U.S. company, quantified as Canadian because it was produced in Canada.[30] *Chatelaine,* in reviewing available children's programming, described it as 'an excruciatingly stilted syndicated preschoolers program. The guests are panicky preschoolers in their Sunday best, kept in line by a gimlet-eyed, syrupy-voiced lady. A super-cheap "economy item" for local stations.'[31]

In all fairness, the recently established 'second stations' in the major city markets had tremendous initial setup costs, upwards of five million dollars between the eight stations during the first year, which left little money for programming. By 1966, however, the original eight second stations were pulling in eight million dollars in profit.[32] There was certainly money available to be spent on Canadian programs, but without regulations requiring a minimum expenditure, there was no reason for stations to bother. Economic rationale meant that station owners followed the path of greatest profitability. These were, after all, not public services or community-minded operations but businesses with an eye on the bottom dollar.

Audiences could turn to the Canadian Broadcasting Corporation for nationally relevant television programming, although in many cases its low-intensity and bizarre mixture of the cultured and the rustic left something to be desired. Masseyesque conceptions of culture continued to underwrite the CBC's operations, while at the same time its mandate required it to air distinctly national programming. Highbrow audiences were offered programs such as *Festival*, with orchestras, ballet, and theatre; the current affairs coverage of *This Hour Has Seven Days*; and the long-running game show, *Front Page Challenge*, in which the panelists attempted to identify the show's guest based on a newspaper headline. Even the CBC flagship game show, then, operated along cultured lines and in significant contrast to the flashy consumerism of programs broadcast by CTV. There were also shows that played upon regional stereotypes as part of providing audiences with a dose of Canadiana. One finds, for example, ideas of the folk in shows such as *Don Messer's Jubilee, Singalong Jubilee, Irish Rovers*, and other 'barn dance' programs based upon Celtic and Western iconography, alongside an attempt to bring Canadians into the lives of a working-class family in Quebec with *La Famille Plouffe* (*The Plouffe Family* in its English-language version), a show quite notable for its popularity with both language groups. Although these shows stand out from the others in terms of cultural brow, they do nonetheless fit with the conservative, slow-paced, and even genteel programming seen as being in the best interest of Canadian audiences.

The CBC went so far as to Canadianize *Sesame Street*, an American icon, in order to increase its level of domestically relevant children's programming. Since the American version contained a Spanish-language component, the idea was hit upon at the CBC to replace the Spanish with a Canadian segment. The nationalized version of *Sesame Street* came to include segments with a six-year-old Cree boy from Manitoba; a six-year-old from Saint-Hilaire, Quebec; a six-year-old son of a lobster fisherman in Richibucto, New Brunswick; and an eight-year-old who lived in Alberta near the Rocky Mountains.[33] This selection played upon regional and ethnic identifiers right down to having the father of the New Brunswick child depicted as a lobster fisherman instead of an office worker or other less regionally identifiable occupation. *Chatelaine* not surprisingly gave the Canadian substitutes a positive review. 'As the Canadian content goes up, the program gets better; the brilliantly produced Canadian inserts have a more lyrical, humanistic tone than most of the American version; great identity-builders for Canadian kids.'[34]

Canada was not alone in nationalizing *Sesame Street*; it is one of the most adapted programs in the world. In *Jolts: The TV Wasteland and the Canadian Oasis*, Morris Wolfe notes that 'there's a *Plaza Sesamo*, a *Vila Sesamo*, a *Via Sesame*, a *Rue Sesame*, a *Sesamstrasse*, a *Sesami Storito*, a *Sezamu-lica*. The children in McLuhan's global village are all watching *Sesame Street*.'[35] Yet a number of broadcasting networks, including the British Broadcasting Corporation, refused to air the original program, let alone nationalize it, because of the show's visual and aural intensity.[36] This criticism certainly seemed true in the Canadian context. Even with the Canadianized version going so far as to replace the American 'zee' with the Canadian 'zed' in alphabet songs, *Sesame Street* still came off as much more American than its slower-paced and low-budget Canadian rivals *Mr. Dress Up* and *The Friendly Giant*. 'None of the frenetic pace of Sesame Street is found here,' Wolfe argues. 'Mr. Dress Up, like The Friendly Giant, assumes that children have an attention span that extends beyond two minutes, an assumption that's reflected in the structure, style and content of both programmes.'[37]

Given the difference between CBC budgets and those of American imports, there is little wonder that domestic offerings had such a down-to-earth pace and feel. According to an assessment made by the CBC in 1959, one that likely stayed true throughout the 1960s (and even until today) in terms of significant differences in expenditures, American thirty-minute dramas cost $41,400 versus the CBC's $11,350; sixty-minute American dramas cost $81,000 versus the CBC's $29,000; and ninety-minute dramas cost on average $135,000 versus the CBC's less than $42,000 expense. The situation was similar in other genres. U.S. half-hour quiz shows averaged $28,250 versus $6,500 for their Canadian counterparts, and one-hour variety programs averaged $112,000 compared to $47,750.[38] Americans thus spent about the same amount on thirty-minute dramas as the CBC did on those lasting ninety minutes, over four times as much on quiz shows, and more than double on variety programs. It is quite understandable that advertisers would prefer the American shows being aired by CTV stations over the Canadian content offered by the CBC.

Canadian content regulations had begun in 1961 as a quantified means of ensuring that the private sector made a return on using the public trust, but the results during the first few years were questionable and raised concerns about station activities. It was with this concern in

mind that federal bureaucrats once again asked Canadian Pulp and
Paper Association president Robert Fowler, who a decade earlier had
chaired the Royal Commission on Broadcasting, to lead an inquiry into
the broadcasting system. The Advisory Committee on Broadcasting of
1965 confirmed the earlier commission's prediction that allowing privately owned broadcasters to form second stations and operate a network free from the Canadian Broadcasting Corporation would lead to
an increase in American programming. Station owners imported twice
as much American programming as the CBC, and although the committee found that a few stations produced some decent shows, most of
the broadcasters too often relied upon mediocre programs of quiz-
show quality.[39] The Canadian Association of Broadcasters, defending
station owners in front of the committee, blamed the Canadian content
regulations and claimed that station owners had limited resources to
produce programs. If the quota level was reduced, the association
argued, then stations could offer fewer but higher-budget programs. Of
course, claiming that they would spend more money was a far cry from
actually doing so, and the committee was not convinced of the CAB's
sincerity, given that stations had plenty of money with which to produce
shows. If anything, the Fowler committee noted, stations should be
required to spend more money on Canadian content at the current
quota level.[40]

Unlike at the previous committees and commissions that looked at
the broadcasting sector, the CBC came under significant criticism for its
selection of shows. American material made up approximately 30 per
cent of the network's programming, much of it, in the committee's
opinion, poor in quality.[41] In all fairness, however, the CBC had little
choice in the matter. In the 1950s the network had had exclusive access
to the major city markets and could coerce advertisers into sponsoring
Canadian programs in exchange for access to American programs. A
decade later the situation was significantly different because, thanks to
the Conservative Party, the CBC now had to go head to head with privately owned stations for the limited pool of advertising revenue. Without sufficient funds from the federal government to cover operation
and program production costs, the CBC had no choice but to rely upon
the same inexpensive, revenue-drawing American shows as its private-
sector competition.[42] Bringing to an end the CBC's regulatory powers
did not result in a greater variety of programming, as the Canadian
Association of Broadcasters had promised the federal government; it
merely made the television experience more homogeneously American.

A lot of the blame for the straits Canadian television found itself in could quite rightly be pinned upon the actions of the Conservative Party, yet the problems now inherent in the system fell upon the Board of Broadcast Governors to correct, and the board had largely failed to ensure that the private sector made good on its obligations. Canadian content regulations were 'impractical' and difficult to enforce, in the assessment of the Fowler committee.[43] The lack of a quality cause or a requirement that a minimum amount be spent on a program led to insultingly cheap offerings. Nor did the committee approve of the 'foreign events of national interest' loophole. 'Compliance with the Canadian content regulations,' the committee complained in its report, 'should clearly not depend, for example, on the number of foreign state funerals or major sporting events that happen to fall within a particular period.'[44]

Perhaps the BBG would not have faced such hostility if it had done more to prosecute offending stations.[45] In 1961 Andrew Stewart, chairman of the BBG, had stated that 'it would be very unwise for a station to assume that it can choose to forget all about its promises and assume that there would not be some repercussions.'[46] Yet only a few years later the promises were going unfulfilled and abuses were rampant. CJOH-TV Ottawa, for example, pledged 69.5 per cent Canadian content during peak viewing hours, including domestically produced programs and live shows featuring Canadian performing arts, but it broadcast only 14 per cent during the summer of 1964.[47] Despite such glaring incidents, the BBG did little to crack down on offenders. Why the lack of prosecution? Broadcasting historian Robert Babe has argued that the reason lay with the problems of bringing a case to court: doing so 'would entail detailed examination and cross-examination before a judge on 365 days of program logs in order to establish the level of Canadian content achieved.'[48] And even if stations were found to be in the wrong, the BBG had limited powers to penalize them. Section 12 of the Broadcasting Act placed the ability to revoke licences or attach conditions with the Department of Transport; all the BBG could do was to make recommendations to the ministry.[49] The result was a rather impotent regulator unable to keep in check a private sector that was flouting promises to make good on profiting from the airwaves.

Television program producers and industry workers in general were certainly not happy with the status quo. Members of the Association of Radio and Television Employees of Canada had expected significant employment opportunities to emerge out of the Canadian content regulations. The disappointment and frustration extended to feature filmmakers, who had hoped that the regulations would mean a market for their goods. And audiences, for their part, experienced a decline in domestic programming on the CBC and received very little of it, particularly in terms of quality material, from the private sector. All of this did not bode well for a sense of contentment with the national television experience and the ability to engage in domestic expression.

Radio Broadcasting and the Struggle for Canadian Music

Radio station owners did not have to worry about placing Canadian content during periods of lowest audience attendance, repeating material, or using any of the techniques popular in the television sector since the BBG had yet to extend the requirements to the radio airwaves. Radio stations were free to emulate their American counterparts in supplying vast quantities of foreign recordings selected for their popularity on American charts. CHUM-Toronto not only based its airplay on the recommendations of American programming consultants and trade papers but also created a 'CHUM Chart' that stations and record retailers from coast to coast relied upon to identify sellable recordings. Music journalist Ritchie Yorke, a pre-eminent music columnist and author of *Axes, Chops and Hot Licks: The Canadian Rock Music Scene (1971)*, a treasure trove of interviews with Canadian musicians, identified CHUM as the station that did 'the least for Canadian talent.'[50]

Not only did radio stations pass over domestic offerings, but, in the opinion of the Australian-born Yorke, other media outlets failed to give substantial attention to a thriving area of entertainment. Canada could learn much from the media exposure being given to musical acts in other countries, he argued. 'Local rock stars made the front pages of Australian newspapers; there were national television programs on which artists were not condemned to sing versions of U.S. hits; and magazines devoted lengthy spreads and regular columns to the domestic music business. England was the same. So was every English speaking country in the world, with the exception of Canada. The first fifteen years of the rock era had slipped away, and Canada was still nowhere in the world of music.'[51] Walt Grealis, a record promoter who had also worked as a police officer and public relations agent, was one of the few people trying to improve the situation. Supported by his friend and industry figure Stan Klees, Grealis launched the first issue of a Canadian-focused music-industry trade paper, *RPM*, in February 1964. The hope was that more exposure for domestic acts would lead to an increase in airplay and a stronger domestic music scene. It was a valiant yet naive endeavour; the duo had no idea of the hostility *RPM* would face from station owners. 'Gradually I began to see clearly the apathy of broadcasters,' Grealis recalled in an interview with Yorke. 'A promotion man would take in a Canadian record and they'd throw it into the garbage right in front of him. Those things actually happened.'[52]

Grealis knew that if Canadian musicians were going to make it, they needed not only airplay but a way of fostering a public awareness of Canadian 'stars.' To this end he created the Gold Leaf Awards during *RPM*'s first year of publication, an initiative later reworked into the still-running Juno Awards. Initially they consisted only of a publicized selection of winners, but in February of 1970 the trade paper hosted its first celebratory event and handed out awards made in the shape of a metronome. The award winners included some well-known names but not a lot of variety over previous years. Andy Kim won as top male vocalist, and Ginette Reno top female vocalist; for five years in a row Gordon Lightfoot won the folk artist award; The Guess Who was the top vocal-instrumental group for three years running; Tommy Hunter took the male country singer award for three years in a row; and Dianne Leigh won the female country singer award five times.[53] The list was a testament to the unwillingness of ratio stations to take a chance on developing new stars.

RPM faced an uphill battle of having to win acceptance station by station, its initial success coming largely outside the Toronto area, in which CHUM had shut out much of the trade paper's influence. Grealis's fortitude was celebrated in 2004 by the Canadian Academy of Recording Arts and Sciences, the organizer of the Juno Awards, with the creation of the Walt Grealis Special Achievement Award. Back in the 1960s, however, Grealis was a thorn in the broadcasting industry's side, his attempt to bring recognition to Canadian music a daunting and frustrating task requiring tremendous resilience and the support of like-minded Canadians who saw popular music as an important component of national life.

Musicians, largely locked out of the radio market, relied heavily upon live music venues.[54] Although clubs and other such venues existed from coast to coast, no city offered a better chance at landing a recording contract than the Toronto scenes that straddled sections of Yonge Street and Yorkville. Interestingly, the musical cornerstone of Yonge Street in the early 1960s was actually an American. Ronnie Hawkins, a rockabilly musician from Arkansas who had hits with 'Forty Days' and 'Who Do You Love,' found himself a comfortable niche in the Toronto club scene and fell so in love with Canada that, over forty years later, he continues to make it his home. His fondness, however, did not extend to Canadian radio stations. 'That's what pissed me off about Canada at first – the way radio stations treated Canadian musicians like they were dirt,' Hawkins has recalled. 'Nobody can tell whether you're good or bad if you're not heard.'[55]

Loosely knit musicians were groomed into tight backing bands by the rough-talking American, including a group that went on to become an icon of American music by adopting historic signifiers: The Band, which included Robbie Robertson, a phenomenal guitarist born in Toronto and raised in the Six Nations of the Grand River Reserve just outside Brantford, Ontario. After years of shaping their chops backing Hawkins as his 'Hawks,' the musicians who would go on to form The Band decided to head off on their own and explore some new sounds and techniques. The attempt to make it under the nationally distinctive name Canadian Squires did not work out well, however. 'You're going to have to forget this Canadian Squires thing,' Hawkins advised the musicians, 'because [record labels] won't touch a Canadian group. Take my word for it. They know the Canadian market is so small they won't get their money back.'[56]

The domestic industry did not want Robertson and his fellow band members, but Bob Dylan certainly did. The legendary folk performer was going electric and needed a rocking backup band to fill out his sound; so on the suggestion of Mary Martin, the secretary for Dylan's manager, Albert Grossman, and a fan of Hawkins's Hawks, he checked out and recruited the musicians for what would become a famous – or, to folk purists, infamous – concert tour. After astonishing international audiences with their musical abilities and with Dylan taking some down-time at his ranch in Woodstock following a motorcycle accident, the backing band decided to go out on its own under the name that had been often used to refer to its members in their capacity of sharing the stage with Dylan: The Band. From then on, Robertson and his band-mates indulged in a melange of American Southern anti-modernism with hits that included 'The Night They Drove Old Dixie Down,' a tale of a Southern railroad worker dealing with the death and destruction wrought by the Civil War. Appropriately, The Band's 1969 self-titled release had a cover photo of the musicians adorned in Civil War era–inspired garb and facial hair – a far cry from their years in Toronto with mohair suits, skinny ties, and slicked-back hair but an image that none-theless speaks loudly about musicians who, having had to leave an unde-veloped industry, had found new personas abroad.

While Yonge Street was lined with venues for rocking crowds, the Yorkville area offered plenty of opportunities for folk, blues, and country musicians.[57] American stars, including blues artists Buddy Guy and Howlin' Wolf and folk artists Ritchie Havens and James Taylor, provided club owners with solid crowds, while slower periods were offered to Canadian musicians hoping to make a name for themselves. Gordon Lightfoot, Murray McLauchlan, Neil Young, Joni Mitchell, and jazz guitarist Lenny Breau all performed at the Riverboat. At the Purple Onion one could see Buffy Sainte-Marie, Bruce Cockburn, and Ian and Sylvia Tyson, at least until the latter duo moved up to the Village Corner and then off to the United States. They were certainly not alone in leaving Canada for the American market; it was rather rare to make a decent career out of Yorkville or even Canada as a whole. Without radio airtime to help promote their careers, Canadians had little choice but to look towards the United States. In a 1969 interview Neil Young recalled, 'I spent some time in Toronto training myself as a folk singer. But I soon realized that nothing was ever going to happen in Toronto. I split and went to Los Angeles. I was just completely fed up with the Canadian scene.'[58] Radio station programmers relied largely upon foreign recordings, which in turn meant that Canadians musicians had to achieve stardom in the United States in order to get airplay at home. There was little reason to stay.

Feature Filmmakers and the Denial of Screen Time

The millions of dollars invested by the Canadian Film Development Corporation led to the production of many movies but did little to alter the preference of theatre owners for American offerings. There was no reason to take risks on domestic reels when imports came with virtually guaranteed profitability. Why screen Canadian movies when one could use screen time for Hollywood hits such as *Doctor Zhivago* (1965), *Bonnie and Clyde* (1967), *The Graduate* (1967), Stanley Kubrick's *2001: A Space Odyssey* (1968), and *Midnight Cowboy* (1969)? The fact that numerous Canadian films had large budgets was not enough to win the attention of exhibitors, and just as they had provided a roster of excuses used for not picking up domestic works, many theatre owners now justified their disinterest in Canadian films by claiming that the films tended to have an unmarketable cinematic style. Whether the films were unmarketable or merely nationally distinctive is certainly debatable, but it is true that many of Canada's up-and-coming feature filmmakers demonstrated techniques they had learned while working at the National Film Board; the cinematic 'realism' and 'authenticity' so important to earlier nationalists was now reason enough for many venues to be biased against domestic offerings. 'The documentary feeling, Canada's legacy from Grierson, became the strongest element in its feature films,' Martin Knelman has noted in *This Is Where We Came In: The Career and Character of Canadian film.*[59] One sees this element, for example, in Don Shebib's *Goin' Down the Road,* a tale of two down-and-out Nova Scotia fellows who move to Toronto in hopes of making it in 'the big city' only to end up unemployed and fleeing the police amidst broken dreams and empty beer bottles, and Claude Jutra's *Mon Oncle Antoine,* a drama about a French-Canadian boy coming of age in a small town. Both filmmakers had spent time at the NFB, *Mon Oncle Antoine* having actually been made during Jutra's time at the board. It should come as no surprise that both films were dismissed by domestic distributors and exhibitors until they received tremendous praise in the American market, at which point they were picked up by Canadian theatres – certainly evidence that it was not so much that the national style was unmarketable as it was that theatres were unwilling to take a risk on an unproven product.

Distributors made no secret of their disdain at being targeted by concerned Canadians or at the unfairness of such treatment. 'We, as distributors, are condemned because we look at film from a commercial standpoint,' as Victor Beattie, past-president of the Canadian Motion Picture Distributors Association, identified the situation.[60] Yet the reason was more underhanded than Beattie admitted. This was not merely a situation of weighing commercial interests: distributors and exhibitors were in cahoots with Hollywood producers, who controlled a large part of the Canadian marketplace. Hollywood's use of vertical integration and block booking ensured a strong lock on the exhibition circuit. Even the United States government had two decades earlier seen fit to pass legislation designed to end Hollywood's use of vertical integration and open the marketplace for independent filmmakers and theatre owners. Canada had not yet done the same.

The economic anemia that came with the denial of screen time was compounded by the removal of ticket monies. Famous Players and Odeon owned two-thirds of commercial theatres in Canada and almost all of those in the big urban centres in the 1960s, taking in 70 to 80 per cent of Canadian film revenues.[61] Even the Quebec market was not immune from this extraction because American interests had entrenched themselves among English-language audiences in the Montreal area. *Le Devoir* reported that '78% des recettes des cinémas de Montréal et de Verdun provenaient des salles contrôlées par les circuits Famous Players, United Amusement et Odéon, 57% des recettes dans les cinémas de Montréal sont recueillies par les films américains ou britanniques en version originale, parlée anglais. 96% de ce montant fut recueilli dans les salles Famous Players-United Amusement.'[62] With such little money left in Canada, filmmakers were virtually dependent upon the support of the Canadian Film Development Corporation.

For the most part, the only Canadian films that routinely attracted the interest of exhibitors were those of a highly sexualized form, which were not Hollywood's forte. It was ironic, given that Canadians had done so much to identify themselves as culturally superior to the Americans, that titillating films were becoming such an important – and subsidized – part of the domestic industry. So many films of this type were being made in Canada that *Time* published an entire section detailing the emergence of 'Maple Syrup Porn' as a new genre of cinema.[63] Two of the highest grossing of these were *L'Initiation* (1970), in which a young girl falls for a famous author and provides audiences with ample nudity, and *Des femmes en or* (1970), a tale of two lonely suburban Montreal housewives who call for home-delivery services and then coax the deliverymen into bed. As the titles imply, sexualized films were particularly popular in Quebec, so much so that this risqué fare actually helped to establish the province as a viable place for film-industry investment.[64]

Shocking to the cultural weltanschauung of some Canadians was the fact that *L'Initiation* and *Des femmes en or* were actually made with taxpayer dollars secured through the Canadian Film Development Corporation. Nor would it be the last time the corporation put its money behind such films. Why was the body vested with the task of developing a domestic feature-film industry so keen to invest in what many people criticized as being soft-core filth? *L'Initiation* and *Des femmes en or* were the only films to return their initial investment to the corporation during its first few years of operation: there seemed to be little choice but to rely upon erotic films to maintain a funding pool that otherwise would dry up quite quickly as a result of so many other films not being screened. It was quite telling that, as of mid-1971, approximately $4 million had been invested and only about $500,000 returned.[65] Film bureaucrats could not afford to cut off a reliable source of economic return. This argument did not, of course, satisfy all critics, particularly those who were struggling to develop a nationally conscious cinematic experience. 'It is better for Canada not to have an industry at all than have it founded on sheer smut and crap,' filmmaker Don Shebib told the *Globe and Mail* in a 1970 interview.[66]

That exhibitors showed little interest in anything other than sexually exploitive films made the frustration of not receiving screen time all the worse. In 1969, the second year in which the Canadian Film Development Corporation was in operation, only 10 of 669 films exhibited in Canada were made domestically.[67] In other words, Canadian content was less than 1.5 per cent. A combination of theatrical circuit interest in established American films and Hollywood's monopolization practices ensured that many Canadian filmmakers, and the audiences who wanted to see their films, were increasingly frustrated and concerned about the stark discrepancy between the growing number of films and the lack of exhibition. There was a lot of disappointment and resentment among Canadian filmmakers, who saw their reels sitting on the shelves and gathering dust. It is not surprising that so many of them would turn to a nationalism laced with anti-Americanism, one seeking to pry open domestic theatres in the name of promoting Canadian nationhood.

Problems in the Publishing Sector

Peter C. Newman's anger at the Paperback and Periodical Distributors Act (1964), the infamous piece of legislation that exempted *Time* and *Reader's Digest* from a clause otherwise limiting tax deductions to advertising taken in Canadian periodicals, speaks volumes about how many of the participants in the periodical sector felt that the federal government had done nothing but serve the interests of continentalists. Nor were magazine publishers alone in the desire to see the fostering of a viable publishing industry. Book publishers, sharing many of the same contributors and resources as their periodical counterparts, were not faring all that well either. For many years the industry had relied upon monies received from foreign companies for reprinting their books in the Canadian marketplace, the economic gains in turn allowing publishers to produce Canadian content – not unlike the CBC showing foreign programs and using the advertising revenue to help fund the production of domestic shows or the Canadian Film Development Corporation investing in sexualized movies and using the returns to fund unprofitable films. During the 1950s and early 1960s, however, American publishing interests decided that it made more economic sense not to renew the publishing contracts held with Canadian presses and instead to establish

American-owned branch plants, a decision that stripped many domestic publishing houses of an important source of income.[68] It was more profitable to cut out the Canadian middleman and, in turn, reduce the supply of monies being used to publish the Canadian works against which the foreign titles competed.

Some Canadian companies did their best to continue publishing domestic books despite the economic handicap. McClelland and Stewart, perhaps the best known of Canadian publishers, certainly stands out as a company that put its weight behind Canadian content. This publishing house was helped out by the fact that the Canada Council offered funds for book publishing, including a grant in 1957 for McClelland and Stewart to publish the New Canadian Library series. This ambitious project, in which a selection of Canadian literary works were to be reprinted as part of a collection, promised great gains in terms of nation-building and in raising the profile of Canadian authors. Over the next few decades the books selected for the series were met with popular approval and even achieved the status of Canadian classics.[69] It should come as no surprise, however, that academic Malcolm Ross and Jack McClelland of McClelland and Stewart chose books not only for their literary merit but also for how they fit into the economic and nationalistic interests of the press.[70] This is why at least one critic, the acerbic John Metcalf, has argued that the New Canadian Library series speaks more about the desire of McClelland and Stewart to nation-build than it does of the literary quality of the works that were chosen.[71] Although the series was well received upon its inception in the late 1950s, a decade later the books would take on a new status as readers flocked to them and other works as part of a 'CanLit' phenomenon brought on by a new wave of Canadianization that resulted in large part from the excesses of American imperialism.

Conclusion

What had happened to the promises of Canadian content and opportunities for domestic expression? Canada continued to be an overrun market, a dumping ground for foreign goods, thanks in large part to domestic distributors more interested in imports than indigenous offerings. The situation was made all the more tense and confrontational by federal policies that permitted, if not encouraged, activities operating counter to national needs, including the funding of foreign-focused and tourism-friendly cultural endeavours that showed little interest in the work of domestic producers, allowing for television quota loopholes, failing to pass Canadian content regulations for radio, exempting *Time* and *Reader's Digest* from the periodical legislation, and investing in feature-film production without securing screen time. Many Canadians had expected state intervention to offer new employment opportunities and access to domestic content, only to find profit-minded distributors getting richer while producers continued to struggle. A growing sense of frustration among many Canadians, particularly those of the expanding middle class whose lives were intertwined with the arts and entertainment sectors, led to a rise in nationalistic sentiments and a popular interest in overhauling the status quo. Canada was on the cusp of a new moment of Canadianization.

5 Creating the Peaceable Kingdom: A New Nationalist Canadian Identity

If we had to have a crime syndicate up here, I would prefer to have a Canadian crime syndicate.

> Thirteen-year-old Stephen Wither, youngest member
> of the Committee for an Independent Canada[1]

Literary historians may remember 1971–72 as the year it became fashionable to have a few Canadian books on the coffee table, or to casually mention the latest Atwood or Aquin in mundane conversations.

> Canada Council, 1971–2[2]

'These absentee landlords – and sometimes the U.S. State Department whose responsibility it is to protect their interests – have a considerable influence on Canadian public policy,' Walter Gordon warned a gathering of University of British Columbia students in 1970.[3] This was the same person who, back in 1964, had been the Liberal Party's finance minister and whose government had buckled to the U.S. State Department and exempted *Time* and *Reader's Digest* from the Paperback and Periodical Distributors Act. Only a few years had passed, but much had changed. Gordon no longer sat idly by while American-based foreign owners and branch plants, the 'absentee landlords' to which he referred, extracted resources and capital from Canada. Despite Gordon's role in the periodical exemption, he had redeemed himself to Peter C. Newman and other concerned Canadians by leaving the Liberal Party in November of 1965 amidst governmental and business-sector concern about his nationalistic tendencies, including an infamous budget debacle in 1963 in which he had proposed a high tax on foreign acquisitions of Canadian companies. Abraham Rotstein, to whom Newman had sent the letter condemning Gordon over the *Time* and *Reader's Digest* exemption, reassured Gordon that 'in my humble opinion, time is on your side. It will not be long before an affirmative and explicit appreciation of what you have trying to do will spread across the country.'[4]

One has to look at 1965 as the starting point of a new model of pan-Canadian nationalism, the so-called new nationalism, and a moment of Canadianization in which a new generation of intelligentsia turned to culture as a means of imprinting a sense of nationhood in a time of crisis. First, in that year Walter Gordon resigned from the Liberal cabinet. Second, philosopher George Grant released *Lament for a Nation: The Death of Canadian Nationalism*, a critique of Americanization and Canada's failure to build a 'more ordered and stable society than the liberal experiment in the United States.'[5] Grant placed Canada's national design within a Masseyesque model of British inheritance, and he decried a shift which, as a result of the Conservative Party's inability to prevent Liberal continentalism, had led to 'the end of Canada as a sovereign state.'[6] Grant's prediction was dire, but in prematurely lamenting Canada's death – although in many ways correctly lamenting the end of an earlier national design – he helped to spark a debate on national sovereignty and the Canadian relationship with the United States. *Lament for a Nation* was 'the most important book I ever read in my life,' academic and influential nationalist James Laxer has reminisced. 'Here was a crazy old philosopher of religion at McMaster and he woke up half our generation. He was saying Canada is dead, and by saying it he was creating the country.'[7]

Many Canadians were beginning to feel that their way of life, and that of their nation, had become intimately tied to the United States through a continentalism not necessarily in their best interests. Uneasy feelings about the American presence at home were amplified by the decline of John F. Kennedy's Camelot into a time of race riots, protests, and militarism under the leadership of Lyndon B. Johnson and Richard Nixon. Political scientist Philip Resnick is not off the mark in noting that 'it is difficult to assess to what extent English Canadian intellectuals (including academics) created the new nationalism ... or to what extent they themselves were merely responding to a political force let loose by the waning influence of the United States.'[8] Had Canada tied itself to a sinking ship?

A generation of intelligentsia, many of whom were part of the expanding middle class, began to articulate a new model of nationhood, one casting off Masseyesque Anglophilic ethnic nationalism and the Liberal Party's continentalism in favour of a civic nation reified from within. Economists Walter Gordon, Melville Watkins, and Abraham Rotstein, academics Robin Mathews, James Steele, Gary Lax, and James Laxer, publishers Mel Hurtig and Jack McClelland, editor and columnist Peter C. Newman, and authors Margaret Atwood and Farley Mowat, to name but a few of the influential thinkers, lent substantial guidance and intellectual capital to this movement. Although this nationalism shared with the Masseyites the use of personal networks and professional relationships, it also drew heavily upon the activities of a like-minded 'baby boom' generation eager to politicize the issue of national identity. Activities within the New Democratic Party and the relatively less partisan Committee for an Independent Canada were complemented by grassroots movements, sit-ins, and rallies on university campuses and in public spaces; this quest for nationhood was being taken to the House of Commons and to the streets.

Further, both the Masseyites and the new nationalists emerged out of periods of destabilization, the former adapting to modernity and the latter confronting the overwhelming presence of the United States. Although the new nationalists shared with the Masseyites a contempt for the United States, this time around the anti-Americanism was based not so much upon fears of commercialism and moral degradation as upon a resistance to economic and cultural imperialism. These nationalists sought not to guide the young and fragile Canada through the colony-to-nation process so much as reclaim its lost sovereignty. 'During the last fifty years we have freed ourselves of traces of colonial status insofar as Britain is concerned,' claimed Walter Gordon to *Star Weekly* magazine in 1967. 'But having achieved our independence from Britain, we seem to have slipped, almost without knowing it, into a semi-dependent position in relation to the United States.'[9] Put more tersely in the words of Margaret Atwood and Farley Mowat, Canada had become an 'exploited colony' and 'satellite of the empire.'[10]

Harsh words from influential figures, yet the new nationalism was not so much a political revolution as it was an ideological happening of middle-class aspirations and assumptions, a movement indicative of a new symbolic order, new ideas of citizenship, and a new use of culture in the quest for nationhood. The weakening of the Canada-Britain relationship, new patterns of immigration, an expansion of the middle class, and steps forward in establishing a social welfare environment were but a few of the factors changing the temper of the quest for nationhood. The Dominion of Canada and its ethnic nationalism was giving way to the idea of a 'Peaceable Kingdom' still present today, a non-violent, multicultural mosaic of understanding and social cohesiveness, with a supportive welfare safety net and solutions to both Canada's and the world's problems.[11]

The Peaceable Kingdom was the 'imagined community' reimagined, a paradigm that proposed a socialist-leaning framework in which to empower a civic nation, paradoxically offering both an escape from the complexities of an increasingly transnational world and a new nationhood through which to experience these complexities. It was certainly with genuine hope for the future and much enthusiasm that William Kilbourn told the readers of *Canada: A Guide to the Peaceable Kingdom* (1970), a collection of writings articulating and celebrating components of the new nationalist design, 'I cannot help feeling ... that Canada, merely by existing, does offer a way and a hope, an alternative to insanity, in so far as there is a way and a hope for any of us in an insane world.'[12] A similar sentiment, one giving more weight to the socialist leanings of the new nationalism, was expressed by Abraham Rotstein in a talk given in the wake of the movement: 'what we hoped for in this movement was the growth in this country of a new mood or new political climate. Not only did we have in mind the self-awareness of cultural and economic domination, but the release of other forces as well – those of mutual concern for our regional, class and personal inequalities, as well as a greater extension of social justice and genuine democracy. We had hoped to create such stronger social bonds to unite us and create a higher level of political expression.'[13]

Whereas the Masseyites had turned to high-cultural devices in defining and pursuing their national design, this new nationalism mobilized multi-brow outlets of expression and identity construction. The earlier attempt to guide the post-colonial project along cultured lines, lifting the nation above the tainted fruits of modernity and developing it into a nation worthy of its British inheritance, had gone the way of Vincent Massey and his Anglophilic cohorts. This new generation of intellectuals consisted largely of middle-class elites and cultural workers interested in encouraging domestic expression across the board – all the more so if the content involved national myths, symbols, figures, events, references, and other signifiers. Nationhood was said to rest within all-things-Canuck.

Of course, it was not coincidental that these nationalists and many of their followers had ideological and economic interests in various areas of cultural activity. These were not highbrow cultural patrons but multi-brow participants; culture was not only a way of life but, for many, their bread and butter. The authority of nationalistic culturists of the early century had given way to that of cultural workers, people who were frustrated with the failure of state initiatives – the Canada Council, Canadian content regulations for television (and lack of them for radio), intervention for periodicals, and the Canadian Film Development Corporation – to establish opportunities for domestic expression and a relationship between producer and audience. That these individuals sought to retool the machinery of Canadianization, then, should come as no surprise: they envisioned a national project in line with their class interests and took upon themselves the responsibility of acting on the supposed behalf of their fellow citizens. As Philip Resnick has noted in *Land of Cain: Class and Nationalism in English Canada, 1945–1975*, 'Marxist analysis would underline the class interests of most of those articulating this so-called classless nationalism. It was the new petty bourgeoisie that stood to be the chief beneficiary of the symbolic investment now called for in "science policy," "cultural policy," "independent foreign policy," and so on. Members of this class would be its interpreters, and in all likelihood, the policy-makers engaged in turning nationalist ideology into state policy.'[14] Further, in looking at how a number of Canadian publishers formed the Independent Publishers Association as a lobby group for state aid, Resnick correctly observed that 'the self-serving connection between the publishing of Canadiana and the espousal of Canadian nationalism need come as no surprise, or put another way, Canadian nationalism could also mean good business. This is not to suggest that [publishers Mel] Hurtig, [Jack] McClelland or the members of the Independent Publishers Association formed in April 1971 did not have a genuine commitment to English Canada's cultural identity above and beyond mercenary motives. *Tout au contraire.* But let's not fool ourselves – class interest played its role.'[15]

That being said, and in full acknowledgment of the economic benefits that some participants stood to collect, it is important to note that the greatest gains were in many ways ideological. The request for state monies to help prevent publishers from going bankrupt speaks not of a desire – and certainly, far from the capacity – to amass monies but of an impassioned yearning to see the national project operationalized in line with the middle-class interests of its advocates. This is why it is not surprising to see so much of the new nationalism being voiced from within the arts, mass media, and universities, sites where the lives of its middle-class participants are often intertwined with the ebb and flow of cultural activity. It is here that one finds canaries in the coal mine of nationhood.

The Coming of the New Nationalism

Walter Gordon is not a name recognized by many Canadians today. He did not make it into the CBC's 2004 viewer-based poll of the Top 100 Greatest Canadians – unlike singer Avril Lavigne (no. 40), controversial First World War pilot Billy Bishop (no. 48), and buxom starlet Pamela Anderson (no. 51) – but the impact of this accountant and economist upon the new nationalism and the ways in which Canadians continue to see themselves as members of a Peaceable Kingdom was quite significant. Gordon holds the distinction, at the very least, of being among the first intellectuals to draw significant attention to problems stemming from the massive influx of American investment. On the surface, all seemed fine as the monies, increasing from U.S. $3.58 billion to $8.33 billion between 1950 and 1957, helped to raise the Canadian GNP to among the highest in the world and let many people indulge in a cornucopia of automobiles, laundry machines, and record players.[16] Much of this investment, however, had occurred with little in the way of checks and balances and had led to American acquisition of vast quantities of key natural resources and industries. In 1957 the federal government asked Walter Gordon, at that time an accountant and not yet a member of the Liberal cabinet, to chair the Royal Commission on Canada's Economic Prospects, an experience that drew his attention to problems of economic imbalance stemming from this influx of monies and sale of domestic resources. If foreign investment was left unmonitored, Gordon reported to the government, it could have negative repercussions on national sovereignty. But this warning was not enough to bring about a change in policy; Gordon's concerns went unaddressed as both the Liberal government and its Conservative successors dismissed the report.[17] American monies were a valuable contributor to federal coffers, and any alteration threatened to impact on economic growth.

Despite a rough welcome for the report, Gordon was very supportive of the Liberal Party, and upon the defeat the Conservatives in the 1963 election, Lester B. Pearson offered him the position of finance minister. Gordon could not have asked for a better opportunity to bring about the changes recommended back in 1957, but his nationalistic leanings – mere economic concerns, really – proved to be problematic both within and outside the Liberal Party. In his position as finance minister, he proposed a budget with high taxes on foreign takeovers and an increase in Canadian equity, a move that upset many of his colleagues in the business sector, who, when the budget began to show inconsistencies, were happy to watch it blow up in his face.[18] Historian Stephen Azzi has recounted that in the wake of the budget proposal, 'Gordon entered the York Club in Toronto, where Harry Wilson, president of National Trust, asked him, "Walter, how does it feel to enter a club where everyone hates your God-damned guts?"'[19] The continentalist business class had no interest in Gordon's nationalistic concerns, and the fact that Pearson's administration felt much the same left him with little choice but to depart from the Liberal cabinet two years later.

Gordon's attempt to draw attention to the impact of American investment upon the Canadian economy was part of a much larger picture of foreign influence and a weakening of national sovereignty. The domestic mass media were chock full of content brought in from the United States to such a degree that one could not avoid daily encounters with American television shows, music, magazines, books, and feature films. Not only was Canada's entertainment industry an extension of the American one, but now, as Gordon noted, so was the economy. Nor did things seem to be slowing down. How was one to feel comfortable upon hearing Secretary of State John Foster Dulles explain that 'one [way] is to gain control of its people by force of arms. The other is to gain control of its economy by financial means'?[20] Or with Undersecretary of State George Ball describing the Canadian struggle against 'integration' and 'economic domination' as futile?[21] Such careless talk did nothing to help Canadians feel at ease with American intentions.

Manifestations of American imperialism at home and abroad certainly did not escape the attention of a generation of baby boomers, particularly those who filled university and college campuses. They held grassroots protests against the American military-industrial complex; gathered for speeches on topics that included workers' movements, civil rights, feminism, and third-world causes; established sit-ins at government buildings and in university quads; experimented with urban communalism within the walls of Toronto's Rochdale College; and shut down streets in the name of reclaiming public space from pollution-spewing automobiles. That so many of the participants came from a middle-class background meant that there was both the economic freedom to engage in such activities and a compelling sense that in doing so, they were exerting their rights within a world they stood to inherent.[22]

The youthful protests and energies harmonized well with the verbal warfare being unleashed by a generation of radicalized intelligentsia. This was no gentlemanly Masseyesque nationalism. As I discussed in '"Kicking Uncle Sam Out of the Peaceable Kingdom": English-Canadian

"New Nationalism" and Americanization,' Margaret Atwood showed no reserve in identifying Americans as 'the killers' and Canadians as 'the killed' in a dichotomy in which 'Canadians too can be hunters, but only by taking a stance towards Nature which is the stance of America towards them.'[23] Likewise, the always fervent Farley Mowat described the United States as a nation of 'overt totalitarianism,' a 'machine for greed' driven by its 'instinct for continental domination' and 'general imperial … cast of mind.'[24] Anti-Americanism, although a powerful means of rallying emotions, was a slippery and often self-defeating discourse that allowed legitimate concerns to be dismissed as extremist and their proponents painted as 'ugly' Canadians. 'It is extremely easy for the "anti-Americanism" red herring to be raised. Once that happens, the whole issue is lost,' as noted Stephen Clarkson, a professor of political economy at the University of Toronto, in a letter to Peter C. Newman in 1970.[25]

Critics proved to be so effective at equating legitimate concerns with anti-Americanism that the Committee for an Independent Canada, established by Gordon, Rotstein, and Newman in 1970, went so far as to publish a pamphlet to address the question 'Are we anti-American?' The response was simple: 'No. We simply believe that good international life comes from the healthy development of free and independent nations. As long as we are dependent we will not find our true voice and will have failed in our responsibilities.'[26] Nationalist discourse was much more effective when it avoided setting up an American 'straw man' to disembowel and instead kept the focus on the problems arising from continentalism. This approach aided in rationalizing concerns and calls for change that might otherwise ostracize 'soft' nationalists and those Canadians who did not self-identify as nationalistic so much as merely concerned citizens.

Dealing with the economic and cultural imperialism of the supposedly 'friendly' United States was not a uniquely Canadian experience, of course. Europeans had relied heavily upon economic investment from the United States following the Second World War, a situation that left them particularly vulnerable to the political influence which rode on the coattails of assistance. Yet prosperity permits a lot of infringement upon national sovereignty, and quite interestingly, many Europeans continued to regard the United States as a shining example of modernization. In Denmark, for example, some intellectuals offered critiques of Americanization, but there was little in the way of public protest. 'The modernity of U.S. culture appealed to the young generation of Danes dissatisfied with the retrospective outlook of postwar Denmark,' Soren Schou has explained in 'The Charisma of the Liberators: The American-ization of Postwar Denmark.'[27] By the turn of the twenty-first century, however, as will be discussed in the last chapter of this book, the Euro-pean Union began forming multilateral mass-media agreements as a means of ensuring domestic discourse in the face of even greater levels of American content, 'Canadianization' becoming the term used in Europe to describe a country that fails to sufficiently bulwark itself against Americanization.

Canadian concern about American investment and cultural influence coincided with a period of public discourse about nationhood and iden-tity, the combination of which underwrote the rise in popular national-ism and idea of Canada as a Peaceable Kingdom. The Royal Commission on Bilingualism and Biculturalism, launched in 1962 and running throughout the decade, raised questions about the relationship between the two dominant groups and opened the door to discussions about the position of minorities within the identity paradigm. In 1965 a new flag replaced the Red Ensign, an emblem of Canada as a dominion of the British Empire, in a controversial and symbolic declaration of nation-hood. The Centennial celebrations of 1967 rallied the population together in a national sense of self by intricately striking familial chords. And in that same year, Expo 67 in Montreal brought together sixty-two countries and attracted over fifty million visitors in an act of reifying Canada's presence in the world of nations.

Given the circumstances, it should come as no surprise that many citi-zens sought to claw back continentalism and ensure the sovereignty of their own national project. A 1967 poll showed that 60 per cent of Cana-dians believed foreign ownership could endanger national sovereignty, and 47 per cent thought the current situation of foreign ownership needed to be addressed.[28] A survey three years later showed that 46 per cent of those polled agreed that 'Canada should buy back a majority control, say 51%, of U.S. companies in Canada, even though it might mean a big reduction in our standard of living.'[29] A large number of Canadians, at least those who answered pollsters, showed a significant willingness to sacrifice material gains for the sake of nationhood.

Many of these people also helped to bring about the rise of the New Democratic Party. 'Canada is rapidly becoming an economic hinterland for the American industrial complex,' declared NDP leader Tommy Douglas to his fellow members of the House of Commons in a statement typical of the party's concern about American influence.

It should be remembered that these United States corporations did not invest in Canada as an act of Christian charity, but rather to assure a guaranteed supply of raw materials to feed the voracious American industry ... I warn the government that the time will come very soon when the Canadian people will no longer allow a cynical and supine government to barter away our birthright in the name of continentalism. The Canadian people are becoming alarmed at this situation, as is shown by the statements of one of the government's former ministers, Hon. Walter Gordon, and others, as well as by editorials appearing in newspapers and periodicals across the nation.[30]

Formed in 1961 with Douglas, a former Saskatchewan premier, at its helm, the NDP carried forward the socialist ideas of the Co-operative Commonwealth Federation and the belief in social equality with which many Canadians popularly identified. Douglas and his political compatriots were doing quite well in the nationalistic climate of the late 1960s; the party offered Canadians an alternative to Liberal apathy, the established kowtowing to business elites, and the wholesaling of Canada's natural resources to the United States. Canada, it seemed, finally had a federal political party that was interested more in the social welfare of its population than the economic strength of its upper tier.

Nationalism was becoming such a defining force in Canadian life that in 1967 Lester B. Pearson tried to win over voters by convincing Walter Gordon – and his nationalist capital – to return to the party. In her autobiography *Memoirs of a Bird in a Gilded Cage*, Judy LaMarsh, secretary of state at the time of Gordon's return, told of how the Liberals brought him back 'because he was so popular with a large segment of the public,' but the administration was also sure to limit his power – offering him the position of president of the privy council – in order to prevent a replication of earlier 'embarrassments.'[31] Gordon agreed to return in exchange for the government's forming the Task Force on the Structure of Canadian Industry, to be chaired by economist Melville Watkins. The task force, in what is popularly referred to as the Watkins Report, backed Gordon's earlier concerns and recommended that a body be created to monitor foreign investment and increase domestic ownership in key areas of the economy. Once again, however, the government showed no interest in the idea and shelved the report, prompting Gordon to resign his position and walk away from a party that seemed hopelessly unwilling to institute changes essential to Canadian sovereignty.

Gordon's departure once again harmed the Liberals' attempt to foster a progressive image, but fortunately for the party, the loss of Gordon and his nationalist capital was offset by the popularity of another member, someone capable of capturing the attention of nationalistic citizens yet able to operate from within party ideology. Pierre Elliott Trudeau quickly became a striking political presence in an age of national revitalization. The excitement of the Centennial celebrations and Expo 67 easily segued into 'Trudeaumania' and his electoral victory in 1968. Audiences loved the middle-aged yet charismatically young prime minister. One could not ask for a more exciting and debonair political figure, a man with one foot in Parliament and the other on the dance floor, a hobnobbing politician as comfortable driving his Mercedes convertible and dating movie stars as he was fighting in the backrooms of Ottawa and debating the minutiae of internationalism. He well travelled, highly educated, and modern; he took strong stances against political corruption, worked with trade unions, and, as minister of justice in 1967, had removed the state from the bedrooms of the nation. Raised in Montreal, in a bilingual family of French and Scottish heritage, he wonderfully combined this pedigree with worldliness.

Trudeau fit well with the sense of a new, energetic, and confident nation. Even George Grant, a strong critic of the Liberal Party, recalled thinking that Trudeau initially seemed to offer a positive change from C.D. Howe's 'worship of the corporation' and Pearson's 'capitalist internationalism.'[32] Nationalists within the intelligentsia soon came to realize, however, that the new prime minister emitted an aura of nationalism that served to rally support for federalism but, in fact, viewed nationalism as an ideology to be adamantly rejected. This was not an uncommon sentiment in the 1960s: many people in the international community equated nationalism with discriminatory and oppressive regimes. Two world wars and countless civil conflicts seemed to have resulted from nationalism gone awry. 'Nationalism' was a 'dirty word,' as Abraham Rotstein complained, an ideology painted with a wide brush as something offering little that was positive.[33] The new nationalists did not agree with such an assessment, of course. 'Defensive nationalism,' such as the strain active in Canada, Robin Mathews and James Steele argued, was significantly different from 'imperialist nationalism.'[34] The presence of the former in Canada was even chalked up as a reaction to an Americanization that contained elements of the latter. 'There is a new surge of Canadian nationalism as a defence against the fall-out from American nationalism,' Melville Watkins explained to the participants of a University of Alberta teach-in on 25 November 1969. 'To brand such feelings as anti-American is to miss the point: What is involved is resistance to imperialism and a thirst for the survival of Canada as an independent nation founded on a distinct economy.'[35]

Where Watkins and like-minded thinkers differed from other nationalistic intelligentsia, however, was in the degree to which the 'independent nation' required a socialist economy. The current political system seemed to be offering 'soft' nationalists just enough in the way of concessions to give the appearance of change. Watkins experienced this first-hand when he chaired the Task Force on the Structure of Canadian Industry, yet he found the government unwilling to implement the recommendations. 'It was the whole damn thing in Ottawa all over again,' he angrily recalled about how the Liberals shelved his report; 'listening to the mandarins talk, listening to them agree with everything you say ... but you're never allowed to do anything.'[36]

A year later, still frustrated with federal hypocrisy and the surrendering of Canadian sovereignty, Watkins joined with academic James Laxer to lead a political movement so leftist that it could not even be contained by the New Democratic Party. The 'Waffle,' a splinter group formed within the NDP, called for a socialist restructuring of the Canadian economy.[37] True, the NDP stood for a welfare state and the protection of natural resources from exploitation, but the Waffle could not accept a party platform that, apart from adding more Crown corporations and increasing domestic ownership in key areas, operated within a system of capitalism privileging the few over the many. Ownership regulations may have looked good on paper, but they tended to benefit a continentalist Canadian business class that had exchanged national sovereignty for profits in the first place. Canadian stability required no less than a dedicated socialism implemented on the behalf of the nation as a whole. For the Waffle, this overhauling of national life was only one part of a larger struggle for international socialism and equal rights; the meetings held and the publications put out by its members tell of a strong devotion to workers' movements, feminist struggles, and the plight of immigrants.[38]

Political divisions within the new nationalist intelligentsia, particularly the rise of the Waffle movement, prompted Gordon, Rotstein, and Newman to form the aforementioned Committee for an Independent Canada (CIC) in 1970 in hopes of ensuring a unified nationalist front.[39] They were, as satirically described by the *Toronto Star*, 'those subversive idealists who are in favour of pure air, clean water and a slightly-used virgin.'[40] Over three hundred people showed up for the committee's first annual meeting in December 1971, including co-founders Gordon, Rotstein, and Newman, CIC chairman Jack McClelland (who was stepping down and would be replaced by Toronto lawyer Eddie Goodman), book publisher Mel Hurtig, editor Claude Ryan, author and broadcaster (and future governor general) Adrienne Clarkson, and political figures John Roberts (Liberal), Gordon Fairweather (Conservative), and Max Saltsman (NDP). Political differences, it seemed, were being put aside for the sake of nationhood. 'I'm a desperate Canadian nationalist,' Saltsman remarked at the conference. 'I'm willing to hold hands with almost anyone in order to preserve an independent Canada.'[41]

Short on research data and lacking representatives from Quebec but full of passion and interest, the gathering was an occasion for networking and policy formation. 'The committee,' as stated in the constitution adopted that evening, 'is concerned with exploring the advantages of the Canadian economy becoming more independent; less dependent on imports of foreign capital, foreign technology and foreign manufactured goods and less dependent on exports, particularly exports of largely unprotected resources.'[42] Independence entailed a 'buying back' of American companies in key areas of the economy and replacing them with domestically owned or Crown corporations.[43] This position was certainly softer than that advocated by the Waffle, but it was one that spoke to a much wider audience, and on that night in December, many people saw it as being within their grasp.

Keeping all these characteristics of the new nationalism in mind, we should not be surprised to see that much of the cultural mobilization involved an anti-imperialist grassroots tone. The Masseyesque romanticization of moral cultivation that had underwritten the first moment of Canadianization was replaced by an idealization of multi-brow content and the desire to widen systems of communication in areas controlled by profiteers collaborating with American imperialists. Nationalists sought out anything with a glint of Canadianness as a tool to be used for the sake of a nation in crisis. At the same time, elements that had previously come under the umbrella of Canadian content but were now counterproductive to the imperatives of nation-building, such as the high-cultural branch plants and quantification of mass-media industrialism, needed to be replaced with 'genuine' indigenous content. Canadianization was once again underway as nationalists mobilized culture in the quest for nationhood.

Nationalism, Publishing, and the Literati

Advances in publishing technology and distribution during the early twentieth century had not only contributed to nation-building in terms

of aiding learned discourse but, with increases in the level of public literacy, offered nationalists the ability to reach the hearts and minds of
readers through space-specific literature. Novels became 'that celebrated artifice of the nationalist imagination in which the community is
made to live and love in "homogenous time,"' as famed post-colonial
theorist Partha Chatterjee put it in *The Nation and Its Fragments: Colonial
and Postcolonial Histories*.[44] They can also be ideological blueprints for
normalizing the community or, in this case, the Peaceable Kingdom, in
which the readers are cast as participants. The new nationalist literati
knew that they needed to take on roles as architects in creating something new out of the old, while like-minded publishing companies,
many of which were little more than grassroots operations – Coach
House Press (1965), Oberon Press (1966), Hurtig Publishers (1967),
Talonbooks (1967), and House of Anansi Press (1967) – did their best
to defy market dynamics and make available dialogues that otherwise
might have been unavailable. Rowland Lorimer, an expert in the history
of Canadian publishing, captures this grassroots phenomenon with particular colour:

> With a great deal of education in their heads, at times a manuscript in their
> pockets, and a total lack of experience in business (let alone the nuance of
> business), the baby boomers came hard upon the blockage to the publica-
> tion of Canadian creative writing and discussion of Canadian issues that
> the branch plant system represented. Their response was to take control of
> the printing press themselves. For approximately $5,000 they became pub-
> lishers of their colleagues and themselves. As they persuaded bookstores to
> accept their titles, and as the political and cultural and intellectual elites
> became aware of these titles and the quantity to the content and writing
> they contained, only one conclusion could be reached. Far from being van-
> ity publishers, this new wave of publishers was bringing forward issues,
> ideas, and writing that had been silenced by the agency system and that
> deserved a hearing in Canadian society if not the world.[45]

The tone of the works should not come a surprise. From treatises on
reclaiming Canadian sovereignty to poetic attacks upon the American
empire, the books offered much to nationalists and critics alike.
Among the works of note are the collection of nationalist dialogue and
poetry *The New Romans: Candid Canadian Opinions of the U.S.* (1968),
edited by Al Purdy; William Kilbourn's *Canada: A Guide to the Peaceable
Kingdom* (1970); Ian Lumsden's *Close the 49th Parallel, Etc.: The*

Americanization of Canada (1970); Margaret Atwood's literary guide *Survival: A Thematic Guide to Canadian Literature* (1972), which she described as 'a cross between a personal statement, which most books are, and a political manifesto, which most books also are, if only by default';[46] Robert Fulford, David Godfrey, and Abraham Rotstein's *Read Canadian: A Book about Canadian Books* (1972); Rotstein and Gary Lax's *Getting It Back: A Program for Canadian Independence* (1974); Kari Levitt's economic analysis in *Silent Surrender: The Multinational Corporation in Canada* (1970); Rotstein and Lax's political treatise *Independence: The Canadian Challenge* (1972); Robert Laxer's *(Canada) Ltd.: The Political Economy of Dependency* (1973); and an overview of the nationalist struggle in Susan M. Crean's *Who's Afraid of Canadian Culture?* (1976), the book's cover warning the prospective buyer that 'the survival of Canadian culture and the Canadian nation is in danger. But there is a way to save us.'[47]

The nationalism that made many of the works appealing to some readers did, on the other hand, ostracize others who could not (or did not want to) see beyond the original impetus. Key to nationalist success in the area of book publishing, then, rested in the ability to maximize the appeal of writings through normative outlets. Educational institutions were a particularly vital site for doing so, as within these venues were not only audiences but an infrastructure capable of vesting literary and educational capital in the works. It was soon evident, however, that many educators had little idea about the availability of Canadian content. Robert Fulford has recalled a conversation with an English teacher who presented him with a disheartening situation. 'She had heard about Canadian Literature courses, she said, and she had been approached by some students with the suggestion that she begin to teach one ... There was only one problem: she didn't know anything about Canadian literature. She had graduated in English from a Canadian university; she had received her specialist's certificate in English, but nowhere along the way had the Canadian novel been so much as mentioned. How does one begin to teach it? What novels do you teach? She had read hardly any.'[48]

Margaret Atwood's *Survival*, perhaps the most discussed 'CanLit' artefact of this period – she attributed its success to a combination of 'good luck, good timing, and good reviews' – was initially conceived as a response to requests for information on Canadian works from people attending her talks.[49] The first version, which Atwood put together for House of Anansi's Dennis Lee and David Godfrey, was little more than a small guidebook with a reading list designed for CanLit programs. But between her nationalistic inclinations and Dennis Lee's editorial hand, the draft quickly expanded into a manifesto. *Survival* traces the 'experience of being a victim in a colonial culture,' the book explains in a phrase not coincidentally attuned to the nationalist discourse of the time.[50] In arguing on the behalf of 'Canadian literature, as *Canadian* literature – not just literature that happened to be written in Canada,' *Survival* moved beyond surveying literary interests and into serving those of nation-builders.[51] Atwood did not chart the path of literature so much as create a way of canonizing it in line with the new nationalist paradigm.

Not everyone was happy with such nationalistic literary activities, of course. Critic John Metcalf is one person who has made a career out of objecting to what he sees as nationalist parochialism. 'I don't use literature as sociology, history, anthropology, or travel guide,' Metcalf once declared.[52] The argument is straightforward enough: nationalists actually prevent a national literature from organically developing by trying to impose upon it abstract notions of nationhood and identity. To Robin Mathews, an acerbic author and strident nationalist unreserved in his use of language – his 1968 poem 'Centennial Song,' for example, compared Canada to a 'whore' selling herself to the United States[53] – Metcalf was little more than a 'barking dog.'[54] Actually, compared to the analogy given for the selling-off of Canada, Metcalf got away with a rather mild rebuke.

Universities in Canada versus Canadian Universities

Robin Mathews certainly knew something about criticism; perhaps no other new nationalist was as much a target of venomous condemnation as Mathews. His combination of passionate oratory and dedication to nationalist interests, particularly those in tied to academia, set the stage for fierce confrontations. Frustrated by the complacent hiring of American academics and a lack of Canadian courses, Mathews and fellow Carleton University professor of English James Steele launched a highly contested and controversial campaign to increase the number of Canadian citizens and Canadian content courses in universities and colleges. It should come as no surprise that academia, as a site of social construction, cultural dissemination, and information consumption, proved to be such a hot spot for conflict. Academics possess significant intellectual capital and are capable of greatly contributing to the task of nation-building. Conversely, there is a strong belief that universities are bastions of independent thought and should not have to kowtow to politicized interests. Any attempt to change the status quo meant a ferocious battle against entrenched interests protected by some very powerful ideas about academic freedom.

The roots of the problem that plagued Mathews, Steele, like-minded faculty, and fellow nationalists are simple enough to pinpoint. Rapid university expansion in the 1960s meant a need for more academics than Canada could supply at the time. In 1960–1 there were 7,760 full-time faculty members in Canada, a number that increased to 24,612 by 1970–1, yet only 8,684 doctorates were awarded during that decade. Given the number drawn into the government, industry, and other non-academic areas, it has been estimated that only 5,600 or so were available for employment by Canadian universities.[55] Universities had little choice but to look elsewhere for academics, and Americans, many of them dodging the draft and heading north, were plentiful. The situation was made all the more problematic given that many of the Canadians who were available had actually been trained abroad and returned home with non-Canadian academic interests and networks. Interestingly, Ernest Sirluck, the University of Toronto's dean of graduate studies, had warned his peers about this phenomenon back in a 1966 issue of *Varsity Graduate*. 'The United States, the United Kingdom, and to a lesser extent certain other countries, have paid for the graduate training of a very large part of our professoriate. We will not escape the vulnerability of our academic colonialism until we cease to bum a free ride.'[56]

This statement was echoed three years later when Robin Mathews and James Steele released their highly influential *The Struggle for Canadian Universities*, a daring and radical call for universities to increase their level of Canadian faculty and course material. This treatise on academic life was a bold statement about the important role played by universities in the national context. To struggle for Canadian universities was to struggle for Canada itself, the duo argued in their book. Without immediate action, 'one of the most important centres of national definition will be sapped of its relevance.'[57] The decade of reliance upon foreign academics without checks and balances, like the problem with American economic investment, had reduced Canadian universities to little more than branch plants for foreign academic endeavours. American-dominated departments tended to dismiss Canadian academics as being of lesser quality and opted to hire new faculty members from the 'foreign institutions which they know and trust,' sometimes being as brazen as to recruit friends directly from their alma maters.[58] The Canadian 'colonial-minded academics' who permitted, if not collaborated in, such activities were judged by Mathews and Steele to be just as guilty as the Americans.[59]

The duo put forth a critique of the common idea – and one which foreign-born academics often hid behind – that the academy operated as a bastion of free thought uninfluenced by national considerations. 'Teaching and research are not ordinarily conducted by disembodied minds in a metaphysical world of learning,' explained *The Struggle for Canadian Universities*. 'They are carried on by particular men, in particular places, at particular times, about particular problems and in the context of particular communities.'[60] In other words, with foreign faculty came a foreign world view and a disinterest in Canadian content to the detriment of the nation and its citizenry. This argument was backed by telling incidents of neglect for Canadian interests, including statistics compiled from the term papers of a first-year university sociology class at Laurentian University. Of the collection of 260 papers, 50 were on 'race relations' but only 5 dealt with 'distinctly Canadian racial difficulties,' while approximately half dealt with 'the American Negro.' A number of the students even used phrasing that made themselves sound as if they lived in the United States.[61]

These two controversial academics were not alone in trying to draw attention to the need for an increase in Canadian content in the academy. In fact, this issue had been attracting attention, albeit on a much more subtle level, over the past few years. Back in 1965, the same year Walter Gordon left the Liberal cabinet and George Grant released *Lament for a Nation*, Trinity College School in Port Hope, Ontario, launched a 'National History Project' to survey the teaching of Canadian course material. Its report, *What Culture? What Heritage?*, presented a compelling platform for increasing the level of Canadian content in course curriculum. Over the next few years a number of groups took up the cause in establishing outlets for discussing Canadian topics. Trent University was at the forefront with the creation of the *Journal of Canadian Studies* in 1966. Three years later Mount Allison University founded an undergraduate program in Canadian Studies, and in that same year the Ontario Institute for Studies in Education hosted a three-day conference on the topic of Canadian Studies. Out of these initiatives emerged the non-profit Canadian Studies Foundation in 1970. At the turn of the decade, then, Mathews and Steele were politicizing elements of something that others had already made steps forward in popularizing.

The Arts in Canada versus Canadian Arts

The new nationalism flourished in radical ways within the high-cultural sectors that had earlier been revered as bastions of gentlemanly refinement and elevation. By the 1960s the focus on international arts as templates for domestic culture had seemed to result in an imbalanced cultural life; venues were continuing to rely upon foreign works instead of providing opportunities for those created by indigenous playwrights, choreographers, composers, and other artists. This situation was far from satisfactory within the new nationalist paradigm. What had once been a core part of offsetting the menace of commercialism and helping Canadians to replicate foreign achievements within the domestic context had itself become an unwanted and even dangerous threat to nationhood. The British cultural inheritance so paramount to the Masseyites now seemingly hindered indigenous expression; earlier cultural convictions now worked against the interests of a new nationalism. What followed was a testament to changing conceptions of cultural constitution and a rise in the idea that high culture was no longer in and of itself worthy of praise.

Grassroots theatres, much like their publishing counterparts, were established as a means of facilitating a radicalized cultural experience capable of challenging the theatrical status quo. Theatre Passe Muraille (1968), Factory Theatre Lab (1970), Tarragon Theatre (1971), and Toronto Free Theatre (1972) all did much to give domestic playwrights opportunities denied by the numerous foreign-focused venues. Operating above a garage in Toronto and only staging Canadian works, the Factory Theatre Lab proudly claimed to have 'produced 100 Canadian plays' in its first three years, 'half of them in full professional production.'[62] It even had a 'Canadian theatre library' and workshops to develop and display Canadian talent.[63]

A nationalistic overhauling of theatrical life was on its way. Performers and audiences gathered together for events such as the First Festival in Toronto, a nineteen-day festival of new Canadian plays held from 19 August to 6 September 1970.[64] With Canadians putting on the works of other Canadians, it should come as no surprise that playwrights seemed increasingly comfortable with situating their works in the domestic context. A month after the First Festival, writer Harvey Markowitz told the *Globe and Mail* that 'from what I've seen, I think [Canadian playwrights] are actually beginning to become less embarrassed about being Canadians. They're placing the action right here in Canada. Why, just a couple

years ago I was too cautious even to mention Yonge Street. Many of my
plays were set in New York.'[65] The new Canadian theatres and their
indigenous plays attracted both the traditional theatre-going public
curious about the new offerings and a new generation of theatre-goers
interested in Canadiana.[66]

Anti-colonialism and a nationalistic desire to construct 'in' and 'out'
groups became a defining characteristic of theatrical life among nationalistic cultural workers at this time. Just as the Group of Seven fifty years
earlier had employed modernist aesthetics to separate their work from
the dominant visual arts, so theatre groups often employed experimen-
tal approaches and non-traditional techniques in order to distinguish
between 'theatre in Canada' and 'Canadian theatre.'[67] New theatrical
aesthetics and methods were combined with topical issues speaking to
the interests and needs of the national community. The Factory Theatre
Lab took this message to heart in reacting to Dunlop Canada's Toronto
plant closing in May 1970, in which six hundred employees were laid off
with only two months' notice, by putting on a play entitled 'Branch
Plant.'[68] On at least one occasion the play was followed by a seminar
explaining how multinational corporations were a threat to Canada.[69]
Within this event cultural nationalists had found something that spoke
to the role of the arts as a means of tackling pressing social issues. 'The
fight against plant shutdowns had become a cause célèbre and the Dunlop workers had become their first martyrs,' in the words of historian
Steven High.[70] Nationalistic playwrights did not have to look hard to
find subject matter of appeal to audiences in this day and age.

Challenging the theatrical status quo of cultural branch plants meant
tackling the Canada Council itself.[71] Forged within a Masseyesque cultural weltanschauung that had identified the international arts as a
means of bringing Canada 'up to standard,' the council was the product
of a nationalist paradigm increasingly out of touch with the needs of
Canadians struggling with the issue of sovereignty. 'Why,' wondered the
Committee for an Independent Canada, was 80 to 90 per cent of
the Canada Council's theatrical funding going to companies – including
the National Arts Centre, the Stratford Festival, and the Shaw Festival –
that presented at most only one Canadian play?[72] In the 1971–2 season
one finds thirty-two of the top-funded theatres receiving approximately
$13,000 a play, despite the fact that of their combined 148 plays, only
18 were written by Canadians. Conversely, most of the plays put on by
the Factory Theatre Lab, Theatre Passe Muraille, Tarragon Theatre, and
Le Théâtre d'Aujourd'hui were Canadian productions, yet these four

theatres received only a combined $35,000 or so in subsidies, or a scant
$1,000 per play.[73] It is telling that Canadian playwrights found their best
market to be not theatre but writing scripts for television (a market established thanks in part to the Canadian content regulations).[74]

The grassroots fight against internationally focused theatres was taken
into the backyard of the Stratford Festival Theatre in 1969. Canadian
Place Theatre, established in the city of Stratford to stage plays by Canadian authors, was a small and far from solvent theatre. Student actors
built props during the day and acted at night, subsisting on seven dollars a week and taking their meals at a local café in return for washing
dishes.[75] A love of theatre and concern for Canadian sovereignty kept
the Canadian Place Theatre alive. Co-founders John Palmer and Martin
Kinch, both in their mid-twenties, hoped to make the theatre a permanent venue for Canadian works. 'The Manitoba Theatre Centre doing
"Hello, Dolly" frankly makes me ill,' Palmer explained to the *Toronto
Telegram's* Jim McPherson in August 1969. 'That whole thing that Canadians won't go to see Canadian plays is ridiculous. The reason they
won't go to see them is because there are too many "Hello, Dolly"s touring around. If you give them Canadian plays, they'll go to see them."[76]
McPherson, although finding the theatre's concept to be interesting
and worthy of support, gave a mixed review to the play he attended.[77]

The Stratford Festival Theatre reacted to its theatrical rival – and the
growing interest in domestic works – by establishing a 'Third Stage' for
Canadian and non-traditional performances. Stratford now had the
ability to exert power over its ideological competition by setting the
grounds upon which the challenge was posited. Yet although the Third
Stage had been created with theatrical performances in mind, it actually
ended up doing much more for the musical community by offering an
outlet to struggling composers and musicians for whom grassroots venues were not a practical option.[78] After all, orchestral composers and
musicians were struggling just as much if not more than their theatrical
counterparts, particularly because venues were not as readily available.

The lack of orchestra-friendly venues was compounded by the disinterest of organizations and associations in domestic talent and works.
No episode is more telling than one in September 1971 involving the
Montreal Symphony Orchestra, an organization that not only had a
track record of failing to hire Canadians but, the *Montreal Star* reported
to its readership, had recently hired five new members without including a single Canadian.[79] Alexander Brott, director of the McGill Chamber Orchestra, pointed out the obvious in telling the *Montreal Star* that

such hiring policies did little to develop a national cultural experience. 'If we are only aiming to present the very best the world has to offer, regardless of Canadian content, we could easily and much more economically present a series at Place des Arts with the finest orchestras, such as the Boston, the New York or even the Vienna and Berlin Philharmonic Orchestras.'[80]

The Atlantic Symphony Orchestra was a notable exception to the Canadian orchestral norm. Formed in 1968 as the first regional-based professional symphony orchestra, the ASO claimed to put on more Canadian works than any of its peers. 'In the four years of the ASO it is doubtful that any Canadian composer of merit has been omitted from performance,' proudly explained Lionel D. Smith, executive director of the orchestra, to the *Halifax Mail Star*.[81] This atypical use of Canadian material attracted praise from the Canada Council and was rewarded with a $190,000 grant for the 1971–2 season.[82] It was an important grant for the council to give, but in a time of heated nationalism and complaints about skewed funding priorities, it would take more than token measures to placate a growing number of nationalistic cultural workers who judged the council guilty of neglecting indigenous national cultural activities. In giving little consideration to Canadian content in grant proposals, the council seemed to be shirking its true purpose. This milestone of the Masseyesque moment of Canadianization was in need of an overhaul, and members of the arts community increasingly seemed poised to stage a coup against a funding council that owed its existence, and much of its cultural direction, to a previous generation of cultural nationalists.

Cinematic Nationalism

Why did filmmakers take so well to the new nationalism? Several reasons stand out. First, perhaps no other area of mass-media activity, with the exception of radio broadcasting, was so saturated with American content. Even the outlets of exhibition themselves were often tied directly to American interests. 'We are told in Canada that our prospective enemies are Russia and China,' argued Henry Comor, president of the Association of Canadian Television and Radio Artists, in the February 1967 issue of *Take One*, a nationalistic film magazine launched the previous year. 'In my opinion, a case can be made for indicating the U.S. as our real enemy and for placing Canadian forces all along our border with their guns aimed at Los Angeles and New York.'[83] Anti-Americanism

was so present in Canadian cinematic life, in fact, that the organizers of
the 1970 Canadian Film Awards decided to exclude American actors
from being nominated for awards for their roles in a Canadian film.[84] A
second factor contributing to cinematic nationalism can be traced to
the undercurrent of disappointment permeating the sector at this time.
The Canadian Film Development Corporation helped filmmakers produce a number of quality movies, only for all of their hard work and
vision to end up sitting on shelves and gathering dust. 'Not making films
you should be making is awful, but making them and then not having
them shown is worse,' as filmmaker Claude Jutra told the *Ottawa Citizen*
in the December of 1971.[85] Third and finally, films are a highly commu-
nicative medium capable of channelling popular opinions and ideas. To
have this outlet neutered in a time of national crisis could only lead to
frustration and provoke a thrust for change.

Filmmakers took so thoroughly to nationalist sentiments, in fact, that
for many, as film critic Geoff Pevere put it, what mattered was not
whether 'something was Canadian, but whether it was Canadian
enough.'[86] Nationalism offered much to the cause of filmmakers, and in
turn nationalism became an ingrained part of their craft, so much so
that, as in other areas of cultural production, there was an interest in
canonizing national distinctiveness. It is worth noting that this is an
ideological trapping that still exists today, even within scholarly work on
cinematography. One finds, for example, Janis Pallister, professor emer-
itus of Romance languages at Bowling Green University, arguing that
'true Canadian content' needs to reflect 'the nature of Canada,' as in
'films that reflect Canadian life and values, and are not easily equated
to American works.'[87] This approach attempts to isolate the national
experience and overlook, if not eliminate, anything that might be shared
with the foreign 'other.' As cultural studies expert Lawrence Grossberg
has noted in 'Identity and Cultural Studies: Is That All There Is?' 'any
identity depends upon its difference from, its negation of, some other
term, even as the identity of the latter term depends upon its difference
from, its negation of, the former.'[88] That Canadians and Americans
share much in their continental North American lifestyle and that both
suffer from the workings of unbalanced capital and power becomes
irrelevant through the use of 'in' and 'out' categories. Not only does
Canadianness become selectively identified, but so too does American-
ness; in cinematic terms one finds Hollywood's representations of
American life being taken as those of the United States as a whole. This
idea was wonderfully – and colourfully – addressed by Harry J. Boyle,

long-time CBCer and chairman of the Canadian Radio-television and Telecommunications Commission, in a talk given on 2 April 1977 to a conference on 'Canadian-American Relations: Culture, Energy and Commerce.' As Boyle insightfully told his audience, 'I am not going to harp about American cultural invasion. I am sick of hearing about it. In the first place most of it is not American anyhow. The wash of television and of highly specialized commercial effort, neutered and homogenized as to time and place, employing devices and sensational effects that bear little resemblance to culture … They originate in America, but God help us all if the Gentle Bens, the Kojaks, and the third film version of "Airport" soon to assail us, are representative of American culture.'[89] The statement was worthy of someone who had spent a quarter of a century at the CBC and now headed the body that regulated the broadcasting sector.

Conclusion

Continentalism and the American investment it entailed helped to increase the Canadian economic standard of living during the 1950s and the ability of many people to indulge in the wealth of American media content and industrial goods offered by distributors and retailers. That so much of the investment had occurred with little in the way of checks and balances, however, increasingly concerned Walter Gordon and a few like-minded (and atypical) figures in the business sector who looked beyond the economic bottom line. Had Canada gone from being a colony to a nation only to fall back into colonial status, this time as part of the American empire? Had national sovereignty been traded for the nickels and dimes of investment and the excitement of media content? Many Canadians began to feel that, at the very least, the country had become too integrated with the United States and that something needed to be done to ensure national sovereignty. This sentiment was made all the more prominent as a result of the celebratory climate of the 1960s and the tarnishing of the United States by internal civil unrest and external militarism. For some people, many of whom were middle-class participants in the arts and mass-media sectors, nationhood required no less than casting off the British post-colonial inheritance and the Liberal Party's continentalism in favour of a new national design, a Peaceable Kingdom of social welfare, multiculturalism, peacekeeping, and Crown corporations which ensured that all citizens benefited from the wealth of domestic resources.

Culture, mobilized during the first half of the century by Masseyites who attempted to navigate Canada through the colony-to-nation process in a time of modernity, now offered a new intelligentsia a means by which to reclaim Canadian sovereignty from forces of imperialism. And just as cultural nationalism rewarded its leading proponents with positions of influence within the social, cultural, and political hierarchies of post-colonialism, so one finds it promising significant gains to the legions of playwrights, artists, actors, composers, academics, and other cultural producers whose way of life was intimately linked to the domestic context. A new model of Canadian nationhood was under construction, one attuned to the middle-class, multi-brow, and leftist ideas and interests of its architects. The Peaceable Kingdom, complete with ivory towers and cultural can(n)ons, offered refuge to a citizenry being dragged into the empire of its southern neighbour. The only problem was that it still needed to be built.

6 Guaranteed Culture: Nationalism and the Question of Intervention

Whatever smacks of censorship or dictation by the patron is suspect. But [nationalists] admit – and sometimes demand – one exception to this rule. Performing arts ask the Council to impose quotas, in the form of ceilings, on the employment by companies of foreign artists; and the creative artists ask for quotas, in the form of floors, on the production of Canadian works.

Frank Milligan, academic and future museum director[1]

The cultural nationalists have attempted to influence the government into Culture by Decree; they have lobbied for subsidy, regulation, and quota. It does not seem to have penetrated with them that culture cannot be imposed.

Literacy critic John Metcalf[2]

The Stratford Festival Theatre had staged a lot of drama since opening in the small town of Stratford, Ontario, in 1952, but few of the scripts matched the real-life excitement that took place in the spring of 1974. With artistic director Jean Gascon preparing to step down, Stratford's board of directors thought it had found the proper replacement in British-born Robin Phillips, an established actor with a strong interest in directing. Phillips had been chosen over William Hutt and John Hirsch, two distinguished Canadians with strong international reputations. Here was yet another instance in which Stratford, it seemed in the eyes of some nationalists, was at best a testament to out-of-date theatre in Canada and at worse a cultural colonizer. Hirsch and six other Canadian directors, with Robertson Davies drafting the *cri de coeur*, scathingly protested the selection of a non-Canadian as artistic director and took it as an opportunity to air their grievances about Stratford's neglect of Canadian cultural life. 'When Stratford was founded, it began a new era in Canadian theatre, and we have benefited from its enterprise and courage. Now, it appears that the theatre we represent is taking one direction, and Stratford another. During the past twenty-five years theatre in Canada has advanced to a direction that Stratford does not reflect. Canadian theatre is now working consistently to present world theatre in Canadian terms, to reveal a truly Canadian sensibility, and to advance, under the best circumstances at its command, Canadian plays, and the work of theatre artists in every field.'[3] Robin Phillips was caught in the crossfire of Canadianization. The situation would repeat itself upon his resignation in 1980, with the festival theatre once again facing calls for a Canadian successor.[4] Herein was a telling episode in which new ideas of nationhood and culture were being played out against the status quo. Stratford offered a site where, as academic Richard Paul Knowles has colourfully described, 'on the one hand, the nationalist hordes are seen to be villainously attacking the temple of transcendent art in which all Canadians should take pride; ... on the other, the arrogant British are accused of colonizing what ought to be a "purely" Canadian institution, using Canadian public funds to produce British high culture.'[5]

The controversy surrounding Robin Phillips was much ado about citizenship, and in this it was far from unique. From the mid-1960s through to the mid-1970s one finds many concerned Canadians calling for fellow citizens to be placed in important sites of identity construction; greater access to Canadian content; an end to taxpayer-subsidized cultural colonialism; and the introduction of subsidies, tax-deduction incentives, federal investment, and quotas guaranteeing the availability of cultural Canadiana. Quotas were the most controversial of possibilities, yet they also offered the best means of making sure that Canadian content was shown on stage and placed on gallery walls, taught in universities, transmitted over radio airwaves, and projected upon the screens of movie houses, and that Canadians were placed in positions of authority in cultural institutions. Although the success of quotas in the television sector had been questionable, the technique appealed to the desire for domestic discourse and expression in areas otherwise bulwarked by profiteers within the systems of distribution and exhibition.

Canadianizers this time around did not seek to elevate high-cultural creativity to a position of great reverence and back it with the cultured offerings of publicly owned broadcasting and film bodies; here was not merely a paradigm in which the cultural community debated the role of culture in national life and what did or did not constitute an appropriation of art for nation's sake. Nationalistic intelligentsia and their like-minded supporters were now mobilizing entire systems of bureaucratic, quantitative, and market-friendly techniques designed to facilitate the utmost in multi-brow Canadian content. Culture and the national design were being put together in a significantly new way with nation-builders employing cultural precepts and proposing forms of intervention that would have horrified their Masseyite predecessors. The reaction among some of their contemporaries, particularly those residing in the sites under siege, turned out to be (to little surprise) just as strong. Offensive language and acerbic defamation became common tools on both sides of the Canadianization debate. But to the new advocates of nationhood, a sovereign Peaceable Kingdom required no less than a willingness to risk careers, make enemies, and sacrifice old friendships.

The Arts Community and the Push for Representation

Vincent Massey and a generation of cultural nationalists had looked to the arts, and the spiritual elevation resting within, as a requisite part of securing Canadian nationhood among the torrents of modernity. The arts continued to have an important role among nation-builders, yet echoing the disinterest expressed by apathetic patrons, critics, and the federal government during the time of the Masseyites, there were also tremendous barriers to be overcome. One of them, ironically enough, was actually something that had been a triumph during the earlier moment of Canadianization: the Canada Council for the Arts. The council had done much for the arts since its creation in 1957, but a decade later many people in the cultural community were not finding themselves all that well served by the fact that a large amount of the council's funding went towards cultural organizations which drew upon foreign talent and compositions. The same internationalism that had been idealized as a template for Canadian cultural growth now seemed to be operating contrary to national cultural needs. Nationalistic culturists began drawing lines between the national and non-national, Canadian culture and cultural branch plants, and in doing so, they found themselves having to confront and challenge the very body that had been so pivotal to cultural life earlier.

The Canada Council had to get with the times, it seemed, by giving greater consideration to Canadian talent and the use of works by Canadian citizens – authors, playwrights, composers, choreographers, and others – in funding decisions. If doing so meant introducing Canadian content criteria into funding decisions, then so be it. Some people were willing to go so far as to call for quotas. Did quotas infringe upon artistic freedom? Certainly. But as these more far-reaching of cultural nationalists were sure to point out, such a measure was merely a counterweight to the discrimination already occurring within many organizations and venues, particularly those oriented towards profitability and tourism, which offered little in the way of opportunities for Canadian talent and works.

Calling upon the Canada Council to change the ways in which it made its funding decisions came as part and parcel of the new nationalism. In 1967, a powerful year in Canadian life, the Composers, Authors and Publishers Association of Canada (CAPAC) issued a request for the council to begin giving greater consideration to Canadian content, arguing that this was necessary in order for the population to access the myths, symbols, stories, and values so essential to Canada's post-colonial survival.[6] Of course, one should not be surprised to see that not only was the idea gaining ground in other cultural organizations but it was proving to be tremendous divisive. Members of the Canadian Conference of the Arts (CCA) spent the summer of 1967 trying to agree upon ways to improve the status quo, only to fail in coming to a unanimous position. Both the CCA's Music and Musical Theatre groups ended up rejecting 'the idea of giving special bonus grants in return for Canadian content,' but the Theatre Group, on the other hand, found the possibility of bonus grants to be interesting because 'while the stick is not effective, the carrot may be.' In the end, the CCA took a middle ground in recommending that the Canada Council introduce an 'effective incentive program' or an 'automatic bonus' to encourage the use of Canadian plays and, most controversially, noted that the council would not be out of line if it chose to consider citizenship criteria when making orchestral grants.[7] Quotas, however, were not something behind which the CCA wanted to put its weight.[8] As late as 1973 the CCA continued to downplay the quota possibility in favour of what it identified as 'more funds for works high in Canadian content or of particular relevance to the Canadian population where these works are of recognized artistic merit or potential.'[9]

Playwrights, suffering alongside other creators of original works, were given a chance to air their grievances and present suggestions for change at a special conference sponsored by the Canada Council in Gaspé, Quebec, in July of 1971. It was here that playwrights could take their concerns directly to the source of cultural monies and call for Canadian content considerations in council funding decisions. Some playwrights went so far as to request that the council require that theatres receiving its funds reserve half their stage time for Canadian works – in other words, a quota.[10] Some theatre directors, particularly those with a track record of putting on foreign works, rejected the idea as being out of touch with the interests of audiences. Canadians did not want Canadian content, the critics complained, although their position was taken in the face of the tremendous popularity of Canadiana at this time and more accurately reflected the desire to continue relying upon foreign works of utmost profitability.[11] The quota concept, in the words of the Canada Council's 1971–2 *Annual Report*, became 'the centre of a lively and some-times angry public debate' at the conference.[12] Faced by such division, the council rejected the request that new considerations for Canadian content be introduced into grant decisions. Instead it was decided that the council would issue an appeal for funding recipients to increase their use of domestic plays.[13] It almost goes without saying that this was an empty gesture. Of greater importance was the debate itself and the atten-tion it drew to the plight of indigenous arts. As the *Vancouver Sun* reported to its readership, 'whether or not a 50 per cent [Canadian con-tent] rule is imposed, it seems certain that the council has caught a whiff of the winds of change blowing across the country and that new means will be sought to foster Canadian dramatic writing.'[14]

Playwrights were understandably disappointed with the council's treatment of their request for greater consideration, but in that same year, and a sign of the changing times, the council decided to start con-sidering – although not requiring, and a far cry from a quota require-ment – an orchestra's use of Canadian talent when assessing grant applications.[15] For a decade now the council had been trying to address the problems that were plaguing orchestras, a particularly anemic area of the arts given that grassroots operations were not much of an option. A special gathering had been hosted by the Canada Council back in 1961, one in which its participants, including Jack McClelland, Leonard Cohen, Robert Fulford, and John Gray of the Macmillan Company of Canada, discussed the possibility of having Canadian content conditions attached to orchestral grants, but the council ultimately decided against the idea.[16] Such a measure was too radical for the council at that time, and even after a decade had passed, Canadian content was now only to receive 'consideration,' not priority. It was not surprising to see that three years into the policy the council still talked of quotas for orches-tral grants as being 'chauvinistic' and not something with which it wanted to get involved.[17]

A quota system for the arts, although not an idea that sat well with the council, made a lot of sense to groups representing the interests of performers. The Association of Canadian Television and Radio Artists (ACTRA), being quite familiar with the Canadian content regulations in television, called for a 50 per cent minimum in government-sponsored theatres as well as an increase in funding for domestically focused venues.[18] It made sense to do so; after all, many of its members worked not only on television but on the theatrical stage as well. The Committee for an Independent Canada, operating upon a strong agenda but many of whose members relied upon the cultural economy, put forth a similar call for a quota system as a means of ensuring that audiences had access to a cultural experience fundamental to their nationhood. It was a strong measure but one which, the committee argued, seemed necessary, given that Canadian content was of less concern to theatre owners than 'new furniture for the theatre's VIP room.'[19] Similarly, quotas should be instituted for publicly funded art galleries at a level of at least 50 per cent Canadian content in terms of holdings, acquisitions, and showings.[20] With taxpayer funds should come a commitment to offer a cultural experience important to the population from which those dollars were drawn.

Guaranteed access to Canadian plays on stages and Canadian art on gallery walls went hand in hand with placing Canadian citizens in positions of leadership in cultural institutions. For the Masseyites, the need to bring the nation up to international cultural standards had entailed attracting as much foreign talent as possible, an approach that by the 1960s seemed counterintuitive to ensuring opportunities for Canadian talent. Stratford, the flagship of Canadian theatre, had to deal with this divisive issue as early as 1964. The British-born Michael Langham, looking to step down as Stratford's artistic director, recommended to the festival's board of directors that a Canadian be hired to succeed him. The members disagreed. In the words of the nationalistic *Toronto Star*, the board 'panicked at the thought of so drastic a loosening of the Britannic cord of dependency and the delegation of the Festival's million-dollar affairs to a native son.'[21] Langham ended up staying on until 1967, at which point he was replaced by two Canadians, Jean Gascon as executive artistic director and John Hirsch as associate artistic director (the partnership lasted for only one season before Hirsch departed and Gascon took over both roles).[22] This would not be the last time Stratford experienced such a controversy, of course. Hirsch hoped to return to Stratford and take on the position of artistic director when Gascon stepped down, only to find, as explored in the opening vignette to this chapter, that the board members had decided to replace Gascon with British-born Robin Phillips. Hirsch would eventually take on the position of artistic director in 1981 when Phillips stepped down.

One of the more interesting moments in which issues of citizenship and cultural bias played out, complete with protestors 'taking it to the streets' and staging rallies, occurred at the Art Gallery of Ontario in June of 1972. The gallery's decision to hire Richard J. Wattenmaker as the new chief curator certainly did not go over well with many nationalistic critics; not only was Wattenmaker not Canadian but, even worse, he was American. 'In order to further an awareness by Canadians of their own artists this country needs curators who know what's been done here, and by whom,' artist Charles Pachter remarked to the *Toronto Star* about the hiring.[23] It was an idea taken to the street by the imposingly named Committee to Strengthen Canadian Culture and, of moderate name but not moderate action, the Canadian Artists' Representation.[24] Wattenmaker was placed in a difficult position, and it was true that, as he told the press, 'I'm certainly being made a symbol for a lot of issues that have nothing to do with me or the gallery.'[25] He was an American but he was not America. The difference mattered little in the mindset of those who led the Canadian Artists' Representation, a group that not only rallied people against the Wattenmaker hiring but also sought to purge 'Americans, Englishmen, and other aliens' from locales such as the Ontario College of Art, *Artscanada* magazine, and Fanshawe College's fine arts department.[26]

Taking important concerns to such parochial ends merely skewed the ability to engage in serious discussion and allowed critics, for their part, to feel free to retaliate in kind. A 'letter to the editor' from Toronto artist and gallery owner Jack Pollock, for example, equated citizenship requirements with one of the most offensive of taboos: 'incest never has and never will broaden and expand the Canadian creative horizon.'[27] Cultural nativism, in painting all foreigners with a broad brush, served the more extremist of ends and limited the ability of non-Canadians to make a genuine contribution to national life. Texas-born Tom Burroughs was but one of many Americans who showed an interest in advancing the presence of Canadian content in theatrical life. He left the Yale Repertory Theatre to accept an appointment at the Shaw Festival in early 1971 and, upon doing so, made clear his intention to provide opportunities for domestic expression. 'I'd ... like to see the Canadian talent drain reversed,' he explained to the *Ottawa Citizen*.

'There's too many exciting theatre people leaving Canada these days.'[28] Of course, while such comments were likely sincere, it is important to consider them in light of the repercussions that came with stepping on the toes of nativists.

The Academy and the Battle for Canadian Content

Rooting out foreigners in Canadian cultural institutions was something Robin Mathews and James Steele found themselves being accused of on a daily basis. These two academics saw themselves as trying to correct an imbalance within academic sites crucial to the 'particular needs and problems of the Canadian community as a whole,' as they phased it, overhauling locales where 'such knowledge and concern is much more likely to be found in citizens of Canada than in non-citizens who owe their allegiance to other communities.'[29] In their view, one shared by many Canadian academics, rapid university growth had led to an influx of American faculty members who brought with them foreign areas of interest and a bias against Canadians and Canadian content. Entrenched and seemingly beyond reproach, foreign-leaning departments could feel free to hire directly from the United States without giving Canadian graduates an equal opportunity for employment (after all, at this time academic appointments did not even have to be advertised in Canada).

For Mathews and Steele, a minimum quota for Canadian faculty was no more than a form of 'employment equity' – a concept more common today than over thirty years ago – as a corrective measure to systemic discrimination. As Yasmeen Abu-Laban and Christina Gabriel describe in *Selling Diversity: Immigration, Multiculturalism, Employment Equity, and Globalization,* 'employment equity measures seek to identify and eliminate barriers to employment as well as to improve the representation and status of these groups within the labour market. To the extent measures focus on issues of substantive quality, employment equity is concerned with social justice and the social rights attached to a post-war understanding of citizenship.'[30] In the nationalist rhetoric of the late 1960s and early 1970s, it meant making space for citizens in cultural institutions co-opted and barricaded by foreigners. After all, as Mathews and Steele pointed out, employment equity was a common international practice: the United States, France, Italy, and Japan, among others, had restrictions on the level of foreign academics as a means of ensuring opportunities for their own citizens.[31] The United

States had even begun to institute proportional-representation legislation in universities in order to make room for its ostracized minorities.[32] Racial tensions and feminism prompted employment equity south of the border, while nationalism led to something similar in Canada.

Calling for a minimum level of Canadian citizens and Canadian content did not, of course, go over well with the non-Canadian academics now making the country their home. Conversely, many academics were happy that someone – or, in this case, two people – had finally spoken up about the disparities and problems faced by Canadian academics. Letters of both support and condemnation, from mild to extreme, made their way to Mathews and Steele.[33] The lengths to which the two were willing to take Canadianization certainly shaped the tone of the reaction. As evidenced in a letter of response from Muni Frumhartz, a peer of Mathews and Steele at Carleton University, Canadian content was an important issue, but the duo's willingness to go as far as a quota or other quantitative means to correct the inequalities risked alienating many academics who might otherwise lend support to the cause.[34]

The Struggle for Canadian Universities, the treatise at the heart of the call for change, attracted its share of rebuke. The Canada Council challenged the book's claim that 68 per cent of Canada Council research grants to York University in 1968–9 had gone to non-Canadians. The council put the level at 61 per cent, a still impressive amount, and explained that so many grants went to Americans because they composed so much of the faculty.[35] Of course, that was exactly the problem which these two academics and their like-minded supporters were trying to address. And then there was the reaction from members of the University of Waterloo, a school given special attention in the book because of its high level of American faculty members. The university's information-services director used an interview in the school newspaper to call *The Struggle for Canadian Universities* 'a witch-hunt in the worse McCarthy tradition,' and the academic vice-president was quoted as exclaming that 'the absurdity of this is absolutely breathtaking.'[36]

Mathews and Steele did not win a landslide of support, but their efforts were in many ways rewarded by the degree to which their ideas were picked up by others in the academy, particularly representative bodies. In *The Canadianization Movement: Emergence, Survival, and Success*, Jeffrey Cormier has told of how 'the movement found a permanent home by taking over and transforming a professional association of sociologists and anthropologists.'[37] The Canadian Sociology and Anthropology Association (CSSA) became a hotbed for Canadianization. In 1971 the CSSA launched a self-examination that revealed a sharp division among its members on the issue of giving Canadians favourable treatment in hiring and research grants.[38] Despite the lack of agreement between its members, at its May 1972 annual general meeting the association passed a motion declaring 'support for the encouragement and development of Canadian content in research and teaching in the social sciences' and recognition 'that there are grave problems of Canadianization that should be faced and worked on constructively in our two disciplines.'[39]

The association did not stop at merely making a statement of support, however. This was soon followed by the formation of subcommittees on Canadianization and Canadian Studies to investigate hiring practices, course content, research funding, and graduate student admissions. The mere existence of these two bodies served to further polarize its members. On one side were academics such as David Schweitzer of the University of British Colombia, who told the *Montreal Star* that the subcommittees served an important purpose because 'the problem of Canadianization is tied in with the broader problem of establishing a distinctive Canadian identity.' Conversely, as the newspaper noted in that same article, some other CSAA members were in an uproar and linked the subcommittees to 'fascism, racism, and encouragement of mediocrity.'[40] In early December 1972 the Canadianization subcommittee reported that there was evidence supporting the conclusions made elsewhere about barriers to employment and lack of interest among foreign faculty members for issues of Canadian concern. The subcommittee in turn recommended that department-head positions be exclusively reserved for Canadian citizens, that existing department heads and deans be encouraged to give Canadian candidates priority in job competitions, and that 75 per cent of graduate student positions be reserved for Canadians.[41]

The fallout from the recommendations hit the desk of Pierre Maranda, president of the CSAA, with little in the way of restraint. 'The Canadianization document is an insult to the intelligence of sociologists and anthropologists,' decried Donald P. Warnick, chair of the Department of Sociology and Anthropology at York University, in a letter to Maranda. 'May I urge a prompt retraction and a note of apology to deans, presidents, and the membership at large.'[42] Or, as Jack Steinbring, chair of the University of Windsor's Department of Anthropology, raged in a similar letter, 'the unrestrained nationalism conveyed in your document is an insult to scholarship.'[43] Letters from the pro-Canadianization contingent were, not surprisingly, just as emotionally powerful in supporting the move. One finds, for example, Elaine Cumming, chair of the University of Victoria's Department of Anthropology and Sociology, letting Maranda know that she would be 'very glad when the Americans are in a minority and view themselves as guests in the house, not masters,' even if this meant preferential hiring for Canadians on an 'all things being equal' basis.[44] A few months later, at its annual general meeting in May 1973, and despite the polarized opinions, the Canadian Sociology and Anthropology Association backed the findings of the subcommittee and passed the recommendation that 'sociology and anthropology departments with more than 50% non-Canadian faculty [institute] a moratorium on the hiring of non-Canadians for any regular academic appointment at or above the rank of assistant professor.'[45] Of course, this was merely a suggestion. The association had no power to bring about such a controversial change.

In one final example, it is worth noting that a similar survey was issued by the Canadian Political Science Association, the report for which made waves in the summer of 1973. The Committee on Canadian Content, formed by the association with an eye to 'the facts regarding the Canadian content of the teaching of political science in Canadian universities,' reported that approximately one-third of courses were to some degree Canadian in content, and that these courses were primarily taught by Canadians – non-Canadians had a distinct disinterest in domestic issues and topics.[46] The survey did, however, suffer from difficulties endemic to such an endeavour. Privacy concerns and the hostility of some survey recipients limited the number and breadth of response. For example, Khayyam Z. Paltiel, chair of Carleton University's Department of Political Science, told the association that he was 'far too busy to answer *any* of these questionnaires and [I] request that you cease and desist from asking me to do so in the future. I think that the whole process of "inquisition" has been pushed to absurdity and I for one do not wish to cooperate.'[47]

It did not take much effort to attack Canadianization; there were more than enough rhetorical tools. The fact that other countries had citizenship regulations in place was disregarded in favour of decrying the idea as a slippery slope to fascism and – one of the most loaded of social ills – anti-Semitism. 'If you say that you must be a Canadian citizen to do this then it's a very easy step to say that you must be a Canadian citizen who has certainly political views, you must be a Canadian citizen with a certain color of skin, you must not be Jewish and so on and so forth,' argued Thomas Perry, an American-born professor of pharmacology at the University of British Columbia, in an interview with the

UBC Alumni Chronicle.[48] The ludicrousness of this comment is breathtaking, but its tone says much about the times.

A less-heated investigation into Canadianization, albeit still a very divisive one, was taking place as part of a survey of Canadian Studies initiated by the Association of Universities and Colleges of Canada. The Commission on Canadian Studies, launched in 1972 and chaired by T.H.B. Symons, a former president of Trent University, experienced – as could be expected – division from the very start. 'Some people clearly felt that the Commission should begin its activities by a ceremonial burning of the American flag on the steps of the Parliament Buildings, others at the other extreme denied the need to give any serious attention at all to the questions that the Commission had been asked to examine,' noted the commission's report, *To Know Ourselves*, commonly known as the Symons report.[49] Not surprisingly, the commission found that Canadian universities lagged behind others in dealing with areas of education, research, and knowledge of national interest and needs.[50] Canada was 'not a sufficiently interesting subject for study and research' and of only 'second-rate academic importance' in the view of many non-Canadian academics.[51]

Here was yet another affirmation of the arguments made by Mathews and Steele. *To Know Ourselves*, however, did not go as far as the duo of Canadianizers and like-minded academics had hoped. The 1975 report called for course curriculum reviews with an eye to Canadian content, an examination of the attitudes towards Canada within academic departments, more effort to facilitate studies on Canadian subjects, support for Canada as an important topic of academic inquiry, and encouragement of Canadian content in curriculums.[52] These were all relatively soft measures – plenty of examination and awareness-promotion but nothing in the way of quotas – thereby leaving the report open to criticism from those who had hoped for a stronger stance. Robin Mathews was among those who dismissed the report for being weak and for failing to offer measures strong enough to address systemic problems.[53] Yet Symons did not view himself as an ardent nationalist, nor did he view Canadian Studies as a tool to be used in the arsenal of Canadianization. 'In promoting Canadian studies,' Symons would explain a few years later, 'we should not confuse nationalism and education. In pointing to the need for such studies, I think we must take care to make sure that they are not turned into an exercise in flag-waving.'[54]

Symons was a temperate voice in a period so radical that even Robin Mathews was occasionally dismissed as being too restrained. Passionate, articulate, and caught up in the movement for change, politicized youths – many of them university and college students – proposed far-reaching solutions to academic problems. Groups such as the New Left Caucus, a Toronto-based student movement and self-identified 'revolutionaries interested in seeing the overthrow of both capitalism and imperialism,' rejected Mathews's 'sentimental nationalism' in favour of a university-wide socialist revolution that included citizenship quotas and a curriculum of socialist content and analysis.[55] And then there was the Canadian Liberation Movement and the like-minded 85% Canadian Quota Campaign, both of which – as the name of the latter organization indicates – advocated a minimum 85 per cent Canadian faulty quota. 'Any lesser demand would put us right where we started – as colonials,' the 85% Canadian Quota Campaign argued in a brochure handed out in early 1971. Sure, they were discriminating, the group acknowledged, but it was justifiable because they were only 'discriminating against the discriminators.'[56]

Student organizations and representatives offered an important discursive outlet for the grassroots energies and interests of budding academics. In the 2 August 1969 issue of the *Toronto Star*, Martin Lowery, president of the Canadian Union of Students, argued that 'when you get too many Americans, you get courses that aren't relevant to Canada. And you also get the old boy network operating. Americans on staff bring in their American friends.'[57] Not an overly radical declaration and certainly one in keeping with the core of nationalist complaints, yet other members of the Canadian Union of Students were willing to go much further. Bob Baldwin, the union's associate secretary, used an opportunity at its 1968 congress to warn his fellow students that American faculty members carried with them 'the values which enslave the worker in the factory, which impoverish and destroy the poor, which objectify women for consumption and which bore the student in the classroom. These are the values which permeate our society and on which U.S. capitalism is thriving.'[58] The desire among students for a change to the status quo not surprisingly also manifested itself among graduate students with much to gain from Canadianization within the academy. Testament to this is Marjaleena Repo's *Who Needs the PhD?* (1970), published by the Graduate Students' Union at the University of Toronto, which requested a 'Canadians first' policy for two-thirds of faculty; the remaining third could be made up of academics from other countries provided no single country made up more than 20 per cent.[59]

Mathews and Steele certainly did not lack support from Canadianizers both within and outside academia. 'Never in the history of the

Canadian academy has there been a finer example of just and dedicated courage than that displayed by these two men,' Hugh MacLennan said of the duo in the 17 May 1969 issue of the *Toronto Star.* Their contribution to the quest for nationhood testified not only to their willingness to make sacrifices in their personal lives and careers but, MacLennan argued, spoke loudly of the need to bring about quotas in the academy, an idea he used the newspaper article to promote.[60] Peter C. Newman, joining MacLennan in attracting the ear of the public, likewise advocated quotas and pointed out that provincial powers could be used to ensure that university faculties consisted of a minimum two-thirds Canadian citizens.[61] That Newman would do so was no surprise, of course; he was a founding member of the Committee for an Independent Canada, a group renowned for pushing the envelope of Canadianization. Its members were certainly not short of rhetoric in advocating on the behalf of disadvantaged Canadian academics. 'Our PhDs are going to be out chopping trees,' as CIC president and book publisher Jack McClelland told the *Toronto Star* in the December of 1971. 'That will be the only occupation left for them.'[62] The committee went so far as to hold its own survey of academic life, the results of which not surprisingly supported the conclusions made by Mathews and Steele. According to its research, foreign faculty levels had more than doubled from 36.2 per cent in 1962–3 to 75.1 per cent in 1971–2.[63] Non-Canadian professors held many of the top positions, hiring often occurred via transnational networking with little or no consideration for domestic candidates, and departmental curricula were dominated by foreign interests. Canadian courses made up only 21.47 per cent of the offerings in political science, 18.67 per cent in history, 6.9 per cent in sociology, and 5.9 per cent in English.[64] 'Today Canadian content is frequently given second place in the university curriculum because American or European topics are already well known to the imported instructor and he is often unfamiliar with Canadian materials,' a committee member argued, echoing the conclusions other investigators, in the summary of the results. 'Even when Canadian content is taught by foreign nationals it may be presented with an alien perspective.'[65] Correcting this imbalance necessitated no less than giving Canadian citizens priority in job hiring and, quite interestingly, requiring that current and future non-Canadian tenure-track position holders take out citizenship as a 'tangible expression' of their commitment to Canada.[66] This latter recommendation stands out as being a little puzzling. Instead of distancing Canadian universities from American values and ideology, such a measure would extend tentative

Canadianness to Americans and their supposedly imperialist weltan-schauung. Were non-Canadian teaching interests and hiring biases to disappear by merely the taking out of citizenship? Perhaps this was viewed as a concessionary measure, or maybe the CIC thought that biases would be eliminated as part of a baptism of nationalization. At the very least, the recommendation speaks loudly of a desire to do whatever was necessary in order to increase the Canadian presence, even if only loosely defined, in the academy.

The Canadian Music Scene and *RPM*'s Push for Canadian Content

Radio stations owners, whether they wanted to admit it or not, were operating on borrowed time. As detailed in chapter 3, the Board of Broadcast Governors in 1959 proposed a requirement that, as of 1961, television stations would have to broadcast a minimum level of Canadian content as identified and quantified via industrial criteria, and in response to the requests of several talent-based organizations, the BBG let it be known that the regulations would likely be extended to radio once the television situation had been sorted out. True, television was still quite a mess of questionable domestic programming and station owners unwilling to meet quota obligations, but the new nationalist climate and a growing appreciation for the importance of popular music in fostering a national sense of self ensured that the idea would not go away quietly.

The coming of rock and roll in the late 1950s did not seem to offer much in the way of a positive contribution to national life; the sexual threat of Elvis's hips and the debaucheries promoted in song lyrics did much to ensure that this form of expression evoked a public outcry. By the 1960s, however, the music had shed much of its earlier threat to social morality, and some of the songs, thanks to artists linking political and social messages with instrumental aesthetics, even seemed to offer insights into national issues. A new generation of listeners were turning to song lyrics as means of exploring not only teenage angst but also the national project they stood to inherit. In the view of sociologist and theorist of popular music Simon Frith, 'we use pop songs to create for ourselves a particular sort of self-definition, a particular place in society. Music can stand for, symbolize *and* offer the immediate experience of collective identity' more effectively than other cultural forms.[67] The gist of this argument has also been put forth by cultural theorist John Storey, who goes as far as to identify popular music as the main instrument of the counterculture.[68] It is no surprise, then, to see American protest and counterculture movements so effectively using music as a means of fostering group identities and tackling social inequality, racism, and the military-industrial complex. Audiences rallied around songs – lyrical treatises really – such as Bob Dylan's 'A Hard Rain's A-Gonna Fall' (1963), Barry McGuire's 'Eve of Destruction' (1965), Country Joe and the Fish's 'I-Feel-Like-I'm-a-Fixin'-to-Die Rag' (1965), Jefferson Airplane's 'Volunteers' (1969), and James Brown's 'Say It Loud' (1969).

Having been forced out of the domestic market because of a lack of opportunities, many Canadian performers had little choice but to establish their careers among the turbulence of American life – and did so to great ends. Neil Young's 'Ohio,' written when he was part of Crosby, Stills, Nash and Young, and Joni Mitchell's 'Woodstock' are only two examples of Canadian-authored protest and counterculture songs defining the period. That Canadians did so well in the United States should come as no surprise; much of the music they had been listening to for years and the musical styles in which they trained themselves came from that country. In '"Dream, Comfort, Memory, Despair": Canadian Popular Musicians and the Dilemma of Nationalism, 1968–1972', historian Robert Wright notes that 'it was the natural affinity of Canadians for the American folk tradition and their uniquely ambivalent perception of American society, not anti-Americanism, that accounted for their remarkable ascendance as heroes of the Sixties generation. Canadians did not simply offer a foreigner's critique of American society – that kind of parochialism would only have alienated them from their American audience. Rather, they had preserved in their music the explicitness, sensitivity, and vitality of a protest tradition that was, in its essence, American.'[69] Instead of having an opportunity to adapt their aesthetic and observational skills to Canadian circumstances, as the Group of Seven had done so many decades earlier in applying European modernist aesthetics to nationalistic sentiments, these musicians found themselves forced to become expatriates, leaving their place of birth but finding comfort in social scenes akin to their musical background.

This exodus of talent certainly had an impact on the ability to integrate musical expertise with issues of Canadian sovereignty. What nationalists did have, however, was Walt Grealis and his *RPM* trade paper. Over the past half a decade *RPM* had done much to rally attention to domestic music, and in 1968 Grealis and his friend Stan Klees set out to do even more by drawing attention to the need for Canadian content quotas in radio broadcasting. In the 20 April 1968 issue of *RPM*, the first article of a ten-part series detailing the value of a regulatory change was presented. 'Nationalism is non-profit so advertising revenue is the chief concern of most programmers,' the trade paper reminded its readers. 'Unfortunately we have to generalize in saying that Canadian programmers do not lead but rather follow and are quite content to exercise his "license" as a vehicle for foreign culture and entertainment with a few domestic tidbits thrown in to assure "license" renewal.'[70]

This argument was reinforced the following year when The Guess Who, a band based in Winnipeg, had a hit with its song 'These Eyes' and, quite tellingly, had to first break the song in the American market before Canadian stations showed a willingness to give it airplay. Bassist Jim Kale has recalled that 'when it started to move in the U.S., CHUM went right on it, and even claimed they'd broken the record, made the first release. Like hell they did.'[71] 'These Eyes' helped to put the spotlight on a major problem in the Canadian music scene: a song usually had to become at hit in the United States before domestic stations would give it sufficient (particularly pan-national) airplay. Soon after The Guess Who's success, *Billboard* magazine decided to investigate and expose this problem in a special issue focused on the Canadian music scene.[72]

Radio station owners found themselves having to scramble to save face in a time of looming Canadian content regulations. A dozen stations, including some owned by CHUM, formed the Maple Leaf System (MLS) in June 1969 in hope of appearing to be supportive of Canadian music. A masterful sense of cunning and calculation was displayed in the decision to ask *RPM*'s Walt Grealis to be the project's coordinator; the MLS was latching onto his nationalist capital as a means of vesting the project with an earnestness. The facade did not impress rock journalist Ritchie Yorke, however. 'The real reason for the formation of the MLS was to try to throw the [broadcasting regulator] off the track, to demonstrate a sincere effort among broadcasters to expose Canadian artists on domestic airwaves, to dismiss the need for legislation,' he argued soon after.[73] Was the MLS too little, too late? The question of Canadian content was now permeating public discourse and seemed poised to put radio broadcasting on the same path as television. At least this would be the outcome if Canadianizers managed to strike the right chords and attract the ear of the regulator of the broadcasting system.

Canadian Films and the Lingering Issue of Quotas

'[You are] trying to lull the House [of Commons] and the public into a false sense of security about government support for Canadian film making.' Wally Gentleman, president of the Society of Film Makers, showed little restraint in making this accusation in his 17 January 1970 letter to Secretary of State Gérard Pelletier.[74] Frustrated and tired of unfulfilled promises, Gentleman was merely voicing a sentiment shared by many filmmakers and would-be audience members. State investment in film production had, given that there was no system of ensured exhibition, resulted in little more than economic subsistence and artistic disappointment. The time had come for something more than investment dollars. The Montreal chapter of the Canadian Society of Cinematographers requested a quota system and a 15 per cent surtax on the gross profits of foreign-made feature films.[75] The Canadian Conference of the Arts' Committee on Film demanded more use of independent films by the CBC, a 15 per cent quota for commercial theatres, a chain of publicly owned theatres for Canadian films, a remittance on ticket revenues to be distributed to filmmakers, new tax incentives, a 50 per cent domestic film quota for boards of education, the establishment of a national film school, and the retraction of Canadian content qualification for co-productions with the United States.[76] The Association of Canadian Television and Radio Artists made the request for a 20 per cent quota for domestic films in movie theatres a component of its platform.[77] The Toronto Film-makers' Co-op and the Canadian Filmmakers' Distribution Centre joined in with their own arguments for a theatrical quota.[78] These were but a few of the organizations making public pitches for intervention.

Amazingly, even the National Film Board was coming onside with the call for overhauling systems of distribution and exhibition. This pillar of the first moment of Canadianization was finding its privileged position in Canadian cinematic – and cultural – life overshadowed in the transition from 'feature films in Canada' to 'Canadian feature films,' and with many of its members active in the feature-film sector, it was coming to terms with the realities of contemporary cultural activity. A 'new era' was about to begin, reported the NFB *Annual Report 1970–71*, one in which 'depth' and 'sincerity' would be balanced with 'a certain show-biz flair ... to excite mass audience[s].'[79] This change came hand in hand with a greater appreciation of the gains to be had through a quota system. Although a draft of the NFB's 1969 'Statement of Policy for the Board as a Cultural Agency' asserted the board's traditional anti-quota position, this stance did not make it into the final draft.[80] In fact, a year later, and in line with the ideas expressed in the *Annual Report*, Film Commissioner Hugo McPherson used a meeting of the Standing Committee on Broadcasting, Film, and Assistance to the Arts as an opportunity to criticize the lack of a legislated film quota or a 'special tax' to aid the industry.[81]

Unfortunately for enthusiastic NFB feature filmmakers and audiences interested in seeing national films created in the feature format, the cinematic revolution proved to be short-lived. In July 1970, just as the film board was embarking on its new direction, McPherson resigned his post. He was replaced by Sydney Newman, someone who viewed the NFB as having 'slipped from its original purpose' and who sought to have its filmmakers get back to the traditional tasks.[82] As he told the *Financial Post* in the autumn of 1970, under his leadership the NFB would return to focusing on documentaries, informational films, government material, theatrical shorts, and programs for television audiences.[83] All of this could be done, Newman argued, without resorting to quotas; in fact, he was sure that by reinvigorating earlier distribution systems, the board could even triple the showings of its theatrical shorts.[84]

Gentrifying an aging pillar of Masseyesque Canadian content meant re-establishing the board's connection with the Canadian Broadcasting Corporation, a like-minded cultural body with a similar nation-building mandate and one at which Newman, along with taking up the post at the NFB, had accepted a directorship. It was time for the two bodies to come together in creating Canadian content of a traditional kind. 'Years of stiff-necked non-co-operation between these two government bodies has driven the National Film Board film-maker further into his own cocoon,' Newman opined to Secretary of State Gérard Pelletier.[85] Yet what the NFB and the CBC ideologically shared did not translate in terms of economics and production, and Newman was unable to reconcile his plans with the fact that the CBC possessed its own in-house facilities and had little need of NFB films. These two bodies actually competed against each other in many areas, particularly in public affairs programming.[86] Even when the CBC found itself interested in showing an NFB film, the situation often led to conflict as the broadcaster and filmmakers argued over the number of commercials that could be shown, the time of airing, and the prices paid for the reels.[87] Filmmakers were not all that comfortable with having their artistic works subjected to – and sliced into chunks for the sake of airing the goods of – commercial interests. 'There have been few issues at the Board to which the film-makers have reacted so strongly,' as one board member remarked during a meeting that October.[88] That the CBC had little interest in NFB content, let alone that it showed a lack of willingness to alter its commercial policy in favour of the cinematic arts, intensified an already tense situation in which filmmakers were trying to come to terms with Newman's unrealistic goals.[89]

The new film commissioner was out of date with the realities of Canadian cinematic – and cultural – life, operating on a Masseyesque model of Canadianization that had faded away during the decades in which he was overseas. Newman had been a participant in an earlier push for Canadian content, overseeing the production and distribution of hundreds of NFB documentaries back in the late 1940s and then, as of 1952, taking on the job of CBC director of features and outside broadcasts and later supervisor of drama. His talents led him to leave for the British television industry in 1958, which turned into an almost twenty-year hiatus from the Canadian scene. The moment of Canadianization to which Newman returned was quite different from the one he had left, the ebb and flow of nationalism having drained the old guard and replaced it with a thriving new nationalism that empowered a different idea of the film board's cultural constitution and role in forging nationhood. It is perhaps no wonder that, as Newman noted in a letter to a friend in January of 1972, he might have been back on Canadian soil, but he felt 'homesick' for London.[90]

Disconnected from the cultural realities of the time, Newman had no qualms over dismissing feature filmmaking as a 'highly risky business' in which the NFB was to have no role.[91] He proved to be just as wary of the push for a cinematic quota system. Harking back to the rhetoric and arguments of a past age, and with little grasp of the realities of feature-film distribution and exhibition, Newman told *Cinema Canada* that cinemas being 'foreign owned has nothing to do with it. You're indulging in a red herring! ... Do you mean to tell me that they wouldn't be delighted to run a film, which will make them as much money as an American film?'[92] Numerous secretaries of state had said the same thing, only to be proven wrong in the face of Hollywood monopolization and the security that came with sticking to tried-and-true films. Revealing of the faulty logic upon which Newman asserted his argument was the question of just how theatres were to know that a film would be profitable until it was actually shown. Giving screen time to unproven Canadian films meant setting aside monies guaranteed by a film already proven in the American marketplace. Newman's unwillingness, or inability, to grapple with a new cinematic age was compounded by his inability to see the failings of trying to turn back time.

Under Newman's leadership, the film board would no longer be putting its weight behind the new nationalist design, but Michael Spencer, executive director of the Canadian Film Development Corporation, proved more resolute in calling upon the state to establish a quota system. Given that the corporation looked like an economic sinkhole, with taxpayer monies being used to create films that did not even receive screen time, something had to be done to save a project otherwise doomed to bankruptcy. On 6 May 1971 Spencer appeared before the Standing Committee on Broadcasting, Film, and Assistance to the Arts and argued that quotas were a necessary part of a national cinematic experience, a remedy to Hollywood monopolization that one found being used in Britain, France, Italy, Spain, and other countries.[93] The federal government, long able to avoid the question of quota intervention, could not continue to stall on a matter of intervention viewed by many as a practical component of ensuring outlets for national expression. Throwing money at the production side of cinematic life had led to little more than industrial subsistence and artistic frustration; the state seemed to be running out of alternatives to a quota system.

Publishing and the Push for Opportunities in the Marketplace

Canadian publishers suffered from the opposite problem to that of filmmakers: distribution was not so much the issue as covering production expenses. Many presses did their best to churn out stacks of nationalist guidebooks, poetry collections, economic analyses, political commentaries, and numerous manifestos, but it was difficult for them to recoup the costs of producing for a small market with an even smaller audience. It was time, argued Michael Macklem of Oberon Press and his like-minded peers, for the federal government and cultural agencies to treat publishers less as businesses and more as cultural operations. 'In Canada, for the serious literary publisher with a reputation to maintain, it's not a question of losing money or not losing money,' Macklem explained to a member of the Canada Council. 'It's a question of how much you lose and on what.'[94] Companies that chose to publish Canadian works did so not for profit but for art, identity, and nationhood, and presses should thus be treated as cultural enterprises deserving economic assistance based on those reasons alone. No one expected artists to live off of their sales; why should the situation be different for publishers?

Economic woes characterized the publishing sector as much as did the content being produced. No concerned Canadian could be comfortable with seeing Gage Publishing and Ryerson Press both being acquired by foreign companies in December of 1970, the latter purchased by McGraw-Hill using money borrowed, ironically enough, from a Canadian bank.[95] Two major book presses were gone in one year, and McClelland and Stewart, a fundamental publisher of Canadian works, also seemed set for the auction block. It took more than heady nationalist times to keep solvent a publisher concerned more about Canadiana than profit margins. The Ontario government had watched two publishers sold off to foreign interests, and it decided – fortunately for Canadianizers – to ante up money to help save McClelland and Stewart. This one-time infusion, however, merely served to extend its survival in the face of a very uncertain future.

Despite distribution not being the primary problem for the publishing sector, one should not be surprised to see the Committee for an Independent Canada put its weight behind the catch-all solution of a quota system. Such an approach 'would not be onerous nor ... exclude foreign books,' the committee argued, and the idea offered a significant opportunity for the educational and paperback sectors.[96] Interestingly, many publishers chose not to support the idea of a quota system. It made sense for the Canadian Book Publishers Council, whose members possessed a roster of foreign authors, to reject the idea of a quota, yet so too did the Independent Publishers Association (later renamed the Association of Canadian Publishers), an organization representing twenty-five Canadian-owned publishing houses. The association's decision was based not on a distaste for quotas but on the possibility of a better solution residing within a program of federal subsidies to be given exclusively to domestically owned publishers. Funds would not only help to rectify the situation, but by limiting them to Canadian presses, 'public funds and the efforts of public servants' would not subsidize and otherwise facilitate 'the operations of foreign-owned and foreign-controlled book publishing firms in Canada.'[97] Although McClelland and Stewart, a publishing house guided by the nationalistic Jack McClelland, found a quota system to be attractive as an idea, the company conceded that it would be impractical to implement and instead joined with others in requesting the start of state incentives for works on Canadian topics and subsidies for domestically owned publishing companies.[98] The answer to the needs of Canadian book publishers, then, seemed to rest with some kind of direct investment along the lines of the Canadian Film Development Corporation.[99]

The periodical publishing sector, on the other hand, was struggling to change the so-called assistance that it had already been given by the government. *Time* and *Reader's Digest*, endowed with de facto national status as part of the Paperback and Periodicals Distributor Act (1964), were still able to attract advertisers seeking a tax deduction for purchasing space in domestic magazines. The legislation seemed even to make the situation worse by encouraging advertisers to take the money previously spent on a breadth of American periodicals and focus it on *Time* and *Reader's Digest*, thereby eliminating the competition the duo had experienced from their American peers.

What had been a slap in the face to domestic magazines in 1964 had now festered into resentment and calls for change backed by new ideas about the role of periodicals in national life. An important contribution to this debate occurred with the publishing of the report of the Special Senate Committee on the Mass Media in 1970. 'Magazines are special,' the committee argued. 'Magazines constitute the only national press we posses in Canada ... Magazines, in a different way from any other medium, can help foster in Canadians a sense of themselves. In terms of cultural survival, magazines could potentially be as important as railroads, airlines, national broadcasting networks, and national hockey leagues.'[100] Within such dynamics, *Time* and *Reader's Digest* could not expect to maintain their privileged position. They had been 'good corporate citizens' but continued to have an unfair economic advantage.[101] Market problems were particularly endemic in French-language Canada, the committee noted, as a tiny market size and the popularity of imports from France ensured double the 'sickness.'[102] *Sélection du Reader's Digest*, the French-language version of *Reader's Digest*, played a role in this situation as well, attracting advertising dollars that might otherwise go to domestic periodicals.[103] The committee concluded that it was time for the federal government to institute ownership regulations and anti-overflow legislation, techniques commonly used in other countries to ensure domestic expression and the availability of goods in skewed marketplaces.[104] One means to this end could involve legislation requiring that a minimum of 75 per cent of Canadian subsidiary stock and 75 per cent of officer and director positions be held by Canadian citizens.[105] In addition – and as called for by many people in the industry – the government could create an investment fund along the lines of the Canadian Film Development Corporation to help address production woes.[106]

Altering the national status quo in regard to American periodical branch plants did not seem to be too much to ask. Periodicals are tremendously influential sites of communication, and ownership regulations were deemed to be merely a means of requiring that corporations show some responsibility to the country in which they operated. The issue now, though, was whether the federal government would bring the recommendations to fruition. It had been only a decade earlier that the Liberals had given into American interests and the desire for an Auto Pact. Yet the years that had passed had become increasingly nationalistic, and this time around the periodical sector showed no signs of sitting quietly on the side while the government failed to act. Canadianization was underway and the state had a role to play.

Conclusion

'You can legislate until hell freezes over, but you can't legislate audiences into the theatres.' Paul Morton of Odeon-Morton Theatres, in making this declaration in a February 1974 interview with the *Globe and Mail*, was propagating the idea that Canadians were not interested in domestic films.[107] Nationalistic filmmakers disagreed, as did half of the general public who responded to a 1973 Gallup poll.[108] No longer able to point to the lack of domestic products as a reason for opposing Canadian films, exhibitors were falling back on characterizing audiences as disinterested in domestic offerings, something quite difficult to do in a time of widespread nationalism. Many Canadians were showing support not only for films and Canadian content of all sorts but also for measures designed to ensure that systems of communication were open to domestic discourse. Something needed to be done to facilitate a relationship otherwise being thwarted by distributors and exhibitors; intervention in the broadcasting sector seemed justifiable because airwaves were a natural resource and thus a public trust, but, it seemed to many Canadians, there were other ways of interpreting just what constituted a (and 'the') public trust. Perhaps being a major social, cultural, and economic force in the national community, with a tremendous influence upon the ability for Canadians to communicate, was sufficient enough a criterion upon which to require state-based checks and balances and reason enough to justify legislation that would oblige its participants to offer, even if only to a small degree, opportunities for Canadians to interact with one another. Was it not socially responsible to make Canadian content available to citizens who were otherwise offered little other than that which served the pocketbooks of the few?

It was all telling of a significant change in the ideological character and composition of Canadianization. New nationalists were taking previously vilified measures and casting them as solutions for a nation struggling with a loss of sovereignty and the desire of its members for a sense of nationhood. That the quotas, tax incentives, and investment dollars recently established by the state had been tailored to the needs of specific industries – and for the purpose of encouraging private-sector economic growth – mattered little to people seeking to apply the precedents across the board for the nation's sake. Nor did it matter that the areas concerned were characterized by commercialism and money-making, since these nation-builders and architects of the Peaceable Kingdom were often themselves members of a middle-brow, middle-class, middle-of-the-road cultural economy that had its roots in the era of the Massey-ites and had come to maturity during the continentalism of the 1950s.

Mobilizing cultural devices for the sake of a national design did not occur without a tremendous struggle, of course. Considerations for Canadian content in Canada Council funding decisions, quotas for galleries and other venues, and citizenship requirements for arts organizations were all part of an art for nation's sake at odds with the idea that art should exist as an end in and of itself. Universities were divided as faculty members fought over job quotas, citizenship requirements for academic positions, and minimum levels of Canadian content. Debates over extending Canadian content regulations to radio broadcasting led to station owners reworking their public image in hope of warding off the tide of change. The failure to secure screen time for Canadian feature films, particularly those funded by the Canadian Film Development Corporation, led to calls for exhibition quotas and box-office remittances from theatres otherwise acting as pipelines for Hollywood films. Book and periodical publishers debated the merits of a quota system and the need for federal subsidies to prevent the loss of even more publishing houses to American conglomerates. And the suggestion that branch-plant periodical publishers should have to divest a large part of their stock to Canadians made the thrust for change all the ideologically richer.

This second wave of Canadianizers was vesting the quest for nationhood with a new temper, but, as with their predecessors, success in this task required pushing the government into tackling controversial ideas and enacting divisive legislation. Even if citizenship influenced how institutions operated and quotas offered opportunities for national discourse, could the state justify such radical intervention? Doing so would require a willingness to engage in loaded debates, the provision of significant economic resources, and a careful handling of heated jurisdictional issues. It was much to ask of a federal government which, outside ad hoc concessions in areas of pressing concern, had done little to risk the wrath that came with offending continentally minded cultural profiteers.

The Toronto Arts and Letters Club, ca. 1922, a hub for artists, authors, academics, and others who were interested in culture and nationhood. Seated at the table are members of the Group of Seven and a co-founder of the *Canadian Forum*. L-R: Frederick Varley, Franklin Carmichael (partially hidden), A.Y. Jackson, Lawren Harris, Barker Fairley (*Canadian Forum*), Frank Johnston, Arthur Lismer, and J.E.H. MacDonald. (LAC, John Vanderpant/e02712907)

Prime Minister William Lyon Mackenzie King on the occasion of the Diamond Jubilee of Canada, 1927, engaging the nation-building power of radio in what was the first coast-to-coast broadcast. Privately owned radio stations were linked in order to make the broadcast possible. Five years later, the federal government established the Canadian Radio Broadcasting Commission, which in 1936 was restructured into the Canadian Broadcasting Corporation. (LAC, The Hands Studio/ PA-126949)

Vincent Massey, cultural patron, civil servant, and nationalist, chatting with Alec Guinness and Amelia Hall after a performance of *Richard III*. No one did more than Massey to elevate Canadian nationhood upon the shoulders of high culture. (© National Film Board of Canada. Reproduced with the permission of the National Film Board of Canada. NFB/PHO-0047)

Group of Seven artist A.Y. Jackson creating a piece of Canadiana in rural Quebec, ca. 1943. (LAC, PA-129918)

National Film Board of Canada information display. The 'Ideas into Images' display told how 'every aspect of Canada's national life is raw material for the lens of the National Film Board, Canada's visual workshop.' The NFB provided a sanctioned, informative, cultured cinematic alternative to feature films; nationalists easily canonized the film board as the provider of 'truly Canadian' content. (National Film Board of Canada, LAC, John Mailer/PA-169678)

Anne Murray started her career as a cast member on *Singalong Jubilee*, one of CBC's many wholesome alternatives to American commercial programming. Her rendition of 'Snowbird' became a favourite choice of radio stations airing tried-and-true songs to fill their Canadian content quota. (CBC Still Photo Collection)

Walter Gordon, a former minister of finance and later a leading 'new nationalist' intellectual, talking with Patrick Watson and Laurier Lapierre on the CBC Television program *This Hour Has Seven Days*, 5 May 1966. Gordon sounded an early alarm about the impact of American investment in Canada and, when the Liberal Party refused to institute measures to regulate the acquisitions, stepped down from his position as minister of finance to raise public awareness about the need to reclaim national sovereignty. (LAC, Duncan Cameron/Duncan Cameron fonds/PA-113492)

Margaret Atwood, literary icon, cultural nationalist, and architect of 'survival' as a paradigm for understanding Canadian literature, ca. 1972. (Margaret Atwood, photograph by Graeme Gibson)

Peter Gzowski, as managing editor of *Maclean's*, centrepiece on *This Country in the Morning* (later *Morningside*), and host of the television talk show *90 Minutes Live*, became an icon within the national identity he often discussed. (CBC Still Photo Collection)

Pierre Trudeau and Gérard Pelletier experiencing Trudeaumania during the election campaign of 1968. Following their electoral success, these two politicians used federal resources to fund cultural events that promoted national unity and invested heavily in what were increasingly identified as 'cultural industries.' (LAC, Duncan Cameron/ Duncan Cameron fonds/PA-180807)

Trudeau: uniting Canada one maple leaf at a time. (LAC, Robert Cooper/PA-139117)

'Canada's Cultural Industries Are Big Business,' a poster by the Department of Communications, ca. 1981–2, identifying and promoting culture as a commodity to be bought and sold. The task of federal cultural guardianship was taken over by the Department of Canadian Heritage in 1993. (LAC, Department of Canadian Heritage collection/Accession 1995-230 DAP 00002)

7 Saving Canada: Pierre Trudeau and the Mobilization of Culture

More government 'investment' … is the word now, not 'subsidies' or even 'grants.'

Calgary Albertan, 1969[1]

'Technology, which brings abundance and material happiness, presupposes an undifferentiated mass of consumers; it also tends to minimize the values that let a human being acquire and retain his own identity, values I am grouping here under the vague term "cultural." The political order created by the state must struggle against this kind of depersonalization by pursuing cultural objectives.' Pierre Trudeau argued this point in an essay written in early 1965 and later published as 'Quebec and the Constitutional Problem' in *Federalism and the French Canadians*, a 1968 collection of his writings, its release coinciding with the first year of his prime ministership. The rest of the passage is even more telling of his views on the cultural intervention that would come to characterize his administration:

> The state must use its legal powers to compel the economic community to favour certain values that would otherwise be destroyed by the pressure of economic forces. In other words, just as the state intervenes in economic matters to protect the weak through social legislation, so it must intervene to ensure the survival of cultural values in danger of being swamped by a flood of dollars.
>
> This principle does not create problems when it is a question of intervening in favour of painting, music, films, the 'Canadian content' of radio or television, and other similar matters. But it may be useful to recall that

even this kind of cultural investment is only achieved at some cost, not only economic, but also cultural. For it supposes that the state knows better than the citizen what is 'good' for him culturally, and such a hypothesis must always be applied with utmost prudence and consideration. More than any other, this kind of value is international and common to all men; in the long term, then, the state should ideally promote an open culture.[2]

Although an internationalist in terms of economic practices, including keeping Canada open to American investment, and well aware of the importance of international cultural exchange, Trudeau made clear his belief that outlets for domestic discourse needed to be ensured in a marketplace which otherwise operated in favour of money-makers and profiteers. Democracy necessitated open discourse. The new nationalist call for state intervention in the cultural sector, then, was not as harshly received as one might have expected. Less acceptable was the sheer size and extent of the request: Canadian content requirements in Canada Council grant decisions and cultural institutions; quota limits on foreign academics, a minimum level of Canadian content in course curriculum, and citizenship requirements in key academic positions; Canadian content for radio broadcasting; guaranteed screen time for feature films; corporations to invest in publishing companies; and the removal of the *Time* and *Reader's Digest* exemption from the Paperback and Periodical Distributors Act of 1964.

Trudeau did not subscribe to the nationalism that underwrote the Canadianization of the new nationalists or the far-reaching socialism advocated by many of its thinkers, but he did share the desire for a Canada of civic rights and freedoms and thought that this goal could be best achieved via a model of Canadianization emphasizing federalism over nationalism. Crafting a new role for the Liberal Party within national life was all the more important to Trudeau because his government was struggling to maintain its leadership of a federation racked by divisive nationalist movements. The Masseyites had turned to high-cultural devices and cultured mass-media alternatives as a means of navigating the colony-to-nation transition amid the upheavals of modernity; the new nationalists had empowered multi-brow cultural outlets in the struggle against American imperialism and the proliferation of cultural branch plants; and now Trudeau was about to radicalize the relationship between the state and cultural activity for the sake of a federalism challenged by Québécois separatism and, to a much lesser degree, the new nationalism (and its political representation within the New

Democratic Party). Gone were the days in which William Lyon Mackenzie King and like-minded civil servants steered clear of investing taxpayer dollars in the cultural pursuits of the longhairs. Earlier in the
century 'culture,' identified as resting within the higher of brows, had
excluded many Canadians, and the government had little interest in
turning over public monies to the activities of the privileged few; culture
was now, however, broadly defined and existed as part of a cultural economy involving many Canadians. For the federal government to not
intervene in culture would be for it to shirk its responsibilities – or so
argued Trudeau and his successive secretaries of state, Gérard Pelletier
(July 1968 – November 1972), James Hugh Faulkner (November 1972 –
September 1976), and John Roberts (September 1976 – June 1979).
Cultural devices offered tools not only for promoting a pro-federalist
nationhood but also for securing Liberal Party leadership in the country
during a time of significant political tension and contestation.

What would start out as federal cultural legislation tailored to private-
sector interests and jurisdictional limitations, carefully disguising the
actions of the state in rhetoric of developing national cultural life on
behalf of the population, would evolve into something much larger.
Over the course of the next decade, the Trudeau administration set the
groundwork for a third model of Canadianization, a cultural industrialism in which the federal government established itself as the guardian
of nationhood and posited Canadian content within massive bureaucracies operating upon industrial precepts – a Canadianization still occurring today under the aegis of the Department of Canadian Heritage.
Cultural industrialism, particularly the ways in which it entailed shifting
monies from public-sector activities to private-sector growth, allowed
federal bureaucrats to enter cultural activities through a backdoor.
Once they were inside, the success of Canadianization amounted to a
leap of faith that the content produced by the subsidized industries, or
at least a significant fraction of that content, would raise public support
for a Canadian nationhood of civic federalism.

Pierre Elliott Trudeau and the Federal Interest in Culture

Establishing restrictions on the influx of American economic investment, an idea supported by many Canadians, was not something with
which Trudeau wanted to get involved. Much like his Liberal predecessors, the new prime minister valued the contribution of foreign investment to the economy and, unlike the new nationalists, did not view it as

a manifestation of American imperialism. This stance was more than evidenced in the lengths he took to dodge the call for a Crown corporation to regulate foreign investment, even when the recommendation was coming from reports commissioned by his own government. As I have discussed elsewhere, 'the 1970 Commons Standing Committee on External Affairs and National Defense, chaired by Liberal MP Ian Wahn, echoed the Watkins Report in calling for a Canadian Development Corporation and a government body to organize foreign investment. A year later, Herb Gray released a report detailing problems posed by foreign investment and also recommended an agency to oversee its development. The findings were supported by the Ontario government's 1971 Interdepartmental Task Force on Foreign Investment, which once again recommended moderate actions to correct problems with foreign investment.'[3] The latter document, originally meant to be internal, was leaked by the nationalistic *Canadian Forum*, and the Liberals had no choice but to go public on a subject they preferred to avoid.

Federal reports and recommendations continued to point to the need for change, yet it took the combination of a rebuff from the United States and poor results in the 1972 federal election for Trudeau to finally take action on the issue of foreign investment. First, Richard Nixon refused to exempt Canada from a 10 per cent surcharge on imports in August 1971, leaving Trudeau grovelling to the American president in a attempt to change his mind. The pressing need to lessen Canada's economic reliance upon the United States prompted Secretary of State for External Affairs and Deputy Prime Minister Mitchell Sharp, someone who had done much to sink nationalist initiatives during his tenure as minister of trade and commerce, into searching for trade alternatives. The 'Third Option,' as Sharp's plan came to be called, was far from successful.[4] The changed climate did, however, push the Trudeau administration into finally creating the Canadian Development Corporation to help 'buy back' areas of industry dominated by American interests.

Second, the lead-up to the 1972 federal election coincided with a broad dissatisfaction with the state of the economy, substantial public support for Progressive Conservative leader Robert Stanfield, and a strong dose of western alienation, particularly in regards to Trudeau's handling of the 'Quebec question.' One western Canadian, for example, wrote to his member of Parliament in late 1972 to declare that he would 'no longer stand silently on the sidelines while a bunch of irresponsible government types down east squeeze hundreds of millions of dollars out of Western taxpayers then shovel it through a hole in the back fence to those Franco-phony-Canadians in Quebec.'[5] (More will be said about Quebec later in this chapter.) With Trudeaumania having faded away and the administration facing some difficult circumstances, the Liberals were returned with a slim minority government of 109 seats to the Progressive Conservative's 107 in the 1972 elections, the results requiring that the Liberals rely upon, and thus make concessions to, the New Democratic Party (which won 48 seats). David Lewis had done much for the cause of social issues in Canada during his years as national secretary of the Co-operative Commonwealth Federation (1936–50) and as a founding member of the NDP. Now, having replaced Tommy Douglas as party leader, he used the electoral results as a way to push the Liberals into forming the Foreign Investment Review Agency (FIRA) to help keep checks and balances on foreign purchases of Canadian natural and industrial resources. FIRA was a step forward, but to some Canadians, particularly those who had long pushed for such a body, it was little more than a token gesture. Walter Gordon called FIRA 'a joke ... designed to deal with the fringes and not with the substance,' while for his part, Melville Watkins dismissed it as 'like having a referee at a rape.'[6]

Trudeau had long made clear his view on economic protectionism. As he put it in a 4 October 1968 debate in the House of Commons, his administration was 'inclined more to institutions which are broadly international rather than toward nationalist approaches.'[7] Cultural intervention, on the other hand, was something he showed a greater willingness – a desire, in fact – to enact. Bringing the state into the cultural sphere offered the state a means of securing opportunities for Canadian content otherwise throttled by profit-minded industries, developing sites of production important to nationalistic cultural workers, and, quite important for the Trudeau administration, offsetting the Québécois separatist nationalism unleashed by the Quiet Revolution, which directly challenged federal leadership. Whereas the new nationalists viewed the threat to Canadian nationhood as being situated south of the border, Trudeau had his eyes fixed on activities occurring in Quebec.

The Quiet Revolution, commonly associated with the 1960–6 period of Jean Lesage's Liberal government in Quebec, brought to the province a number of changes tied to rapid industrialization, modernization, the decline of Catholicism, and a growing interest in shifting powers from the federal to the provincial level. During this period the Lesage administration established provincial corporations and departments to aid in the centralization of economic and social capital and power, going so far as to create a Department of Cultural Affairs in 1961, which consisted of the Office de la Langue Française, the Departement du Canada Français, d'Outre-frontières, the Conseil Provincial des Arts, and the Commission des Monuments Historiques. For some French Canadians the goal was to increase opportunities in areas of provincial life otherwise dominated by English-speakers, but a number of Quebecers saw the situation as a step towards securing the long-denied birthright of a separate post-colonial project. Herein laid an opportunity to facilitate a transition from a colonized French Canada to a nationalized Quebec. And despite the name, the Quiet Revolution certainly was not quiet once the Front de Libération du Québec (FLQ), composed largely of radicalized youths seeking an independent Quebec state, began shaking neighbourhoods by bombing federal buildings and postal boxes in 1963.

In the same year as the bombings, Trudeau's predecessor, Lester B. Pearson, had tried to reduce tensions by forming the Royal Commission on Bilingualism and Biculturalism. The hope was that enhancing the position of French Canada at the federal level, including establishing more federal opportunities for French-speakers, would make the Québécois feel more included in the federal framework. Opening the door to discussions about identity and nationhood, however, led to an interesting turn of events in which other groups walked in and aired their grievances. Marginalized ethnic communities, long glossed over in the national master-narrative, took the opportunity to assert their positions within a nation increasingly consisting of more than the two traditional 'races.' The commission had been formed with 'bilingual' and 'bicultural' in its name, but it would end up having to position itself much more broadly. The earlier ethnic national design was evolving into a civic one, and the commission was placed in the difficult position of placating Québécois separatism while addressing a variety of ethnic groups rallying for position within the national narrative. Out of this dilemma, after half a decade of hearings and publications, emerged a federally sanctioned portrayal of Canada as a bilingual but multicultural nation, a move in line with demographic realities requiring that the architects of nationhood replace ethnic privilege with civic rights.[8]

It would take more than a federal commission to satiate the passions of a generation of Québécois, however. Both Jean Lesage's Liberal Party and Daniel Johnson's Union Nationale offered the voting public an empowered platform in the lead-up to the 1966 election. Lesage's re-election promises included 'soft' reforms such as control over old-age pensions and family allowances and transferred monies upon Quebec's opting out of federal programs. For Daniel Johnson, on the other hand, Quebec required no less than a radical shift of entire sectors of federal activity to the provincial level, including control over currency and jurisdiction over broadcasting. Johnson even implied that the provincial government might strive for complete sovereignty if federal bureaucrats did not acquiesce to its demands.[9] The electoral result was close, with Lesage's Liberals winning 46 per cent of the vote to the Union nationale's 40 per cent, but with the Union nationale receiving a greater number of seats, it was Johnson who formed the government. The Quiet Revolution had given way to a Québécois regime.

Among the Liberal Party members who won their seats was former journalist and Radio-Canada host René Lévesque, someone who had stepped into the political limelight back in 1960 as part of Lesage's government. Lévesque had contributed much to the changes associated with the Quiet Revolution through his positions as minister of Hydro-electric Resources and Public Works (1960–1), Natural Resources (1961–5), and Family and Welfare (1965–6). Increasingly uncomfortable with his party's direction, he left the Liberals a year after holding onto his seat in the 1966 election and sat briefly as an independent before forming the Mouvement Souveraineté-Association. The following year Lévesque merged his party with the Ralliement National to form the Parti Québécois – under Lévesque's leadership, of course – to bring about far-reaching changes associated with the ethnic politicizing of Quebec society. 'We are *Québécois*,' explained Lévesque in his *An Option for Quebec* (1968). 'What that means first and foremost – and if need be, all that it means – is that we are attached to this one corner of the earth where we can be completely ourselves: this Québec, the only place where we have the unmistakable feeling that "here we can be really at home."'[10]

Lévesque and like-minded Québécois intellectuals were negotiating the transition of an ethnic identity into a modern world of civic states. Theorist of nationalism Anthony D. Smith has described this process as the work of an 'ethnie' adapting itself to 'the transformations wrought by modernity' by 'retaining or reconstructing an "authentic" and particularistic ethnic heritage.'[11] Ethnic identifiers provide the character and foundation for 'in' and 'out' groups of the new political system, with a particular emphasis on the use of a shared name, language, myth of descent, traditions and rituals, and association with a specific territory.[12] This politicization of ethnic nationalism, just like its civic alternative, required leading intellectuals to actively mobilize cultural outlets as a means of identifying and reifying the national project in line with their envisioned design.[13] Without an effective and successful use of cultural devices, the transition would not have been possible.

The Canadian Broadcasting Corporation and the National Film Board, publicly owned, nationally mandated bodies essential to generations of pan-national Canadianizers, became just as important to the builders of this alternative national project. Radio-Canada, the French-language wing of the CBC, offered the Québécois an important outlet for engaging audiences in a nation-building discourse. From discussions on topical events to the songs of *Chansonniers* and *boîtes à chansons* rallying audiences to a shared experience, broadcasting presented an opportunity to construct narratives of a communal past and collective future. '*Les belles histoires* reminded people of the life on the soil of days not long gone by; the Plouffe family was new to city life,' as the Task Force on Broadcasting Policy (1986) recalled.[14] Life at Radio-Canada was so politicized by 1968 that some of its employees protested the fact that the new Broadcasting Act described the CBC as having an obligation to foster national unity.[15] By the following year the CBC was such a target of federal criticism for the separatism among its ranks that Donald Davidson, speaking on the behalf of the corporation, found it necessary to explain to the Standing Committee on Broadcasting, Film and Assistance to the Arts that 'you cannot expect separatism not to reflect itself in the Canadian Broadcasting Corporation or in the programming ... if separatism exists in the body politic of Canada itself.'[16]

The directors of the National Film Board found themselves just as caught up in division and controversy as their CBC peers. The reason for this situation was due, at least in part, to the decision to relocate the NFB's production facilities from Ottawa to Montreal in 1965 and the creation of linguistically separated filmmaking sections. It was a decision that served the politicized interests and aspirations of Québécois filmmakers; they now had the ability to create films speaking primarily to a like-minded audience. One can see the tension and division between filmmakers of different national projects manifesting itself that year at the Montreal International Film Festival: as film critic Gerald Pratley commented in the 7 August 1965 issue of the *Toronto Telegram*, 'everything French-Canadian is avidly received, and no English-Canadian film stands the ghost of a chance of winning a prize.'[17] The division increased over the next few years to such a degree that the majority of Québécois filmmakers decided to boycott the 1971 Canadian Film Awards. Director

Claude Jutra, one of the few Québécois in attendance, won eight awards for *Mon Oncle Antoine*, taking home more awards than any other film-maker. In a seminal moment in Canadian cinematography, Jutra took the stage at the awards show and left his mark by declaring, 'Vive le cinéma québécois.'[18] His film, created during his tenure with the NFB, was about a boy coming of age in a time of rapid change, a story that spoke loudly about the maturation of Quebec in the era of the Quiet Revolution. The NFB had become a production house for films contributing to different quests for nationhood – so much so that, as Gary Evans colourfully describes it, the Parti Québécois's provincial electoral victory on 16 November 1976 was met with Québécois filmmakers at the film board engaging in a 'raucous day-long celebration' while 'most English staff took their lunch outside the building that day.'[19]

Cinematic activity offered a significant contribution to the Québécois national project because it was not as encumbered by Hollywood's linguistic, economic, and ideological monopolies. Filmmakers, exhibitors, and audiences came together in celebrating the latest cinematic works of the community they envisioned. As Arthur Lamothe, president of Quebec's Association des Producteurs du Film, told the *Montreal Gazette* in the August of 1971, 'our public, our preoccupation, and our interests are quite different to those of the English-Canadian producer.'[20] Of course, as plagues all attempts to use art for nation's sake, the content spoke to a limited audience – and not just in terms of the non-Québécois citizens of Canada. Exporting the films proved to be problematic. 'The greatest problem with Québec cinema today is that our filmmakers produce films about Quebecers for Quebecers,' film producer Louis Laverdière noted in an interview with the *Chronicle Herald*, and 'the only interest these films have for Europeans is that they show how our houses are decorated and how we speak French and nothing more.'[21]

Although Québécois separatism threatened the pan-national project envisioned by the new nationalists, some of the latter's intellectuals could not help but feel sympathy and even empathy with the Québécois quest for nationhood. Margaret Atwood likened the Quebec government's attempt to reduce federal control to her own concerns about the need to roll back the American presence.[22] For his part, Walter Gordon was more than willing to grant concessions and special status to Quebec, but he rationalized doing so as a means of keeping the province within a united front against Americanization.[23] 'There is not much point in working out the difficulties between French and English speaking

Canadians,' Gordon argued in a 1968 address to the Canadian Management Centre of the American Management Association, 'only to find that we have become a kind of economic dependency of the United States and have lost the power to control and influence our own destiny.'[24] For Gordon, American imperialism was the much bigger threat to be addressed; Québécois separatism was second on the list.

Democratization and Decentralization in the Arts

Pierre Trudeau disagreed with Walter Gordon's assessment: Québécois separatism was a much greater threat than American imperialism because it challenged the federal status quo and jeopardized national unity. Faced by not only a politicized Québécois nationalism but also the challenges posed by the new nationalism (and its voices within the NDP), Trudeau was willing to undertake measures favouring the stabilization of a Liberal-led federalism. Canada was in crisis and the only solution was to mobilize pre-existing cultural devices and legislate into existence a roster of new ones. That the government could guise its act of self-preservation in responses to public requests for intervention promised to make the process all the easier.

Success in bringing the state closer to culture required proactively recasting the ways in which the public viewed both the role of the state and the constitution of culture. 'It may be necessary to transform completely the notion of culture,' explained Gérard Pelletier, the first of several secretaries of state to serve in the Trudeau administration, to an audience in Lethbridge, Alberta, in October of 1969. 'Why should the theatre and opera have a monopoly on culture? Why should not movies, jazz, popular songs, and psychedelic happenings also not be a means of cultural expression?'[25] This was not a novel idea in 1969, of course: Pelletier was not suggesting anything that was not already commonly accepted. Yet in making this bureaucratic stance, the secretary of state was sanctioning the idea that there were many dimensions to cultural life and, in turn, that the federal government had an important role to play.

What followed was a cultural program of 'democratization,' designed to broaden the definition of and accessibility to national cultural resources, and 'decentralization': making publicly owned cultural bodies more representative of the country as a whole (a corrective measure to policies and initiatives often criticized as being Ontario-centric). Susan M. Crean, author of the nationalistic *Who's Afraid of Canadian Culture?*, has recalled how 'at that time, democratization, a term nobody seemed able to define exactly, was on everyone's lips in arts administration circles. The Department of the Secretary of State was said to be busy formulating Canada's first comprehensive cultural policy, to embrace publishing and film-making as well as museums and the performing arts. The objective was to afford all Canadians access to what were becoming known in government lingo as "our cultural resources."[26] The Arts and Cultural Policy of 1968, as it came to be known, was formed two decades after Louis St Laurent had announced the Royal Commission on National Development in the Arts, Letters and Sciences. That the contents would have thoroughly distressed Vincent Massey and his contemporaries speaks volumes as to how conceptions of culture and nationhood had changed in that time. The policy lay a foundation for a federal mobilization of cultural activity in line with the needs of the state. It's objectives were

(a) to improve the quality of the collective and personal life of Canadians;
(b) to study the Canadian personality thoroughly;
(c) to forge national unity;
(d) to stimulate the two founding cultures and to integrate the original contribution of the native peoples and New Canadians;
(e) to develop and promote bilingualism;
(f) to give a cultural dimension to our political and economic democracy and a more democratic dimension to our cultural activities;
(g) to give the artist and researcher the means to enrich Canada's cultural heritage.[27]

The policy was so focused on the needs of the government, in fact, that grants were to be provided only 'for purposes that are clearly of national benefit.'[28] The policy of earmarking funds for endeavours promoting national unity signified a radical departure from previous federal cultural involvement; this was not art for art's sake or even art for nation's sake but art for federalism's sake, designed to forge a sense of allegiance and unity in a time of political threat.

With the new policy came an enlarged federal cultural bureaucracy, much of it placed within the portfolio of the Department of the Secretary of State. First, the government created the Arts and Culture Branch to aid in formulating cultural policy and administer cultural agencies.[29] By the 1973–4 fiscal year the Arts and Culture Branch had $4.2 million to dole out to theatres, galleries, museums, and other recipients with an eye to funding federally friendly Canadiana.[30] Second, the Cabinet

Committee on Culture and Information, operating in parallel to a new Department of Communications, was formed to implement cultural activities and handle information. National Film Board commissioner Hugo McPherson, already frustrated at the government's approach to the NFB, cited this centralization as one of the reasons for quitting his position in July 1970. He told *Time* magazine that

> the Trudeau government seems to be centralizing cultural activity in a way that I find completely out of tune with the Canadian tradition. A great deal of the success that agencies like the Film Board and the CBC have had, has been because of the freedom they've been given. If the planning now is going to be done within the minister's office, who is going to do it? … If the government decides to coordinate our whole cultural scene we are approaching the idea or possibility of state-voiced culture. I'm not suggesting that [Secretary of State] Mr. Pelletier is trying to do this deliberately, but it is possible to move inadvertently into a situation where control is so concentrated that it becomes difficult to maintain cultural freedom.[31]

Ironically, decentralization required establishing a large centralized cultural bureaucracy; it led to the rise of a bureaucratic cultural czar with more power to shape the temper of nationhood than that possessed by any non-bureaucrat.

The Policy and New Roles for the Arts

The Canada Council had done much for the cultural activities of the Masseyites, and even though it received rough treatment from the new nationalists, the council managed to hold its own in the face of protest and conflict. Dealing with the federal government, however, proved less successful. Federal monies given to the council were now, as part of the Arts and Culture Policy, earmarked for specific purposes. The historic arm's-length relationship was eroded as bureaucrats attempted to appropriate the council for federalist interests. For example, the council was offered a large sum of money earmarked for an Art Bank to purchase and loan domestic works, an initiative that over the course of decade led to the acquisition of more than eight thousand works by more than nine hundred artists.[32] Earmarked funding was taken up a notch following the success of René Lévesque's Parti Québécois in 1976, a political threat meriting a $1.7 million federal grant to the Canada Council to be used specifically for national-unity purposes.[33] The following year almost $1 million was given to the council for a national book festival, while at the same time the National Arts Centre was awarded a special $1.1 million grant to be used for a bilingual theatre company that would travel the country and promote national unity.[34] Funding pro-federalist artistic happenings, some going so far as even to orchestrate the nature of the events, spoke volumes about the state's boldness in venturing into taboo activities.

The council not only had to give funds to events chosen by the federal government but conversely was pressured not to fund artists who were politically separatist. Gertrude Laing, speaking on the behalf of the Canada Council, explained to the Standing Committee on Broadcasting, Film, and Assistance to the Arts that 'it is not our role to exert any kind of control or censorship over those artists or organizations that benefit from the grants of the Canada Council in any area other than their qualifications as arts and scholastic organizations, so long as they are not actually breaking the law.'[35] The artistic integrity of the council required no less than an adamant willingness to fund artists of all political orientations.

Federal bureaucrats had better luck teaming up with members of the arts community than it did with the council. The arts were becoming an industry, and its participants were eager to join with the government in treating it as a sector worthy of economic development. As the *Toronto Star* reported in February of 1969, in an article titled 'The Pelletier Plan for a people's culture,' the secretary of state viewed culture as 'a legitimate industry – like fishing or farming – with the right to a consolidated cultural budget instead of piecemeal grants.'[36] It was an approach that worked well for bureaucrats seeking a greater role in cultural activities, those Canadians who desired an economic justification for the state using taxpayer dollars to support the arts, and artists who were willing to treat their craft as a commodity for the sake of a higher income. Michael Macklem of Oberon Press has colourfully noted that the desire for monies has meant that 'the arts are dressed up – by their friends, be it admitted – as an *industry*. An industry that creates employment and contributes to the Gross National Product. What would Michelangelo have thought if he'd been told that the building of St. Peter's created employment (which of course it did) and *that that was why it mattered?*'[37]

There was certainly no lack of support for the idea within the arts community. In October of 1968 the Canadian Conference of the Arts asked the federal government to start giving more credit, and funding, to the arts based upon their contribution to the economy.[38] The arts were not only 'an integral and necessary part of life in a healthy society' but also the provider of employment and tax monies and facilitators of tourism activity. Local economies owed much to the arts.[39] It was thus deemed unfair that the arts sector 'has never even been recognized as an industry.'[40] If the ideological benefits of cultural activity were not enough to attract state funds, there was now an economic justification to boot.

The new approach to conceptualizing, rationalizing, and justifying cultural expenditures on an economic basis was soon picked up by the newspaper press. 'Culture brings money into smaller towns' announced the title of a *Financial Post* article in the summer of 1969, the text telling of how Stratford attracted approximately $1.2 million a year.[41] 'Shaw Festival has grown up,' read a *Toronto Telegram* story that same summer, with the festival's maturity apparently evident in how it had brought approximately $250,000 to the local economy outside festival revenue in a mere eleven weeks.[42] What the big foreign-focused theatres had lacked in Canadian content they more than made up for in economic activity; a cultural approach that had drawn vilification from the new nationalists conversely attracted great praise from those who viewed culture in monetary terms. Gérard Pelletier was so keen to develop the contribution of the arts to tourism economies, in fact, that he offered the Shaw Festival a plot of land for a new building capable of accommodating larger audiences and increasing the festival's monetary potential. Although the festival organizers appreciated the offer, they instead opted to expand the theatre's downtown location. By the turn of the decade the federal government was well on its way to reposition itself away from an arm's-length patronage of the arts and into proactively developing the cultural economy, searching out economically lucrative projects, and, at the same time, getting to claim a lion's share of credit for the vibrancy that resulted from its initiatives.

The CRTC, Pierre Juneau, and the Desire for Canadianization

Not only did broadcasting offer much to federal designs, but it was one area where the government had jurisdictional authority. A new Broadcasting Act was passed in 1968 to help bring the system in line with what the Trudeau administration was hoping to accomplish. First, the previous description of 'predominantly Canadian in content and character' was replaced by the more industrial 'predominantly Canadian creative and other resources'; gone was the qualified 'character' in favour of something more economic and bureaucratically friendly. Second, station owners were now to be more accountable for Canadian content through

'Promises of Performance' requiring that stations maintain program logs, classify programs (game show, news, drama, etc. – although no minimum amount of each had to be provided), and be subject to occasional monitoring to confirm the airing of Canadian content.[43] From here on in, it would supposedly be more difficult to not live up to programming promises. Third, tighter ownership regulations limited broadcasting licences to Canadian citizens and corporations headed by Canadians, with a maximum 20 per cent of voting shares available to non-Canadians.[44] The Committee for an Independent Canada applauded this 'repatriation of several hundred million dollars of assets in the broadcasting industry.'[45] On the other hand, as the NDP's Waffle splinter group would surely point out, domestic ownership merely meant domestic capitalism, and all that private ownership ensured was that more profits stayed in Canada to the benefit of stations doing much to inundate Canadians with foreign content in the first place.

Canadianizing the broadcasting sector required not only a new Broadcasting Act but also a new body capable of implementing Liberal Party interests. The Board of Broadcast Governors, the Tory-based body established a decade earlier by John Diefenbaker, was replaced by the Canadian Radio-Television Commission (CRTC; as of 1976 the Canadian Radio-television and Telecommunications Commission). Unlike the Board of Broadcast Governors, this new regulator possessed the licensing powers – and thus the ability to not only issue warnings but also make licensing decisions – previously held by the minister of transport (the lack of which had made prosecution difficult for the BBG).[46] Trudeau chose the Quebec-born Pierre Juneau, an old friend from his days in Paris and one of the people with whom he had started *Cité libre* in 1950, to take the reins of the new commission. Juneau had developed his administrative skills at the National Film Board in the years from 1949 to 1966, followed by a short stint as vice-chair of the Board of Broadcast Governors. He possessed skills and connections that made him a solid candidate for an important part of Trudeau's Canadianization.

The idea of extending Canadian content regulations to the radio sector was certainly nothing new. The Board of Broadcast Governors had considered the idea back in 1961 but had decided to delay the move until the television regulations had been sorted out.[47] By the late 1960s it was clear that regulations for radio were a necessary part of correcting a systemic imbalance in the music industry: the success of Canadian musicians abroad testified to both the level of talent and the fact that radio stations had failed to offer opportunities to domestic artists. It helped that Walt Grealis and Stan Klees of *RPM* were doing much to convince the CRTC of the gains to be had through Canadian content regulations. 'We made sure that all the members of the CRTC received copies of *RPM*,' Grealis recalled. 'They needed advice and help. They were not entirely familiar with the broadcasting-record business in Canada. But they were open-minded.'[48]

It did not take the CRTC too long before it stepped into the fray. On 12 February 1970 the commission proposed increasing the level of Canadian content from 55 to 60 per cent on television and instituting it at 30 per cent for AM radio (the dominant radio band at that time), effective a year from that date.[49] Why a smaller amount for radio stations? Juneau explained that this was an opportunity to see if radio broadcasters would spend more money on Canadian content if they could provide it at a lower level, a policy that television station owners had long requested for themselves.[50] There was also the concern that, despite the recent musical success stories, there might not be a sufficient volume of quality domestic music to go any higher.

As in television, Canadian content was to be measured on an industrial scale, with regulations requiring that a song meet two of four points: 'the instrumentation or lyrics were principally performed by a Canadian,' 'the music was composed by a Canadian,' 'the lyrics were written by a Canadian,' and 'the performance was wholly recorded in Canada.' The system became know as MAPL, or 'Maple,' an acronym of M=music, A=artist, P=producer, and L=lyrics. In 1975 the CRTC extended the regulations to the FM band, but given that it was less active and largely consisted of specialty programming, the required amount varied according to the type of station specialization: country 30 per cent, easy listening 10 per cent, middle-of-the-road 15 per cent, and contemporary 20 per cent.[51] Over the next two decades, however, the FM band would become more popular because of the clarity of its signal, and in 1991 the requirement was increased to the standard level for mainstream stations.[52]

It is interesting that, despite chronic problems with program quality in the television sector, the CRTC decided to continue measuring Canadian content quantitatively. In 1968, just as the Board of Broadcast Governors was winding down, there had been discussions about integrating a point system measuring quality.[53] Gérard Pelletier, having just taken up his position as secretary of state, also showed an interest in implementing a measure of quality in the regulations. He worried that the quantitative approach was merely 'an exercise in mathematics, and if you're good enough at mathematics, the rules can be circumvented.'[54] But as Pelletier later acknowledged, a measure of quality would be very difficult to implement.[55] The 'catch 22,' as his compatriot Pierre Juneau pointed out to members of the Standing Committee on Broadcasting, Film, and Assistance to the Arts in June of 1971, was that 'if we proposed a system of regulation which would introduce a judgment of quality we would receive much more criticism than we have had about almost anything else.' In staying with the existing quantitative system, Juneau conceded, one just had to hope that stations would attempt to offer quality content – a leap of faith taken in the face of all evidence to the contrary.[56]

The new regulations did not come without a mix of the old responses. During the month of April 1970, the CRTC held numerous hearings into the proposed regulations and received submissions from over a hundred groups and individuals. The Canadian Broadcasting Corporation not surprisingly supported the proposal and offered suggestions on how to fix existing problems.[57] The Association of Canadian Television and Radio Artists, already enjoying the employment benefits of the regulations in the television sector, called for the television quota to be increased to 85 per cent on the CBC and to 60 per cent by 1975 for private stations (a level to be raised to 70 per cent by 1980).[58] An all-star cast, including Pierre Berton, Farley Mowat, Fred Davis, and Adrienne Clarkson, showed up to support ACTRA and the new Canadian content regulations.[59]

Conversely, and quite predictably, the Canadian Association of Broadcasters lashed out at the regulations. For years the CAB had tried to convince the government that regulations were not necessary because there was plenty of Canadian content on the radio airwaves. J.A. Pouliot, president of the association, even went so far as to claim that Canadian content was already between 75 and 80 per cent.[60] The CRTC, on the other hand, estimated the level to be between 4 and 7 per cent.[61] All the traditional arguments against regulations were dusted off for this new series of hearings, including cries of censorship, quantity not equating with quality, and, quite boldly given the abundant evidence to the contrary, that Canada lacked talent.[62] And if all of that was not enough, the association forced a seven-hour filibuster at one of the hearings.[63]

Opponents of Canadian content regulations were supported by some like-minded politicians. These were the people that Juneau had to face off with at the Standing Committee on Broadcasting, Film, and Assistance to the Arts, but fortunately he was well armed thanks to the recent success of the Winnipeg-based band The Guess Who. 'American

Woman' hit no. 1 in Canada on 25 April 1970, the date of one of the CRTC hearings on the proposed Canadian content regulation changes, and two weeks later the album topped the American charts, just in time for Juneau's appearance in front of the standing committee.[64] It would prove to be a tough moment in the history of Canadian content. Juneau was pushed to answer such questions as what 'well-known and good Canadian music ... the Canadian people would want to listen to,' prompting the CRTC chairman to boldly retort that 'on the American listings this week the top record is a Canadian one. It is called *American Woman* by The Guess Who.' The dissenters were confused by the idea of having a Canadian album with 'American' in its name hitting the top of the U.S. charts, but Juneau explained that the album was indeed Canadian. Doing their best to bypass this fact, critics continued to hammer away at Juneau and the proposed radio regulations, telling him that audiences would not want to listen to 'Squaws along the Yukon' and 'The Log Driver's Song.' 'Do you think this is the kind of music that the Canadian people are going to be rushing to their radios to listen to more than they do now?'[65] The archaic and hackneyed songs were far from representative of popular Canadian works, but they did serve the purpose of launching a vitriolic attack on behalf of station owners.

The battle over Canadian content regulations was brought into the House of Commons as well. Conservative MP Gordon Ritchie, who later went on to be Canadian deputy chief negotiator for the Free Trade Agreement, had this to say to his fellow MPs:

> If Canadians have any obsession, it appears to be over national identity. The latest episode of this self-indulgence is in the CRTC ruling that more Canadian content is required in both the CBC and private television. All the clichés since confederation have been dusted off and our new jingoistic nationalism about Canadian culture is once again to the fore ... I say ... that the Canadian content provision is simply a device whereby the CRTC hopes to tighten the screws on already groveling Canadian broadcasters. If they do not toe the line, they will simply be told their culture content does not measure up. This is a purely totalitarian approach. It is the same approach used by Dr. Goebbels when he threatened people with the awful charge of non-Aryanism. Here we have non-Canadianism.[66]

It was an amazingly skewed declaration. Ritchie not only displayed a lack of concern about opportunities for domestic expression; he intentionally and completely misconstrued the elements measured by the regulation and the status of broadcasters, going so far as to equate the regulation with Nazi racial persecution for no reason other than shock value. It is disturbing to hear this analogy from the person who would later have a leading role in protecting culture during the Free Trade Agreement negotiations.

The complaints of station owners, the 'grovelling' broadcasters on whose behalf Gordon Ritchie was eager to fight, needed to be taken with a grain of salt. The Board of Broadcast Governors, and later the Canadian Radio-Television Commission, kept in mind the importance of helping station owners make profits. Television quotas were lowered to match drops in audience levels during the summer, and prime time was scheduled widely enough to let broadcasters place Canadian programming at the margins and American material in the peak viewing slots. 'The revenues and profits of licensees had to be protected, particularly in television,' Herschel Hardin has noted. 'If television licensees weren't financially healthy, they could not contribute to Canadian objectives, even if keeping them healthy meant sacrificing the level of Canadian content.'[67] And although stations baulked at having to provide the public with a return on the privilege of using a natural resource to make money, it is quite true, as Pierre Juneau noted in March of 1972, that station owners did not turn in their licences.[68] Broadcasters made plenty of profit; it was just that they could not expect to do so without giving something back to the population whose airwaves they used to amass monies.

As for audiences, they seemed to be on the topic of the new regulations. According to a 1970 Gallup poll, 47 per cent of Canadians supported increasing Canadian content to 60 per cent, while 42 per cent disapproved.[69] If the responses are broken down along linguistic lines, it is interesting to note, one sees significant differences: 65 per cent of French-speakers supported Canadian content regulations, while 22 per cent were opposed. For English-speakers the results were flipped, with only 39 per cent approving and a massive 53 per cent opposing. 'Other' language groups, as they were categorized in the poll, were reported as being 48 per cent in support the regulations to 37 per cent opposed. English-speakers, it appeared, were the least likely to support the increase and the only group more opposed than supportive. A significant amount of the opposition seemed to come from rural areas that lacked access to multiple stations and cross-border American signals; their television reception was largely limited to CBC's combination of arts programming and low-budget barn dances instead of the exciting car chases and gun fights offered by American shows. Leo Del Villano, mayor of the small town of Timmins, Ontario, told the newspaper press that 'Northern Ontario residents don't want things shoved down their throats' and that they should have access to the same types of programs enjoyed by those Canadians who lived within range of American stations.[70] Or, as it was put in a letter to the editor published on 26 March 1970, 'why not the same rule for all Canadians? Remove cable [television] from Toronto, Hamilton, Ottawa, etc. and make them watch 60 per cent of inferior Canadian shows such as [the CBC's performing arts program] *Festival*. The CRTC and the government haven't got the guts.'[71]

Cable television, referred to in this letter to the editor, was a new distribution technology being used in several major cities to offer audiences a variety of American programming. Although many subscribers certainly enjoyed the content, other Canadians decried the existence of yet another pipeline of American content and the fact that this technology infringed upon the ability to use television in the task of Canadianization. Cable television providers did not use airwaves, the natural resource and public trust which justified requiring that distributors offer Canadian content, and thus they had an edge over their broadcasting counterparts. The Committee for an Independent Canada wanted this new threat addressed by having the government nationalize cable television distribution: that way Canadians would be ensured access to domestic content no matter what the form of dissemination.[72]

This idea, although attuned to stronger nationalistic sentiments, flew in the face of economic realities. Pierre Juneau instead hoped that cable providers would contribute to Canadianization through the creation of 'community channels' (or 'public access channels'), which would offer a 'place for a new politics of cultural pluralism, a politics of family and neighbourhood.'[73] This optimism was soon quashed, however. As of 1972, only about a third of cable companies provided some form of community programming, and by 1975 the CRTC conceded that cable would not be a revolutionary outlet for Canadian content.[74] Making the economic best out of a culturally bad situation, the broadcasting regulator ended up treating cable television as an opportunity for commercial industry growth. 'The CRTC worked to Canadianize cable,' historian Paul Rutherford has recalled, 'if only by forcing the companies to delete random American commercials in their offerings to the public' and replace them with ones made by Canadians.[75] This requirement lasted only until Parliament passed Bill C-58 in 1975, however, which removed the tax deduction for advertising spots purchased on American border stations targeting the Canadian audience as of 1 January 1976. The hope, as with the Paperback and Periodical Distributors Act of 1964, was that advertisers would redirect their dollars towards domestic stations, although this move seemed to benefit broadcasters and the producers of commercials much more than it served the desire to increase the availability of Canadian programming. Nonetheless, the legislation seemed to have had the economic impact hoped for by bureaucrats. Political scientist John Meisel has reported that 'Canadians spent about $21.5 million on U.S. TV advertising in 1975. This represented roughly ten percent of all Canadian television advertising. As the result of the legislation, the revenue of American border broadcasters dropped to $6.5 million by 1978.'[76]

Bringing commercials into the fold of Canadian content made a lot of sense for a government that pursued industrial growth as a means of achieving a sense of nationhood. In fact, commercials were often even more valuable than the programming they interrupted because, as the Association of Motion Picture Producers and Laboratories of Canada pointed out, 'a one-minute commercial in one of those ghetto program hours with someone playing the organ for an hour' cost more to produce and employed more Canadian talent.[77] Given the amount of money at hand, the Association of Canadian Television and Radio Artists was willing to go so far as to request 'a ban on the importation of foreign produced commercials, except for commercials produced by Canadian producers and using Canadian talent outside the country for reasons of climate or locale.'[78] The lack of employment in the anemic television industry could, some people hoped, be offset if only in part by sucking milk from the commercial production industry. Pierre Berton, an active voice in the association, folded economic interests into cultural ideology in telling the CRTC that 'the commercial, like it or not, is part of our cultural fabric and it is just as important to me as a Canadian when I view commercials ... to view them in the Canadian context.'[79]

That being said, one cannot be quick to link such a declaration solely to the desire for economic gain, as it did speak of changing cultural times. Even Duncan F. Cameron, the national director of the Canadian Conference of the Arts, was willing to lend weight to commercials as a form of artistic expression. As he rhetorically asked a UNESCO conference in Ottawa in 1970, were billboards 'less important art forms in Canadian society than those of the "fine" arts? We'd be fools to think they were.'[80] To have the Canadian Conference of the Arts come onside with commercialism as a form of cultural expression spoke loudly of the new ways in which culture was being conceptualized. Advertisements were becoming what Paul Rutherford has called 'the art of our times,' a form of communication employing consumer identifiers – 'modern,' 'cool,' 'easy,' and so on – within national contexts.[81]

At the very least, and in more critical terms, having the CRTC let station owners count commercials as part of the Canadian content regulations consituted a gain for the production industry. Station owners also stood to benefit from actually being paid – through advertising dollars – to air Canadian content that cost them nothing to produce or acquire. In the spirit of the times – or 1976, to be more precise – and in line with industry interests, Pierre Juneau and the CRTC introduced measures by which domestic commercials could be included in Canadian content requirements. It was telling of a federal approach to broadcasting that focused on economic growth (and appeasing cultural workers) over the qualitative elements of the content produced; entering culture through an industrial backdoor left little other option.

Trudeau, Radio-Canada, and Separatism

Pierre Juneau did much to lead the cause of Canadianization in the privately owned television and radio sectors, but for Trudeau the big problem rested with the CBC or, more specifically, Radio-Canada, the French-language wing of the national broadcasting service. Again one finds the prime minister more concerned about Québécois separatism than the Americanization that consumed the new nationalists and, as with the pressure being put upon the Canada Council, with a desire to root out separatism in the public sector. The exposure given by Radio-Canada to separatist discourse was, after all, a threat to the federal foundation upon which the government operated. In 1973 Trudeau had hoped that the problem was in decline because, in his assessment, 'although the CBC, French side, is by no means perfect it is no longer as strong a vehicle of separatism as it was four or five years ago.'[82] Yet even if that had been the case, the victory of René Lévesque's Parti Québécois in the 1976 provincial election brought the spotlight back on the CBC. Al Johnson, the network's president at that time, has reminisced about how his presidency 'was characterized by the omni-present problem of the Parti Québécois having been elected ... and by the obsession of the members of Parliament from Quebec and the élites of Quebec with the notion that CBC, Radio-Canada, had contributed to separatism and was responsible for the election of the Parti Québécois. They believed that.'[83]

By the following year the situation had intensified. Future prime minister Jean Chrétien, at that time minister of Industry, Trade and Commerce, had attracted controversy for telling the *Toronto Star* that Radio-Canada had become 'Radio-Quebec' and that the broadcaster had intentionally stopped airing the national anthem for three months – Radio-Canada brashly attributed the absence to a technical error despite the length of time it took to have it corrected.[84] This issue was minor, however, compared to the statements made by Trudeau. Over the course of the 25 February 1977 House of Commons debate, for example, the prime minister displayed his willingness to engage in no-holds-barred criticism of the broadcaster:

> Almost everyone, including the high officials of the CBC, would be prepared to concede that the overwhelming majority of employees in the CBC are of separatist leanings. I have heard them say that.

> We merely say that the CBC, the property of the Canadian people, should not be used to help destroy the country.

> The private stations seem to carry less separatist propaganda messages than does the CBC.

> There is a very real concern on the part of many citizens, particularly those who listen to Radio-Canada, that that can be a separatist propaganda machine. Indeed, it can be used to get the people of Quebec to believe more in separatism than in federalism. This government is very worried about that. We are trying to act on that in a proper fashion. I hope we will have the support of hon. members opposite who believe in freedom of speech but still believe it is the duty of the CBC to promote Canadian unity and not separation.[85]

That Québécois nationalists threatened a federal state was problematic enough to Trudeau, but that they did so by employing nationally mandated public institutions frustrated him no end.

It was only a matter of time before the prime minister turned his sights on the national broadcasting system. Two weeks after making the above statements in the House of Commons, Trudeau let his fellow members of Parliament know that he had been in talks with the CRTC about launching an examination into both the television and the radio services.[86] A decision was soon made to have Harry Boyle, Pierre

Juneau's recent successor as chair of the CRTC, preside over a Committee of Inquiry into the National Broadcasting Service. Boyle was certainly being put in an awkward position, given that he had worked at the CBC for a quarter of a century (1943–68), rising from covering farm reports to becoming a program director and eventually an executive producer. It is interesting, then, to find that under his leadership the committee concluded that there was no conscious attempt to 'hand over' Radio-Canada to Québécois separatists or any clear bias in support of separatism over federalism.[87] Instead of trying to hunt out separatists, Boyle argued in the committee's report, one needed to look at the national network's larger problem of centralization and lack of regional input. 'Boyle had succeeded in diverting the assault on the CBC French network for its separatist bias by berating the English network for its failure to reflect the country,' legendary CBC figure Knowlton Nash noted in *The Microphone Wars: A History of Triumph and Betrayal at the CBC*.[88] It was a cunning way of parrying Trudeau's attack on the Radio-Canada while at the same time providing the prime minister with a means of saving face. On 21 July 1977, the committee having issued its report, Trudeau defended his inquiry in the face of criticism in the House of Commons by carefully stating that 'the Boyle report indicates that they are guilty of malpractice and they are guilty of not uniting Canada. It seems to me that this was the essence of the charge.'[89] Canadianization might not have led to a purging of separatism from the broadcasting body politic, but it did provide Trudeau with a chance to chastise the orchestrators of a Québécois separatist project operating at odds with his federalist one.

A Subsidized Solution to Publishing Woes

Gérard Pelletier was no amateur when it came to spinning cultural activity in terms of cultural nationalism. 'Our poets, novelists, sociologists, authors of school texts, are indispensable. If the publication of their books is not commercially possible, government subsidies must make it so.' The secretary of state, making this statement to a conference in Ottawa in early 1971, was laying forth a position that increasingly defined the Trudeau administration's approach to cultural activity: Canadian content needed to be made available even if doing so necessitated federal monies. Subsidies, Pelletier explained to his audience, were a much better option for the book sector than Canadian content quotas for distributors or any other measure bordering on censorship.[90]

Of course, rhetoric was cheap, and unlike in broadcasting, where the public trust ensured that stations were the ones paying for Canadian programs, aid to the book publishing sector had to come from government coffers. It was an expensive proposition but one that served the federal interest in developing cultural industries. By the end of the year Pelletier had not only put his weight behind subsidies but also offered up a plethora of other ideas that the state might be able to pursue in order to foster national unity and an economically strong publishing sector, including a publishing development corporation, grants to translate English- and French-language books from one to the other (something also serving the pro-unity agenda), and $500,00 towards 'quadrupling the present level of export of Canadian books in the next five years.'[91] Two other ideas raised by House of Commons members for Pelletier's consideration were a Canadian-owned book distribution system and the establishment of a publishing house in the United States to popularize Canadian authors and expand the market for their works.[92] Not everyone shared this interest in Canadianization and measures that would come out of the pockets of the federal government, of course, but interestingly, the list of naysayers included Jean-Luc Pepin, the Liberals' minister of Industry, Trade and Commerce, who wanted to leave the responsibility – and expense – of aiding the publishing sector to the provincial governments.[93]

If Pepin got his wish, then Ontario would have had to handle much of the problem because that province was home to many of the big publishing houses. So much so, in fact, that the purchase of Gage Publishing and Ryerson Press in 1970 by American interests prompted the provincial government to investigate the industry. The Ontario Royal Commission on Book Publishing, reporting in 1972, offered an articulate assessment of a situation in which having 'Canadian publishers' did not necessarily mean having 'Canadian publishing.'[94] Advocating a 'moderate cultural nationalism in book publishing,' the commission argued that intervention was reasonable 'to the extent that furnishing [the publishing sector] will enrich and protect the cultural life of the people of Ontario and Canada.'[95] Support did not extend so far as to include a quota system, however, which was rejected as a 'simplistic solution' to market problems.[96]

In the same year as Ontario bureaucrats were perusing this report, the Trudeau administration acted on the recommendations of Gérard Pelletier and introduced the Federal Book Publishing Policy, an initiative to be administered by the Canada Council in what was another instance of the state earmarking funds. 'Canadian Publishing Gets $1,092,500 assist with strings attached,' announced a 9 November 1972 article in the *Toronto Star*. Compared to the $10 million to the Canadian Film Development Corporation, the $1,092,500 offered the publishing sector – $500,000 of it for purchasing books from Canadian-owned publishers to be distributed in Canada and abroad – seemed awfully skimpy.[97] But then again, there were fewer mouths to feed than one might think, particularly given that the 'block grants' were – as requested by nationalists and domestic publishers and in line with the government's own interests – limited to what Pelletier described as the 'genuinely Canadian sector of the industry (that is, the sector under Canadian control).'[98]

The new policy was a far cry from the extensive changes called for by many Canadians, and their displeasure found its way to the desk of the secretary of state. Hugh Faulkner, Pelletier's replacement as of November 1972, received stacks of letters from people seeking a stronger measure than that offered by the block-grant program, Canadian content quotas for retailers being a popular choice.[99] Yet the federal government could do only so much, Faulkner noted in responses to the letter writers, since many areas – including school curricula, library purchases, and book retailers – came under provincial jurisdiction.[100] The Trudeau administration was trying to economically assist a sector for which it was not even responsible; the reason for doing so, of course, was because intervention offered much to federal bureaucrats attempting to establish a sense of nationhood.

Periodicals and the *Time* and *Reader's Digest* Exemption

Time and *Reader's Digest* were dirty words to some people in the periodical sector and a lingering point of contention between nationalists and the federal government. Exempting these two American periodicals in the Paperback and Periodical Distributors Act of 1964 had left bureaucrats vulnerable to criticism which, a decade later, after years of nationalist fervour and a growing appreciation for magazines as positive contributors to cultural life, had fermented into intense bitterness and hostility. Why had the state yet to correct what was clearly a legislative anomaly? 'The right kind of encouragement and protection can have spectacular results,' argued Doris Anderson, editor of *Chatelaine*; in the editorial space of the July 1974 issue.[101] *Chatelaine* was not merely a consumer magazine; it was a consciously Canadian one, combining articles such as 'What Makes a Couple Marry,' 'Is There a Link between Potato Blight and Birth Defects,' and 'Budget Cookery' with 'What It's Like to Be English in Montreal' and 'Heirloom Quilts from the Royal Ontario Museum.'[102] 'Chatelaine made its promise of Canadian content in reportage, fashion, food, and fiction its chief editorial hook,' as historian Valerie J. Korinek has noted.[103] Not only did readers depend upon Chatelaine, but, Doris Anderson contended in the December 1974 issue, so did the industry: 'over the years we've discovered and published hundreds of new Canadian writers, illustrators and photographers.'[104] The quest for nationhood, at least one in line with the idea of the Peaceable Kingdom, would be set back in a number of ways without the contribution made by Chatelaine and similar magazines.

As 1974 came to an end and the new year moved into the month of April, Hugh Faulkner announced that Bill C-58 would alter, effective 1 January 1976, the Time and Reader's Digest exemption. Advertisers would be able to deduct advertising expenditures only in magazines with at least 75 per cent Canadian ownership or 80 per cent in original content. This was the same bill which, as noted earlier in this chapter, excluded advertisers from receiving tax deductions for spots purchased on American television stations targeting the Canadian market. Doris Anderson, speaking on the behalf of Chatelaine and echoing the words of the Special Senate Committee on the Mass Media in 1970, praised the measure as a step forward in acknowledging that 'a strong periodical press is as necessary in Canada as is a national railway, an airline or a Canadian television or a Canadian radio network, but the kind of vigorous, challenging, magazine industry we need does not exist in Canada and has not existed for 30 years.' Canada had the talent, she noted; all that the industry needed was a level playing field against the branch plants.[105] Jubilance over alterations to the Paperback and Periodical Distributors Act soon turned to concern, however, as in the autumn of 1975, merely a few months before the legislation was to take effect, the Liberal cabinet began discussing the possibility of reducing the 'original content' criterion from 80 to 60 per cent. Doing so elicited a protest from the Canadian Periodical Publishers' Association, the Book and Periodical Development Council, and nationalists Abraham Rotstein, Pierre Berton, Peter C. Newman, Robert Fulford, and Claude Bissell, among others, who asked for it to be left as it was.[106] Too much work had gone into winning the alteration to allow the government to back down.

The publishers of Time and Reader's Digest, not surprisingly, came out swinging in protection of their marketplace advantage. 'We wonder how many of our readers and how many members of the journalistic community really want to see a precedent set whereby rigid rules of "difference" are established by the Government,' remarked Stephen S. LaRue, president of Time Canada, in regards to the 80 per cent original content criterion.[107] LaRue's statement, published in the 10 March 1975 issue of *Time*, was a clear attempt to guise economic interests under the spectre of censorship, a charge that Hugh Faulkner later rebuked by noting, 'Time (Canada) is fighting for money, not principle.'[108] The point was so clear that even former *Time* (Canada) editor and special correspondent John Scott identified Bill C-58 as more of an economic constraint than a restriction on freedom of thought.[109] Of all the complaints, though, perhaps the most true to heart was made by E.P. Zimmerman, president of Reader's Digest Canada. 'It makes me want to vomit,' he candidly told members of the Standing Committee on Broadcasting, Film, and Assistance to the Arts on 24 November 1975.[110]

As with other attempts to aid the production of Canadian content, the Liberals had to face off against Conservatives eager to equate intervention – even though it was merely a refining of pre-existing legislation – with vile historical events. One Conservative MP went so far as to compare Bill C-58 to the propaganda techniques of Joseph Goebbels and the Nazis, the Russian occupation of Czechoslovakia, and government corruption in Vietnam and Cambodia.[111] Yet the difficulties plaguing the domestic industry could not be ignored, as not only did *Time* and *Reader's Digest* gobble up tremendous amounts of tax-deductible advertising revenue but, as was noted during a House of Commons debate in the autumn of 1975, publishers had to contend with thirteen of the fourteen national magazine distributors being American-owned.[112] Conservative Party complaints proved to be insufficient in stopping a long overdue piece of legislation.

The U.S. Department of State, having a decade earlier coerced the Canadian government into the exemption, requested that the Liberals hold off passing the bill in order to allow time for negotiations. That the Americans would suggest such a thing made David Lewis of the New Democratic Party livid, yet the decision fell upon Trudeau, who, in appreciating the need to maintain good relations with Canada's largest trading partner, told members of the House of Commons that 'we do not have to follow their advice, but we certainly can hear what they have to say.'[113] In the end, and to the cheers of concerned Canadians, the bill was passed unamended, and the exemption from ten years earlier was finally brought to an end. The Conservatives could be left to complain and the Americans to possibly retaliate, but Trudeau and like-minded intelligentuals understood that Canadianization required a tremendous amount of fortitude.

Feature Films, Voluntary Quotas, and the Capital Cost Allowance

Few bureaucrats showed such an ability to cut to the heart of a situation, and to do such with heartfelt conviction, as Pierre Juneau. He showed no lack of forthrightness when, in speaking at a meeting of Ottawa's Canadian Club, he rhetorically asked whether Canadians would 'be deprived if instead of thirty American films being shown there were a few less American and a few Canadian thrown into the mix?'[114] The obviousness of the answer was only surpassed by the sensibility of the question. This type of declaration was necessary, however, as distributors and exhibitors had long managed to keep discussions about cinematic activity focused upon the supposed lack of quality films. More and more this facade was crumbling under the millions of dollars spent by the Canadian Film Development Corporation: many movies now had big budgets and offered much in terms of cinematic excitement. The real reason, now evident to many filmmakers and supporters, was that distributors and exhibitors had no reason to deviate from the system of Hollywood block booking and vertical integration. The American film giants had, as the Toronto Film-makers' Co-op complained to the secretary of state in May of 1972, a 'functional, if not legal, monopoly' over distribution and access to exhibitors.[115]

Theatre owners, quite content to act as pipelines for American films, showed no signs of feeling pressured into making concessions to filmmakers. Instead they seemed to take solace in the fact that film exhibition came under provincial jurisdiction and that, with much of the effort for legislated screen time being directed at the federal government, there would be little in the way of change. It probably did not seem much of a threat, then, when on 30 March 1973 Hugh Faulkner told members of the Standing Committee on Broadcasting, Film, and Assistance to the Arts that a quota was 'something we should look at; I am not sure it is practical, but it is certainly an option.'[116] Faulkner was not going out on a limb in making this statement: there certainly seemed to be public backing for the idea. According to a 1973 Gallup poll, 65 per cent of Canadians supported the idea of having Canadian theatres reserve eight weeks of every two years for Canadian films, 17 per cent disagreed and 18 per cent were undecided.[117] The following summer, still struggling with jurisdictional issues, Faulkner decided to take the idea of a quota system to the provincial premiers. This initial foray proved to be unsuccessful, however, as the premiers showed no interest in instituting a quota or box-office levy.[118] They did not seem to share the Trudeau administration's desire to mobilize Canadian content for the sake of nationhood; for them, intervention presented more headaches than gains. Only the Quebec government, certainly to no surprise, showed interest.[119] In fact, that province was already exploring the possibility of a quota.[120]

It was a tough position for this would-be Canadianizer. 'Legislative jurisdiction in this field is clearly provincial,' Faulkner conceded during a House of Commons debate in May of 1975. 'I am simply making representations to the provinces on behalf of the industry in regard to both the question of quotas and levies.'[121] Perhaps it was the resolve with which Faulkner engaged the provinces on the quota issue or maybe because Quebec seemed poised to pass a quota (something that could lead to other provinces doing the same). Whatever the reason, in early 1976 Famous Players and Odeon Theatres (Canada) Ltd decided that the best option was to try to deflect the push for quotas by conceding to a 'voluntary' quota system. According to the agreement made between these two chains and the Department of the Secretary of State, Canadian films would be screened for four weeks per theatre per year (one week a year at drive-ins), and a $1.7 million fund would be created from ticket revenues to be put towards domestic film production.[122] 'Some form of quota was necessary,' Faulkner explained to his fellow members of the House of Commons on 6 February 1976, and a voluntary system seemed to be 'an improvement' over the status quo.[123] It was an idea he had mentioned to them the previous autumn, identifying a voluntary quota as possibly the best solution to a bad situation.[124] Now he just had to wait and see if it was much of a solution at all.

To help things along and to reassure exhibitors that there would be no lack of high-budget films, the secretary of state agreed to increase the Capital Cost Allowance from 30 to 100 per cent. It was a move designed to encourage private-sector investment in film production, the next logical step in an ever-present shift from funding the public sector to investing in the private alternative. Canada was coming closer to creating a Hollywood North of subsidies and backstage talent offering much to American companies happy to maintain their monopoly thanks to Canadian taxpayers.

The Academy and the Issue of Jurisdiction

It is an understatement to describe the Ontario Conservative government's minister of Education and minister of University Affairs (and soon premier) William G. Davis as not being in favour of Canadianization. 'The university is part of the contemplative tradition,' he argued to the thirty-first National Conference of the Canadian University Press in early 1969. 'It is not an experiment in political democracy. Politicizing a university can distort its aims and disrupt its functions.'[125] That universities were inherently politicized as a result of the nature of pedagogy went unacknowledged. Nonetheless, as with film exhibition and much of the publishing sector, education fell under provincial jurisdiction, and because so many of Canada's universities were located in Ontario, a substantial part of the call for changes to academic life needed to be addressed to Davis. But *The Struggle for Canadian Universities*, the influential treatise put forth by Robin Mathews and James Steele, did not convince this minister of education. Davis responded to the book by calling Mathews and Steele 'anti-American' and rejecting their 'extreme conclusion' about the problems in the academy. As he put it in a letter to Mathews, 'higher learning, which emphasizes academic excellence, hardly seems to me an area where the most important qualification for a professor should be Canadian citizenship.' The employment equity that Mathews and Steele were suggesting, Davis warned, was no less than a violation of the Ontario Human Rights Code.[126] Mathews disagreed, of course, and he did not mince words in a September 1971 letter to the man who had recently replaced John Robarts as the premier. 'I believe that you (who control the Ontario Human Rights Commission) are doing all in your power to support the rape of Canadian rights.'[127]

Robin Mathews no doubt relished seeing Premier Davis undermined by the investigations launched by his own administration. In 1972 the Ontario Royal Commission on Book Publishing found that American professors taught courses intimately linked to areas of foreign interest, to the detriment of domestic discourse.[128] A year later the Select Committee on Economic and Cultural Nationalism, Colleges and Universities in Ontario reported that Canadian academics were at a disadvantage because of the lack of citizenship regulations, a measure that other countries had seen fit to establish.[129] The problem was found to be so systemic that the committee recommended legislation to ensure that all chancellors, members of boards of governors or equivalent, presidents, vice-presidents, deans, and chairs of departments be Canadian citizens; and that, further, 'for each university in Ontario, averaged over the 7 subsequent years, 80% of new appointments be Canadian citizens at the time of appointment, and 70% of new appointments be from among those who have obtained most or all of their graduate training at Canadian universities.'[130] Such legislation might be interpreted as being contrary to the Ontario Human Rights code, as Davis had stated to Mathews, but the committee recommended that an amendment be passed in order to make it legal in the case of university faculty hiring.[131] Finally, in order to properly address discrepancies in course offerings, departments were to provide annual reports on Canadian content courses, curricula, planning, and development.[132] All in all, the issue was well summarized in one comment: the committee members did 'not feel that careless recruiting and lack of sensitivity to matters of Canadian importance and concern are justifiable under the guise of academic freedom.'[133]

What had started as an academic manifesto penned by Robin Mathews and James Steele had, as of the mid-1970s, gained widespread support and credibility, so much so that the federal government decided to work its way around jurisdictional issues and address the issue by implementing changes in the area of immigration law. As of 15 April 1977, colleges and universities were required to advertise teaching positions in Canada. But since they did not actually have to interview any Canadian candidates, problems continued largely unabated. Appointments of Canadians increased by only 3.9 per cent in the first year of the policy.[134] After a few dismal years, the government took the added step of requiring that departments interview Canadians for positions before advertising abroad.[135] This requirement still left departments able to dismiss Canadian candidates as insufficiently qualified and then hire abroad with no need to fill a proportional representation quota, but at the very least, hiring practices now operated under a greater degree of scrutiny. Bypassing trained Canadians would be more difficult to do as a result of federal action.

Much less controversial, but very telling of a federal government putting its resources behind the quest for nationhood, were the contributions made to Canadian Studies programs at home and abroad. The Department of External Affairs actually took an early lead by making Canadian Studies an official part of its mandate in 1974, building upon years of organizing and arranging cultural displays, student exchanges, travelling art exhibitions, touring musical groups, lectures by Canadian academics, and even the establishment of a Canadian Culture Centre in Paris in 1970. Initially focusing on developing Canadian Studies programs in the United States, Britain, and Japan, the department as of 1976 had extended its support to programs in Belgium, Italy, and Germany.[136] The Department of the Secretary of State had much catching up to do. In a memorandum to the cabinet back in 1970, Gérard Pelletier had suggested 'the introduction of a new Canadian Studies program designed to encourage, for the direct benefit of the general public, the preservation, enlargement and diffusion of that part of the Canadian heritage that lies within the domain of the humanities and social sciences.'[137] Yet it took until 1979 for the department to put substantial effort – and money – towards Canadian Studies programs. Still, the three-year monetary commitment of over a million and a half dollars to the Canada Studies Foundation, the Association of Canadian Community Colleges, and the Association of Canadian Studies was a testament to a government interested in reifying nationhood by making the nation itself a topic of study.[138]

Conclusion

In all the agreement and disagreement surrounding federal intervention taken in the name of Canadian content, few points are as matter-of-fact as one made by Pierre Juneau in response to those people who decried Canadianization as a form of censorship. 'Fiddlesticks!' he told the fifty-seventh annual Advertising Seminar of the Association of Canadian Advertisers on 1 May 1972. 'There is just about the same risk of [being deprived of American content] as there is of lacking snow in Kapuskasing, mosquitoes in the Laurentians or bureaucrats in Ottawa.'[139] All one had to do was to look at magazine racks, bookstore shelves, movie advertisements, and television schedules to see that the nation was open to the importation of American products.[140] In Juneau's view, Canadian content regulations were a means of ensuring variety and making available content that would otherwise be censored by distributors and exhibitors only interested in material proven to be popular in foreign marketplaces; money-making was as much a form of selection control – in fact, even more so – as a requirement that domestic programming be made available to the population. Two weeks later Juneau followed up this idea by telling the Chamber of Commerce of Victoria that the victims of censorship were those Canadians who had little programming choice other than that determined by broadcasters and their advertisers.[141]

Juneau was testifying on the behalf of Canadianization, as well as to the importance of opening pathways of communication within a society, but not to the reasons why and the problematic ways in which the federal government had engaged in such activity. The Trudeau administration was encouraging relationships between producers and audiences, yet it did so in ways that often first and foremost served the goals of federalists. Bureaucrats had unabashedly taken the state from passively assisting to proactively structuring cultural activity on the supposed behalf of the population when, in fact, intervention promised significant rewards to a government willing to navigate contested terrain and deploy a combination of coercive quotas and consensual investment. Federal initiatives were not self-sacrificial. A Liberal-defined, pro-federalist Canada, one facing the political threat of Québécois separatism, required no less than a willingness to mobilize culture as thoroughly as possible, a relationship between the state and culture that Vincent Massey and the architects of the first moment of Canadianization had feared.

The Trudeau administration had ideological goals in mind, but the means had a distinctly industrial character. Federal intervention, undertaken with consideration of the need to satisfy cultural workers and manoeuvre around jurisdictional issues, set the foundation for a cultural industrialism that has come to define Canadianization since the early 1970s. The prime minister and his cultural lieutenants – namely, successive secretaries of state Gérard Pelletier, Hugh Faulkner, and John Roberts and CRTC chairman Pierre Juneau – established an impressive list of federal accomplishments in the cultural sector. The Arts and Cultural Policy, with its catchwords 'democratization' and 'decentralization,' let the government portray itself as acting on behalf of all Canadians in funding events that promoted national unity and invested in local tourism economies. The CRTC increased Canadian content regulations for television, introduced them for radio, dealt with the cable television revolution, and further posited Canadian content in industrial terms by classifying commercials as cultural. The Federal Book Publishing Policy allowed the secretary of state to bypass jurisdictional issues by providing subsidies for domestically owned publishers together with funds for translating books as a means of encouraging industry growth and helping to bridge the English-French divide. The *Time* and *Reader's Digest* exemption was removed from the Paperback and Periodical Distributors Act in order to strengthen the magazine industry. The lack of feature-film exhibition, with the Canadian Film Development Corporation increasingly seeming to be a money pit, was addressed through a voluntary quota system – the easiest way of dealing with the lack of federal jurisdiction – and an increase to the Capital Cost Allowance designed to lure investors into putting their money into film production. Finally, concerns about Americanization in the academy were dealt with through immigration-law changes requiring that universities assess Canadian candidates for positions before interviewing non-Canadians, and in addition, the government spent millions of dollars on Canadian studies programs. Much of the intervention distilled into a combination of coercion where possible (including quotas and ownership and citizenship regulations) and the obtaining of consent (largely through subsidies and funding programs) where jurisdiction and private-sector resistance needed to be overcome.

It was amazing that the federal government had managed to do all of this with little backlash. Certainly, there were plenty of complaints, especially from whose who were effected by quotas, rather than those who benefited from the subsidies, of course. Television and radio broadcasters objected to Canadian content regulations. Movie theatre owners decried the move towards a quota requirement. The publishers of *Time* and *Reader's Digest* complained about the removal of their exemption. Many academics and even the Ontario minister of education himself objected to any attempt to alter departmental hiring practices and course criteria. Yet state intervention occurred with less resistance than one might have assumed. The sheer breadth of intervention satisfied many soft nationalists; the focus on industrial investment and subsidies made many cultural workers happy and satiated those Canadians who sought an economic return on federal monies to the arts; and aiding production without a requirement that the content contain national identifiers helped the state largely to avoid the issue of censorship. A 1979 survey even showed that 83 per cent of Canadians actually favoured state intervention in culture.[142] It was a radical change from decades earlier, when the state had done all it could to avoid entangling itself in the cultural sphere.

As the new nationalism waned during the 1970s, the government in power found itself sitting comfortably as the guardian of nationhood and the administrator of cultural devices. Never before had the federal state had such a free hand in cultural activity. And for the most part, it seemed that the past decade of state intervention had contributed to a rise in cultural activity. In positing Canadianization upon an industrial foundation, the state made Canadian content more plentiful, more economically valuable, and much more quantitative. But what did this mean for audiences? Just what did cultural industrialism have to offer in qualitative terms?

8 Littlest Hobos and Kings of Kensington: Canadian Cultural Melange in the 1970s

We are 100 per cent behind Canadian content, but ... we do not favour 100 per cent of Canadian content.

Special Senate Committee on the Mass Media[1]

Neither Canadian crews nor Canadian locations themselves necessarily imbue a television program with Canadian values or concerns.

Task Force on Broadcasting Policy[2]

Pierre Trudeau, coming to power in a time of not only political challenge from the New Democratic Party but also, and much more pressing, the threat of Québécois separatism, took the federal government from passively to proactively structuring national cultural activities. The model of Canadianization launched by his administration, that of cultural industrialism, entailed a careful combination of regulation where jurisdiction permitted and monies where intervention proved to be more controversial (or simply where funds were most needed). The result was substantial sector-by-sector change to the cultural status quo. Direct investment and earmarked funds to the arts community were granted in line with economic (particularly tourism) and pro-unity interests. Canadian content regulations were increased in television and extended to radio. Subsidies were distributed to domestically owned book publishing houses. The *Time* and *Reader's Digest* exemption was removed as a means of helping periodical publishers. A voluntary film quota system and an increase in the Capital Cost Allowance were instituted for the film sector. And changes to immigration laws helped to open employment opportunities to Canadian academics, while federal funds aided in the development of Canadian Studies programs.

The list is impressive, but intervention alone does not a nation make. The Canadian content coming out of Trudeau's model of Canadianization was highly mixed in quality, reception, and impact, and it did not necessarily do much to promote a national sense of place. This consequence should come as no surprise, of course, as cultural industrialism works better for bureaucrats and cultural workers than it does for those whose primary concern is the opening of systems of communication to greater domestic discourse. One can see how, looked at critically, the Trudeau administration's mobilization of cultural devices was in some ways more successful than the content it fostered. And although many cultural workers enjoyed new employment opportunities and audiences had a greater access to domestic goods, the biggest beneficiary of state involvement was the state itself.

Federalism, Separatism, and the Arts

Famed author and literary figure George Woodcock showed no sign of pulling punches when it came to federal incursions into the arts. 'Trudeau's view was basically that the control of the nation's cultural life, especially of its arts, is essential for the consolidation of political power, and cultural policies should be directed towards supporting a government's principal aims,' he argued in *Strange Bedfellows: The State and the Arts in Canada*.[3] Woodcock felt threatened by Trudeau's appropriation of the arts for federal interests and the reduction of art to merely another form of cultural expression. For him there was a difference between 'culture' and 'cultural,' and the unique status of the arts seemed to have been lost in the Trudeauvian paradigm of cultural 'democratization.'

Woodcock and like-minded culturists were not alone in their concerns. The Canada Council found itself quite uncomfortable with the direction taken by the administration. Earmarking funds for pro-federalist cultural activities placed the council in a difficult position by using it as an intermediary in the face of its own monetary difficulties. 'The willingness to fund "national unity" through the arts, but not adequately to fund the arts themselves,' chairman Gertrude Laing pointed out in the council's 1977–8 *Annual Report*, 'is evidence of an attitude to cultural policy which gives me great concern.'[4] This use of earmarked funds in some ways even more infuriated those arts institutions that sought monies free from the obligation of having to provide opportunities to Canadian talent. Stratford's Robin Phillips, the English-born artistic director at the centre of the hiring controversy three years earlier, chastised the federal government for not giving the funds to the council and, in turn, the traditional recipients: 'I am angry that the secretary of state has seen fit to do any funding at all. The Canada Council is the agency best equipped to handle funding of the arts. It was established for this purpose and it has been doing the job effectively for years.'[5] Stratford's focus on British works seemed to leave it out in the cold in a time of monies earmarked for nationalist purposes. The reality of the situation, however, was that Stratford's importance within the economy of cultural tourism ensured that the festival theatre would not go without state support. The festival was evolving from a Masseyesque celebration of high culture to the pinnacle of cultural tourism, and the state was not going to stop sending money to its organizers. So much so, in fact, that it is worth looking ahead in time to see that the Stratford Shakespearean Festival Foundation of Canada was actually granted four million dollars from public coffers between 2001 and 2004 as part of a three-year donor-matching program.[6] Four million dollars to one theatre group! As long as Stratford could draw tourists, it would continue to receive more than its share of taxpayer dollars.

Fiscal hardships in the face of federal self-interest, the impact of nationalism on the cultural psyche, and new leadership led to a change in priorities at the council. Consideration for elements of Canadian content had begun for orchestral grants back in 1971, but as of 1978, under the chairmanship of Mavor Moore – who had once described the National Arts Centre (and its lack of domestic works) as money spent on 'pride and tourism'[7] – support for Canadian content became a 'priority' and 'a matter of policy' for the arts as a whole.[8] The council even put its weight behind the call for Canadians in key positions of publicly funded theatres. Quality was still paramount, of course, and the Canada Council would not support poor-quality work simply because it was Canadian; nor would grant applications lacking Canadian content be excluded from funding.[9] But in terms of council priorities, there was now a solid leaning towards indigenous expression and engagement. The council was coming to terms with the shift towards supporting the idea that it was not enough merely to have high culture but that culture should also do much to involve the works of Canadians. Out of this concept emerged an attempt to better balance the needs of both performers and producers – actors and playwrights, musicians and composers, dancers and choreographers – in the face of apathetic exhibitors who employed many of the former and few of the latter.

The results of the change at the council were quite telling. Seventy-five of the ninety-five works performed by council-supported dance companies in the 1978–9 season 'were original Canadian choreographies,' the council's *Annual Report* proudly exclaimed.[10] A year later the council reported that 'more Canadian plays were produced in 1979–80 than in any previous season and only Canadians or landed immigrants were hired in senior artistic and administrative positions in our theatres.'[11] New priorities not only helped to overcome systemic disadvantages for the creators of original pieces but, as many nationalists had predicted, the quality proved to be top-notch. According to a 1979 Statistics Canada survey, music groups and opera companies staging Canadian compositions drew larger crowds than those offering no Canadian material.[12]

Not all arts organizations, of course, not even the publicly owned ones, felt a need to change their offerings. The National Arts Centre, which began operating in 1969 and drew scorn at that time for failing to support domestic works, continued to schedule little in the way of Canadian orchestral music. In fact, the Task Force on the National Arts Centre (1986) found it necessary to recommend that the level of Canadian content be brought up to 'a minimum of one-third of total programming.'[13] Ottawa's cultural showpiece still had far to go in living up to the 'national' part of its name.

Television, Canadian Content, and the National Contrast

The fallout at the CBC from Trudeau's attempt to purge it of Québécois separatism was not too difficult for the network to bear and did, interestingly enough, open the door to a significant change in the Canadian content offered by the national broadcaster. CBC president Al Johnson endured the Committee of Inquiry into the National Broadcasting Service thanks to the skilful way in which Harry Boyle, CRTC chairman and head of the committee, diverted the blame from the French-language service to the broader problems of centralization and lack of regional representation. The unintended, yet quite positive outcome was that the crisis offered Johnson an opportunity to overhaul the broadcasting network and bring it up to date with the interests of audiences. 'He was captivated by the idea of "Canadianizing" the airwaves,' recalled Knowlton Nash, the ghost writer for what would become the 'Touchstone' policy of 1977. 'That would be, he decided, his moment. It would also reinforce the "Canadianization" Pierre Juneau had sought during his years at the CRTC and would be Johnson's answer to accusations from Quebec Liberals that the CBC was betraying Canada.'[14] Here lay a chance for the national broadcaster to put to rest once and, it was hoped, for all the accusations that had plagued its operations and at the same time serve the interests of audiences and the advertisers upon which the corporation depended for revenues.

The Touchstone policy tried to move the CBC away from being a pillar of Masseyesque Canadianization, with its combination of high-culture and clichéd Canadiana, and towards supporting a Canadian content experience that was both national and popular.[15] An important component of this policy entailed combining established templates with shows built upon celebrities and 'star power.' In the 1978–9 season, for example, the network aired the dramatic *Riel* (4 million viewers) and *Duplessis* (1.9 million) alongside flashy Anne Murray and Rich Little *Superspecials* (3.5 and 3 million respectively).[16] All of this home-grown glitz and glam in turn meant less money being spent on American imports: 95 per cent of program expenditures went to Canadian productions in that season.[17]

CTV, formed a decade earlier as the first non-CBC television network, was not much effected by this wave of Canadianization. The decision by the CRTC to increase Canadian content from 55 to 60 per cent and to implement tighter 'promises of performance' was little more than a tweaking of the status quo, and many of the domestic programs continued to reflect what one would expect from the profit-minded network: inexpensive, generic shows such as *Stars on Ice, The Bobby Vincent Show, Headline Hunters, Grand Old Country, The David Steinberg Show, The Amazing Kreskin,* and *Sports Beat.*[18] *Excuse My French,* a half-hour comedy drawing a large audience in Quebec, displayed national characteristics but was soon cut from the schedule because its production cost outweighed the advertising revenue.[19] Efforts in the area of dramatic programming, among the most expensive of formats, were even more scarce and, even when offered, did not impress Canadianizers. CTV's dramatic series *Police Surgeon* (1972–4) was dismissed by the CRTC as being little more than a low-quality, co-produced, made-for-export program.[20] The lack of dramatic programming, quality or otherwise, drove the CRTC to tie CTV's 1979 licence renewal to a promise to increase its output of drama. This decision was not as oppressive as one might think, however, because – and in the spirit of cultural industrialism – CTV stood to gain extra Canadian content credits if a dramatic program achieved a minimum 'points' total on an industry-based checklist. This new obligation in some ways even served CTV interests, broadcasting analyst Herschel Hardin has noted, since 'the programming can still easily be Americanized or internationalized (that is, de-Canadianized) for foreign sales – a typical arrangement.'[21]

CTV's actions were predictable and thus were in some ways much less shocking than those of Global Television. In 1972 the CRTC agreed to grant Global Television a broadcasting licence based upon its promise to air a large amount of Canadian content. Global went so far as to pledge a minimum of $8 million for domestic programming during the first year alone. Here was a golden opportunity, in the eyes of the CRTC, to offer Canadians a new outlet for domestic expression. And at first everything seemed to be right on target, with the programming schedule including the variety show *Everything Goes*; a conversation circle discussing relationships called *This Program Is about Sex*; two shows hosted by Pierre Berton (*My Country* and the *Great Debate*); *Witness to Yesterday*, with actors portraying historical figures being interviewed; cartoonist Ben Wick's interview program *World of Wicks*; coverage of World Hockey Association games, with Peter Gzowski and Ken Dryden as commentators; and numerous French-language films dubbed into English.[22]

The abundance of Canadian content, however, soon came to an end as Global struggled with its economic bottom line. Having secured its licence, the broadcaster responded with the simple – and profitable – solution of breaking its Canadian content promises and replacing domestic programs with American imports. The result was startling. Global's revenues went, Robert Babe has explained, 'from $2.9 million for the eight months ended August 31, 1974 to $8.6 million for the year ended August 31, 1975, to $15.4 million for 1976, and to $22.1 million for 1977.'[23] Not only was the CRTC bamboozled, but with Global now competing for the rights to American programming, the price of imports jumped 'by 35 to 40 percent between the 1975–76 and 1976–77 years.'[24] Instead of increasing the level of Canadian content on the airwaves, Global ended up making the situation worse; now all the broadcasters had even less money in their programming budgets to spend on Canadian content.

The draw of inexpensive American programming was just too much to resist; that advertisers put such a premium on imports made the choice inevitable. In the mid-1970s CTV placed the cost of American programming at approximately $4,000 an hour and its advertising revenue as $30–50,000. Or, comparatively, American prime-time programming was 22 per cent the cost of its Canadian equivalent, while its revenues were 163 per cent higher.[25] Cheaper, more profitable, and made with higher budgets, American shows offered a lot to station owners and investors.

What did these relative costs mean for audiences? The result was a television experience of high-budget, high-intensity, high-excitement

American programs and low-budget, low-intensity, and low-excitement Canadian content. The shootouts and backstabbings on *S.W.A.T.* and *Dallas* were well matched with the high-impact glitzy consumerism of *The Price Is Right* and its tanned host, Bob Barker. Even John Bassett, owner of CFTO, admitted to tuning into a rival station in order to watch *M*A*S*H*.[26] With Canadian stations getting to select from the most jam-packed of American offerings and no need for the slower-paced ones and audiences probably received a much more one-sidedly violent image of the United States than did American audiences.

The tone and appeal of the imported programming was more than clear to viewers. 'No one denies that much of the U.S. fare we now get is frivolous junk,' noted the *Calgary Herald* in the wake of the CRTC's proposal to increase the level of Canadian content. 'But at least it is well-produced junk.'[27] It was also tremendously violent junk, particularly compared to domestic programming. The CRTC's Symposium on Television Violence in 1976 found that 47 per cent of the half-hour American programs broadcasted in the Toronto area were significantly violent, compared to only 3 per cent of the Canadian offerings.[28] A year later the Ontario Royal Commission on Violence in the Communications Industry concluded that CTV was the most violent network on the continent; the United Nations took this assessment to the next level by identifying it as one of the most violent in the world.[29] CTV, in an ingenious if implausible move, blamed its use of a large amount of violent material on the Canadian Broadcasting Corporation. If the CBC did not purchase the non-violent, family-oriented American programs, CTV would not have to rely on violent, action-adventure material in order to offer audiences an alternative.[30]

Canadian shows, with their budget-minded sets, awkward filming techniques, and stumbling storylines, seemed to plod along when compared to the American offerings. An extensive use of inexpensive local programming – approximately 15 per cent of CBC and 25 per cent of CTV Canadian content as of 1968 – helped to impart a realistic tone.[31] This phenomenon was furthered by the proliferation of shows such as *Don Messer's Jubilee*, *The Littlest Hobo*, *La Famille Plouffe*, *Beachcombers*, the *Degrassi* series, and *King of Kensington*, all of which seemed honest, sincere, and heartfelt thanks to the subject matter and the relatively low production budgets. One could not help but be struck by the difference between Canadian and American shows. In the Canadian cop drama *Sidestreet* the officers did not use weapons; *Wojeck* and *Quentin Durgens* could not outrun, let alone outshoot, *Starsky and Hutch*, *Charlie's Angels*, or *Magnum P.I.*; and Peter Gzowski was much more down-to-earth in *90 Minutes Live* than was Johnny Carson on *The Tonight Show.* Canadian programming had many fewer 'jolts per minute,' Morris Wolfe has argued. 'Compared to the people on *King of Kensington,* those on American shows such as *All in the Family* seemed speeded up. *King of Kensington* felt like a 1950s American comedy rather than one from the 1970s.'[32]

The result was that Canadian content often stood out from the American alternatives. 'You can turn on your TV in the middle of a program and immediately know whether it is a Canadian production,' as one viewer noted in a newspaper 'letter to the editor.'[33] Such an impression has actually become canonized to the detriment of contemporary television program producers. Academic Elspeth Cameron has explained that the 'slick professionalism' and use of heroes in the Heritage Minutes popular in the late 1990s 'prompted criticism that American production values overwhelm the communication of "Canadian" values ... glitzy one-minute "bytes," some viewers argue, are better suited to American subjects than to their Canadian counterparts.'[34] The strength of this sentiment among audiences and industry people has led popular culture theorist Will Straw to note that 'while there is a widespread belief that Canadian films and television programs offer a distinct (i.e., more restrained) tone than those imported from the U.S., insistence on a Canadian tone as a requirement for certain kinds of public support seems both ludicrous and unnecessarily authoritarian ... More to the point, a valorization of tone risks enshrining, as the expression of a national cultural sensibility, an aspect of Canadian films or television programs that might simply be an effect of their lower budgets and production values.'[35] Quantitative Canadian content regulations, then, paradoxically contributed to fostering a qualitative sense of Canadianness within the television sector, although low-budget and amateur are not qualities with which many people would wish to identify.

City-TV, a Toronto-based independent that was issued a broadcasting licence on the basis of serving and reflecting the local community, is unique in putting a distinctive twist on the Canadian content tone. 'City was designed by Moses [Znaimer] to be everything conventional TV (like the CBC, maybe?) was not: fast, adventurous, noisy, multicultural and impolite,' as Geoff Pevere and Grieg Dymond noted in *Mondo Canuck: A Canadian Pop Culture Odyssey.*[36] Unlike the CTV's use of imported excitement, Znaimer put City-TV's money into creating bargain-basement thrills. From late-night *Baby Blue* soft-core pornographic movies to the energetic celebrity exhibitionism of *The New Music, Fashion Television,* and *Movie Television,* City-TV assembled a roster of domestic shows offering much in the way of visual intensity. Even *City-Pulse News* was fast-paced in the ways in which its newscasters reported the latest happenings and information. All of that being said, City-TV's production budgets nonetheless imparted an amateurism and realism on the excitement and thrills that gave the shows much of the same feel as other Canadian programs. Shaky camera work, visible teleprompters, the casual demeanor of on-air personalities, the man-on-the-street interviews, and the general means by which the station put Toronto itself on the air meant that the experience had a strongly domestic feel. City-TV offered viewers a sexy, if not racy, side of Canadian content.

Radio and the Impact of Canadian Content Regulations

Whereas the television experience was characterized by low budgets and programming that stood out as quite different from that of the American alternatives, radio broadcasting offered much in the way of top-notch content. The sheer need to fill Canadian content quotas led to tremendous investment in recording technologies and, in turn, the recording of high-quality albums and singles. There was only one 16–track recording studio in Canada in 1970; four years later there were five 16–track and one 24–track studios in Toronto, a 32–track studio in Montreal, and a variety of other recording facilities across Canada.[37]

Many Canadian musicians showed an immediate appreciation for what Juneau had done. A sample of comments, taken from rock journalist Ritchie Yorke's *Axes, Chops and Hot Licks: The Canadian Rock Music Scene* (1971), testifies to the contribution made by the regulations:

> Gary Peterson, drummer for The Guess Who: 'It shouldn't have been necessary to legislate it. Eventually, I think, there'll be no need for it. But something was needed to get the ball rolling, and I believe the CRTC regulations are the answer. It would have made our career a lot easier if they had started ten years earlier.'[38]

> Skip Prokop, drummer for the band Lighthouse: 'They are helping – not just us, but everybody. Some shit is being played, but you'll hear that anywhere. Finally the guys who are great players will be able to make a living as rock musicians.'[39]

Pierre Senecal of Mashmakhan: 'I don't think any of us are going to have to move away anymore. I think Canada has become an international music country, from inside and outside.'[40]

Bruce Cockburn: 'I believe the CRTC has definitely helped me. It's at least drawing everybody's attention to what's happening with Canadian artists. That can only be good.'[41]

Anne Murray: 'I don't know if I'd have been able to make it without the thirty percent business.'[42]

Not all musicians were quick to praise the impact of the Canadian content regulations, however. Many radio stations chose to overplay the music of a few artists, primarily those who had already made their reputation in the United States, and thereby caused some of these artists to feel that the regulations had actually harmed their careers. Perhaps no one complained as much as did Gordon Lightfoot, a tremendously talented singer-songwriter who, despite having been canonized as a national troubadour, showed no interest in the quest for nationhood or any willingness to tolerate the fallout resulting from Canadianization. In a declaration similar to that of Bryan Adams twenty years later, as discussed at the start of this book, Lightfoot told *Maclean's* that 'the CRTC did absolutely nothing for me. I didn't need it, ab-so-lute-ly *nothing* ... and I don't like it. They can ruin you, man. Canadian content is fine if you're not doin' well. But I'm in the music business and I have a huge American audience. I'm going to do Carnegie Hall for the second time. I really like to record down there, but I like to live up here. I really dig this country, but I'm not going to bring out any flags. I'm an entertainer. *I'm in the music business.*'[43] Lightfoot was not alone in terms of experiencing overplay. 'Last week ... the percipient listener might well have gotten the impression that AM radio stands for Anne Murray,' half-joked an article in *Time* magazine following the start of the regulations.[44] Or, as Geoff Pevere and Grieg Dymond described the situation in *Mondo Canuck*, 'if you listened to pop radio in the early seventies, it was easy to believe that Burton Cummings was the voice of Canada.'[45]

Yet despite the overplay, the Canadian content regulations offered performers and audiences a greater opportunity to engage in a relationship through the publicly owned airwaves and, quite tellingly, artists now had a better chance at making a career in Canada without first having to become a hit in or move to the United States. The Federal

Cultural Policy Review Committee in 1982 correctly summarized the situation by stating that

> the single step by the federal government released an immense volume of creativity in the Canadian music world – especially in the popular music field. Many new performing groups were created, recording studios emerged, record producers proliferated and many small companies were formed, leading eventually to the development of a substantial Canadian record production industry. Above all, much new music was created. A new crop of Canadian singers and musical groups arose in response to the content regulations, reaching large audiences at home and around the world, with the result that some of our 'pop' artists and groups are stars not only in the eyes of Canadians, but to fans in other countries as well.[46]

For its part, the radio wing of the CBC was undergoing an overhaul of its programming format, a significant change given that, as in television, CBC radio was still largely operating in line with the Masseyesque model of Canadianization. An internal CBC report written in early 1970 noted what many listeners already knew: 'Canadians generally do not care much for what CBC radio is providing at present.'[47] What followed was a 'radio revolution' headed by Laurent Picard, president of the CBC from 1972 to 1975. Knowlton Nash, the CBC's English television news and current affairs director at the time, has noted how the radio network avoided the pitfalls of competing against the private sector with similar programming – as the television network was trying to do – by instead carving out a distinct niche. A new and larger audience was won 'by offering more meaningful programs than the commercials, pop music, snippets of news, and opinionated phone-in shows that dominated private radio.'[48] In line with Trudeau's ideas of 'democratization' and 'decentralization,' this strategy meant that high-cultural precepts were cast to the side in favour of a more populist approach. Programs such as *As It Happens* with Barbara Frum and *This Country in the Morning* (later *Morningside*), hosted by Peter Gzowski, helped to make over CBC radio into an accessible, down-to-earth, audience-friendly network. The new direction, however, took a toll on its cultured arts and music programming, a situation unaddressed until the reorganization of the FM service into a 'cultural' wing.[49] Picard's 'radio revolution,' in offering something of interest to a broad audience, helped the CBC to increase its hold on the listening public to approximately 10 per cent by the 1980s. Not only did more Canadians tune in; they tended to do so for long periods of time and for specific programs.[50] The revolution was clearly a success.

The Film Industry and the Production of Hollywood Films

Hugh Faulkner spent a lot of his time as secretary of state fighting on the behalf of Canadianization in the film industry, only to find his effort leading to little in the way of screen time. Jurisdictional issues, together with apathetic provincial governments, meant that the best he could wrangle was a voluntary quota with Famous Players and Odeon Theatres (Canada) Ltd, yet this proved to be little more than a disappointment. 'I am not satisfied with the results of this agreement,' explained Faulkner to the Standing Committee on Broadcasting, Film, and Assistance to the Arts in early 1977, a year after establishing the voluntary system. 'Quota systems have been found to be necessary and have been successfully implemented in many countries, including France and Great Britain. I am convinced, particularly because of our close proximity to the large and very successful American film industry, that an effective quota system is essential in Canada.'[51] Faulkner's frustration with the voluntary agreement was not about to go away anytime soon. In 1977–8 only a third of Famous Players theatres filled their voluntary quota and barely half even reached the 50 per cent mark.[52] In that same period only a fifth of Odeon theatres lived up to the promise and less than half screened 50 per cent.[53] It seemed as if the biggest winners of the voluntary agreement were the foreign interests and their cinematic allies, who were able to delay the push for intervention and wait out nationalist pressures until the quota issue began to fade away. The voluntary quota agreement continued to be so unsatisfactory that in 1978 the new secretary of state, John Roberts, revived the attempt to bring the provincial premiers on side with a legislated quota. As with previous approaches, he came up empty-handed, however, as no province other than Quebec was interested in involving itself in such a controversial idea.[54] Roberts then tried to renegotiate and improve on the voluntary quota, but to no avail.[55] The final nail in the coffin came soon after as Odeon merged with Canadian, forming Canadian Odeon Theatres, and withdrew from the agreement.[56] Provincial apathy, it seemed, had worked well for distributors and exhibitors.

The Trudeau administration's decision to increase the Capital Cost Allowance (CCA) fared no better as an aid to filmmaking. Robert Fulford, writing under the alias Marshall Delaney in *Saturday Night*, called it 'the national disgrace of the movie industry … a tax-shelter playground for unemployed stockbrokers and overpaid dentists.'[57] Or, as Gary Evans noted in his history of the National Film Board, 'dozens of producers took the money and ran, leaving much paper and few films worthy of distribution.'[58] Quality and distribution did not matter to many of those who viewed the CCA in economic terms, as all that one needed to do was make sure that the final product employed a minimum level of Canadians. As in other areas where Canadian content was quantified upon the use of industrial resources, the CCA turned out to merely be a numbers game. Keith Acheson and Christopher Maule have noted that 'Canadian content depended on obtaining enough citizenship points for different key functions such as director, leading actors, cinematographer, screen writer etc., and having 75% of the budget spent on Canadian inputs.'[59] These requirements did not, however, mean that Canadians were always readily employed. According to a report by the Canadian Conference of the Arts, CCA films costing under one million dollars had 97.3 per cent Canadian participation, while those costing over five million only had 55 per cent.[60] Bigger budgets meant a decrease in the use of Canadian resources. Hugh Faulkner was not off the mark in complaining that 'it is unfortunate but true that most Canadians consider Paul Newman and Robert Redford a safer investment than our home product.'[61]

The result was an increase in film production – from six features in 1968 to about twenty in 1977 – but many of them were not screened. The ones most likely to be picked up were those forged on Hollywood templates or created as cheap B-level fillers, films serving the interests of exhibitors much more than those of Canadianizers. These included *Death Weekend, Shadow of the Hawk, Pleasure Palace, City on Fire, Meatballs,* and *In Praise of Older Women.*[62] *Porky's,* a heavily sexualized teen comedy infamous for a scene in which a boy gets his penis painfully pulled when he is caught peeping on girls in the high school gym shower, made it clear that Canadians could make smut as well as anyone by taking in $150 million (U.S.) worldwide, a new Canadian record.[63]

That such questionable films were usually made to look American in origin – with the Canadian flag, currency, and licence plates replaced with the more marketable American versions – actually helped Canadianizers to continue defining Canadian content as being qualitatively superior to American offerings. These sorts of films were, after all, a far cry from the cinematic ideals embodied by *Goin' Down the Road* and *Mon Oncle Antoine,* and they threatened to include questionable elements within popular conceptions of Canadian cinematography. As Robert Miller sympathetically noted in *The Canadian Film Development Corporation: Promoting the Feature Film Industry in Canada*, disguising the origin of these sorts of films might be 'a blessing after all.'[64]

Perhaps even harder for nationalists to swallow was the idea that Canadian cinematography owed something to the success of morally questionable films. Just as the profits from American television programs helped stations to fund the production of domestic shows, so trashy Hollywoodesque films were among the few to return dollars to the Canadian Film Development Corporation. The point is well encapsulated in the words of Michael Spencer, someone who contributed greatly to the success of the CFDC during his time as executive director and later took on the position of secretary general of the Canadian Motion Picture Distributors Association (a body tied to American cinematic interests): 'If we produce *Porky's* and *Meatballs* and things like that, the money flows back into the industry. From that, we are able to produce quality material.'[65] It was a valid point, at least in monetary terms, because by 31 March 1978 only 13 of 193 funded films had returned a significant amount of money to the corporation.[66] That being said, one has to keep in mind that these films were the sole cash cows because other films, particularly those with distinctively Canadian elements, were not given screen time and the opportunity to attract audiences (and monies).

The Trudeau administration could do only so much in an area of cultural activity outside its jurisdiction, and given that the provinces continued to dismiss the idea of a quota system, the national cinematic industry became increasingly characterized by its ability to subsidize low-budget Hollywood knock-offs (and, in time, to subsidize high-budget films for Hollywood itself). Yet in terms of cultural industrialism, this outcome could be interpreted as a great success. As of 1977, there were 271 film production companies and laboratories with a gross revenue of $79.1 million and 1,609 employees. For their part, theatres paid over $69.6 million in salaries and generated over $14 million in amusement taxes for the government.[67] These figures were exactly what Secretary of State and Minister of Communications Francis Fox, who took on the portfolios in early 1980, sought as evidence of effective federal cultural guardianship. 'While the quality of some of the films has been called into question, there is no doubt that over the past few years we have successfully created a Canadian film industry in Canada,' he proudly announced to his bureaucratic colleagues in June of 1980.[68] Canadian talent and world-class production facilities were coming to stand as signs of cinematic achievement, and in turn the actual content became, for many, a non-issue.

Publishing and Ad Hoc Support

At first, the Federal Book Publishing Policy of 1972 seemed to be a great step forward for the members of an anemic industry. Kildare Dobbs of the *Toronto Star* told his readers that the policy was 'a victory for the new publishers, many of them radical nationalists who have lobbied and agitated with vigor and skill to win public assistance for the home-grown book business.'[69] The Trudeau administration, finding itself in agreement with nationalists and domestic publishers, opted to make funds available only to publishing houses in which Canadians had a majority ownership. Canadian books were in turn identified on the basis of the citizenship of the author (an approach that included landed immigrants), although, much like the infamous 'special interest' clause in the television regulations which included American presidential speeches and World Series baseball games, there was a loophole for any book by a foreigner if of 'a particular interest for Canada by virtue of its subject' or 'by the personality of the author or his ties with the country.'[70]

Distributing the monies directly to domestically owned publishing houses instead of to authors themselves served the agenda of cultural industrialism but in turn meant leaving some writers out in the cold. Morley Callaghan, Hugh MacLennan, and Robertson Davies, for example, were all on the roster of the foreign-owned Macmillan Company of Canada. The policy left the secretary of state open to criticism for supposedly identifying who was and who was not Canadian, but, in fact, it was an aid to the industry and not a judgment of identity. There was more than enough justification for limiting the funds to domestic presses, given that foreign-owned presses operated without the economic difficulties plaguing their Canadian counterparts and the authors on the rosters of foreign presses were usually there because they had already achieved a significant level of success. Hugh Faulkner hoped that authors who were not included in the program would take solace in the idea that they stood to benefit from gains made in raising the status of Canadian authors generally.[71]

That being said, not even the recipients were very happy because the program did little more than provide block grants; as Rowland Lorimer has explained, although these offered 'greater predictability and longer term planning, they were still essentially maintenance programs and did little to assist publishers to build their companies.'[72] The impact was certainly negligible. Foreign-owned book publishers made up approximately 63 per cent of the market in 1973, and four years later the number was still hovering around 65 per cent.[73] It was not until 1979, with the launching of the Canadian Book Publishing Development Program, that the federal government embarked on a more ambitious policy. Keeping in stride with the rhetoric Gérard Pelletier had used to introduce the previous publishing policy, John Roberts launched the new program by lauding how 'books by Canadians – books that articulate the ideas, attitude and values of Canadians and that provide information concerning every aspect of our individual, regional, and collective identity – are essential to the development of a greater knowledge of ourselves.'[74] Such rhetoric gave qualitative colour to an industrial initiative, one which, unlike its predecessor, did not assist struggling publishers but instead rewarded those that were already successful. 'While the bottom line was still cultural,' Rowland Lorimer has noted, 'the vehicle for addressing industry needs was to be industrial development assistance on top of assistance for cultural titles based on sales level and supported by the Canada Council.'[75] The federal government spent $5.7 million in 1979–80 and $6.8 million in 1980–1, and although the program was initially created to last two years, it was continually renewed until it was replaced in 1986 by the Book Publishing Industry Development Program, an initiative with a name that speaks volumes as to its industrial purpose.

The Trudeau administration, in limiting its economic aid to domestically owned publishing houses, was rather successful in helping to establish opportunities for expression in which authors did not have to pander to the interests of foreign publishers.[76] Talented authors and Canadian publishers still struggled against the dynamics of publishing in a small marketplace, yet at least there was state assistance to help get works into the hands of audiences. Opportunities for expression in defiance of market dynamics contributed to the ability of authors to show off their talent and in turn rewarded them with a standing that escaped many in other areas of cultural activity. As Paul Audley has noted in *Canada's Cultural Industries*, 'public attitudes toward television are totally different from public attitudes toward Canadian books. The public think of Canadian writers as bloody good, as good as anybody has, but when it comes to television, they think about it as, first of all, coming from central Canada and second, being low budget.'[77] Authors had the ability to operate on par with their foreign competition, while television producers, in attempting to create American-style products without American-style budgets, could be nothing but second-rate.

State intervention in the periodical sector, in avoiding subsidies in favour of removing the decade-old *Time* and *Reader's Digest* exemptions from legislation limiting income tax deductions for advertising to that taken in domestic periodicals, had just as telling an impact. 'It is with reluctance and deep regret that we announced last week the suspension of Time Canada after a third of a century of publication,' explained Stephen S. LaRue, president of Time Canada, in the 8 March 1976 issue. 'Canadian readers will now receive the U.S. edition of *Time*. Though it will continue to contain Canadian advertising, the magazine will no longer contain a Canadian editorial section.'[78] The statement reeked of LaRue's rubbing in the idea that the periodical would likely continue to attract domestic advertisers but that audiences would not benefit from the few pages of Canadian coverage. In other words, the federal government had accomplished nothing in its agenda of Canadianization other than harming its own citizens. LaRue may have been rather pretentious in downplaying the importance to national life of the removal of the exemption, given that, in the assessment of cultural industry expert Paul Audley, it dissuaded other publishers from launching split-run versions of their magazines.[79]

While Time Canada closed its split-run, Reader's Digest Canada was not so quick to surrender its privileged position in the Canadian marketplace. With the amendment to Bill C-58 requiring only that companies be Canadian-owned but not necessarily Canadian-controlled, Reader's Digest Canada placed 75 per cent of the company's shares in a charitable foundation with Canadian directors. Surprisingly, the backlash at this use of a loophole was not as severe as one might imagine. Unlike Time, which had printed its split-run in the United States, Reader's Digest had a plant in Canada. Many Canadians owed their wage to the periodical, and it had no lack of support. So much so, in fact, that a number of authors – including Kenneth Bagnell and Bruce Hutchinson – signed a letter sent to the federal government in defence of *Reader's Digest*. 'Over the years, *Digest* editors in Canada have been consistently fair and professional in their dealings with us,' the authors explained. 'The *Digest's* superior rates of payment help many writers and artists to survive in the precarious field of magazine journalism. Those fees also enable Canadian contributors to apply to Canadian subjects the time, depth of research and creativity they deserve.'[80] The monies made off the periodical, then, were being defended as a source of revenue for the production of Canadian content. If the marketplace could not be completely overhauled, then at least the revenue could be tapped into for domestic endeavours. That being said, one would not find such a positive spin on the situation if Time Canada had attempted to squeak through the loophole; *Reader's Digest* did not directly suffocate the livelihood of a nationally focused competitor as *Time* did with *Maclean's* in the highly valued area of newsmagazine coverage. Canada needed a national newsmagazine more than it did an indigenous version of *Reader's Digest*.

Academia, Hiring Changes, and Canadian Studies

In all the talk and controversy about Canadianization in academia, perhaps the most important issue was not whether universities were subject to the ebb and flow of the society in which they existed but that, if room was not made for Canadian academics and content, then the space would inherently be filled by foreign interests. The federal government had shown an awareness of this problem in passing legislation designed to help correct systemic discrimination against Canadian academics and, by offering funds for Canadian Studies programs, in making available opportunities for students to engage in content connected to the communities in which they lived. The $1.5 million allocated in 1979 was increased to $3.8 million in 1981 as part of the National Program of Support for Canadian Studies, helping to fund projects that included the publication of the colloquium proceedings of Le Centre d'Études Franco-canadiennes de l'Ouest, aid to a field study in the Arctic undertaken by Trent University's Department of Anthropology, and monies for the Atlantic Regional Studies Program at the University of New Brunswick.[81] A firm annual commitment was made as of 1984 with the establishment of the Canadian Studies Program (which had an initial annual budget of $3.7 million).

Further, the Department of External Affairs did much to assist programs and publications abroad. Among these were the Association for Canadian Studies in the United States (1971) and the *American Review of Canadian Studies*; the British Association for Canadian Studies (1975) and the *British Journal of Canadian Studies*; the French Association for Canadian Studies (1976) and *Études canadiennes/Canadian Studies*; the Italian Association for Canadian Studies (1979) and *Rivista di studi canadesi*; the Japanese Association for Canadian Studies (1979) and

Kanada kenkyu nenpo; the International Council for Canadian Studies (1981) and the *International Journal of Canadian Studies*; and the Association for Canadian Studies in Australia and New Zealand (1982) and *Australian-Canadian Studies*. All of this federal activity speaks loudly of a desire to reify the national project, at home and abroad, by placing it within influential sites of learned discourse. The scale would have astonished the intelligentsia who had founded the *Canadian Forum* half a century earlier.

The availability of Canadian Studies programs owed much to federal aid, but its ongoing popularity, at least at home, continued to derive from the nationalism of its participants. T.H.B. Symons, chairman of the Commission on Canadian Studies and architect of its report, *To Know Ourselves*, spoke out in 1979 about nationalism as 'a problem which is bedeviling Canadian Studies to a greater or lesser extent at many institutions.'[82] Making Canada a topic of academic study yet keeping it free of the sentiments that had led to its creation proved to be quite difficult. This was certainly the result in part of a lack of central guiding principles and curricula. Academic Jill Vickers has pointed out that the interdisciplinary structure has 'resulted in a lack of coherence in the sense that many universities in Canada, and now around the world, offer programs in Canadian Studies to undergraduates without any agreement on the basic parameters of the field, or key thinkers, key concepts or core texts.'[83] Nonetheless, in terms of Canadianization, the mere making of the nation itself into a topic of study stands out as a testament to the ability of nationalists and federalists to reify nationhood through the academy.

Conclusion

The Trudeau administration certainly left its mark on Canadian culture. The arm's-length relationship between the state and the arts was retracted through the earmarking of funds, while at the same time, cutbacks to the Canada Council pushed the funding body into giving greater consideration to Canadian content. In television the government seemed positively philosophical in its conviction that a quantitative change would ultimately lead to a qualitative transformation, although this leap of faith went unfulfilled as marketplace dynamics continued to ensure that Canadian content was based upon the minimum broadcasters could spend and still attract advertisers and audiences. Canadian content regulations for radio broadcasting led to a boon in the music industry and plenty of domestic albums, but station owners often limited the selection to artists who were already successful in the United States. At the very least, the regulations helped to facilitate a relationship between performers and audiences via publicly owned airwaves and offered artists the ability to develop a domestic presence without having to relocate to the United States. The feature-film sector did not fare very well in qualitative terms, but federal bureaucrats certainly found much to praise in the way of industry growth. Famous Players and Odeon (Canada) slipped out of the voluntary quota – after doing little to meet their obligations in the first place – and the increase to the Capital Cost Allowance led largely to the production of generic Hollywood-style films that padded the pocketbooks of producers. Despite the glaring problems, cultural bureaucrats found themselves able to point to industry activity as evidence of cinematic success. As for the publishing sector, many book publishers were able to remain more solvent, or at least subsistent, thanks to federal subsidies, while bringing an end to the *Time* and *Reader's Digest* exemption helped to level the playing field for domestic periodicals. Finally, changes in the academy meant that Canadian academics now had a better chance of securing employment, and for their part, students interested in studying Canada as a topic at the university level had an increasingly large number of courses and programs from which to choose.

Having boldly grasped cultural devices in the face of Québécois separatism, the Trudeau administration had intervened in systems of communication and identity creation in ways that led to results which both supported and confounded the quest for Canadian nationhood. Initial forays were rife with problems, but federal bureaucrats showed a tremendous awareness of the fact that the success to be had from mobilizing cultural devices depended in large part upon a willingness to endure the conflicts. And, quite fascinatingly, the state's cultural agenda came to fruition with a minimum of conflict. Bureaucrats found it increasingly easy to satiate nationalistic cultural workers and conciliate private-sector profiteers by developing the industry from which both sides drew their incomes; money-making, if only as the beneficiary of a subsidized lifestyle, proved to be popular with many people on the pro- and anti-intervention sides of the debate. The government, with so much of cultural industrialism entailing a shift from funding the public sector to investing in the private alternative, could not help but be happy with the evidence of monies well spent.

There was no lack of statistics testifying to the accomplishments of bureaucrats. Royalties to members of the Composers, Authors and

Publishers Association of Canada (which merged in 1990 with the Performing Rights Organization of Canada to form the Society of Composers, Authors and Music Publishers of Canada) rose from $364,000 in 1968 (the first year of Trudeau's prime ministership) to $419,000 in 1969, more than doubled to $871,000 by 1971, leaped to $1,315,000 in 1973, and by 1977 reached the whopping level of $2,256,000. It was a staggering increase, more than quadrupling in the five years between 1968 and 1973 and, measured on a longer time scale, increasing 519 per cent between 1968 and 1977.[84] With so much in the way of economic activity – and bureaucratically assembled statistics – testifying to the impact of federal intervention, one cannot be surprised that many people supported the initiatives. In turn, the fact that so much of the content actually failed to promote the national project envisioned by Trudeau and that some of it even worked against the desire to open outlets of communication to domestic discourse increasingly came to be a non-issue.

Federal bureaucrats oversaw an extended alteration to the cultural sphere serving their interests by, in large part, securing the support of cultural workers and industrialists. Not everyone embraced the changes with open arms, of course; cultural industrialism was not fully in accord with the desires of many nationalists, the artists who sought to keep the state at an arm's-length distance from culture, and those in the private sector who decried the federal attempts to increase levels of Canadian content. Pleasing all sides was an impossible task. The federal government did manage, however, to negotiate its way through a minefield, and in doing so, it secured itself a position of cultural leadership. Bureaucrats now had the ability to influence the grounds upon which cultural activity, economically and ideologically, took place. Canadianization and the quest for nationhood came to rest within the hands of the very government that had long done much to avoid cultural entanglements. Vincent Massey would have been aghast.

9 From Citizens to Consumers: Cultural Industrialism and the Commodification of Canadian Content

Cultural grants looked at exclusively in economic terms can be strongly justified in those terms alone, leaving aside all the cultural arguments that could be brought to bear in support.

Secretary of State James Hugh Faulkner, 1975[1]

Although 'culture' defies precise definition, its dispersion depends more and more on an industrial base.

Francis Fox, secretary of state
and minister of Communications, 1980[2]

At the 1979 Juno Awards, the annual celebration of Canadian music, an unlikely presenter walked on stage, and although his appearance there was slightly out of place, it made sense in a Canadian content sort of way. Pierre Trudeau was officially at the award show in order to induct Hank Snow into the Canadian Music Hall of Fame, but his presence had a much greater resonance. The Trudeau administration had overseen the growth of the Canadian recording industry during the previous decade thanks in large part to the efforts of Pierre Juneau and the Canadian Radio-television and Telecommunications Commission. It was not surprising, then, that Trudeau used the award show as an opportunity to rationalize the state's role in cultural activity and to argue that intervention was not a choice but a responsibility in order to ensure Canadian content.

If an artist creates and performs for himself or herself, he's also up against industrial competition. In Hollywood, in New York, in Europe and other parts of the world. And that's why it's not any more possible for any country to be without a cultural policy than it is to be without an industrial policy ... It's extraordinarily important that a policy be set up to make sure that the artist is not overwhelmed by the industry. And that the artist in a small country has equal chance with the artist in a large country – no matter the industrial power of that country. And that is why you find some policies like Canadian content in television and you find a policy which wants the book and magazine publishing distribution industry to have a greater Canadian content. Or you have a policy which wants to insure a greater distribution of Canadian films.[3]

Therein lay a testament to the importance of cultural industrialism, as it had been taking shape during the previous ten years, in the quest for nationhood.

Much had indeed happened over the course of the decade. The need to stabilize federal leadership and achieve national unity in the face of political challenges had prompted Trudeau into mobilizing cultural devices, but doing so, particularly given the need to justify the presence of the state, meant that much of it took on an industrial tone. This was a telling component of the shift in the paradigm of Canadianization. Whereas the new nationalist model of Canadianization had sought a Peaceable Kingdom via support for Canadian content no matter what the economic margin, the cultural industrialism launched by the Trudeau administration promised to achieve a similar form of civic nationhood (one rooted within a strong federalism) through opportunities for discourse piggybacked upon strong cultural industries. Yet this policy meant that cultural activities were increasingly conceptualized and operationalized in accordance with industrial precepts. Canadian content needed to not only be produced but also sold, its saleability enhanced through commodification and its vibrancy measured in terms of economic tallies. Much of the content coming out of cultural industrialism, then, was made as similar as possible to foreign works in order to make it of interest to distributors.

Thus out of the 1970s emerged a stark reversal of Trudeau's desire, yet – and very tellingly – the results worked well with the cultural bureaucracy of his making. From here on, cultural industrialism would define the temper of Canadianization under not only the Liberals but the Progressive Conservatives as well. Bureaucratically friendly and providing much in the way of economic rewards, cultural industrialism offered something to bureaucrats of all political stripes. That the last two decades of the twentieth century were marked by a turn towards neo-conservatism among both the Liberals and the Conservatives made this vein of Canadianization all the more attractive. Yet there would certainly be rough patches. Cultural workers, including many in the arts, had supported federal industrial initiatives as a means of securing greater state monies, only to now find themselves subject to cutbacks in times of fiscal restraint. Further, the free trade negotiations with the United States in the mid-1980s exposed how the cultural industries – and thus nationhood itself – were vulnerable to federal trade-policy decisions. But for federal bureaucrats seeking fiscal growth as evidence of successful cultural guardianship, and with a large number of Canadians drawing their income from the cultural economy, there was much benefit to be had by treating Canadian content as a commodity to be bought and sold.

Consumer Desire and Star Systems

Content of high-cultural constitution towards which Canadians were to 'naturally' gravitate; plays, books, and poetry addressing Canadian socio-economic concerns; media goods created with low budgets and offering little in the way of action and adventure – these were all characteristics of Canadian content at different points in the century, and all of it had limited success in attracting distributors and exhibitors who preferred the guaranteed profitability that came with imports. Canadian audiences were just as interested as their foreign counterparts in the glitz and glam of American celebrities – Elvis Presley and Bob Dylan in music, Lee Majors and James Garner in television, and Doris Day and Marlon Brando in film. Sometimes the stars were even expatriates whose work was imported by distributors seeking profitable 'American' content. Rich Little, William Shatner, Neil Young, and The Band all fall into this category. An interest in foreign content was just as true of the arts sector. William Shakespeare and George Bernard Shaw, for example, had festival theatres dedicated to their plays; arts institutions and organization knew that they could not go wrong in offering audiences a selection of 'classic' works.

The lack of interest in Canadian content, at least on the part of exhibitors, meant that Canada had an underdeveloped star system. 'There are too few Canadian stars, although there is plenty of talent,' as the Special Senate Committee on the Mass Media noted in its report in 1970.[4] One of the big reasons for this lack was that much of the top talent left and become famous in countries which offered more in the way of money and opportunities. At least such was the case in pan-national terms, as regional exceptions certainly exist, nowhere more so than in French Canada. The committee correctly pointed out that 'Quebec has its own Top Forty, its own sex goddesses, its own totem-intellectuals, its own feature-film industry, its own penny-dreadful press, its own little magazines, night talk shows, its own Bob Dylan.'[5] The sense of existing within a distinct community, as well as the role of like-minded exhibitors in contributing to this situation, allowed for one part of the country to have a thriving celebrity system isolated from the pan-national project.

The lack of a star system was certainly due in part to the activities of the Canadian Broadcasting Corporation. Creating Canadian content within a non-commercial paradigm had meant downplaying the presence of individual actors. The Committee of Inquiry into the National Broadcasting Service, the investigation into separatism at the CBC established by Pierre Trudeau in 1977 and headed by Harry Boyle, went so far as to berate the broadcaster for its 'no star' policy and failure to 'popularize our acting talents.'[6] Audiences, not the broadcaster, had made some performers, including Don Messer, Juliet, and Wayne and Shuster, into celebrities. The lack of stars was a problem that the CBC, in the wake of Boyle's investigation and in line with ideas held by President Al Johnson, hoped to correct as part of the Touchstone policy, discussed in the previous chapter. The turn towards celebrity-based programming at the CBC was a clear sign of the changing times of Canadianization and how even the national broadcaster found itself coming on board with a model that emphasized celebrities, marketing, name recognition, and so forth in selling Canadian content.

A star system is only one means by which content can be sold, of course. Nationalism offers much to commoditizers seeking a marketplace advantage. The MAPL identifier in the music industry, for example, is a small pie-shaped symbol divided into four quarters with the letters M, A, P, and L – music, artist, producer, and lyrics – identifying which component was provided by a Canadian. Back in 1971, following the establishment of radio Canadian content requirements, Stan Klees of *RPM* magazine created the symbol to help broadcasters figure out which releases counted towards their quota requirement, but it soon caught on among sellers hoping to lure nationalistic buyers. 'The *RPM* MAPL logo was so popular that many record companies requested permission to utilize the logo on record labels,' an *RPM* study reminisced.[7] The logo was so effective, in fact, that Jack Shapiro, chair of the Canadian Publications Committee of the Periodical Distributors of Canada, wanted the publishing industry to create something similar. His hope, as he told readers of *Quill & Quire* in May of 1973, was for 'a common distinctive "Canadian logo" which would readily identify a book as Canadian in the eyes of the consumer … some appropriate symbol would improve the merchandising potential … With the prevalent feeling of Canadianism and with effective promotion and merchandising the consumer is willing to pay more for a Canadian title.'[8] This idea has more recently been implemented to great effect by Magazines Canada (a body that includes the former Canadian Magazine Publishers Association), which, as of 2002, has provided a 'Genuine Canadian Magazine' emblem for use by its members.

A Federal Commoditization of Canadian Content

Few things are as telling of cultural industrialism as the ways in which federal bureaucrats, in needing to continue the economic growth upon which they justified their presence in cultural activities, turned from aiding domestic discourse to encouraging the creation of content of interest to foreign buyers. 'We are not just talking about a quaint Canadian culture but about developing a business which we can then export and compete with in the marketplace, in exactly the same way that the Americans and others have done so successfully here,' argued a member of the Standing Committee on Broadcasting, Film, and Assistance to the Arts in May of 1973.[9] This was not as controversial a statement as one might think. Even Pierre Juneau, the highly praised Canadianizer of the broadcasting system, had told the committee a few years earlier that it was 'indispensable to find a way to encourage export of Canadian programs.' Juneau went so far as even to support the use of co-productions favouring the interests of foreign markets. 'It is through co-production between Canadian broadcasters and foreign broadcasters that large and viciously expensive productions will take place. Those productions will be easier to export.'[10]

In other words, Canadians were to collaborate in Americanization not only at home – as distributors and exhibitors had long been doing – but abroad, creating Canadian content attuned to the interests of foreign distributors largely attracted to American-style material. The idea certainly appealed to profit-minded industrialists. Don Brinton, vice-chair of television at the Canadian Association of Broadcasters, showed no shame in using this concept as a defence for member stations choosing to make programs as similar as possible to the American competition; he told the CRTC in December of 1981 that 'production must be attractive to foreign customers, who often express the concerns, rightly or wrongly, that Canadian themes will not attract audiences especially in the U.S. In any business "the customer is always right," and their views must be respected if a sale is to be made.'[11] The customers here, the people supposedly being served, were not the Canadians whose airwaves were used by broadcasters to make money but the foreign buyers who offered more in the way of sales. This focus meant that program producers needed to strip Canadian content of national identifiers in favour of American equivalents. *The Littlest Hobo*, a series about a dog named London who travelled from city to city helping strangers, and *Night Heat*, a CTV and CBS co-production, are memorable examples of this approach in television. It was a technique which, as explored last chapter, also aided in the economic success of Capital Cost Allowance films such as *Porky's* and *Meatballs*.

Sales, whether at home or abroad, required more than merely producing the goods, of course: Canadian content had to be made sellable through the use of marketing and advertising campaigns. Given that doing so was often beyond the means of producers barely able to cover production expenses, the federal government had to begin subsidizing not only production but marketing as well. After all, the bureaucrats justified federal intervention into cultural activities on industrial terms, and if the industry failed, then so too did the government. The two areas requiring the most support were those that lacked quotas and suffered from the difficulty of recouping production expenses in a small marketplace: book publishing and feature-film making. For the book industry, the Department of the Secretary of State put funds towards the development of export markets and advertising. In 1975, for example, $1.5 million was allocated to these ends.[12] The non-profit Association for the Export of Canadian Books, founded in 1972 to catalogue works, conduct foreign market research, advise publishers on accessing foreign markets, and support information campaigns abroad, was a primary recipient from this fund.[13] A few years later this assistance was taken up a notch with the start of the Canadian Book Publishing Development Program (1979).

Initiatives undertaken in book publishing, although quite impressive, were overshadowed by those in the feature-film sector. Year after year during the 1970s one finds federal bodies allocating money for the marketing of films both in Canada and abroad. The Canadian Film Development Corporation began sending reels to the Cannes Film Festival at the beginning of the 1970s and, as of 1971, teamed up with the National

Film Board, the Department of Industry, Trade and Commerce, the Canadian Government Exhibition Commission, and representatives from the private sector to operate an advertising booth at the festival.[14] A year later the Department of the Secretary of State – or more precisely, the Film Division of its Arts and Culture Branch – created a Festivals Office to coordinate Canadian participation at Cannes and a variety of other international film festivals. The goal of the Festivals Office, as stated in the Department of the Secretary of State's 1973 *Annual Report*, was to develop 'effective methods of promoting, advertising and disseminating Canadian films both at home and abroad.'[15] In 1973 the Association of Canadian Television and Radio Artists called for a Canadian film-marketing board, and in that same year these concerns were addressed by a decision at the Canadian Film Development Corporation to 'extend its financial assistance so that more funds could be used for promotion to ensure better marketing and wider distribution of its films in Canada.'[16] In 1974 the corporation funded the advertising campaigns of nine English-language and six French-language films, including *The Apprenticeship of Duddy Kravitz, Black Christmas, Les Ordres*, and *Bingo*, the success of which were singled out as evidence that 'this type of investment is worthwhile.'[17] The next year the corporation supported eleven English-language and nine French-language films because, as its *Annual Report* explained, 'one of the most critical aspects of box office success is the creation of advertising and promotional material with strong impact and motivation.'[18] By 1977–8 the corporation was spending almost half a million dollars on the publicity campaigns of a whopping thirty-six films.[19]

Federal initiatives in the feature-film sector reveal not only an interest in marketing and exporting Canadian content but, and much more telling of cultural industrialism, a shift from investing in the production of films to the developing of an industry in and of itself. Bureaucrats determined the success of Canadian content upon the ability to attract foreign investment and boost employment levels; not only did films need to be marketed internationally but so too did the notion that Canada possessed a vibrant film production industry. The Canadian Film Development Corporation, it explained in its *Annual Report* for 1979–80, was now putting an 'emphasis on promoting Canada as a major filmmaking country.'[20] It was a controversial decision. Filmmaker Allan King was one of many cinematic craftspeople who took offence at this industrial imperative. 'We have the CFDC going to Cannes with an advertising campaign to say that Canada "really" is in the film business, that we make *real* films here,' complained King (whose films included a cine-matic adaptation of W.O. Mitchell's *Who Has Seen the Wind*) in the spring 1981 issue of the *Journal of Canadian Studies*.[21] Bureaucrats and cultural industrialists

> want to advertise that they really are in the film business and they spend a lot of money convincing the world and, of course, themselves that they are really in it. I can understand the impulse, but it certainly creates skepticism in the rest of us. When [CFDC executive director] Michael McCabe says that what he did was create a film industry in the two years he was in office, and I hear other people agreeing that that was the case, I find it all a little laughable. I wonder what the rest of us have been doing for the past twenty-five years? Those of us who have been making features for the last ten years, what have we been doing in all that time? There has been film activity here for a long time.[22]

'Activity' and 'industry,' however, are not the same thing when tabulated in bureaucratic ledgers. Cultural industrialism required economic evi-dence, whereas, for other approaches, the measurement was in terms of artistry and expression.

That commoditization became so predominent in areas of mass media was in many ways less surprising than the degree to which it occurred within the arts. Of course, that being said, an overview of the relationship between the arts and industry shows a clear progression towards the commoditization of craftsmanship. During the first half of the twentieth century the arts were increasingly professionalized, much to the disapproval of those who viewed them as an amateur experience best kept away from commerce; in the 1960s much was done to sell the federal government on the idea that the arts were a major contributor to the economy and should be funded as an industry; and by the 1970s many in the cultural community had fully subscribed to the merits of commoditizing their craft. Testament to this shift is the provocatively titled *A Strategy for Culture: Proposals for a Federal Policy for the Arts and the Cultural Industries in Canada*, published by the Canadian Conference of the Arts in 1980. A few of its recommendations are worth quoting at length:

> International activity should be regarded as a direct extension of our domestic cultural policy. Encouragement to create Canadian materials and

enable them to compete effectively for interest in our domestic market should be supported by policies designed to develop ways and means to distribute these materials internationally on a continuing basis.

Provided that efforts are made to actively develop international market demand for Canadian books, periodicals, films, recordings, television programs, paintings, sculpture, craft objects and other Canadian cultural materials, we are convinced that Canada can reap significant political, social and economic benefits.

Quite apart from the direct economic benefits resulting from foreign sales of our cultural products, heightened international interest in Canada's culture can lead to long-term trade benefits for other sectors of the Canadian economy.

The recommendations put forward ... are designed to create a less unbalanced competitive relationship between Canadian cultural products and their foreign counterparts. [23]

The Canadian Conference of the Arts was by no means alone in calling for the arts to be commoditized. As the Canada Council noted in 1981, the idea of the arts as a 'cultural industry' was 'in the process of becoming the new dogma of arts support theory.'[24] It should come as no surprise, then, to see the Federal Cultural Policy Review Committee, chaired by composer Louis Applebaum and the first wide-scale survey of cultural life since the Massey Commission, in 1982 also putting forth ways in which the arts could be better commoditized.

Canadian artists and their work must be publicized – and marketed – more effectively than they have been in the past. Success in these efforts will stimulate demand for and consumption of the cultural output of the country. In the process, public recognition of our artists will be expanded and their financial rewards improved.

In the same way that buyers of everyday goods and services – peas, shoes or tennis balls – economize on information by responding to goodwill, brand names and trademarks, so do buyers of artistic and cultural products economize on information by a reliance on 'stars,' which can be performing arts companies as well as individuals.

> If this marketing and promotion organization [proposed by the committee in its report] is to be successful, one of its goals will be to promote stars. Stars not only help buyers choose but also serve to highlight various kinds of excellence. They should be recognizable not only among rock musicians and film actors, but also among composers, choreographers, painters, writers, and performing arts companies.[25]

The government had a responsibility, the committee argued, to 'take the lead' in marketing Canadian content by creating an institution dedicated to this task.[26] Similarly, in 1986 the Task Force on the National Arts Centre called upon the NAC to do more to advertise the arts at home and abroad. An entire chapter of its report was even dedicated to developing marketing strategies.[27] It would be hard to imagine a greater reversal of the recommendations put forth by the Massey Commission a mere thirty years earlier.

Culture and Cutbacks in the Eighties

'Culture is not only a matter of artistic creation and appreciation, it is an economic activity that has become a multi-billion-dollar-a-year industry in Canada.'[28] To hear such a statement from the Department of Communications, the chief administrator of federal cultural industrialism as of the beginning of the 1980s, was not surprising. Economic growth was in the air. Statistics would later show that employment in the cultural industries had increased 74 per cent between 1971 and 1981, almost double the rate of the rest of the workforce.[29] The Department of the Secretary of State had done very well in its guardianship of cultural life and nationhood, at least in terms of cultural industrialism, but the massive bureaucracy of cultural bodies, subsidy programs, and private-sector initiatives developed by Trudeau and his cultural lieutenants increasingly necessitated a more appropriate administrator. For this role the government chose the Department of Communications, created back in 1969, during the early years of the Trudeauvian cultural bureaucracy boom, and one well situated for expanding federal interests in cultural activity.

Industry growth, although characterizing the cultural sector throughout the 1970s, certainly could not continue unabated. The bubble had to burst at some point – in this case at the end of the decade amid a slumping economy and fiscal problems that prompted the federal government to tighten the nation's belt. It was a wake-up call for all those who had tied their cultural prosperity to industrial precepts and the ebb and flow of the economy and political interests. Cultural workers found out that in a time of downturn their income was as subject to cutbacks as any other areas of state subsidy and investment; the many artists who had fought for recognition and support on an industrial level now had to deal with the problems entailed in doing so.

At the CBC, where relations with the government had become quite strained, some people felt that the failure to deliver the heads of separatists on a silver platter to Trudeau had something to do with the decrease in state funds. In the opinion of Knowlton Nash, 'the government was becoming tight-fisted and less supportive of the CBC president, at least partly because it was losing faith in his ability or desire to clean house in the French network. Retribution came financially as the government initiated its restraint program and reneged on earlier promises of increased and long-term funding.'[30] These initiatives included cutting $71 million from the proposed $574 million budget for the CBC's 1979–80 season, a move that left the network with even less money to put towards its dynamic new Touchstone agenda of producing solid Canadian entertainment.[31] And the CBC was but one site facing a drop in federal funds. The spectre of cutbacks was powerful enough to make the issue important in the lead up to the federal election on 22 May 1979, the results of which brought the Progressive Conservatives, led by Joe Clark, to power for the first time since Diefenbaker's era, although this administration would last only until the following February, when another election was held and Pierre Trudeau was returned one last time.

But unlike Clark's prime ministership, fiscal conservatism was not about to go away any time soon. The Trudeau administration continued to claw back federal expenditures in the cultural sector, particularly from the public institutions that did not provide a substantial economic return to federal coffers, a policy taken to further lengths following the election of Brian Mulroney and the Progressive Conservatives in September 1984. Coming into power was an administration with little interest in federal intervention and measures promoting domestic cultural and economic sovereignty. The Canadian Development Corporation, a body that had done much to help 'buy back' key industrial areas from American investment, was sold off, while the Foreign Investment Review Agency was replaced by Investment Canada, a body geared towards increasing levels of foreign investment. The watchtowers of the Peaceable

Kingdom, essential to reifying the paradigm of nationhood imagined by the new nationalists and a generation of like-minded Canadians, were apparently under siege by an administration interested more in economic growth than in national sovereignty.

Nor would the public component of the cultural sector be spared similar treatment. 'Was it by good satiric management or sheer ironic chance,' the *Financial Post* noted, that when the new minister of Communications, Marcel Masse, made a presentation at the 1984 Junos, 'the award was for an album [by Bryan Adams] called "Cuts Like a Knife"?'[32] The comment came on the heels of the Conservative Party's decision to cut over a hundred million dollars of funding to the public sector, an area geared more towards encouraging domestic discourse than making money.[33] The cuts not only made neo-conservative sense but also testified to the fact that the public sector had little to offer the administrators of a cultural paradigm favouring the profits reaped from private-sector investment. The Canadian Broadcasting Corporation took the brunt of the hit with a $85-million decrease, while other cuts included $9.8 million from the Department of the Secretary of State's budget for cultural purposes, $7 million from the Department of Communications, $3.5 million from the Canada Council, $1.5 million from the National Film board, $1.5 million from the Canadian Radio-television and Telecommunications Commission, and $1 million from the National Arts Centre.[34] These cultural bodies needed to be treated as if they were any other business, Masse told the House of Commons, not only when it came to funding but also in their operations and production of Canadian content. Denying the CBC a sizeable chunk of its annual funding was a way of prompting it to 'better management' and making 'its international sales operations more aggressive than they have been in the past.'[35] Even the nationally mandated CBC, then, was to focus its production and sales not on the needs of Canadians but on those of foreign markets weaned on American entertainment. It would be hard to envision a more difficult position in which to place the national broadcaster.

The National Film Board, to no surprise, was undergoing just as radical a reworking. This long-standing cultured alternative to the private sector, one that did much to create a cinematic experience of national relevance, not only faced budget cuts but was also subjected to the National Film and Video Policy of 1984, a piece of legislation that retooled the board into a facility to aid in the development and training of talent for the private sector. Offering domestically relevant content was no longer a sufficient contribution to Canadian cultural life;

cultural industrialism dictated that the nationally mandated board must now aid in the economic growth of the private sector.

Bringing the Canadian Film Development Corporation, an initiative designed to develop the private sector, up to date with the demands of the cultural economy necessitated a different sort of treatment. In 1984 the corporation was replaced by Telefilm Canada as a means for the government to administrate initiatives in the television and film industries, with almost all of the effort and money being put towards the private sector. Telefilm was responsible for handling the new Canadian Broadcast Program Development Fund, which matched every two dollars put up by the private sector with one dollar from the fund; the Feature Film Fund, designed to increase the size of film budgets; the Canadian Production Marketing Assistance Fund, which advertised films, conducted test marketing, and launched foreign advertising campaigns; and the Festival Bureau, which was to assist Canadian participation in international film festivals.

By the late-1980s, cultural industrialism had become so paramount to federal cultural policy that it took on an almost untouchable status among bureaucrats. No document makes this clearer than *Vital Links: Canadian Cultural Industries* (1987), an eighty-page guide published by the Department of Communications as a means of informing the companies about issues ranging from market trends to risk-reduction techniques to ways of accessing foreign markets. 'These industries are the principle conveyors of Canadian culture to Canadians,' declared Minister of Communications Flora MacDonald in the preface to the book. 'They are the main investors in and developers of our cultural potential. Without a normal measure of financial predictability for such industries, our cultural development will suffer, as will our voices, our collective strength as a country and indeed the quality of our lives.'[36] In MacDonald's words one finds a stark reversal of the Masseyite desire to use culture to combat the ills of industrialization, commercialization, and commodification. Canadian nationhood now hinged upon those very elements. The individual had given way to the industry; arts organizations had been replaced by bureaucracies as the sites of cultural orchestration; the social value of the public sector had been supplanted by the economic value of the private sector. That the federal government could pursue a rigidly economic agenda yet brazenly guise it within the rhetoric of strengthening Canadian 'voices' and 'the quality of our lives' testified to the strength of cultural industrialism as both a policy and a measure of cultural vitality.

Keeping Culture 'off the Table'

One of the big problems with positing nationhood upon the economic strength of cultural industries, apart from all of the qualitative setbacks and depersonalization it entailed, was about to become more than apparent to many Canadians. In May 1986 the governments of Brian Mulroney and U.S. president Ronald Reagan began discussions about the possibility of a free trade agreement, the establishment of which would, in the view of many Canadians, subject Canadian industries – including the cultural ones – to the interests of a much larger and more dominant power. The marketplace, which had been vested with developing cultural life and nationhood, now seemed like a rug about to be pulled out from under Canada's feet. One poll reported that half of Canadians thought that including cultural industries in the proposed agreement would threaten the nation.[37]

Yet Mulroney had few qualms about engaging in the talks, an initiative backed in large part by business interests, principally represented during the debates by the Canadian Alliance for Trade and Job Opportunities and the Business Council on National Issues, which viewed continentalism as a great opportunity for money-making. For the government to place the national project in jeopardy for the benefit of profiteers did not, of course, go unchallenged. The Council of Canadians, a group uniting nationalist veterans such as Melville Watkins with newer activists such as Maude Barlow and the Pro Canada Network, was at the forefront of the anti-free-trade movement. This faction, as with previous nationalist movements, attracted both intellectuals and industry bodies, including the Alliance of Canadian Cinema, Television and Radio Artists, the Canadian Conference of the Arts, and the Writers' Union of Canada, who sought to protect ideological and economic interests. The *Toronto Star,* long a supporter of nationalist sentiments, explained to its readership that 60 per cent of publishing revenue went to twenty-nine American subsidiaries, 67 per cent of film distribution revenue went to nineteen American subsidiaries, and 89 per cent of sound recording revenue went to foreign companies.[38]

That the two sides would act out their conflict on the national stage was quite predictable. In some ways more telling, however, was the actual composition of the government's negotiating team – the people who were supposedly there to protect the Canadian interests. Gordon Ritchie was selected for the position of deputy chief negotiator, the same person who in 1970, as noted earlier in this book, had attacked Canadian content regulations, compared the CRTC to Nazi propagandist Joseph Goebbels, and described television station owners as grovelling victims kept under the thumb of the broadcasting regulator. The delegation also included Michael Hart, someone whose published recollections about the negotiations display a tremendous narrow-mindedness if not bigotry in describing the anti-free-trade side: 'mischief makers' who 'fall into three broad types: nationalists, idealists [including "radical feminists and church groups"], and protectionists.'[39] Arguments from the 'culture mafia,' as he called them, should be dismissed because cultural issues 'deal less with the head than with the heart.'[40] A Conservative Canada, it appeared, had little interest in issues of the heart.

Brian Mulroney and Joe Clark (as secretary of state for External Affairs) worked to placate public naysayers by assuring audiences that culture would not be included in the agreement. The problem with making this claim, however, was that, as the Americans would more than testify, there was little in the way of agreement as to what constituted culture. American trade negotiators equated 'culture' largely with 'entertainment' and wanted full access to all the related industries. Political scientist G. Bruce Doern has described how 'throughout the negotiations, because the special access that U.S. cultural industries had to President Reagan, the Americans insisted on treating culture as just another name for the entertainment business, rather than something central to Canadian identity.'[41] Consequently, the Canadian request that the cultural industries be exempted from the negotiations appeared to the American delegation to be, or at the very least was identified and criticized as being, no more than a Canadian desire to protect a lucrative industrial sector. Little if any sympathy was shown for the struggle to ensure cultural discourse in a domestic marketplace favouring imports, let alone the broader importance that Canadians placed upon culture as a means of consolidating nationhood.

The American delegation showed no qualms about characterizing Canadian cultural subsidies as unfair, yet, and quite tellingly, the United States government actually did as much if not more to protect its cultural industries at home and abroad. Historian Graham Carr has noted that the difference between Canadian and American cultural intervention and aid, and the reason why the American delegation was able to target Canadian protectionism with little concern about jeopardizing its own, was because of the virtual invisibility of American cultural assistance. 'The emphasis on direct subsidization disguises the fact that the bulk of [American] government support comes indirectly, in the form of hidden subsidies to artists and institutions, and through tax exemptions designed to encourage individual and corporate sponsorship of culture ... From the conventional American standpoint, the beauty of this system lies in its ability to preserve the myth that state intervention is unnecessary and potentially dangerous in the cultural sphere, and that private philanthropy and corporate "giving" are sufficient to do the trick.'[42]

In addition, American cultural intervention at home was accompanied by significant incursions into foreign markets on the behalf of its industries and the government's ideological interests. A few examples are state assistance to Hollywood during the 1930s by securing markets in Canada and overseas, tying funds for European reconstruction to the opening of markets for American products (including entertainment goods), and the American government acting on the behalf of Henry Luce and other periodical publishing moguls in threatening to not ratify the Auto Pact if the Paperback and Periodical Distributors Act (1964) was passed without exemptions by the Canadian government.[43] In fact, during the time of the free-trade negotiations, Flora MacDonald proposed the Film Products Importation Bill as a means of increasing the access of distributors to Canadian films – at the expense of the Hollywood monopolies – through a licensing system, only to have the Motion Picture Association of America complain to Washington; the American government in turn warned that the Free Trade Agreement might not be ratified if the legislation was passed. The result was that the Conservative government backed down and instead introduced a watered-down Film Distribution Policy focused on economic aid instead of correcting infrastructural imbalances.[44]

Despite promises to the contrary, Brian Mulroney did not keep culture off the table. Canadian negotiators conceded to including in the agreement the 'inputs' and 'products' of cultural industries (including recording and photographic equipment) on the duty-free list; a measure regarding ownership and the selling of the subsidiaries of cultural industries; provisions for cable transmission rights; and a cancellation of the provision in the Paperback and Periodical Distributors Act that magazine material be re-edited in Canada in order for a foreign-based periodical to be classified as Canadian and thus that advertisers be allowed a tax deduction for space purchased.[45] Yet these concessions were minor compared to a major concession made by the Canadian negotiators. Article 2005, paragraph 1, allows the Canadian government to exempt cultural products, but it is followed by paragraph 2, a 'notwithstanding clause' that allows the United States to retaliate through equivalent action in any other trade area. This provision has led John Herd Thompson to comment that 'the Canadian government's claim that Canada's cultural legislation has any privileged position in the FTA is specious; the most generous interpretation would be that the FTA restores the cultural *status quo ante bellum*: Canada can keep the policies it already has, but the United States has the power to retaliate against them in any sector it wishes.'[46] The Canadian delegation let the Americans use culture as a bartering chip – the ability to retaliate against Canadian cultural protectionism – and win what was no less than an ipso facto inclusion of the cultural industries.

The passing of the Free Trade Agreement hinged on the 1988 election, and despite early signs of Canadians voting against it (and the Progressive Conservative Party), in the end Mulroney was given a second majority government and the fate of the Free Trade Agreement was sealed. It was with much less conflict that the Canadian and American governments expanded the agreement in 1994 to include Mexico as part of the North American Free Trade Agreement. In the end, perhaps the most telling part of this process was not that culture was included in the agreement but that, as testified to by the degree of public concern about the negotiations, the very existence of a 'cultural industry' to be protected, subsidized, debated, and 'kept off the table' suggested a reified concept of culture conforming to globalization and neo-liberalism. Keeping 'it' off the table confirmed culture as a commodifiable 'it.'

Conclusion

Back in 1980, Brian Arnott and Sonja Tanner, in 'Hard Art/Soft Art,' a contribution to the David Helwig–edited collection *Love and Money: The Politics of Culture*, criticized the fact that 'business, it is now reasoned, can be called upon to save culture.'[47] Yet as both the 1970s and the 1980s made clear, the saviour was not only business but all the tools and techniques of commodification that aided in making, measuring, and selling culture. The federal government, as the architect of the third and current model of Canadianization, cast off the qualitative elements that had been fundamental to the new nationalism, purged Canadianization of the difficulty entailed in identifying the ambiguous and elusive sense of what constituted Canadianness in the contemporary age, and placed the success of cultural activity within the elements that culture had been once used to offset. The Masseyites had posited Canadian content in qualitatively based high-cultural terms in hope that by the raising of public tastes the nation would be 'elevated' above all-things-mass. A strong interest in ensuring qualified, if not quality, Canadian content permeated the new nationalism and the popular interest in engaging in discourse and content that did not have to conform to foreign templates or profitability. But now, with federal bureaucrats having taken the reins of Canadianization and with cultural workers and industrialists seeking employment and economic gains, this configuration had all changed. Identifying cultural vitality with market value; Canadian content as a commodity to be marketed, advertised, and exported; industrialism and commercialism as fundamental to the quest for nationhood – none of these ideas fitted with the earlier paradigms of Canadianization, but they all made sense within cultural industrialism.

The belief that production in and of itself would contribute to national discourse turned out to be unfounded as distributors and exhibitors continued to show an unwilling to open the systems of communication to works other than those forged on American templates of proven profitability. The federal government then had little choice but to begin subsidizing the means by which consumer desire could be fostered not only for the sake of selling subsidized goods but also because sales and industry statistics were being used to justify and legitimize the state's incursion into cultural activities. This reality meant that Canadian content had to be made sellable by employing the same techniques used by Americans to get their goods into foreign marketplaces – celebrities, big budgets, marketing and advertising campaigns. Budgets had to be increased by securing foreign sales and engaging in co-productions with other countries. And the approach seemed to work. Money rolled in as investors and financial institutions, long unwilling to take a chance on investing in domestic cultural production, tuned into the profits to be had by the creation of big-budget goods in line with the interests of domestic and foreign distributors. The cultural economy boomed, and bureaucrats, with plenty of economic evidence of their successful cultural guardianship, continued to pursue Canadianization along the lines of cultural industrialism.

What worked for bureaucrats and cultural industrialists did not, however, necessarily contribute to the quest for nationhood. Tailoring Canadian content to foreign markets meant limiting the ability to produce something primarily of interest to Canadians. Instead of securing outlets for Canadian content at home, the administrators and economic beneficiaries of cultural industrialism placed the focus upon competing against the Americans on similar terms and with similar goods. The variety and selection of Canadian content was thus inherently narrowed in the name of cultural growth. That federal bureaucrats financially encouraged this phenomenon speaks volumes as to how the self-appointed guardians of culture and nationhood were more than happy to reap the economic benefits of subsidizing Canadian content made for foreign markets, instead of ensuring opportunities for domestic discourse first and foremost on Canadian terms.

Federal resoluteness in the face of such contradictions not only continued, thanks to the strength of the cultural economy, but even managed to survive the problems arising from the Free Trade Agreement negotiations. The government showed a tremendous ability to equate economic growth with social good and cast industrial activities in the rhetoric of aiding national expression and exchange. The will of Canadians to operationalize culture upon the industrial precepts would continue to be tested, however, as continentalism turned into globalization, and like modernity a century earlier, new technologies and international forces introduced challenges that needed to be addressed by those who employed culture in the quest for nationhood.

10 Canadianization in a Time of Globalization

Those who apply for federal funding know that you raise your chances of success if you get 'marketing' into the title of your brief. Add 'international' and you're home free. Theatre companies requesting money to pay actors may get nowhere; they should instead ask for twice as much but stipulate that it's for 'expanding our subscriber base in the Greater Chicago Area.' The cheque arrives by return mail.

Robert Fulford, columnist, 2001[1]

The sheer size of the subsidies and of the attendant bureaucracies combine to give the illusion of cultural health.

John Metcalf, literary critic, 1988[2]

Modernity, unleashing a surge of technologies a century earlier, had both challenged and aided the ability of nation-builders to imprint a national design; globalization similarly brought forth new technologies and cultural interaction, complicating the use of culture in the quest for nationhood. Looking at globalization in broad terms, political scientist Stephen McBride has succinctly summarized how,

economically, globalization is marked by major increases in international trade and investment, the evolution of global production by transnational corporations, and unregulated flows of capital. Politically, globalization theorists point to the erosion of nation-states as the key unit in which political decisions are made; the leakage of sovereignty to supranational organizations on the one hand and to subnational units on the other; and, sometimes, to the emergence of neo-liberalism as a global ideology.

Culturally, globalization is held to bring a rather chaotic mix of homogenization (the McDonaldization of the world) and differentiation (the rise of ethno-nationalism on one side and identity politics on the other).[3]

This analysis rings true in the case of Canadianization in a time of globalization. Federal bureaucrats attempted to increase the influx of foreign cultural economic investment and the outflow of co-produced, branch-plant, and multinational content, only to find, with increasing frustration yet no sign of disillusionment, that transnationalism entailed producing goods tailored to external interests and surrendering key elements of domestic cultural policy. The economic benefits did, however, seem to give the orchestrators of Canadianization plenty of justification for continuing along the same path, particularly since rhetorical grandstanding allowed for the contribution made by culture to nationhood to be taken as a given. Quantification stood in as evidence of qualitative success. Or, looked at in another way, the fact that production and opportunities for expression were not one in the same became a non-issue.

Bureaucrats had no problem coming up with the most heartening of speeches. 'Rapidly growing exports not only strengthen the bottom line and the vitality of Canadian cultural industries, but also help brand Canada around the world as the diverse and innovative country it has become,' exclaimed the Department of Canadian Heritage in introducing its Tomorrow Starts Today program, an initiative involving more than $500 million in subsidies, investment, and economic development for the cultural industries.[4] Announcing the new program to an audience in Toronto on 2 May 2001, Minister of Canadian Heritage Sheila Copps blended the traditional rhetoric of cultural guardianship with praise for the industries through which cultural vitality was to be achieved.

The Government in Canada is demonstrating, in the most concrete way possible, its support for Canadian arts and culture. We are giving our creative people, we are giving Canadians the tools they need to bring Canadian arts and culture into the 21st century ... To foster a diverse, inclusive and enriching society, we need not only buildings and bridges, and doctors and soldiers, we need also words and images, songs and dance, artists and creators ... In today's increasingly borderless world, it's more important than ever we make sure our children have the opportunity to see reflections of their lives, their realities, and their stories, when they open a book, switch on the television, buy a CD, or surf the Internet ... The cultural sector contributes over 22 billion dollars to our Gross Domestic Product. It employs over 640,000 Canadians ... I am proud to be a member of a government that recognizes the critical role of arts and culture plays in our lives, and in our society. And that realizes that if our own culture is to flourish, it must be cultivated.[5]

Herein lies an amazing echo of the Masseyites: culture as the way a population learns about itself; cultural activity as being as important to the nation as science, defence, and trade; and cultural growth as something requiring cultivation. Yet there are significant differences. One cannot but detect the intertwining of culture and economics, how cultivation is equated with industrial development, how spiritualism and enlightenment have been replaced by employment and sales, and how, in some ways most telling, the fact that all of this praise and exaltation was coming not from artists and culturists but the government itself. Much had changed since the Masseyites fought with gentlemanly vigour to convince federal bureaucrats that culture was essential to nationhood. That the state now had significant influence over defining culture and its outlets of expression and engagement, however, would have left them horrified.

Vincent Massey, as discussed in the vignette to chapter 2, warned against the creation of a 'Ministry of Fine Arts' or 'Department of National Culture.' Yet had bureaucrats not built themselves something quite similar? The first comprehensive federal cultural policy, formed back in 1968 by the Trudeau administration, seems prehistoric compared to the extensive influence possessed by the Department of Canadian Heritage, created in 1993 as the new monolithic arm of federal cultural guardianship. The department's purpose was spun within the traditional acting-on-behalf-of-all-Canadians rhetoric of 'promoting the creation, dissemination and preservation of diverse Canadian cultural works, stories and symbols reflective of our past and expressive of our values and aspirations.'[6] Such language works well for press releases, but much more telling is the scale and character of the department's cultural roster. The Canadian Heritage portfolio has the big names one would expect: the Canada Council, the Canadian Broadcasting Corporation, Telefilm, the National Gallery, the National Arts Centre, the Canadian Radio-television and Telecommunications Commission, and the National Film Board. But this is not all. The true nature of the department is in some ways better evidenced in its vast array of programs and initiatives designed to develop the cultural economy, a sample of which includes Arts Presentation Canada, the Book Publishing Industry

Development Program, the Canada Magazine Fund, the Canada Music Fund, the Canadian Arts and Heritage Sustainability Program, the Canadian Film or Video Production Tax Credit, the Film or Video Production Services Tax Credit, the Canadian Independent Film and Video Fund, the Canadian Television Fund, Cultural Spaces Canada, the National Arts Training Contribution Program, the National Training Program in the Film and Video Sector, the Publications Distribution Assistance Program, the Publications Assistance Program, and Trade Routes.

That the department was offering more than $500 million as part of its Tomorrow Starts Today program testified to its deep involvement in the cultural economy and the conviction that Canadian nationhood rested upon the success of its cultural industries. Of course, ever the perceptive cynic, columnist (and important contributor to the second wave of Canadianization) Robert Fulford wondered aloud whether the $500 million merely entailed repackaging 'funds from other programs for the sake of making fresh-sounding news? Ottawa money pools are so murky that the question will remain forever unanswerable ... [Sheila Copp's] job is to brag about how good a job Canada and her department are doing even as she promises to improve it. And, in the meantime, do her best to make something old look new again.'[7] Fulford noted something increasingly apparent to those who concerned themselves with the cultural economy: the department's declarations about the massive amounts of money being invested seemed first and foremost to serve the need of bureaucrats to justify – and even praise – their presence in cultural life. And as long as money was being passed around, the state would not lack support from the many economic beneficiaries. The actual character and social contribution of the content was a non-issue.

Bureaucrats could not help but feel secure in the cultural devices of their own making. Globalization contributed to a situation in which the government could point to the tremendous economic value of the industries, the pile of reports charting employment growth, and all the nickels and dimes the private sector was investing in the production of the 'next big thing.' But success was not that clear-cut: a closer examination reveals a questionable underwriting of the Canadian cultural industries. The commodification of Canadian content underway with great gusto over the past decades was now being taken up by multinational corporations whose branch plants (with a Canadian face on their Janus head) take domestic talent straight to international fame and, in so doing, further a situation in which foreign success is used as a measurement of cultural merit; co-productions are being tailored to the interests of co-producers and foreign markets before fabrication even gets underway; and foreign production companies (particularly from Hollywood's film and television industries) and their Canadian collaborators show no qualms in exploiting the talent and subsidies of a domestic industry mobilized to make content for other countries. Such questionable results of federal cultural guardianship, although serving the interests of bureaucrats, are compounded by problems arising from new technologies that are capable of evading federal control, the surrendering of cultural policy to binding decisions made by the World Trade Organization, and new obligations placed upon the Department of Foreign Affairs and International Trade in securing foreign markets for domestic goods. Cultural industrialism may be benefiting from globalization, but as the situation increasingly makes clear, this outcome may not necessarily be in the best interests of those Canadians who are more concerned with domestic discourse than foreign sales.

Arts, Publishing, and Cultural Industrialism in the Global Age

A century had passed since Vincent Massey and a generation of cultural intellectuals had begun vesting the arts with a new and decisive role in national life; now the organizations that owed their existence to earlier moments of Canadianization needed to redefine themselves in a time of globalization. Art for art's sake, art for nation's sake, and even art for federalism's sake were all giving way to a new role for the arts. The National Arts Centre showed great skill at spinning its place – and its worthiness for grants – within a globally based cultural industrialism: 'The future of our children depends ... on the legacy we leave to them. Among other things, that legacy must include a strong, caring nation and a solid economy. Canada's arts sector is a vibrant component of that economy. The arts contribute to the "creative capital" that cities require for economic growth and competitiveness. Moreover, the arts also reflect our national identity as a diverse, multinational people and country – enhancing both our global reputation and our trade position.'[8] Likewise, the Canada Council was retooling itself in line with the realities of a new age. Whereas the arts once served to save the fragile nation from the debauchery of commercialism and homogenization, now the various outlets of cultural activity, as well as the council itself, stood as a vanguard of peace and understanding. Jean-Louis Roux, chair of the Canada Council, told readers of its 2002–3 *Annual Report* that 'today, more than ever before, the arts and culture represent a social lifeline, a bulwark against the rise of violence and aggressiveness in global society. The arts and culture are the salvation of humanity and the guarantors of universal peace.'[9] Civilizing the nation had been replaced by saving the world; a new challenge offered a new purpose for a council needing to continually defend its use of taxpayer dollars.

Book publishing houses were not as capable of reworking their existence to the demands of globalization. Echoing the economic instability of decades earlier, a period remembered for the sale of Gage Publishing and Ryerson Press to American interests and McClelland and Stewart coming close to being on the auction block, Coach House Press, established at the start of the new nationalism in 1965, collapsed in 1996. Fortunately for the press's roster of authors and readers, it was given a new life thanks to original founder Stan Bevington and editor Victor Coleman. The future of McClelland and Stewart, on the other hand, lay along a different path, one more telling of globalization and the presence of multinational publishing houses. In 2000 McClelland and Stewart sold a quarter of itself to Random House of Canada, a division of the German-owned Bertelsmann AG company (which also includes Doubleday and Bantam, among others). That the most important publisher of Canadiana, once led by the fiercely nationalistic Jack McClelland, would enter into such an agreement was a sign of the changing times.

The problems faced by the domestic publishing industry are unfortunately often overshadowed by the success of individual authors on the world stage – success which, quite ironically, is making the domestic marketplace even more alluring to multinational corporations scouting talent to pluck for their rosters. The list of international awards is quite impressive. The 1990s started off with Rohinton Mistry's *Such a Long Journey* placing as a finalist for the Booker Prize in 1991. Michael Ondaatje co-won the Booker in 1992 for *The English Patient* (along with Barry Unsworth for *Sacred Hunger*). The next year Carol Shields's *The Stone Diaries* was short-listed for the Booker and went on to win a Pulitzer Prize. Anne Michaels's *Fugitive Pieces* won the Guardian Fiction Award in 1996, and a year later the book scooped up both the Orange Prize and the Lannan Foundation Award for fiction. Then in 1998, the year after Michaels's success with the Orange Prize, Shields won it for *Larry's Party*. The turn of the century brought much of the same. Margaret Atwood won the Booker Prize in 2000 for *The Blind Assassin*, while her *Oryx and Crake* was a finalist for both the Man Booker Prize, as it was now called, in 2003 and the Orange Prize in 2004. Alistair MacLeod's *No Great Mischief* won the 2001 International IMPAC Dublin Award. Yann Martel won the Man Booker Prize in 2002 for *Life of Pi*. A year later, Martel, Mistry, and Shields were three of the six nominees for the Man Booker. The list is certainly impressive and says much about the level of talent in Canada; taking it as a barometer of the vitality of the domestic literary scene as a whole, and not merely the success of a few Canadian works abroad, is less feasible.

Canadian Music and the Global Connection

Canadian authors attract much acclaim, yet they are less household names than are Bryan Adams, Céline Dion, Alanis Morissette, Shania Twain, and Avril Lavigne, a roster of famous – or in the view of some critics, infamous – popular music acts. The celebrity system so important to the selling of mass goods has contributed to a situation in which musicians are not only identified as cultural producers but also upheld as figures in which Canadians are to take pride. That all five of these artists have left Canada becomes a non-issue among nationalists eager to assemble a fresh roster of names to add to the myth-symbol complex.

The ease with which some Canadian artists integrate themselves into the American music scene ironically owes much to the nationalist push for intervention in the 1960s and the federal alterations to radio airplay that followed. The Canadian content regulations, which took effect in 1971, opened the airwaves to musicians previously avoided by station owners interested in the proven profitability of foreign, primarily American, recordings. The regulations led to the creation of new studios, record-pressing plants, managers, trade papers, and so on to meet the need for Canadian records. Many musicians owed Ottawa a debt of gratitude for an opportunity to make a living without having to jump the border. Radio stations, which initially stonewalled domestic industry development – first, through refusing albums and then, post-regulations, by overplaying established artists – made a significant contribution to the industry in 1982 with the creation of the Foundation to Assist Canadian Talent On Record (FACTOR). In its first year, FACTOR received $355,255 in contributions from member stations and spent $295,000 on thirty-seven projects; loans to musicians and bands ranged from 2,000 to 25,000, the average being $7,767.[10] This initiative was backed by the federal government's Sound Recording Development Program (1986). One also needs to note the role of City-TV, as in its pursuit of the youth demographic, the station produced *The New Music* and Moses Znaimer later built upon this success in creating MuchMusic, which brought Canadian musicians – not only their music but their life-styles – into the view of audiences. Even fringe acts attracted mainstream attention thanks to MuchMusic's interest in profiling independent and regional music scenes.

By the 1990s the Canadian music scene seemed to have 'come of age,' at least in the narrative offered by music critics. Bands such as Sloan and Thrush Hermit showed that the East Coast offered more than merely Celtic sounds; Hayden and the Barenaked Ladies turned their independent releases into launching pads for big-label recording contracts; and Blue Rodeo, Big Sugar, and 54–40 achieved success on Canadian terms by cultivating large fan bases through airplay and the coast-to-coast touring circuit. Considerable credit for the presence of Canadian acts both at home and abroad, however, needs to be attributed to the activities of multinational music conglomerates. American-based multinationals, including EMI, RCA, Columbia, Warner Brothers, BMG, Sony, and Capitol, invested heavily in the Canadian music industry during the 1980s, establishing branch plants capable of seeking out artists with the potential to bring top profits.[11] By 1992, as music columnist Nicholas Jennings noted in *Maclean's* in January of that year, 'an unprecedented 84 Canadian musicians are signed to the seven major, foreign-owned labels, which this year alone have invested $25 million in them – an all-time high.'[12]

With a number of Canadian acts being marketed in the United States (and elsewhere) by multinational record labels, the stage was set for the musical climax of the decade: in 1999 Canadian musical acts, including Céline Dion, Sarah McLachlan, Shania Twain, and Alanis Morissette, received twenty-six Grammy Award nominations. Media outlets and eager fans were keen to spin this event as a sign of 'homegrown' talent reversing the America-to-Canada flow of music, a nonsensical idea only taking root with those who had short memories. Canadian acts had long done well south of the border. The difference now, though, was that instead of artists heading to the United States to make it big, as Neil Young and Joni Mitchell had done, or living in Canada and making excursions south of the border to draw American attention – Gordon Lightfoot, The Guess Who, and others – one finds the branch plants of American-based multinational record labels reaping the bounty of domestic talent and grooming stars for the international stage. That this phenomenon can now occur with lightning speed testifies to the degree to which multinationals have expanded into every component of production and sales: signing talent, writing and recording music, producing videos, setting up media appearances, and launching expensive promotion campaigns. Artists are picked up or even created out of nowhere and made into celebrities through an established star-making machine. Little time was spent in taking Avril Lavigne, for example, from hanging out in a pizza shop in Napanee, Ontario, to working with songwriters and image consultants in New York City and then onto a series of stadium dates around the world.

It is a testament to the nature of globalization that Canadian acts now relocate not only to the United States but to any country of their choosing with no hampering of their careers. Although Céline Dion has followed Paul Anka in moving to Las Vegas (where an entire theatre was created exclusively for her performances), Shania Twain, Canada's country-music sweetheart who redefined the American 'Nashville' sound, has opted for homes in Switzerland and New Zealand, while Bryan Adams, who did much for Americana rock and roll and called for an end to the Canadian content regulations, has made his home in London, England. But, and quite crucially, the difference between those who left in the 1960s and those leaving now is that it is no longer necessary to relocate in order to receive airplay, especially once one has already achieved stardom. That many of these artists are rewarded with honorary doctorates, the Order of Canada, achievement awards from the Junos, and other Canadian recognition, says much about cultural industrialism fostering a situation in which international sales are taken to be more important than residency and participation in the domestic music scene. Or, as one might point out, there is a perplexing irony in how the choice to leave Canada is rewarded with the highest of honours.

Film, Television, and the New Production Industry

The massive size and economic value of the Canadian television and film industry – technology and media mergers increasingly placing these two areas of production under the same industrial (and corporate) umbrella – owes much to the cultural industrialism launched by the Trudeau administration. The emphasis on co-productions and developing cultural goods for export; industries trained to create content stripped of national identifiers (or in which identifiers had been replaced with American equivalents) of interest to foreign distributors; the top-notch facilities and cheap talent which resulted from the belief that increasing the economic strength of the production industries would lead to more distribution and exhibition; the volume of subsidies that required nothing more than a minimum number of Canadian employees in the production of an item – all of this helped to bring Canada in on the ground floor of globalization and attract American-based multinational corporations seeking production subsidies. Back in 1981, in an article in the *Journal of Canadian Studies*, Michael A. Levine noted how 'it is increasingly apparent that the major American studios are aware of the potential of Canadian production and are showing interest in entering into a variety of arrangements with Canadian producers ... Canada enjoys a unique opportunity with its cheap dollar, its skilled technicians and creative people and the largest English-speaking market in the world at its doorstep.'[13] These were accurate observations, but the situation took a twist that many people did not foresee (and many continue to blindly overlook). The abundance of talent and technology, with little in the way of distribution for domestic works, has led to the creation of a subsidized film and television industry that creates goods based upon the interests of foreign investors who already have a lock on the outlets of distribution and exhibition. Taxpayers have in turn been placed in the ironic position of subsidizing the monopolization of their market by American media interests. Canada began attracting so many American production companies, in fact, that representatives of the American industry, including the Directors Guild of America and the Screen Actors Guild, launched anti-Canada campaigns and petitioned their governmental representatives.[14]

Canadian production companies have shown no reluctance to join with foreign firms, thanks to federal subsidies offered in the name of encouraging domestic discourse and expression: the Capital Cost Allowance was replaced by the Canadian Film or Video Production Tax Credit (1995); the Canadian Television Fund (1996) was created through a combination of the Department of Canadian Heritage, Telefilm Canada, and the private sector; and the Canadian Film or Video Production Services Tax Credit (1997) provides economic assistance while requiring only that the producer be a Canadian and that a minimum total of six on a ten-point scale of key positions consist of Canadians. Provincial governments, following in the footsteps of earlier federal initiatives, have created their own bodies to lure American film companies with the offer of subsidies, among them the Alberta Motion Picture Development Corporation (1981), Manitoba Film (1984), the Ontario Film Development Corporation (1986), and Saskfilm (1989).

These monies have helped cultural industrialists to go from producing goods for export to engaging in multinational co-productions tailored to the interests of foreign distributors who already have access to markets. In the 1990s a number of companies did so to great success. Alliance (which merged with its competitor Atlantis in 1998 to form Alliance Atlantis) took a position at the forefront with such shows as *Night Heat* and *E.N.G.*, but the most notable in terms of cultural paradoxes is without question *Due South*, a co-production pairing a gentlemanly and polite Mountie with a rough-and-tumble Chicago cop.[15] The Canadian elements echo the old Hollywood Mountie stories with a principled, dedicated, and unarmed Mountie surrounded by fawning women and with Canada depicted as a barren wasteland of snow, trees, and the occasional Native or Inuk. That is, in the few times when viewers saw Canada. The show was situated in Chicago, despite the fact that it was filmed in Toronto, leaving Canada to be little more than an exotic snowy outback. The rationale behind all of this was simple enough. First, the American market was the primary target for the show and Chicago was much more sellable than Toronto as a city of excitement and drama. Second, *Due South* and other shows produced by Alliance relied heavily upon governmental subsidies; so production had to take place in Canada in order to cash in on the money. Ted Magder reports that Alliance's television material was 80 per cent prepaid before production commenced, a testament to the ability to sell goods before even making them, and that federal subsidies covered approximately 75 per cent of the cost of its domestic feature-film production.[16]

Alliance was not alone in using taxpayer dollars to fund co-productions and goods for foreign distributors: the list includes Atlantis, with earlier hits including *Neon Rider* and *Destiny Ridge*; Nelvana Ltd, the producer of such classics as the *Care Bears, The Edison Twins*, and *T and T* (staring Mr T. in a post-A-Team role); and Lions Gate Films, one of the largest film producers and distributors in the world. Having big-league Canadian companies contributing to the economy certainly satisfied bureaucrats, but as economist and cultural industry expert Christopher Maule has observed, 'many of the productions promoted by Alliance Atlantis and Lions Gate Films hardly fulfill [the concept of] "Canadians telling Canadian stories to other Canadians" that is espoused by cultural lobbyists as one purpose of Canadian content and other broadcasting policies.'[17]

That being said, few examples of 'subsidy abuse' come as readily to mind as *Bubbles Galore* (1996). Directed by Cynthia Roberts (a Canadian) and starring porn legends Nina Hartley and Annie Sprinkle, this self-billed 'feminist sex fantasy' tells the tale of a porn star who makes a film of her own with the assistance of her guardian angel, the result being a highly sexually explicit, crude, and, ironically, misogynistic work with enough in the way of grinding body parts to put it on par with soft-core pornography. Many Canadians were angered to discover that the film had received $127,000 in grant money from the Canada Council, the Ontario Arts Council, the Toronto Arts Council, Telefilm Canada, and the Ontario Film Development Corporation.[18]

But should one be surprised to see such a use of taxpayer monies? Qualitative criteria have no place within a Canadianization, or with its bureaucratic administrators, concerned first and foremost with the economic bottom line. 'Every dollar of federal investment in feature film generates another $3.88 in investment from other sources,' praised the Department of Canadian Heritage in its *Report of the Feature Film Advisory Committee: The Road to Success* (1999).[19] It made plenty of sense, at least in terms of cultural industrialism, to increase the Canadian Film or Video Production Tax Credit from $100 million in 1998 to $170 million by 2003.[20] With coffers of nickels and dimes as evidence of cultural vibrancy, the lack of mainstream theatrical release for Canadian films made on Canadian terms becomes a non-issue. A few Canadian feature films, such as David Cronenberg's *Crash*, Atom Egoyan's *Exotica*, and Sara Polley's *Away from Her*, do get made and receive theatrical distribution, but filmmakers, actors, and technicians usually have to align themselves with American production houses in order to receive distribution. Operating as an independent means coming to accept the fact that exhibition will entail no more than small 'alternative' theatres and film festivals in major urban centres. It is a situation in which American films exist as the norm and Canadian films are marginalized alongside non-Hollywood imports and specialty films. This outcome has led Ted Magder to present the following reflection: 'The net result of the policies and practices over the last generation has been an industry with two faces: one, tanned by the California sunshine, poised, eager and able to exploit the international marketplace with film, television and video (and multimedia) productions that, in many cases, seem to be Canadian only by virtue of the workers they employ; the other, hardened by the chill of the Canadian winter, resolute, eager and able to explore the dramatic diversity of everyday life in Canada.'[21]

Or, as bureaucrat Gordon Ritchie complained in his monograph on the Free Trade Agreement negotiations, 'The trickle-down theory seemed to be that by increasing the wealth of Canadian investors in the cultural sectors we would increase the opportunity for the creation of

Canadian works. A study we commissioned by a former Finance Department expert found that while this system had significantly increased the bottom-line profits at a number of leading companies, its contribution to increased Canadian product was much less clear. As my brother acidly commented, it had produced more jobs for grips and gaffers but little in the way of leading parts for actors.'[22] Canada has developed a sophisticated film and television production industry. That so little of it involves content other than that of interest to foreign markets and their Canadian collaborators, though, is telling of its questionable success.

The CRTC and Canadian Content on the Internet

Whereas the music, television, and films sectors offered the state plenty of quantitative evidence in support of cultural industrialism, bureaucrats were less fond of the content being offered by a new technology intimately linked to globalization: the Internet. Existing with little in the way of regulation, the Internet appeared to be what radio broadcasting was a century earlier, a system of communication threatening – as the watery rhetoric often went – to engulf the population. 'Canadians could once again become swamped by the availability of foreign cultural products whose costs have already been recouped in larger domestic markets, with the threat that new and existing Canadian providers could be overwhelmed and silenced by foreign products,' warned the Canadian Content and Culture working group, one of five working groups established in 1994 by the federal government's Advisory Council on the Information Highway. 'This threat is all too real.'[23]

But the Internet is not radio. It does not involve a medium with limited pathways, as is the case with airwaves. Setup costs are low, technology is readily and affordably available, and access to content selection is nearly unlimited. As this situation became more and more obvious, the CRTC backed down from regulating the Internet.[24] The official reason, announced on 17 May 1999 in a CRTC news release simply titled 'CRTC Won't Regulate the Internet' and framed in the rhetoric of cultural industrialism, was that intervention 'might put the industry at a competitive disadvantage in the global marketplace.'[25] More obvious, however, was the fundamental fact that the medium does not lend itself to regulation unless the state is willing to engage in extreme tactics, such as the government of China has done with questionable results. As the president of an Internet service provider told the *Toronto Star* in the wake of the CRTC's announcement, 'there's no way the CRTC can dictate that

Canadians see X amount of content. Once I'm on the Net, I can go any-where I want. If I decide to visit sites in Sweden, there's nothing anyone can do about that. The notion that you can impose a bureaucratic fiat does not exist.'[26] Canadianization in this area was largely moot anyway not only because of the fluidity of the medium but also because there was little need to ensure Canadian content. The CRTC discovered that approximately 5 per cent of Internet content was Canadian in origin, a pretty high amount given the technology's global input.[27]

Satellites, Split-Run Periodicals, and the World Trade Organization

The spectre of the Internet was joined by the threat of satellite commu-nication, another technology contributing to the sense of living in a glo-bal village and one which, it soon became clear, not only jeopardized the domestic periodical industry but also revealed the precarious situa-tion into which the government had led its cultural industries. In the early 1990s the publishers of *Sports Illustrated*, part of Time Inc., discov-ered that satellite transmission offered a means of bypassing the legisla-tive language used in the 1964 Paperback and Periodical Distributors Act (1964 and 1976 amendment) limiting tax deductions for advertise-ments in magazines to those that fulfilled domestic criteria.[28] 'The sig-nal has gone out that it is now possible for non-Canadian magazines to enter the Canadian advertising market, notwithstanding the measures in place since 1965 to discourage this phenomenon,' warned the Task Force on the Canadian Magazine Industry in 1994. 'Other publishers are already exploring the opportunities of launching a split-run in Canada.'[29] The task force recommended that the federal government introduce an excise tax of 80 per cent of the amount that a split-run would charge for its advertising. A year later, Bill C-103 was passed to bring about this change and amend the legislation to include satellite transmission. All, it seemed, would be fine.

But it turned out that all was not fine. Federal bureaucrats had com-mitted Canada and its cultural industries in international trade agree-ments bound to the rulings of external mediation bodies. The United States government argued that Bill C-103 infringed upon the Free Trade Agreement and the General Agreement on Tariffs and Trade, and bypassing NAFTA's infamous retaliation clause, it took the issue straight to the World Trade Organization. The Canadian delegation claimed that advertising constituted a service, not a trade, and thus it fell under the General Agreement on Trade in Services. The WTO disagreed, however, and ruled in favour of the United States. Here was a startling wake-up call as to how the pursuit of foreign markets had led to a surrendering of control over cultural policy and the ability to ensure domestic discourse on Canadian terms. Historian Mary Vipond had predicted back in 1989 that 'if Canada attempts aggressively to seek overseas markets for its communications products it may well be attacked for the controls it imposes at home.'[30] This prediction proved to be quite true.

Saving face meant passing Bill C-55 (1999), a watered-down replacement for Bill C-103 that focused on advertising dollars instead of import barriers. In retaliation and making use of the clause in NAFTA, the U.S. government threatened to block imports of steel and lumber if Canada did not change Bill C-55. In other words, the free trade agreement had placed Canada on the brink of a trade war based upon an issue of culture, just as had been foreseen by its critics. Tellingly, federal bureaucrats backed down and offered the United States greater access to the domestic market in exchange for the ability to pass legislation designed to help Canadian periodicals.[31] One could not ask for a clearer sign that culture had indeed been on the table.

Nor would these be isolated cases. The United States showed no qualms over filing a complaint about preferential mailing rates for Canadian material. Once again the World Trade Organization sided with the Americans, and in 1998 the Canadian government was forced to rework its Publications Assistance Program to bring it in line with the WTO's interpretation of the General Agreement on Tariffs and Trade. The result was that preferential mailing rates were replaced by a system of direct subsidy. Instead of being able to enact protectionist legislation, the government had to fall back on throwing money at the problem. In 2003–4, for example, $49.4 million was spent on almost twelve hundred Canadian magazines and community newspapers.[32] It was a costly way of making up for a blow to federal cultural guardianship.

Culture, Markets, and New Directions in Foreign Policy

Comprehensive federal initiatives into developing markets for cultural exports, as discussed in the previous chapter, dated back to the early 1970s. By the 1990s the responsibility for this area rested with the Department of Canadian Heritage and the Department of Foreign Affairs and International Trade. One finds, for example, the state continuing to team up with the non-profit Association for the Export of Canadian Books (AECB), formed in 1972 as an industry-based attempt to expand the market for domestic works. It was more important than ever, the association noted in its 2002–3 *Annual Report*, to 'help Canadian exporters compete and succeed in international markets and, in more general terms, promote Canada's image abroad and promoting Canadian culture around the world.'[33] Or, in the words of Bob Tyrrell, chair of the board of directors at the AECB and also president of Orca Book Publishers, 'the AECB will continue to remind government and the industry's funding agencies of the success of our industry and the key role the Association plays in this partnership to introduce Canada to the world. We will continue to emphasize the importance of their commitment and responsibility to aid in providing Canadian content on the international front.'[34] It was not a hard sell. The Department of Canadian Heritage was more than interested in supporting major publishing endeavours. Significant work was being undertaken to make 'improvements in the Canadian book supply chain, business planning, internships, marketing and promotion projects, professional development, book industry research and international marketing activities.'[35] As of 2004, the department's Book Publishing Industry Development Program – its name evocative of its purpose – provided approximately $39 million per year to the publishing sector.[36]

More telling is the government's move beyond subsidizing the activities of like-minded cultural exporters and into making the securing of external markets an official part of its foreign policy. In 1995 the mandate of the Department of Foreign Affairs and International Trade was changed to officially include the task of promoting Canadian content abroad and ensuring markets for distribution. From where did such a far-reaching idea come? The spectre of *Sports Illustrated* infiltrating the Canadian marketplace and the increasing dollar value of cultural exports had led the Special Joint Parliamentary Committee Reviewing Canadian Foreign Policy (1993) to call for greater representation and protection of national cultural-industry interests abroad. Out of this recommendation came a radical change with substantial ideological repercussions. 'The new international cultural agenda overtly places foreign policy in a relationship with culture and identity that challenges the terms on which the legitimacy of foreign policy was traditionally built,' incisively argued political scientist Louis Bélanger in the fall 2000 issue of the *International Journal of Canadian Studies*.

Whereas foreign policy is presented as the external political expression of an independent identity and culture, thus contributing to the reification of the political and national character of this cultural reality, cultural insecurity associated with globalization is generating demands on the state, suggesting that the independence of culture vis-à-vis foreign policy is being called into question. And, in fact, the state's emerging new international cultural mission implies a foreign policy which is no longer satisfied with simply promoting an already existing culture abroad, but which is actively defending it and ensuring its development internationally.[37]

In other words, the federal government was now officially doing what its American counterpart had done for almost a century – exerting influence over foreign markets in order to sell domestic goods. That so much Canadian content resembled American offerings merely added to the irony of the phenomenon. Not only has this new policy undermined the respectability and effectiveness of the Department of Foreign Affairs and International Trade in the international community, but, as Christopher Maule has noted, the difficulty of acting upon this cultural agenda has left the department open to criticism at home for its lack of effectiveness in fighting on the behalf of the cultural industries.[38]

These setbacks, however, have not been enough to convince federal bureaucrats to decouple cultural industrialism and foreign policy. The Tomorrow Starts Today campaign launched in 2001, for example, included funds for the Cultural Export Development program, a joint initiative between the Department of Foreign Affairs and International Trade and the Department of Canadian Heritage. Its purpose was guised in the media-friendly rhetoric of helping cultural producers to be 'ambassadors, sharing Canadian voices and values with the world.'[39] That same year the two departments teamed up to create the Trade Routes program, a three-year, $23-million program designed to assist in the marketing and selling of cultural goods abroad. Once again the Department of Canadian Heritage justified the activities through a fusion of cultural and economic rationale, paradoxically equating domestic expression with foreign sales: 'Canada's innovative arts and cultural products and services help to express our diversity, values and identity. They are also a vibrant element of Canada's new economy and an essential part of our country's export story. With almost $5 billion per year in exports of products and services from Canada's cultural sector already, Canadian arts and cultural producers are responding to diverse international appetites.'[40]

Canadian success in the international marketplace with goods co-produced with American companies, a core part of the government's strategy of cultural industrialism, is beginning to face a backlash. Foreign governments and their citizens are showing tremendous concern about being overwhelmed by American-style content and ending up in a situation similar to that in Canada; it would certainly interest Canadians to know that many people see Canada as having lost the attempt to bulwark itself against Americana. 'Canadianized here means Americanized!' Kim Christian Schroder has noted in 'Can Denmark Be Canadianized? On the Cultural Role of American TV-Serials in Denmark.'[41] Television consumption is of particular concern, as the combination of satellite transmission and abundant American-style program production has threatened to, in the words of sociologist Richard Collins, 'replicate in Western Europe the effects of American television in Canada, namely damage to polity and culture, destabilizing one and debasing the other.'[42]

Some countries are seeking strength in numbers not only as a means of defending themselves against this wave of content but also, and quite importantly, as a way of securing opportunities for their own industries. In 1989 the European Union established Television Without Frontiers, an audio-visual directive designed to increase the presence of domestic programming. Non-EU member countries can engage in an offshoot of the program called the European Convention on Transfrontier Television. For the film sector there is the European Convention on Cinematographic Coproduction, designed to encourage co-productions and the dissemination of films (telling of the cultural industrialism taking root in other countries, 'Europeanness' is measured as a minimum of fifteen of nineteen points of industrial/talent usage, among other requirements). European initiatives have been joined by the Conferencia de Autoridades Cinematográficas de Iberoamérica, created in 1997, which brought together Argentina, Bolivia, Brazil, Colombia, Chile, Cuba, Mexico, Peru, Portugal, Spain, Uruguay, and Venezuela in a co-production film agreement with strict quantitative criteria almost exclusively requiring that all 'talent' be citizens of member countries.[43]

Canada has co-production agreements with many of these countries, yet the government has not entered into any of the multilateral agreements. Discussions with the European Union in the late 1990s went nowhere, but Canadian bureaucrats still seem interested in the possibility. François Macerola's report for the Department of Canadian Heritage, *Canadian Content in the 21st Century in Film and Television Productions: A Matter of Cultural Identity* (2003), recommended that 'Canada seek to secure preferential treatment and special association status with the most important multilateral initiatives, particularly those within the European Union.'[44] Country-by-country co-production agreements, long a staple of television and film production, no longer seem to be sufficient; a global era requires a multilateral approach, one that many countries seem to be taking without an interest in including a Trojan Horse of Americanization.

Conclusion

Some areas of cultural activity are adapting, with mixed success, to the realities of globalization. Arts organizations are casting their cultural worth (and justification for receiving taxpayer dollars) in global terms; the book industry is dealing with both traditional economic woes and the absorption of presses into multinational corporations, although this situation is in some ways overlooked by the popular attention given to the success of authors in winning international literary awards; the domestic music scene is operating upon a new multinational dynamic facilitating both domestic and international success while further separating big-name artists from their domestic context; and the television and film sectors are thriving, at least in economic terms, thanks to subsidies for foreign production companies and domestic collaborators making Americana for international audiences. Crises in content are accompanied by those presented by new communication technologies and federal cultural policy-making. The Internet, satellite transmission, World Trade Organization verdicts, fusion of cultural and foreign policies, and exclusion from multilateral cultural directives all testify to cultural industrialism as not being the most stable bedrock upon which to build a sense of nationhood.

Yet the Department of Canadian Heritage has little reason to feel anything other than comfortable with its approach to cultural guardianship in a time of globalization. The cultural economy is worth billions of dollars; many Canadians are employed; American monies and production companies are coming northward – statistics are not in short supply when evidence is needed to justify the presence of the state in cultural activities. The almost effortless ability to guise this economic agenda in the rhetoric of aiding domestic expression is telling of both bureaucratic skills and the degree to which the words have lost any actual qualitative meaning. Federal bureaucrats, as well as those who benefit from state cultural guardianship, are proving to be more than capable of conflating industry with identity in the face of the cultural insecurity, instability, and blatant contradictions that arise in a system which relies upon domestic profiteers and multinational corporations to develop Canadian content. Out of these contradictions runs a very questionable path upon which to articulate and orchestrate a civic nationhood serving the interests of the citizenry as a whole.

Conclusion: Building Canada – Culture and the Quest for Nationhood

The Department of Canadian Heritage had much to say about national cultural life in the two-page introduction to its *Culture and Heritage: Connecting Canadians through Canada's Stories* (2003), the title alone playing upon the idea that the goal was first and foremost to encourage domestic discourse on domestic terms. Rhetoric told of how 'it is our culture that defines us as Canadians. In our arts and through our heritage, we live our values and create our identity. It is through our country's rich cultural diversity that we convey our sense of community, to each other and to the world.' And as one would expect, the report slotted the contribution of Canada's cultural activity to nationhood into a historical lineage, with the department going so far as to vest nationhood upon civilizations long predating the concept: 'Culture is the hallmark of great civilizations. From the Phoenicians to the Egyptians, the Greeks and the Romans; from the Incas to the Algonkian, ancient peoples made their mark and left their legacy through the art and culture they created and we inherited. Pictographs or papyrus, pyramids or poems – symbols and stories represent the identity of a people and the soul of a nation.'[1]

The declaration was fit for the Masseyites of a century earlier, but by this point in Canadianization the words came across as little more than rhetorical window dressing for a more pressing purpose. Of all the statements made in the two-page introduction, only one was separated from the rest, only one received italics and an enlarged font. Like a company reporting year-end results to its stockholders, the Department of Canadian Heritage used special formatting to single out the fact that 'the cultural sector contributes more than $22 billion a year to our economy and employs more than 640,000 Canadians.'[2] That the monetary worth of something did not necessarily indicate its value, that economic activity did not equate with domestic discourse, and that numbers did not a nation make continued to elude bureaucrats caught up in reaping the financial rewards of a lucrative cultural economy.

The Department of Canadian Heritage stands out as antithetical to the cultural vision dreamt of by Vincent Massey and a community of like-minded intellectuals, but the fact that the department exists speaks volumes about how the quest for nationhood has continued. Just as the Masseyites benefited by mobilizing culture in support of their nation-building interests, so a massive federal bureaucracy now reaps the economic returns of a Canadianization shared with cultural industrialists. Out of the contrast emerges a telling picture of the evolution of the idea that Canadian nationhood could be achieved through culture: the Dominion of Canada, based upon a British inheritance, was replaced by – or more accurately, reimagined into – a Peaceable Kingdom of multiculturalism, civic rights, and a social safety net; culture went from being construed as a force of social morality and enrichment to being valued for its contribution to the economy; guiding the population along an enlightened path above all-things-mass gave way to strategies of cultural employment and economic growth; the United States changed from producing threatening commercialism and escapist content to becoming a collaborator in the Canadian attempt to do the same; the earlier faith in high culture was replaced by one in the economy and money-making; and the efforts to suppress commercialism and commodification have been superseded by a turn to marketing, celebrity 'star systems,' and quite crucially, exporting Canadian content by creating it in accordance with foreign interests.

Much has changed in culture and the quest for nationhood. By the turn of the twenty-first century the very federal government that had long avoided the controversies and pitfalls of cultural intervention now held the reins of Canadianization and chose to define, measure, and value culture not upon qualitative elements but by how well commodities sell. And there is certainly no indication that Canadianization is about to be abandoned. Culture continues to serve the interests of Canadianizers facing the threat of Québécois separatism (and the implications of being a 'nation within a united nation'), the need to consolidate multiculturalism, and the daunting task of negotiating a transnationalization of capital and cultural policy that increasingly ties the ebb and flow of Canadian life to forces outside governmental control. The tensions being felt by Canadians are, of course, merely

microcosms of larger global struggles with ethnic conflicts and civil
wars, new patterns of immigration, the expansion of communication
and information technologies, and the integration of economic markets, all of which defy the ability to carve the globe into neatly organized
nation-states. The 'building block' approach and 'single civic nation
with a homogeneous national identity which could be used as a model
for "healthy" national development,' as Anthony D. Smith described the
phenomenon, has become obsolete.[3] The world of nations is increasingly polarized between civic states and ethno-territorial nations, and
there is no end in sight to this pattern.

There is little question that the state needs to play a role in cultural
activity, but is the current model of Canadianization serving the needs
of the population? Cultural industrialism offers a subsidized cultural
marketplace through which cultural capitalists can compete internationally, drawing upon state funds and tax deductions to create material
for export; yet by its very nature this paradigm encourages, if not limits
itself to, content forged on American templates (and thus stripped of
Canadian characteristics). Out of this process comes a series of enduing
paradoxes – industry as a means to identity; Canadian content tailored
to the interests of foreign audiences; struggles to negotiate a special
position for the cultural industries within trade agreements; the reduction of the public sector to the status of a business; and, quite tellingly,
positing the solution to Canada as an overrun market upon the ability of
Canadians to participate in their own cultural subjugation. To these
problems are being added the complications of globalization – issues of
ownership and control become distorted as media corporations merge
into multinational conglomerates; protectionism is losing its earlier
rationale; new technologies are changing conceptions of space, time,
and trade; the binding judgments of international tribunals are altering
the ability of governments to enact cultural policies on the behalf of
their populations.

Cultural industrialism does little to serve the need for domestic discourse on domestic terms and free from considerations of profitability in
a skewed marketplace. If Canadians are to benefit from state activity
within the cultural sector and not the other way around, then more
needs to be done to allow the population to engage in discourse valued
not for its monetary worth but simply based on the need to open systems
of communication and expression. Out of such an approach would come
a greater ability to debate issues of nationhood and, in some ways even
more pressing, negotiate and adapt the social and political infrastructure

to the changing needs of Canadians as individuals and as a society. Necessary steps include reversing the federal shift from public- to private-sector investment and guaranteeing that public-sector institutions can operate free from the need to attract advertising dollars or create content for export. At the very least, federal bureaucrats need to come to terms with the fact that economic strength and industry growth do not equate with opportunities for national discourse and expression. The federal government needs to back down from its assumption – and leap of faith – that marketplace parameters offer a positive means of achieving national goals. Until it does so, citizens will continue to be bound to a paradigm of Canadianization at odds with their best interests.

Notes

Introduction

1 These three statements are originally from separate interviews, as quoted in
  Pevere and Dymond, *Mondo Canuck*, 2. The three statements have also been
  previously assembled by Greg Potter in *Hand Me Down World*, 125.
2 'Bryan Adams to Government: "Get Out of the Music Biz,"' *Billboard*,
  25 Jan. 1992, 44.
3 Quoted in 'Cancon Debate Heats Up Toronto Meet,' *Billboard*, 11 April
  1992, 66.

4 Ibid.; emphasis in original.

5 A task force headed by industry figures recommended that 'in order to recognize the increased amount of collaboration between songwriters in the
creation of songs, the existing regulation should be modified so that where a
song is co-written by a Canadian and a non-Canadian, where the Canadian
songwriter is credited with at least fifty percent of the composer's share
respecting the music and at least fifty percent of the writer's share respecting
the lyrics, that song should qualify for one of the two required "points"'
(CRTC, Public Notice 1992–32, 30 April 1992). The CRTC later announced
that it would implement this recommendation (Public Notice 1993–5,
29 Jan. 1993).

6 Testa and Shedden, 'In the Great Midwestern Hardware Store,' 207.

7 For more on 'imagined communities,' see Anderson, *Imagined Communities.*

8 For an overview of 'reconnaissance' as an historical approach, see McKay,
'The Liberal Order Framework.'

9 For example, Heritage Minutes on Canadian television present a mixture of
history and myth that evoke a deep-seated nationalist sentiment. They were
initiated in 1991 with funding from the Charles R. Bronfman Foundation, in
reaction to Bronfman's experience of being awarded the Order of Canada
and the desire to make Canadian history more appealing to the population.
See, for example, Cameron, 'Heritage Minutes'; see also McGinnis,
'Heritage Minutes,' for the moments as 'commercials for Canada.'

10 Kedourie, *Nationalism,* 9.

11 Ernest Gellner's *Thought and Change* was his first significant articulation
of this argument and underwrites his later work. Similarly, the respected
theorist Eric Hobsbawm has identified nations as the product of a post-
Enlightenment period in which political forces competed for leadership and
control. See *The Invention of Tradition* and *Nations and Nationalism since 1780.*

12 Anderson, 'Staging Antimodernism in the Age of High Capitalist Nationalism,' 98.

13 See Francis, *National Dreams,* chapter 6, 'The Ideology of the Canoe: The
Myth of the Wilderness,' and Berger, 'True North Strong and Free,' 84.
National identifiers and invented traditions are often tremendously narrow,
if not false, characterizations of complex social occurrences serving the purposes of those constructing them. See, for example, McKay's *The Quest of
the Folk.*

14 The 'space-binding' media had, by Innis's time, largely replaced earlier
'time-binding' media, including oral traditions, which he thought were
more effective at providing a strong sense of community. See Innis, *Empire
and Communication, Bias of Communication,* and *The Strategy of Culture.* See also

Stamps, *Unthinking Modernity*, for an interpretation of Innis's work as a reaction to modernity.

15 Vipond, *The Mass Media in Canada*, xi. See also Rutherford, *The Making of the Canadian Media*, for an examination of media as a 'fourth estate.'

16 Williams, *Keywords*, 76–9.

17 Simons, *Gramsci's Political Thought*, 43, 44. The intelligentsia is a loose collection of cultural and political intellectuals seeking to define the national construct and employing nationalism as the means of securing their leadership. In Gramscian terms, 'Every social group, coming into existence on the original terrain of an essential function in the world of economic production, creates together with itself, organically, one or more strata of intellectuals which give it homogeneity and an awareness of its own function not only in the economic but also in the social and political fields' (Gramsci, *Prison Notebooks*, 5).

18 Historical writing has reflected this division. Arthur R.M. Lower's *Colony to Nation* is perhaps the most notable attempt to identify Canadian nationalists as those who fought for the creation of a Canadian nation separate from British 'control.' See Edwardson, '"Narrating a Canadian Identity."' On the other hand, Carl Berger's *The Sense of Power* explores the idea that those who espoused an imperialist direction for Canada at the turn of the twentieth century were in fact just as nationalist by advocating a British-based national direction that placed Canadian prosperity within an imperial framework. Some of the semantic and conceptual problems in the book, particularly Berger's use of nationalism and imperialism, have recently been examined by Douglas Cole, Terry Cook, and Graham Carr. See, for example, Carr, 'Imperialism and Nationalism in Revisionist Historiography.'

19 See Bhabha, *Nations and Narration* and *The Location of Culture.*

20 This idea was common among many colonies shifting into nationhood. See Raymond Williams's introduction to *Culture and Society, 1780–1950.*

21 Litt, *The Muses, the Masses, and the Massey Commission*, provides a thorough examination of the members of the commission, while Massolin, *Canadian Intellectuals, the Tory Tradition, and the Challenge of Modernity, 1939–1970*, connects Tory intellectualism with an anti-modernism and the attempt to renegotiate an Anglo-Celtic inheritance.

22 Rutherford, *The Making of the Canadian Media*, 77. See also Owram, *Born at the Right Time.*

23 See Litvak and Maule, *Cultural Sovereignty.*

24 Rotstein and Lax, *Getting It Back*, xii.

25 See Edwardson, 'The Many Lives of Captain Canuck.'

26 Committee for an Independent Canada (Hendry), 'Theatre in Canada,' 12.

27 Trudeau, 'Federalism, Nationalism and Reason,' 193.
28 United States, National Foundation on the Arts and the Humanities Act of 1965.
29 Baudrillard, *The Consumer Society*.
30 John Metcalf offers some similar arguments in *What Is a Canadian Literature?*
31 Ostry, *Cultural Connection*, 42.
32 Richler, *Barney's Version*, 5.
33 See, for example, Cook's *Canada and the French-Canadian Question*; *French-Canadian Nationalism*; *The Maple Leaf Forever*; and *Canada, Quebec, and the Uses of Nationalism*.
34 Cook, *Canada, Quebec, and the Uses of Nationalism*, 173–4.
35 Ibid., 15.
36 Ibid., 13.
37 Cook, 'Nationalism in Canada or *Portnoy's Complaint* Revisited,' 19. On the copy in LAC, MG 31– D190, vol. 24, file 24–22, someone (quite possibly Robin Mathews) penned at the end of the article, 'Ramsay Cook is a Fascist C.I.A. Pig.'
38 Lee, *Consumer Culture Reborn*, 48.
39 Historian Robert Wright has offered great insights into the current relationship – or lack of one – between youths and nationalism. See *Hip and Trivial* and 'L'État, c'est Molson? Youth and the Decline of Canadian Nationalism,' in his *Virtual Sovereignty*, 153–91.
40 For a look at state intervention that includes assistance to amateur athletes and promotes physical activity as an important part of childhood development, see Harvey and Proulx, 'Sport and the State in Canada.'
41 Many sports have been credited with contributing to the national sense of self, including hockey, curling, lacrosse, and even baseball, football, and basketball. The relationship with baseball is explored in Barney, 'Whose National Pastime?' Football is examined in Stebbins, 'Ambivalence at the Fifty-five-Yard Line.' The CRB Foundation has released a Heritage Minute depicting basketball as the creation of a Canadian and thus a part of the national fabric.

1. Colony to Nation

1 *Canadian Forum*, no. 1 (Oct. 1920): 3.
2 Johnston, 'The Emergence of Broadcast Advertising in Canada, 1919–1932.'
3 Wallace, *The Growth of Canadian National Feeling*, 7. Originally published in the *Canadian Historical Review* in 1920.
4 Interestingly, such periodicals often emulated foreign alternatives because established templates, historian Graham Carr has noted, lent

Canadian periodicals an air of international credibility. See Carr, 'Design as Content.'

5 Vipond, 'The Nationalist Network,' 32. emphasis in original.
6 Ibid., 33–4.
7 Ibid., 46.
8 Tippett, *Making Culture*, 7.
9 McKay, 'Historians, Anthropology, and the Concept of Culture,' 226.
10 Campbell, 'From Romantic History to Communications Theory.' For a look at Ryerson Press's earlier assistance to authors, see Peterman and Friskney, '"Booming" the Canuck Book.'
11 Young, 'The Macmillan Company of Canada in the 1930s.'
12 Carr, '"All We North Americans."'
13 Vipond, 'Best Sellers in English Canada, 1899–1918,' 98–9.
14 Tippett, *Making Culture*, chapter 4, 'Volunteers, Subscribers, and Millionaires: The Character of Private Patronage.'
15 Finlay, *The Force of Culture*, 157.
16 LAC, MG 30–D111, vol. 1, file 4; emphasis in original.
17 Quoted in Hill, *The Group of Seven*, 58.
18 Edwardson, 'A Canadian Modernism.'
19 See, for example, Jessup, 'Prospectors, Bushwhackers, Painters' and 'The Group of Seven and the Tourist Landscape in Western Canada.' See also Davis, 'A Study in Modernism'; Cameron, '"Our Ideal of an Artist"' and 'Tom Thomson, Antimodernism, and the Ideal of Manhood.'
20 *Canadian Forum* 1, no. 2 (Nov. 1920): 37.
21 *Canadian Forum* 2, no. 18 (March 1922): 558.
22 *Canadian Forum* 1, no. 2 (Nov. 1920): 37.
23 *Canadian Forum* 1, no. 10 (July 1921): 293.
24 This offer was made in 1937. See Finlay, *The Force of Culture*, 155.
25 Cupido, 'Sixty Years of Canadian Progress,' 19.
26 Brison, 'Cultural Interventions'; and Lazarevich, 'Aspects of Early Arts Patronage in Canada.'
27 LAC, MG 30–D401, vol. 1, file B, letter B-5.
28 Berman, *All That Is Solid Melts into Air*, 17. See also Lears, *No Place of Grace*, and Walden, *Becoming Modern in Toronto*.
29 *Life*, 23 Nov. 1936.
30 *Maclean's*, 15 Nov. 1936.
31 *Year Book of the Canadian Motion Picture Industry*, 1951–2, 21.
32 Ironically, *Evangeline* was based on the work of an American poet, Henry Wadsworth Longfellow, and the actors and director were American. See Walz, *Canada's Best Features*.

33 James, *Film as a National Art.*

34 Magder, *Canada's Hollywood*; and Pendaukr, *Canadian Dreams and American Control.* See also Ulff-Møller, 'The Origins of the French Film Quota Policy.'

35 Pendakur, *Canadian Dreams and American Control*, 61.

36 Peers, 'The Nationalist Dilemma in Canadian Broadcasting,' 255.

37 CBC, *Broadcasting in Canada*, 1, 2.

38 Litvak and Maule, *Cultural Sovereignty*, 19–20. See also Strange and Loo, *True North, True Crime*, for an exploration of Canadian-produced pulp magazines.

39 Vipond, 'Canadian Nationalism and the Plight of Canadian Magazines in the 1920s,' 45.

40 James, *Film as a National Art*, 344.

41 Dickinson and Street, *Cinema and State*, 40. For a look at the popularity of quotas and taxation among a number of European governments, see Victoria de Grazia, 'Mass Culture and Sovereignty.'

42 Vipond, 'Canadian Nationalism and the Plight of Canadian Magazines in the 1920s,' 47.

43 Cupido, 'The Medium, the Message and the Modern,' 119.

44 Canada, Royal Commission on Radio Broadcasting, *Report*, 9.

45 Litvak and Maule, *Cultural Sovereignty*, 23–4.

46 Ibid., 26–7.

47 House of Commons, *Debates*, 18 May 1932.

48 Babe, *Canadian Television Broadcasting Structure*, 25.

49 CBC, *Broadcasting in Canada*, 12.

50 Maurice Charland has noted that 'Canada's prowess in developing space-binding technology celebrated as a national achievement in the [Pierre Berton book on the railway] *National Dream*, ironically serves now to undermine Canada's cultural autonomy.' See Charland, 'Technological Nationalism,' 215.

51 Litvak and Maule, *Cultural Sovereignty*, 27.

52 Ibid., 28.

53 Ibid.

54 Pendakur, *Canadian Dreams and American Control*, 84, 85.

55 See Nelson, *The Colonized Eye*, for a revisionist look at Grierson's role in the film body.

56 See Rodger, 'Some Factors Contributing to the Formation of the National Film Board of Canada,' for an overview of the change from the bureau to the board.

57 Historian Mark Kristmanson describes it as 'not art for art's sake but a means of saturating the field of filmic communication with a generalized audiovisual rationality suitable to national government.' See Kristmanson, *Plateaus of Freedom*, 50.

58 Morris, 'After Grierson,' 3.

59 Kristmanson, *Plateaus of Freedom*, 50.

60 Magder, *Canada's Hollywood*, 70.

61 The U.S. Department of Justice overturned the decision in 1985, allowing
    for the development of the major media conglomerates that now dominate
    production and distribution. See also Morris, *Embattled Shadows*, for an
    authoritative survey of the early film situation.

62 NFB Archives, 5–A, AMPPLC, box 77, 'Supplementary Notes – Aid to the
    Canadian Motion Picture Industry,' 18/1/60, 21(2).

63 The meeting occurred in January 1948. See Miller, 'The Canadian Film
    Development Corporation,' 74.

64 NFB Archives, 5–A, AMPPLC, box 77, 'Aims outlined by MPPA president
    Eric Johnson,' quoted in NFB's 'Supplementary Notes – Aid to the Canadian
    Motion Picture Industry,' 18/1/60, 21(2).

65 Apostle, 'The Display of a Tourist Nation.'

66 C.D. Howe, House of Commons, *Debates*, 10 Feb. – March 1948, 1475, 1477.

67 Ibid., 1494.

68 Pierre Berton provides an insightful look at the project in *Hollywood's
    Canada*. See part 4, 'Canadian Cooperation, Hollywood Style.'

69 Canadian Co-operation Project, *Annual Report 1949*; NFB Archives, A-151,
    file 1494, vol. 2, extract from *Kinematography Weekly* (London England), 12
    April 1951, 'Close-Up – Canadian Capers by a Correspondent in Canada.'

70 NFB Archives, 5–A, AMPPLC, box 77, 'Supplementary Notes – Aid to the
    Canadian Motion Picture Industry,' 18/1/60, 21(5).

71 Canadian Co-operation Project, *Annual Report*, 1949, 4.

72 Pells, *Not Like Us*, 219.

2. Culturing Canada

1 Massey Commission, *Report*, n.p.

2 Originally in a speech given at Prince of Wales College in Charlottetown;
   Ferdinand Vandry in the *Dalhousie Review* 31, no. 2 (summer 1951): 74.

3 Metcalf, *What Is a Canadian Literature?* 100. Nationalist Robin Mathews has
   critically noted that Metcalf, a British-born literary critic residing in Canada,
   'has been and is the recipient of quite generous support from the state
   granting agencies – support which he continues to take – while condemning
   state support of the arts.' See Mathews, *Treason of the Intellectuals*, 120.

4 Massey, *On Being Canadian*, 47, 48; emphasis in original.

5 Ibid., 48.

6 Brison, 'The Kingston Conference, the Carnegie Corporation and a New
   Deal for the Arts in Canada.'

7 Ibid.

8 Quoted in Tippett, *Making Culture*, 73.

9 Lewis and Scott, *Make This Your Canada*, 176.

10 See Litt, *The Muses, the Masses, and the Massey Commission*, chapter 1, 'The Origins of the Commission,' and Tippett, *Making Culture*, 183.

11 Kuffert, *A Great Duty*, 4.

12 Massey Commission, *Report*, 7, 65.

13 As Paul R. Gorman puts it, mass culture 'had come to designate a system of popular leisure practices and arts that were considered wholly new to urban and industrial society. And the system was believed to be almost synonymous with corruption and decay.' See Gorman, *Left Intellectuals and Popular Culture in Twentieth-Century America*, 1, 2.

14 LAC, RG 33–28, vol. 13, Canadian Federation of Home and School, *Brief*, 1359.

15 Massey Commission, *Report*, 18.

16 Ibid., 35.

17 Ibid., 284.

18 CBC, *Submission to the Royal Commission on Development in the Arts*, 36.

19 Ibid., 36.

20 Ibid., 6, 32, 33, 35.

21 Stewart, *From Coast to Coast*, 147. At this point in time, English-speaking Canadians were served by two networks. Trans-Canada was the CBC's original network, with twenty-four CBC stations and thirty privately owned affiliates, and was primarily responsible for providing Canadian material. The Dominion Network commenced in January 1944 as an alternative network, with one CBC and forty-nine privately owned stations, and provided a large quantity of commercial material. See CBC, *Annual Report*, 1962, 44.

22 CBC, *Submission to the Royal Commission on Development in the Arts*, 40. Interestingly, there is no mention of British Commonwealth or France commercial programming, which may have been included in the calculation of Canadian material.

23 Ibid., 1, 3, 18, 19.

24 Ibid., 23, 24.

25 At the very least, the CBC provided crucial employment to the cultural sector. See Woodcock, *Strange Bedfellows*, chapter 3, 'The State as Employer of Artists.'

26 LAC, RG 33–28, Vancouver Branch of the Association of Canadian Radio Artists, *Brief*, 2–3.

27 LAC, RG 33–28, American Federation of Musicians of the United States and Canada, *A Submission to the Royal Commission on National Development in the Arts, Letters and Sciences*, 1–2.

28 Massey Commission, *Report*, 33.
29 LAC, RG 33–28, Canadian Writers' Committee, *Brief*, 2.
30 LAC, RG 33–28, Vancouver Branch of the Association of Canadian Radio Artists, *Brief*, 10.
31 Massey Commission, *Report*, 283.
32 Ibid., 284, 298, 305.
33 Ibid., 47, 280.
34 Ibid., 301.
35 Ibid.
36 Ibid., 305.
37 See Kristmanson, *Plateaus of Freedom*, chapter 2, 'Love Your Neighbour: The RCMP and the National Film Board, 1948–1953.'
38 Morris, 'After Grierson,' 3.
39 National Film Board, *Annual Report*, 1950–1, 6.
40 Ibid., 10.
41 See Morris, 'After Grierson,' for an exploration of these three films and the social drama genre.
42 LAC, RG 33–28, Canadian Writers' Committee, *Brief*, 10.
43 Massey Commission, *Report*, 50.
44 Ibid.
45 LAC, RG 33–28, Hearings, Association of Motion Picture Producers and Laboratories of Canada (AMPPLC), 906, 910. The AMPPLC did not give evidence to support its claim about quotas in other countries.
46 Frank Underhill in the *Canadian Forum* 31, no. 367 (Aug. 1951): 102.
47 Massey Commission, *Report*, 58.
48 Ibid., 59.
49 LAC, RG 33–28, Canadian Writers' Committee, *Brief*, and National Conference of Canadian Universities, *Brief*, July 1949.
50 LAC, RG 33–28, Hearings, Mr Gordon Couling, Northern Ontario Art Association, 104.
51 LAC, RG 33–28, National Conference of Canadian Universities, *Brief*, July 1949, 9.
52 LAC, RG 33–28, Federation of Canadian Artists, *Submission to the Royal Commission on Development in the Arts, Letters and Sciences*, 6.
53 Massey Commission, *Report*, 193.
54 Ibid., 186.
55 Ibid., 189.
56 Ibid., 164.
57 Ibid., 272.
58 Ibid., 109.
59 Ibid., 275.

60 Ibid., 272.

61 Ibid., 18.

62 Ibid., 165.

63 Ibid., 273.

64 *Canadian Forum* 31, no. 366 (July 1951): 73.

65 Ibid., 74.

66 Massey Commission, *Report*, 408.

67 Legget in the *Dalhousie Review* 36, no. 3 (Autumn 1951): 276.

68 Ibid., 282.

69 Underhill in the *Canadian Forum* 31, no. 367 (Aug. 1951): 102.

70 Ibid.

71 See Litt, 'The Massey Commission as Intellectual History.'

72 Litt, *The Muses, the Masses, and the Massey Commission*, 238.

73 House of Commons, *Debates*, 1951, 4933.

74 Jeffrey, 'Private Television and Cable,' 207.

75 A. Davidson Dunton, CBC, Special Committee on Radio Broadcasting, Minutes, 11 May 1950, 22.

76 LAC, MG 30–E481, vol. 41, file 'TV Government Policy,' document 'Government Statement on Television Policy,' 23 March 1949.

77 A. Davidson Dunton, CBC, Special Committee on Radio Broadcasting, Minutes, 10 Dec. 1951, 451.

78 A. Davidson Dunton, ibid., 14 April 1953, 84.

79 CBC, *Broadcasting in Canada*, 33.

80 Ibid.

81 See ibid., 33-4, for more details.

82 Ibid., 35.

83 Committee member, SCoB, Minutes, 29 April 1955, 262.

84 Jim Allard, vice-president of the Canadian Association of Broadcasters, ibid., 24 May 1955, 595, 603, 623.

85 Committee member, ibid., 19 May 1955, 557.

86 A. Davidson Dunton, CBC, ibid., 19 May 1955, 554.

87 Massey Commission, *Report*, 406.

88 Canada, Royal Commission on Broadcasting, *Report*, 25.

89 See Rutherford, *When Television Was Young*, for an exploration of these early years of CBC Television.

90 Canada, Royal Commission on Broadcasting, *Report*, 41, 146.

91 Ibid., 123.

92 Ibid., 185.

93 Ibid., 87.

94 Ibid., 64.

95 Ibid., Appendix XIV, 29.
96 Canada Council Act, 1957, section 8 (1).
97 Ostry, *Cultural Connection*, 99.
98 Quoted in Canada Council for the Arts, *Opening Proceedings*, 15.
99 Canada Council for the Arts, *First Annual Report*, 1958, 22.

3. From Institution to Industry

 1 Knelman, *This Is Where We Came In*, 5.
 2 House of Commons, *Debates*, 26 July 1955, 6844.
 3 Nash, *Swashbucklers*, 178.
 4 Ibid., 178.
 5 Bassett later became chairman of the Security Intelligence Review Commission, a member of the Privy Council of Canada, and companion of the Order of Canada.
 6 Gittins, *CTV*, 25.
 7 Nolan, *CTV*, 201.
 8 Board of Broadcast Governors, SOR/59–456. The 1958 Broadcasting Act required stations to broadcast 'varied and comprehensive broadcasting service of a high standard that is basically Canadian in content and character.'
 9 SCoB, Minutes, no. 1, 13 Feb. 1961, 31. The CBC calculated Canadian content at 66 per cent on the English-language network and 85 per cent on the French-language network, but affiliates put it closer to 45–50 per cent. See Stewart and Hull, *Canadian Television Policy and the Board of Broadcast Governors, 1958–1968*, 31, 32.
10 Board of Broadcast Governors, SOR/59–456, section 6.4. This system was used until the 1970s, at which time a point system was created. See Robert Babe's *Canadian Television Broadcasting Structure, Performance and Regulation*, a balanced exploration of the infrastructure upon which an important part of Canadianization took place, for a detailed overview of the Canadian content regulations, their means of assessment, and changes to them, including the adoption of a more quantitative point system in the early 1970s. See also Marc Raboy's *Missed Opportunities* for a look at the state's inability to use the broadcasting system in accordance with nation-building desires.
11 LAC, MG 30–E481, vol. 42, 'Statements by and before BBG,' CBC to BBG, 'Re: Proposed Television Broadcasting Station Regulations,' 23 Oct. 1959, 5; SCoB, Minutes, no. 11, 11 June 1959, 403.
12 LAC, RG 41, vol. 669, microfilm T3044, 'CBC Minutes of Meetings of the Board of Directors,' 61st meeting, 9–12 Sept. 1959, 118.
13 Ibid., 8th meeting, 3–5 Dec. 1959, 189.

14 LAC, RG 100, vol. 34, file 183, Association of Radio and Television Employees of Canada, 'Brief to BBG regarding proposed television regulations,' Nov. 1959, 6; SCoB, Minutes, no. 2, 16 Feb. 1961, 41.

15 SCoB, Minutes, no. 1, 13 Feb. 1961, 27.

16 BBG, 'Comment by the Canadian Association of Broadcasters,' 26.

17 Ibid., 25.

18 LAC, RG 100, vol. 29, file 163, 'Position Papers,' CAB, 'Comment Concerning the proposed new television regulations submitted by the Board of directors and television section of the Canadian association of broadcasters,' 20 Oct. 1959, 6.

19 BBG, 'Comment by the Canadian Association of Broadcasters,' 18.

20 Ibid., 23.

21 Jhally, *The Codes of Advertising*, 15.

22 LAC, RG 100, vol. 34, file 183, Association of Canadian Advertisers and Canadian Association of Advertising Agencies, 'Brief to the Board of Broadcast Governors,' 1959, 5. See also in the same file the collection of briefs and community response to BBG's regulatory proposals, including Procter & Gamble Company of Canada letter to CAB, 28 Sept. 1959, 'Appendix A' of CAB response to BBG regarding proposed regulations.

23 CRTC, *Symposium on Television Violence*, 161.

24 SCoB, Minutes, no. 3, 20 Feb. 1961, 72, 84.

25 Ibid., 42, 73.

26 Ibid., 73.

27 Murray T. Brown, CAB, ibid., no. 4, 23 Feb. 1961, 93, 98. Ralph Snelgrove, vice-president CAB, ibid., 101–2.

28 LAC, RG 100, BBG, microfilm M-3074, Public Hearing, Television Regulations, 2–3 Nov. 1959, Ottawa, 218–19. See also SCoB, Minutes, no. 2, 16 Feb. 1961, 45.

29 Murray Chercover, president and managing director of the CTV Network, to SCoBFA, Minutes, 23 April 1970, 21:51.

30 SCoB, Minutes, no. 3, 20 Feb. 1961, 86.

31 LAC, RG 100, vol. 34, file 183, Canadian Council of Authors and Artists, 'Brief to BBG regarding proposed television regulations,' Sept. 1959.

32 Andrew Stewart, 'Canadian Broadcasting,' Address to the Hamilton Association, Hamilton, Ontario, 28 Jan. 1961, quoted in Stewart and Hull, *Canadian Television Policy*, 43.

33 CAB, quoted in SCoB, Minutes, no. 4, 23 Feb. 1961, 107.

34 The first few years required occasional changes to the level as a means of assisting stations in achieving them. The original quotas were to be 45 per

cent from 1 April 1961 to 30 March 1962 and to be increased to 55 per cent following 1 April 1962. In May 1962 the Canadian content regulations were amended to include a minimum of 40 per cent Canadian content from 6:00 p.m. to midnight. In June 1962 the board added subsection (3a) to section 6 to reduce it to 45 per cent for the summer months, to help stations deal with the decrease in summer television viewing. The board did the same for the summers of 1963 and 1964. In the summer of 1964 the regulations were amended to change the measurement from four-week periods to a four-quarters-of-a-year system, making it easier for stations to program over the summer. See Babe, *Canadian Television Broadcasting Structure.*

35 Don Jamieson, SCoB, Minutes, no. 1, 13 Feb. 1961, 32; Murray T. Brown, CAB, ibid., no. 4, 23 Feb. 1961, 104.
36 CBC, *Broadcasting in Canada,* 24.
37 Ibid., 45.
38 See Edwardson, 'Other Canadian Voices.'
39 BBG, *Report of the Consultative Committee on Program Policy 1967–68,* 36.
40 James, *Film as a National Art,* 347; *Year Book of the Canadian Motion Picture Industry, 1952–1953,* 134.
41 Morris, *Canadian Feature Films, 1913–1969.* Number tabulated from Morris's listings, 4–12.
42 NFB Archives, NFB, Minutes, 1 Nov. 1954, 12, 13.
43 Ibid., 27 Jan. 1958, 4.
44 NFB Archives, 5–1: AMPPLC, box 77, Lochnan to Mulholland, 'British Quota – What it means,' 17 Oct. 1959, 2, 3.
45 Ibid., Department of External Affairs, letter, 16 April 1959, 2, 3.
46 Ibid., U.S. Department of Commerce, 'Production of Movies in India Maintained at High Level,' 23 Sept. 1959.
47 Ibid., file 2477, 'Presentation to the Government of Canada by the Association of Motion Picture Producers and Laboratories of Canada Concerning the Development of the Film Industry in Canada,' Oct. 1959, 24, 25.
48 Ibid., 'Presentation to the Government of Canada by the Association of Motion Picture Producers and Laboratories of Canada Concerning the Development of the Film Industry in Canada,' Oct. 1959, Appendix IV, 'Theatrical Feature Production (Section 7),' 1, 2.
49 NFB, Minutes, 26–27 Oct. 1959, 5.
50 NFB Archives, 5–1: AMPPLC, box 77, file 3021, 'Summary of Comments of Conclusions offered by the National Film Board,' regarding Association of Motion Picture Producers and Laboratories of Canada brief, unnumbered draft version, Oct. 1960, 24 and 25(5).

51 Ibid., 'AMPPLC Brief,' 24.

52 Ibid., file 3021, 'Summary of Comments of Conclusions offered by the National Film Board,' regarding Association of Motion Picture Producers and Laboratories of Canada brief, unnumbered draft version, Oct. 1960, 24.

53 The full list consist of Argentina, Australia, Austria, Belgium, Brazil, Burma, Chile, Columbia, Denmark, Egypt, Finland, Formosa, France, Greece, Hong Kong, Indonesia, Israel, Italy, Japan, the Netherlands, New Zealand, Norway, Pakistan, Paraguay, the Philippines, Portugal, Spain, Sweden, Turkey, the United Kingdom, and the West Indies. See ibid., 1954 MPEA Annual Report, cited in 'Summary of Comments of Conclusions offered by the National Film Board,' regarding Association of Motion Picture Producers and Laboratories of Canada brief, unnumbered draft version, Oct. 1960, 24(2)–24(3).

54 Ibid., 25(5).

55 Ibid., file 2477, 'Brief prepared for Minister's use for the meeting between Minister and representatives of AMPPLC Nov. 2–60,' 27 Oct. 1960, 9.

56 Ibid., 10.

57 Ibid., 'Minutes of the AMPPLC,' Montreal, 4 Nov. 1960, 7.

58 Ibid.

59 Ibid., 1–3–23, vol. 3, 'Report of the President of the AMPPLC to the Thirteenth Annual Meeting,' AMPPLC, Toronto, 12–13 May 1960.

60 *Canadian Film Weekly*, 13 Jan. 1960, 5.

61 *Year Book of the Canadian Motion Picture Industry*, 1959–60, 89.

62 *Year Book of the Canadian Motion Picture Industry*, 1960–1, 121.

63 Magder, *Canada's Hollywood*, 103.

64 Miller, 'The Canadian Film Development Corporation,' 109–10, 114.

65 Massey Commission, *Report*, 60.

66 Ibid., 64.

67 Ibid.

68 Ibid.

69 Litvak and Maule, *Cultural Sovereignty*, 30, 31.

70 Ibid., 32.

71 Established by Order in Council, PC 1270–16, Sept. 1960.

72 LAC, RG 33–47, vol. 10, Transcripts, vol. 20, 4–5, Lloyd M. Hodgkins, president, Magazine Publishers Association of Canada.

73 Ibid., 15.

74 Korinek, *Roughing It in the Suburbs*, 57.

75 Canada, Royal Commission on Publications, *Report*, 16; LAC, RG 33–47, vol. 10, Transcripts, vol. 20, 15.

76 Jack Pickersgill, House of Commons, *Debates*, 13 July 1960, 6236.

77 LAC, RG 33–47, vol. 7, Transcripts, vol. 3, 67.

78 Ibid., vol. 4, 29, E. Paul Zimmerman, president Reader's Digest Association (Canada) Ltd.

79 Ibid., 22.

80 Ibid., vol. 19, 99, Commissioner J. George Johnston.

81 Ibid., vol. 20, 7.

82 Canada, Royal Commission on Publications, *Report*, 7.

83 Ibid., 71.

84 Ibid., 215.

85 Ibid., 75.

86 LAC, RG 33–47, vol. 10, Transcripts, vol. 21, 68, Claude Bissell, Canada Council.

87 Ibid., H.T. Mitchell of Mitchell Press Ltd.

88 Canada, Royal Commission on Publications, *Report*, 79.

89 LAC, RG 33–47, vol. 10, Transcripts, vol. 19, 103, Allan B. Yeates, president of the Association of Canadian Advertisers, speaking on the behalf of the Canadian Association of Advertising Agencies and Association of Canadian Advertisers.

90 LAC, RG 33–47, vol. 27, 'Newspaper Clippings,' *Toronto Daily Star*, 5 Sept. 1961.

91 Ibid., Diefenbaker, quoted in 'O'Leary Plan to Be Watered Down,' *Toronto Telegram*, 12 Sept. 1961.

92 John G. Diefenbaker, quoted in 'PM Stands His Ground on Curbing Magazines,' *Globe and Mail*, 25 Jan. 1962, 19.

93 Litvak and Maule, *Cultural Sovereignty*, 71.

94 For a sampling, see *Financial Post*, 7 March and 18 April 1964; *La Presse*, 21 March 1964; *St. John's Telegram*, 25 June 1964.

95 NFB Archives, box 5, file 4125, 'Film Distribution Practices, Problems, and Prospects,' vol. 2, A Report for the Interdepartmental Committee on the Possible Development of Feature Film Production in Canada, May 1965, 10, 13–14. See also chapter 10 below.

96 Ibid., 28.

97 Statement from the guild's brief to the committee, quoted in *Canadian Broadcaster*, 21 May 1964. Almost a decade later a survey commissioned by the secretary of state would confirm this as a significant problem. See LAC, RG 97, box 359, file 5800–0, pt.1, 25 Jan. 1966 – 15 Sept. 1972, Social Survey Research Centre Limited, 'An Assessment of the Problems in the Distribution of Canadian Films,' for the Film Distribution Committee, Undersecretary of State, circa.1972, ii.

98 House of Commons, *Debates*, 20 June 1966, 6621; CFDC, *Annual Report*, 1968–9, 7–8.

99 Maurice Lamontagne in *Time* (Canada), 22 Oct. 1965, 21.

100 Judy LaMarsh, 'Close-up on Bill C-204,' *Take One* 1, no. 1 (Sept.-Oct. 1966): 4–5.

101 'The Trials of Judy the Movie Maker,' *Globe and Mail*, 10 Sept. 1966.

102 Ibid. A year later she reiterated her position that the corporation would not 'produce licentious films, but we want to produce films which are of good commercial quality and of value.' See LaMarsh, House of Commons, *Debates*, 27 Jan. 1967, 12376.

103 CFDC, quoted in 'Film Corporation Bows to Sex,' *Toronto Star*, 6 Oct. 1970.

104 LaMarsh, House of Commons, *Debates*, 27 Jan. 1967, 12378–9.

105 Magder, *Canada's Hollywood*, 137.

106 Bertrand, '"National Identity"/"National History"/"National Film."'

107 Lamontagne, quoted in '$10,000,000 Government Pledge a First Step to $50,000,000 Film Industry,' *Toronto Telegram*, 14 Oct. 1965; LaMarsh, House of Commons, *Debates*, 27 Jan. 1967, 12368.

108 LaMarsh, quoted in 'Canadian Film Fund Looking for a Hard-Headed Manager,' *Montreal Star*, 6 May 1967.

109 'Fourteen Films in the Running for Etrog's Approval,' *Globe and Mail*, 19 Sept. 1970.

4. Canadian Content Woes

1 LAC, MG 31–D73, vol. 4, file 78, Peter C. Newman to A. Rotstein, 7 July 1965; emphasis in original.

2 Ibid., Newman to Rotstein, 18 May 1965. This letter has also been discussed in Edwardson, '"Kicking Uncle Sam Out of the Peaceable Kingdom."'

3 Robert Fulford in *Saturday Night*, March 1982, 36.

4 Granatstein, *Canada 1957–1967*, 151. Of course, the Canada Council was neither the first nor the only source of governmental patronage. Provincial support for the arts was provided by the Alberta Cultural Development Branch (1946), the Saskatchewan Arts Board (1949), the Quebec Department of Cultural Affairs (1961), the Ontario Council for the Arts (1963), the Manitoba Arts Council (1965), and the British Columbia Centennial Cultural Fund Committee (1967).

5 Canada Council, *Annual Report*, 1960–1, 4.

6 LAC, MG 28–I189, vol. 15, file 19, *CCA Seminar '65 Report*, 1.

7 Ackroyd, *Anniversary Compulsion*, 83; Woodcock, *Strange Bedfellows*, 104.

8 Ackroyd, *Anniversary Compulsion*, 82, 85.

9 Ackroyd, *Anniversary Compulsion*, 83; Woodcock, *Strange Bedfellows*, 104.

10 G. Hamilton Southam, quoted in Ackroyd, *Anniversary Compulsion*, 87.

11 Member, SCoBFA, Minutes, 13 June 1966, 1171.

12 Ibid., 1172.

13 'First Arts Centre Director Named,' *Ottawa Journal*, 10 March 1967.

14 'Canada Music Council Attacks Program for Opening of Arts Centre,' *Ottawa Citizen*, 24 March 1969.

15 Mavor Moore, quoted in 'Moore Blasts Spending on the Arts in Canada,' *St. John's Evening Telegram*, 17 April 1969.

16 Jim Gerrard, former director of the Theatre Passe Muraille, interview with Betty Lee, 'Can These Directors Come Up with an Answer,' *Globe and Mail*, 21 Feb. 1970, Supplement, 15.

17 LAC, RG 97, vol. 288, file 5120–1, pt.2, artistic director of the Factory Theatre Lab Ken Glass to Faulkner, 8 March 1973.

18 Richard Paul Knowles, a professor of drama at the University of Guelph, describes Stratford as 'the solidification of a delayed colonial celebration of a 19th-century brand of Canadian nationalism configured on an imperialist British model (one that allows Canada's national theatre to be dedicated to the plays of *the* canonical British writer).' See Knowles, 'The Stratford Festival, Free Trade, and the Discourses of Intercultural Tourism,' 20.

19 Martin Kinch, artistic director of Theatre Passe Muraille, interview with Betty Lee, 'Can These Directors Come Up with an Answer,' *Globe and Mail*, 21 Feb. 1970, Supplement, 15.

20 LAC, MG 28–I278, 'Arts Clippings,' vol. 8, file 1, Ron Evans, 'No Meaning for Canadians,' *Toronto Telegram*, 7 July 1966.

21 *Times* drama critic Irving Wardle, quoted in 'U.K. Critic Finds Stratford "Uneasy",' *Toronto Star*, 11 Aug. 1971.

22 Gittins, *CTV*, 73.

23 Ibid., 73, 78, 87, 89, 102.

24 LaMarsh, House of Commons, *Debates*, 1 Nov. 1967, 3748.

25 House of Commons, *Debates*, 24 Nov. 1964, 10438.

26 BBG, *Report of the Consultative Committee on Program Policy 1967–68*, 37.

27 *Canada Gazette*, part II, 23 May 1962, 573.

28 BBG, *Report of the Consultative Committee*, 37.

29 LAC, RG 100, vol. 33, file 178, 'BBG Correspondence,' Ross McLean, Research Director – Programs, to T.J. Allard, Exec. VP CAB, 28 Jan. 1963.

30 Babe, *Canadian Television Broadcasting Structure*, 26.

31 'Kids' TV: The Best and Worst,' *Chatelaine*, Sept. 1974, 39.

32 Gittins, *CTV*, 69, 79.

33 'Sesame Street Program Now Giving Viewers Canadian Material,' *Daily Gleaner*, 10 March 1973.

34 'Kids' TV: The Best and Worst,' *Chatelaine*, Sept. 1974, 39.

35 Wolfe, *Jolts*, 17.

36 Ibid.

37 Ibid., 23, 24.

38 SCoB, Minutes, no. 5, 21 May 1959, Appendix A, 'CBC Television Program Cost and Revenue Notes,' 131–2. The currency is not specified, but it is likely that both amounts are in Canadian dollars.

39 Canada, Advisory Committee on Broadcasting, *Report*, 30, 35.

40 Ibid., 63. Interestingly, the CAB reiterated the possibility two years later to the SCoBFA, but once again met with little interest (Minutes, 9 Jan. 1967, 1473).

41 Canada, Advisory Committee on Broadcasting, *Report*, 36.

42 Alphonse Ouimet, CBC, SCoBFA, Minutes, 22 Nov. 1966, 1336.

43 Canada, Advisory Committee on Broadcasting, *Report*, 46.

44 Ibid., 49.

45 Ibid., 46.

46 SCoB, Minutes, no. 2, 16 Feb. 1961, 46.

47 Grant, 'The Regulation of Program Content in Canadian Television,' 361.

48 Babe, *Canadian Television Broadcasting Structure*, 146.

49 Grant, 'The Regulation of Program Content in Canadian Television,' 348.

50 Yorke, *Axes, Chops and Hot Licks*, 5.

51 Ibid., 202.

52 Walt Grealis, quoted ibid., 4.

53 'Kim, Reno, Lightfoot among award winners,' *Globe and Mail*, 23 Feb. 1970.

54 For an interesting autobiography of a Canadian musician who did well on the live music scene but was continuously overlooked by radio stations, see Tom Connors's *Stompin' Tom before the Fame* and *Stompin' Tom and the Connors Tone*.

55 Ronnie Hawkins quoted in Yorke, *Axes, Chops and Hot Licks*, 68.

56 Ronnie Hawkins quoted in Nicholas Jennings, *Before the Gold Rush*, 59.

57 See Jennings, *Before the Gold Rush*, for an anecdotal survey of this musical scene.

58 Neil Young quoted in Yorke, *Axes, Chops and Hot Licks*, 140.

59 Knelman, *This Is Where We Came In*, 47.

60 Quoted in Miller, 'The Canadian Film Development Corporation,' 239.

61 LAC, MG 28–I189, vol. 30, file 2, The Toronto Film-maker's Co-op, 'Proposals for Canada's Film Policy: A Brief to the Honourable Gérard Pelletier, Secretary of State,' May 1972, 12.

62 'Les cinéastes à Lesage: aider la production du long métrage à même les revenus de la taxe d'amusement,' *Le Devoir*, 23 March 1964.

63 *Time* (Canada), 28 Sept. 1970.

64 Miller, 'The Canadian Film Development Corporation,' 166.

65 *Montreal Star,* 24 July 1971.

66 Donald Shebib quoted in 'Fourteen Films in the Running for Etrog's Approval,' *Globe and Mail,* 19 Sept. 1970.

67 LAC, MG 28–I189, vol. 30, file 2, The Toronto Film-maker's Co-op, 'Proposals for Canada's Film Policy: A Brief to the Honourable Gérard Pelletier, Secretary of State,' May 1972, 4.

68 Audley, *Canada's Cultural Industries,* 99.

69 See Robert Lecker's comments about the series and his experience with the topic in his introduction to *Making It Real,* 18, 19.

70 See Lecker, 'The New Canadian Library.'

71 Metcalf, *What Is a Canadian Literature?* 43.

5. Creating the Peaceable Kingdom

1 Quoted in 'Attack on Ottawa's Economic Policies Led by Liberal MPs at CIC Convention,' *Globe and Mail,* 13 Dec. 1971.

2 Canada Council, *Annual Report,* 1971–2, 39.

3 LAC, MG 32–B44, vol. 38, file 1, Walter Gordon, Notes for Remarks at the University of British Columbia Alma Mater Society, Student Orientation Program, 24 Sept. 1970, 1.

4 LAC, MG 31–D73, vol. 4, file 61, Rotstein to Gordon, 14 Jan. 1966.

5 Grant, *Lament for a Nation,* 4. Bernard Ostry has argued that 'Grant's thesis relates most deeply to his belief that we are witnesses to the end of Western Christianity and whatever the merits of his argument, it seemed to herald the growth of a new consciousness of the vital role of culture in national life, and of increasing demands from artists and intellectuals that Canadian governments should do something more about it.' See Ostry, *Cultural Connection,* 96.

6 Grant, *Lament for a Nation,* 2.

7 James Laxer quoted in Taylor, *Radical Tories,* 148. Grant denied trying to spark a new nationalist consciousness, but as his biographer William Christian noted, *Lament for a Nation* 'argued with enormous cogency that Canada was finished as an independent nation in North America, yet it was one of the most significant factors in creating the Canadian nationalist movement of the 1970s.' See Christian, *George Grant,* 271.

8 Resnick in *Land of Cain,* 165.

9 Quoted in Levitt, *Silent Surrender,* 1–2.

10 Atwood, *Survival,* 41; Grant, *Technology and Empire,* 219.

11 Interesting to note, a wonderfully multinational origin underwrites the term 'Peaceable Kingdom,' as explored in Kokotailo, 'Creating *The Peaceable Kingdom*.' The phrase originally comes from nineteenth-century American Quaker minister and folk artist Edwards Hicks's paintings of 'The Peaceable Kingdom,' a series initially based on an engraving by English artist Richard Westall titled *The Peaceable Kingdom of the Branch*. In 1965 Northrop Frye employed the phrase in the conclusion to his *Literary History of Canada*. It was then picked up by William Kilbourn. Fry used the Peaceable Kingdom idea, according to Kilbourn, 'to identify that which is most essentially Canadian in our literature.' See Kilbourn, *Canada*, xvii.

12 Kilbourn, *Canada*, xi.

13 Rotstein, 'Is There an English-Canadian Nationalism?' 16. Or, in a less flattering description offered by political scientist Philip Resnick, 'there was a bit of bravura, even *prepotenza*, in the air as English-Canadian nationalists of one stripe or another set about the task of charting their brave new society of the future.' See Resnick, *Thinking English Canada*, 58; emphasis in original.

14 Resnick, *Land of Cain*, 174.

15 Ibid., 159.

16 Thompson and Randall, *Canada and the United States*, 206.

17 See Azzi, *Walter Gordon and the Rise of Canadian Nationalism*, chapter 3, 'The Gordon Commission.'

18 See ibid., chapter 4, 'It Was Walter Gordon's Budget.'

19 Ibid., 109.

20 Quoted in Gordon, *A Choice for Canada*, 82–3, and Mowat, 'Letter to My Son,' 3.

21 Quoted in Gordon, *A Choice for Canada*, 72, and *Storm Signals*, 42–3.

22 For an overview of the period, see Kostash, *Long Way from Home*, and Versuh, *Underground Times*.

23 Edwardson, 'Kicking Uncle Sam Out of the Peaceable Kingdom,' 139.

24 Mowat, 'Letter to My Son,' 5. Mowat's anti-Americanism in this article was so intense that when, almost twenty years later, he was denied entrance into the United States, he listed it as a possible reason why. See *My Discovery of America*, 38.

25 Quoted in Edwardson, 'Kicking Uncle Sam Out of the Peaceable Kingdom,' 140.

26 Pamphlet produced by the Committee for an Independent Canada. See ibid.

27 Schou, 'The Charisma of the Liberators,' 65.

28 A 1967 Gallup Poll, cited in Owram, *Born at the Right Time*, 300.

29 Canadian Institute of Public Opinion, *Gallup Report*, 14 Oct. 1970.

30 T.C. Douglas, House of Commons, *Debates*, 9 Oct. 1970, 39, 40.

31 LaMarsh, *Memoirs of a Bird in a Gilded Cage*, 77.

32 Grant, introduction to 1970 edition of *Lament for a Nation*, viii.

33 Rotstein in *Foreign Affairs*, Oct. 1976.

34 Mathews and Steele, *The Struggle for Canadian Universities*, 40–1.

35 Melville Watkins at a University of Alberta teach-in, 25 Nov. 1969; quoted in Godfrey, *Gordon to Watkins to You*, 127.

36 Watkins, ibid., 61.

37 See Bullen, 'The Ontario Waffle and the Struggle for an Independent Socialist Canada.'

38 See LAC, MG 31–D190, vols. 34 and 35.

39 The CIC ended in 1981 and was replaced by the Council of Canadians four years later.

40 LAC, MG 32–B44, vol. 29, file 'Committee for an Independent Canada 1971,' *Toronto Star*, Feb. 1971.

41 Quoted in 'Independence Talk Would Have Baffled C.D. Howe,' *Toronto Star*, 13 Dec. 1971.

42 Quoted in 'Eddie Goodman Leads Independence Group: Committee Decides Canada Still Worth Saving, Adopts a Constitution,' *Globe and Mail*, 13 Dec. 1971.

43 Gordon, *A Choice for Canada*, 53; *Storm Signals*, 87, 120.

44 Chatterjee, *The Nation and Its Fragments*, 8.

45 Lorimer, 'Book Publishing in English Canada,' 60.

46 Atwood, *Survival*, 13.

47 This list of books was previously published in Edwardson, 'Kicking Uncle Sam Out of the Peaceable Kingdom,' 139.

48 Fulford, Godfrey, and Rotstein, *Read Canadian*, viii.

49 Atwood, 'Survival Then and Now,' 49.

50 Atwood, *Survival*, 238.

51 Ibid., 13.

52 Metcalf, *What Is a Canadian Literature?* 29.

53 Mathews, 'Centennial Song.'

54 Mathews, *Treason of the Intellectuals*, 114.

55 Commission on Canadian Studies, *Report*, vol. 3: 29.

56 Sirluck, 'An Opportunity to Achieve Emergent-Nation Status in Higher Education,' 15.

57 Mathews and Steele, *The Struggle for Canadian Universities*, 3.

58 Ibid., 67.

59 Ibid. and Mathews and Steele, 'The Universities,' 175.

60 Mathews and Steele, *The Struggle for Canadian Universities*, 18.

61 Ibid., 177.

62 LAC, RG 97, vol. 288, file 5120–1, pt.2, Ken Glass, artistic director of the Factory Theatre Lab, to Faulkner, 8 March 1973.

63 'Another Theatre for New Talent Is Taking Shape,' *Toronto Star*, 3 July 1970.

64 See Johnston, *Up the Mainstream*, for an interesting examination of this movement.

65 Harvey Markowitz quoted in 'It's Still a Bumpy Road for Canadian Plays, Playwrights,' *Globe and Mail*, 10 Oct. 1970.

66 Arnold Edinborough in *Financial Post*, 3 April 1971.

67 See, for example, Usmiani, *Second Stage*.

68 See, for example, *Globe and Mail*, 3 May 1971; *Toronto Telegram*, 3 May 1971; *Montreal Gazette*, 4 May 1971.

69 *Toronto Star*, 20 May 1971.

70 Steven High, '"I'll Wrap the F*#@ Canadian Flag around Me,"' 206–7.

71 For an interesting episode in this challenge, see Martin Kinch, artistic director of Theatre Passe Muraille, in interview with Betty Lee, 'Can These Directors Come Up with an Answer,' *Globe and Mail*, 21 Feb. 1970, Supplement, 15.

72 Committee for an Independent Canada (Hendry), 'Theatre in Canada,' 1.

73 Ibid.

74 LAC, RG 63, vol. 1360, file 'Periodical Appraisal,' document: 'The Literary Arts. Report of a meeting held in Toronto Prior to the Canadian Conference of Arts to discuss the Policy of the Canada Council in Relation to the Arts,' 2–3 May 1961, 3.

75 'Stratford May not Want Canadian Plays,' *Globe and Mail*, 5 Aug. 1969.

76 John Palmer quoted in 'CPT Proving Audiences Want to See Canadian Plays,' *Toronto Telegram*, 16 Aug. 1969.

77 Jim McPherson, ibid.

78 Pettigrew and Portman, *Stratford*, 32.

79 'MSO Getting Wider Support from the Public,' *Montreal Star*, 28 Sept. 1971.

80 Alexander Brott, director of the McGill Chamber Orchestra, Letter to the Editor, *Montreal Star*, 27 Nov. 1971.

81 'ASO Is not Neglecting 20th Century Composers,' *Halifax Mail Star*, 20 July 1972.

82 'Granted $190,000,' *Telegraph-Journal* (Saint John, NB), 12 July 1971.

83 Henry Comor, 'American TV: What Have You Done to Us?' *Take One*, Feb. 1967, 6.

84 The film not only contained Americans in the lead roles but was also financed in part by American money. See 'U.S.-Financed Film Centre of Row,' *Toronto Star*, 8 Oct. 1970.

85 *Ottawa Journal*, Dec. 1971, quoted in LAC, MG 28–I189, vol. 30, file 2, The Toronto Film-maker's Co-op, 'Proposals for Canada's Film Policy,' a brief to the Hon. Gérard Pelletier, secretary of state, May 1972.

86 Geoff Pevere, 'On the Road Again: The Making of a Canadian Classic,' *Take One*, no. 8 (summer 1995): 9.

87 Pallister, *The Cinema of Quebec*, 432, 433.

88 Lawrence Grossberg, 'Identity and Cultural Studies,' 89.

89 LAC, RG 97, vol. 293, file 5250–1, pt.6, Harry J. Boyle, CRTC chairman, 'Cultural Considerations,' presentation to 'Canadian-American Relations: Culture, Energy and Commerce' seminar, Montreal, 2 April 1977, 4.

6. Guaranteed Culture

1 Milligan, 'The Ambiguities of the Canada Council,' 66.

2 Metcalf, *What Is a Canadian Literature?* 102.

3 Quoted in Pettigrew and Portman, *Stratford*, 47.

4 See Knelman, *A Stratford Tempest*.

5 Knowles, 'The Stratford Festival,' 28.

6 Composers, Authors and Publishers Association of Canada, letter to Robert Stanbury, Chairman of the Committee on Broadcasting, SCoBFA, Minutes, 14 Feb 1967, Appendix 18, 2078.

7 LAC, MG 28–I189, vol. 18, file 2, *CCA Seminar '67 Report*.

8 Ibid., 7, 23–4, 27.

9 LAC, MG 28–I189, vol. 34, file 3, CCA, 'Declaration of Cultural Concern,' draft, 1973, 26.

10 Canada Council, *Annual Report*, 1971–2, 21. Don Rubin has claimed that 'it was out of this conference that the original demand for 50 per cent Canadian content was first heard.' See Rubin, *Creeping toward a Culture*, 26.

11 Usmiani, *Second Stage*, 28.

12 Canada Council, *Annual Report*, 1971–2, 21.

13 Ibid.

14 'Canadian Theatres Looking Inward,' *Vancouver Sun*, 19 Nov. 1971.

15 Canada Council, *Annual Report*, 1971–2, 13.

16 LAC, RG 63, vol. 1360, file 'Periodical Appraisal,' document: 'The literary arts, Report of a meeting held in Toronto Prior to the Canadian Conference of Arts to discuss the Policy of the Canada Council in Relation to the Arts,' 2–3 May 1961.

17 LAC, RG 63, André Fortier, director, Canada Council, 'Is There a Future for the Symphony Orchestra in Canada?' (notes for a talk at the Joint Conference of the Association of Canadian Orchestras and the Ontario Federation of Symphony Orchestras, Hamilton, 28 April 1974), 9.

18 ACTRA, 'A Policy for the Seventies,' Oct. 1973, 26.

19 Committee for an Independent Canada (Hendry), 'Theatre in Canada,' 8.

20 Committee for an Independent Canada (Pachter), 'The Visual Arts in Canada,' attached proposals and voting results numbered 27, 28.

21 'Stratford '68: All-Canadian to the Top,' *Toronto Daily Star,* 8 June 1968.

22 Ibid.

23 'A Plea for a Canadian as Art Gallery Curator,' *Toronto Star,* 22 June 1972.

24 'Art Gallery Elects Its New President,' *Toronto Star,* 22 Sept. 1972. The Banff Centre for the Arts in 1973 faced a similar situation when a group of artists called for a Canadian artist be appointed to lead the centre. See LAC, MG 28–I278, vol. 2, file 2, 'Banff Festival of the Arts, 1972,73,' 'Banff Centre Protest Mounting,' *Edmonton Journal,* dated 11 Aug. 73.

25 'Protests Puzzle Art Gallery Curator,' *Toronto Star,* 8 July 1972.

26 MG 28-I189, vol. 23, Canadian Artists' Representation (CAR), Ontario Region, 'Brief to "Direction Ontario" Conference of the CCA,' Toronto, Jan. 1973, 5.

27 LAC, MG 28–I278, 'Arts Clippings,' Jack Pollock (likely the Toronto artist and gallery owner), Letter to the editor, unidentified newspaper, n.d., circa 1972.

28 LAC, MG 28–I278, vol. 34, file 3, Tom Burroughs, quoted in 'Manager appointed to festival,' *Ottawa Citizen,* 22 May 1971.

29 Mathews and Steele, *The Struggle for Canadian Universities,* 66.

30 Abu-Laban and Gabriel, *Selling Diversity,* 131.

31 Mathews and Steele, *The Struggle for Canadian Universities,* 113.

32 See Wolf-Devine, *Diversity and Community in the Academy.*

33 Mathews's archival fonds include an immense collection of letters ranging from support and personal anecdotes to criticism and questioning of his statistics. It is also worth noting that at this time the Canadian Association of University Teachers decided not to support the idea of a quota system or any other measure designed to ensure 'some fixed proportion' of Canadian citizens in universities. See LAC MG 31–D190, vol. 24, file 24–20, Canadian Association of Universities Teachers, '"Canadianization" and the University,' 27 June 1969, Report of the Committee of Inquiry into Non-Canadian Influence in Alberta Post-Secondary Education, Appendix A, 88.

34 Muni Frumhartz to Robin Mathews, 7 Jan. 1969, in Mathews and Steele, *The Struggle for Canadian Universities,* 51.

35 'Professor Fighting: 61 Per cent of Research Grants Go to "Non-Canadians,"' *Ottawa Citizen,* 16 Feb. 1970, 12.

36 LAC, MG 31–D190, vol. 30, file 30–9, 'Americanization study causes local furor,' *The Chevron* (University of Waterloo), 20 Aug. 1969, 1.

37 Cormier, *The Canadianization Movement,* 191.

38 LAC, MG 28–I-187, vol. 2, file 2–3, CSAA subcommittee on the future of anthropology, *Annual Report,* 1971.

39 LAC, MG 28–I-187, vol. 4, file 4–13, 'Motion Passed by the Annual General Meeting of the CSAA on May 30/31, 1972,' 1.

40 'Studies Found to Be too American: Canadian Sociologists Out to Cut U.S. Role in Discipline,' *Montreal Star*, 31 May 1972.

41 LAC, MG 28–I-187, vol. 5, file 5–1, CSAA Canadianization Subcommittee Resolutions, 9 Dec. 1972.

42 Ibid., Donald P. Warwick, Chair of York University Department of Sociology and Anthropology, to CSAA president Pierre Maranda, 19 Feb. 1973.

43 Ibid., Jack Steinbring, chair of the University of Windsor Anthropology Department, to CSAA president Pierre Maranda, 1 Feb. 1973.

44 Ibid., Elaine Cumming, chair of the University of Victoria's Anthropology and Sociology Department, to CSAA president Pierre Maranda, 7 Feb. 1973.

45 LAC, MG 28–I-187, vol. 4, file 4–12, CSAA, Annual General Meeting, 30 May 1973.

46 LAC, MG 28–I-187, vol. 5, file 5–1, 'Report of the Committee on Canadian Content,' Canadian Political Science Association, Annual Meeting, Aug. 1973, 1, 24.

47 Letter from Khayyam Z. Paltiel, chair, Carleton University Department of Political Science, to Jean Laponce, Canadian Political Science Association, 23 Feb. 1973; LAC, MG 28–I-187, vol. 5, file 5–1, 'Report of the Committee on Canadian Content,' Canadian Political Science Association, Annual Meeting, Aug. 1973, Appendix III; emphasis in original.

48 Thomas Perry quoted in 'Are Canadian Universities Committing Cultural Genocide,' *UBC Alumni Chronicle*, winter 1969, 15.

49 Commission on Canadian Studies, *To Know Ourselves*, vol. 1: 2.

50 Ibid., 16.

51 Ibid., 133.

52 Ibid.

53 Mathews quoted in the *Ottawa Citizen*, 9 March 1976, 3.

54 LAC, RG 97, vol. 282, Consultant's Papers – Symons, T.H.B., 'Directions in Canadian Culture: Education' (paper presented to the Symposium on Directions in Canadian Culture convened by Mount Allison University to celebrate the tenth anniversary of the establishment of the university's Program in Canadian Studies and of the Davidson Chair in Canadian Studies), 20 Oct. 1979, 6.

55 LAC, MG 31–D166, vol. 2, file 2, New Left Caucus, 'American Imperialization of the University,' 3, 4.

56 LAC, MG 31–D190, vol. 26, file 30–20, 'Canada Must Have Canadian Universities: Urgent Nationwide Campaign for an 85% Quota for Canadians in Canadian Universities,' distributed in Toronto by the 85% Canadian Quota

Campaign. According to the handwritten note on the document in
Mathews's fonds, 'Picked up during my speech at Sidney Smith Bldg, Jan 26,
1971, 1:10 pm → Re: sit-in at Dundas & University Immigration Office.'

57 LAC, MG 31–D190, vol. 24, file 24–9, Martin Lowery, president of the Canadian Union of Students, in *Toronto Star*, 2 Aug. 1969.

58 Baldwin, 'An Analysis of U.S. Imperialism,' 23.

59 Repo, *Who Needs the PhD?* 80.

60 Hugh MacLennan, in *Toronto Star*, 17 May 1969; MacLennan quoted in
Mathews and Steele, *The Struggle for Canadian Universities*, 143.

61 LAC, MG 32–B44, vol. 32, file 4, Peter C. Newman, editor, *Maclean's*, 'Brief to
the Select Committee of the Province of Ontario on Nationalism,' 27 Jan.
1972.

62 Jack McClelland quoted in 'Time Running Out for Free Canada Nationalists
Told,' *Toronto Star*, 11 Dec. 1971.

63 Committee for an Independent Canada (Page), 'Faculty Citizenship in
Canadian Universities and Colleges,' 4.

64 Ibid., 10. See ibid., Appendix A, for a breakdown per university.

65 Ibid., 2.

66 Ibid., 4.

67 Frith, 'Towards an Aesthetic of Popular Music,' 140.

68 Storey, '"Rockin" Hegemony,' 185, 186.

69 Wright, '"Dream, Comfort, Memory, Despair,"' 39.

70 'Legislated Radio: A License to Make Money?' *RPM*, 20 April 1968, 3.

71 Jim Kale quoted in Yorke, *Axes, Chops and Hot Licks*, 28.

72 Ibid., 9.

73 Ibid.

74 LAC, MG 28–I189, vol. 29, file 40, Wally Gentleman, president, Society of
Film Makers, to Pelletier, 17 Jan. 1970.

75 LAC, MG 28–I189, vol. 27, file 13, Montreal chapter of the Canadian Society
of Cinematographers, brief on 'Certain Problems Vital to the Interests of the
Canadian Film Industry,' Part two, Feb. 1969, 5, 6.

76 LAC, MG 28–I189, vol. 30, file 2, CCA 'Direction Ontario,' Committee on
Film, 29 Jan. 1973.

77 ACTRA, 'A Policy for the Seventies,' 25.

78 LAC, MG 28–I189, vol. 30, file 2, Toronto Film-makers' Co-op and
Canadian Filmmaker's Distribution Centre, 'How to make a profit doing
what we really should be doing anyway,' a brief to the Ontario Film Study
Group, Jan. 1973.

79 NFB, *Annual Report*, 1970–71, 5–6.

80 NFB Archives, Minutes, 18 July 1969, 13.

81 McPherson, SCoBFA, Minutes, 12 May 1970, 45.

82 LAC, R-738–O-7–E, vol. 8, file 21, Newman to film producer Stan Jacobson, 18 Oct 1971.

83 'Good Image for Film Board at Home, New Chairman's Aim,' *Financial Post*, 12 Sept. 1970.

84 LAC, MG 28–I-278, vol. 18, file 3, 'Arts Clippings,' 'Newman Push for Canadian content,' *Telegram*, 6 Oct. 1970.

85 LAC, R-738–O-7–E, vol. 7, file 29, Newman to Pelletier, 28 July 1970, discussing the NFB job for Newman.

86 NFB Archives, Minutes, 22–23 Oct. 1971, 2.

87 Ibid., 2, 3.

88 NFB Archives, Minutes, 17 Oct. 1970, 3. See also the minutes for 10 July 1970 and 23 Oct. 1971.

89 See the debates in NFB Archives, Minutes, 22–23 Oct. 1971.

90 LAC, R-738–O-7–E, vol. 8, file 21, Newman to Alan Brien (*Sunday Times*, London), 4 Jan. 1972.

91 Sydney Newman quoted in 'Good Image for Film Board at Home, New Chairman's Aim,' *Financial Post*, 12 Sept. 1970.

92 Sydney Newman quoted in *Cinema Canada*, Aug/Sept. 1974, 46.

93 Spencer, SCoBFA, Minutes, 6 May 1971, 27, 30.

94 Michael Macklem in a conversation recalled in his 'Seed Money,' 35.

95 LAC, RG 97, vol. 296, file 6450–3, pt. 1, 'Rohmer Says Ottawa Both Early and Late in Aiding Publishers,' unidentified newspaper, n.d., circa 1972.

96 Committee for an Independent Canada (Research and Policy Staff), 'Book Publishing in Canada,' 18.

97 LAC, RG 6, vol. 830, file 1420–190/A125, president of the Independent Publishers Association Peter Martin to Pelletier, 6 July 1971.

98 McClelland & Stewart, 'Brief to the Royal Commission on Book Publishing,' Nov. 1971, 59, 27 (seen at Queen's University Library, CA2 ON Z1 70A24).

99 It is worth noting that the idea also attracted support from the Special Senate Committee on the Mass Media (1970) and a gathering of publishers at a conference in March 1971. See Canada, Special Senate Committee on the Mass Media, *Report*, 79; *Globe and Mail*, 2 Feb. 1972.

100 Canada, Special Senate Committee on the Mass Media, *Report*, 153.

101 Ibid., 159.

102 Ibid., 99.

103 One member of the House of Commons even stated that when the French-language version occasionally offered a piece of Canadian writing, it tended to be a translated English-language work instead of one produced by a French-language author. See SCoBFA, Minutes, 25 Nov. 1975, 33.

104 Canada, Special Senate Committee on the Mass Media, *Report*, 157.
105 Ibid., 166.
106 Ibid., 79.
107 Paul Morton of Odeon-Morton Theatres, quoted in *Globe and Mail*, 9 Feb. 1974.
108 Canadian Institute of Public Opinion, 30 May 1973, in Canada, Department of the Secretary of State, *The Film Industry in Canada*, 55.

7. Saving Canada

1 'Arts "Lobby" Will Battle for Dollars,' *Calgary Albertan*, 8 Jan. 1969.
2 Trudeau, 'Quebec and the Constitutional Problem,' in *Federalism and the French Canadians*, 28–9.
3 Edwardson, 'Kicking Uncle Sam Out of the Peaceable Kingdom,' 143.
4 Thompson and Randall, *Canada and the United States*, 273.
5 LAC, RG 97, vol. 295, file 5870–1, pt.1, Francis J. Holmes, to James Richardson, MP, 16 Dec. 1972.
6 Quoted in Azzi, *Walter Gordon and the Rise of Canadian Nationalism*, 183.
7 Trudeau, House of Commons, *Debates*, 4 Oct. 1968, 795.
8 Official multiculturalism was followed by the creation of a minister of state for Multiculturalism portfolio and a Multiculturalism Directorate in the Department of the Secretary of State. Then in the 1980s a series of legislation affirmed official multiculturalism, including the Canadian Charter of Rights and Freedoms (1982), the Official Languages Act (1988), and the Canadian Multicultural Act (1988).
9 Finkel, *Our Lives*, 189.
10 Lévesque, *An Option for Quebec*, 14; emphasis in original.
11 Smith, *The Ethnic Origins of Nations*, 13, 15.
12 Ibid., 22–31.
13 See Raboy, *Movement and Messages*.
14 Canada, Task Force on Broadcasting Policy, *Report*, 211.
15 LaMarsh, *Memoirs of a Bird in a Gilded Cage*, 270.
16 Donald Davidson, CBC, SCoBFA, Minutes, 18 Feb. 1969, 541. See the SCoBFA minutes between October 1968 and February 1969 for intense debates about separatism and Radio-Canada.
17 Gerald Pratley in *Toronto Telegram*, 7 Aug. 1965.
18 Jutra quoted in 'Canada's Very Own Fiasco,' *Vancouver Sun*, 2 Oct. 1971.
19 Evans, *In the National Interest*, 225–6.
20 'Quebec Movie Maker "indifferent" to Canadian,' *Montreal Gazette*, 26 Aug. 1971.

21 *Chronicle Herald,* 14 April 1976, 23.

22 Atwood, *Survival,* 32.

23 Azzi, *Walter Gordon and the Rise Canadian Nationalism,* 169, 170.

24 LAC, MG 32–B44, vol. 37, file 9, Walter Gordon, 'Notes for Remarks to the Canadian Management Centre of the American Management Association, Inc., Montreal, March 26, 1968.'

25 LAC, RG 97, box/vol. 359, file 5400–0, pt.2, Sept. 2/69 – Nov. 17/69, Speech by Secretary of State Gérard Pelletier, 'From an Address in Lethbridge, Alberta, 1969,' cited in Suzanne Rivard to C.J. Lochnan, director, Aide aux Arts et à l'Activité Culturelle, 29 Oct. 1969.

26 Crean, *Who's Afraid of Canadian Culture?* 1.

27 LAC, RG 97, box 359, file 5400–0, pt.2, Sep. 2/69 – Nov. 17/69, 'Summary of the Brief on the Government's Cultural Policy,' no page numbers or date.

28 LAC, RG 97, vol. 358, file 5400–0, pt.1, Undersecretary of State, 'Arts and Cultural Policy,' 13 June 1968, signed by G.G.E. Steele, 2.

29 Ostry, *Cultural Connection,* 129–30.

30 Canada, Department of the Secretary of State, *Annual Report,* 1974, 5.

31 Hugo McPherson in *Time* (Canada), 3 Aug. 1970, 7.

32 Ostry, *Cultural Connection,* 120.

33 Woodcock, *Strange Bedfellows,* 117.

34 Ibid.

35 Gertrude Laing, Canada Council, SCoBFA, Minutes, 24 March 1977, 24.

36 'The Pelletier Plan for a People's Culture,' *Toronto Daily Star,* 8 Feb. 1969.

37 Macklem, 'Seed Money,' 39; emphasis in original.

38 LAC, MG 28–I189, vol. 34, file 1, CCA brief to the Government of Canada, 'A Crisis in the Arts,' Oct. 1968.

39 CCA brief to Pelletier, Jan. 1969, quoted in *Canadian Composer,* Feb. 1969, 16.

40 LAC, MG 28–I189, vol. 33, file 29, Duncan F. Cameron, national director of the CCA, to SCoBFA, Minutes, 15 April 1969, 1299–300.

41 'Culture Brings Money into Smaller Towns,' *Financial Post,* 21 June 1969.

42 'Shaw Festival Has Grown Up,' *Toronto Telegram,* 14 June 1969.

43 Babe, *Canadian Television Broadcasting Structure,* 35.

44 For details of the modifications to the ownership regulations, see CRTC, *Canadian Ownership in Broadcasting.*

45 LAC, MG 32–B44, vol. 29, file 6, CIC, 'Chronology or Canadian Policy on the Foreign Ownership Issue,' 1972, 2.

46 Babe, *Canadian Television Broadcasting Structure,* 31.

47 At the time, the board predicted that the percentage format as applied to television might not be the best way of measuring it in radio. See SCoB, Minutes, no. 1, 13 Feb. 1961, 27, 30.

48 Grealis quoted in Yorke, *Axes, Chops and Hot Licks*, 7

49 See CRTC, 'Proposed Amendments to the Radio (TV) Broadcasting Regulations,' Conflict with broadcasters led to renegotiating the increase at several points during the next few years. See Babe, *Canadian Television Broadcasting Structure*, chapter 7, 'Promotion of Canadian Content,' for a detailed overview of the changes to the regulations.

50 Pierre Juneau, SCoBFA, Minutes, 5 May 1970, 21. See also Juneau, ibid., 7 May 1973, 26.

51 CRTC, *FM Radio in Canada*. It is worth noting that single ownership of both AM and FM stations initially involved simulcasting the same programming on both bands. By the early 1960s there was interest in using the FM band to bring a different selection of material, but it was not until 1967 that the BBG instituted regulations to bring about this change, slowly increasing the amount of separate FM band material from two to six hours a day over the next three years. See Foster, *Broadcasting Policy Development*, 235.

52 See 'New Regs Redraw Canadian FM Map,' *Billboard*, 21 Sept. 1991.

53 BBG, *Report of the Consultative Committee*, 58.

54 Secretary of State Gérard Pelletier in *Commentator*, Nov. 1968, 8.

55 Pelletier, SCoBFA, Minutes, 26 May 1970, 64.

56 Juneau, ibid., 22 June 1971, 21.

57 'Submission by the Canadian Broadcasting Corporation to Canadian Radio-Television Commission Re: Proposed Amendments to Broadcasting Regulations,' CRTC, Public Hearing, Ottawa, 14 April 1970, 24.

58 ACTRA, 'A Policy for the Seventies,' 20, 21. ACTRA also called for 50 per cent on radio by 1974 (22).

59 Hardin, *Closed Circuits*, 21.

60 J.A. Pouliot, president of the Canadian Association of Broadcasters, SCoBFA, Minutes, 9 Jan. 1967, 1473.

61 CRTC, *Special Report on Broadcasting in Canada*, 74.

62 There had even recently been petitions to have the CBC reduced to 'a wholesale manufacturer' of Canadian content programs for private stations. See *Calgary Herald*, 14 March 1970.

63 See Hardin, *Closed Circuits*, for an overview of the hearings.

64 Canadian CHUM Radio Chart, 25 April 1970, in Hall, *The CHUM Chart Book*. It is worth noting that two relatively recent rankings have placed the song as the no. 1 Canadian track of all time, including in *Chart* (July–Aug. 2000) and a reader poll held by Sun Media (*Toronto Sun*, 2 July 2000). See more about this appearance and the song itself in Edwardson, 'Of War Machines and Ghetto Scenes.'

65 See SCoBFA, Minutes, 5 May 1970, 22:25–22:27 for the full debate between Juneau and the critics.

66 Gordon Ritchie, House of Commons, *Debates*, 18 June 1970, 8317.

67 Hardin, *Closed Circuits*, 40.

68 UTL, 'Pierre Juneau to the Chamber of Commerce of Victoria, British Columbia,' 19.

69 'Gallup Poll of Canada: 47 Per cent Give Approval to Canadian Content Ruling,' *Toronto Star*, 4 July 1970.

70 LAC, MG 30–D304, vol. 6, file 6–7, Mayor Leo Del Villano of Timmins, unidentified newspaper clipping, n.d.

71 LAC, MG 30–D304, vol. 22, file 22–27, Bob Ross, Letter to the editor, unidentified newspaper, 26 March 1970.

72 LAC, MG 32–B44, vol. 28, file 3, CIC Press Information, 22 April 1971, regarding CIC submission to CRTC about cable television.

73 UTL, Pierre Juneau, 'Local Cablecasting – A New Balance,' 12, 13.

74 Raboy, *Missed Opportunities*, 203; CRTC, 'Policy Announcement on Cable Television,' 17 Feb. 1975, 10.

75 Rutherford, *The Making of the Canadian Media*, 115.

76 Meisel, 'Escaping Extinction,' 260.

77 John Ross, past president, Association of Motion Picture Producers and Laboratories of Canada, SCoBFA, Minutes, 27 March 1969, 1272. The Directors Guild of Canada also requested the inclusion; see LAC, RG 97, vol. 288, file 5120–1, pt.2, John Trent, president, Directors Guild of Canada, to Hugh Faulkner, 30 Jan. 1973, 1.

78 ACTRA, 'A Policy for the Seventies,' 26.

79 Pierre Berton, Association of Canadian Television and Radio Artists, CRTC, Public Hearing, 21–24 Sept. 1971, 89.

80 LAC, MG 28–I189, vol. 32, file 9, Duncan F. Cameron, national director of the CCA, 'Arts Education and the General Public,' a Canadian commentary prepared for UNESCO conference 'An International Meeting of Experts on Arts Education and the General Public,' Ottawa, Feb. 1970, 16.

81 See Rutherford, *The New Icons?*

82 Trudeau, House of Commons, *Debates*, 12 Sept. 1973, 6471.

83 Al Johnson quoted in Nash, *The Microphone Wars*, 425.

84 Jean Chrétien, minister of Industry, Trade and Commerce, House of Commons, *Debates*, 25 Feb. 1977, 3427.

85 Trudeau, ibid., 3421, 3425.

86 Although Trudeau had originally asked only about the television service, he was informed by the CRTC that it would take only a little extra effort to extend the task to radio as well (Trudeau, House of Commons, *Debates*, 8 March 1977, 3745).

87 CRTC, 'A Content Analysis,' 35.

88 Nash, *The Microphone Wars*, 433.

89 Trudeau, House of Commons, *Debates*, 21 July 1977, 7908, 7855.
90 LAC, MG 28–I189, vol. 24, file 18, 'Publishing – A Cultural Approach,' notes for an address by the Honourable Gérard Pelletier to 'Consultation 2: Edition Conference,' Ottawa, 2 March 1971, 4, 5. See also LAC, RG 97, box 361, file 6400–0, pt.3, Department of the Secretary of State, 'A Federal Policy on Book Publishing,' 1 Dec. 1971, 2.
91 LAC, RG 97, box 361, file 6400–0, pt.3, Department of the Secretary of State, 'Summary of the memorandum to Cabinet,' 1 Dec. 1971, 1.
92 House of Commons, *Debates*, 9 Dec. 1971, 10335.
93 'Pelletier Aid Plan for Book Publishers Stalled in Cabinet,' *Globe and Mail*, 2 Feb. 1972.
94 Ontario, Royal Commission on Book Publishing, *Canadian Publishers & Canadian Publishing*, 16.
95 Ibid., 76–7, 219.
96 Ibid., 52.
97 LAC, RG 97, vol. 297, file 6430–C1, pt.1, *Toronto Star*, 9 Nov. 1972.
98 LAC, RG 97, box 361, file 6400–0, pt.3, Department of the Secretary of State, 'Developments in Federal Policy on Financing Assistance to Canadian Publishing,' 1972. See also ibid., Department of the Secretary of State, 'A Federal Policy on Book Publishing,' 1 Dec. 1971, Appendix C, 'Criteria of nationality.'
99 See letters in LAC, RG 6, vol. 830, file 1440–9, pt.3, and file 1410–5.
100 See, for example, LAC, RG 6, vol. 830, file 1440–9, pt.3, Faulkner to Mrs Helen Lindenberg, 14 April 1975; Faulkner, 'On Publishing Policy,' 34, 35.
101 Doris Anderson in *Chatelaine*, July 1974, 1.
102 *Chatelaine*, Jan. 1974.
103 Korinek, *Roughing It in the Suburbs*, 38.
104 Doris Anderson in *Chatelaine*, Dec. 1974, 1.
105 Doris Anderson, editor of *Chatelaine*, SCoBFA, Minutes, 11 Nov. 1975, 48, 49.
106 Canadian Periodical Publishers' Association, *Newsletter*, no. 19 (1 Oct. 1975): 1.
107 *Time* (Canada), 10 March 1975, 5.
108 Faulkner in *Time* (Canada), 9 Feb. 1976, 5.
109 John Scott, former editor of *Time* (Canada) and special correspondent, SCoBFA, Minutes, 24 Nov. 1975, 29.
110 E.P. Zimmerman, Reader's Digest, SCoBFA, Minutes, 24 Nov. 1975, 13.
111 Member, House of Commons, *Debates*, 23 Feb. 1976, 11166, 11167.
112 House of Commons *Debates*, 17 Nov. 1975, 9126.
113 Trudeau, House of Commons, *Debates*, 10 June 1976, 14362.

114 UTL, Pierre Juneau, 'The 25 Hour Week,' 5.

115 LAC, MG 28–I189, vol. 30, file 2, Toronto Film-makers Co-op, 'Proposals for Canada's Film Policy: A Brief to the Honourable Gérard Pelletier, Secretary of State,' May 1972, 12.

116 Hugh Faulkner, SCoBFA, Minutes, 30 March 1973, 10–11.

117 CFDC, *Annual Report*, 1973–4, 8.

118 Faulkner, House of Commons, *Debates*, 7 May 1975, 5554. See also Faulkner, Ibid., 17 Nov. 1975, 9126. There was no discussion of a 'voluntary' form of quota during these early talks. See Coline Campbell, parliamentary secretary to secretary of state, House of Commons, *Debates*, 3 June 1976, 14114.

119 Faulkner, House of Commons, *Debates*, 17 Nov. 1975, 9126.

120 CFDC, *Annual Report*, 1974–5, 9.

121 Faulkner, House of Commons, *Debates*, 7 May 1975, 5554.

122 Faulkner, ibid., 3 March 1976, 11464.

123 Faulkner, ibid., 6 Feb. 1976, 10706.

124 Faulkner, ibid., 17 Nov. 1975, 9126.

125 Ontario Minister of Education and University Affairs William G. Davis addressing the thirty-first National Conference of the Canadian University Press, in 'Licensed Premises: A Potpourri of Opinion,' *Canadian University*, March 1969, 68.

126 LAC, MG 31–D166, vol. 2, file 2, William G. Davis to Robin Mathews, 8 Aug. 1969, 2, 3.

127 LAC, MG 31–D166, vol. 18, file 18–16, Robin Mathews to William G. Davis, 9 Sept. 1971, regarding Ontario Humans Rights Commission, the possibility of ensuring appointments for Canadians, and Davis's rejection of the notion.

128 Ontario, Royal Commission on Book Publishing, *Canadian Publishers & Canadian Publishing*, 68.

129 Ontario, Select Committee on Economic and Cultural Nationalism, *Interim Report*, 14, 29.

130 Ibid., 33.

131 Ibid., 34.

132 Ibid., 33.

133 Ibid., 29.

134 Granatstein, *Yankee Go Home?* 213. See also Commission on Canadian Studies, *To Know Ourselves*, vol. 3: 42.

135 As of the 1982–3 academic year. See Granatstein, *Yankee Go Home?* 213. See also Commission on Canadian Studies, *To Know Ourselves*, 42.

136 Canada, Department of External Affairs, *Annual Review*, 1974 and 1976.

137 LAC, RG 63, vol. 1362, 'Policy File-Canada Council,' memorandum to the cabinet from the secretary of state, 'Re: Canada Council Policy-Research Programs Background,' 22 June 1970.
138 Canada, Department of the Secretary of State, *Annual Report*, 1979, 43.
139 UTL, Pierre Juneau, 'Broadcasting: A Perspective for Management,' 1972, 11.
140 UTL, Pierre Juneau, 'The 25 Hour Week,' 1971, 4.
141 UTL, 'Pierre Juneau to the Chamber of Commerce of Victoria,' 4–5.
142 Audley, *Canada's Cultural Industries*, xxv.

8. Littlest Hobos and Kings of Kensington

1 Canada, Special Senate Committee on Mass Media, *Report*, 201; emphasis in original.
2 Canada, Task Force on Broadcasting Policy, *Report*, 315.
3 Woodcock, *Strange Bedfellows*, 107.
4 Gertrude Laing in Canada Council, *Annual Report*, 1977–8, 7.
5 Quoted in Pettigrew and Portman, *Stratford*, 129.
6 Canada, Department of Canadian Heritage, *Report on Plans and Priorities 2004–05*, Appendix 2.
7 Mavor Moore quoted in 'Moore Blasts Spending on the Arts in Canada,' *St. John's Evening Telegram*, 17 April 1969.
8 Canada Council, *Annual Report*, 1978–9, 15; 1979–80, 15.
9 *Mail Star*, 28 March 1979.
10 Canada Council, *Annual Report*, 1978–9, 12.
11 Canada Council, *Annual Report*, 1979–80, 15.
12 Cited ibid., 14.
13 Canada, Task Force on the National Arts Centre, *Accent on Access*, 25, 90.
14 Nash, *The Microphone Wars*, 436.
15 Nash provides an overview of the Touchstone policy in *The Microphone Wars*, 436–77.
16 Canadian Conference of the Arts, *A Strategy for Culture*, 122.
17 Ibid.
18 Gittins, *CTV*, 106.
19 Ibid., 104.
20 Ibid., 103.
21 Hardin, 'Pushing Public Broadcasting Forward,' 222.
22 Wolfe, *Jolts*, 69–71.
23 Babe, *Canadian Television Broadcasting Structure*, 85–6.
24 Ibid., 85, 86.

25 Ibid., 65.

26 Gittins, *CTV*, 105.

27 'Ludicrous Spectacle,' *Calgary Herald*, 9 March 1970.

28 CRTC, *Symposium on Television Violence*, 163.

29 Wolfe, *Jolts*, 64.

30 CRTC, 'CBC Television,' 36.

31 The amount is taken from a CRTC report to Parliament quoted in Foster, *Broadcasting Policy Developments*, 255.

32 Wolfe, *Jolts*, 51.

33 LAC, MG 30–D304, vol. 22, file 22–27, R.E. MacMillan, letter to editor, unidentified newspaper, 6 April 1970.

34 Cameron, 'Heritage Minutes,' 19–20.

35 Straw, 'Dilemmas of Definition,' 102.

36 Pevere and Dymond, *Mondo Canuck*, 233.

37 UTL, 'Pierre Juneau to the Chamber of Commerce of Victoria, British Columbia,' 19.

38 Quoted in Yorke, *Axes, Chops and Hot Licks*, 33.

39 Quoted ibid., 89.

40 Quoted ibid., 94.

41 Quoted ibid., 58.

42 Quoted ibid., 102.

43 Gordon Lightfoot to Robert Markle in 'Early Morning Afterthoughts,' *Maclean's*, Dec. 1971, 28; emphasis in original.

44 *Time* (Canada), 1 Feb. 1971, 9.

45 Pevere and Dymond, *Mondo Canuck*, 71.

46 Canada, Federal Cultural Policy Review Committee, *Report*, 236.

47 Peter Meggs and Doug Ward, 'CBC English Radio Report, May 1970,' quoted in Stewart, *From Coast to Coast*, 166.

48 Nash, *Cue the Elephant!* 260.

49 Stewart, *From Coast to Coast*, 181, 182.

50 Ibid.,184.

51 Faulkner, SCoBFA, Minutes, 9 May 1977, 20:5.

52 Coline Campbell, parliamentary secretary to secretary of state, House of Commons, *Debates*, 3 June 1976, 14115.

53 CFDC, *Annual Report*, 1977–8, 8.

54 Roberts, SCoBFA, Minutes, 11 April 1978, 17.

55 Ibid.

56 CFDC, *Annual Report*, 1978–9, 7.

57 Marshall Delaney [Robert Fulford] in *Saturday Night*, March 1982, 61.

58 Evans, *In the National Interest*, 205.

59 Acheson and Maule, 'It Seemed Like a Good Idea at the Time,' 266.
60 Canadian Conference of the Arts, *A Strategy for Culture*, 152.
61 Faulkner, SCoBFA, Minutes, 9 May 1977, 20:6.
62 Canada, Department of the Secretary of State, *The Film Industry In Canada*, 184.
63 Telefilm Canada, *Annual Report*, 1982–3, 6.
64 Miller, 'The Canadian Film Development Corporation,' 205.
65 Michael Spencer, secretary general, Canadian Motion Picture Distributors Association, SCoCC, Minutes, 21 April 1983, 35.
66 Miller, 'The Canadian Film Development Corporation,' 168.
67 Ibid., 101.
68 Hon. Francis Fox, secretary of state and minister of Communications, SCoCC, Minutes, 26 June 1980, 31.
69 LAC, RG 97, vol. 297, file 6430–C1, pt.1, Kildare Dobbs, 'A Political Victory for New Publishers,' *Toronto Star*, 9 Nov. 1972.
70 LAC, RG 97, box 361, file 6400–0, pt.3, Department of the Secretary of State, 'Developments in Federal Policy on Financing Assistance to Canadian Publishing.' See also ibid., Department of the Secretary of State, 'A Federal Policy on Book Publishing,' 1 Dec. 1971, Appendix C, 'Criteria of nationality.'
71 Faulkner, 'On Publishing Policy,' 34, 35.
72 Lorimer, 'Book Publishing in English Canada,' 64.
73 Canada, Department of the Secretary of State, *The Publishing Industry in Canada*, 54, 55.
74 'Notes for a Statement by the Secretary of State, John Roberts, on the Canadian Book Publishing Development Program,' Toronto, 7 March 1979, 1; quoted in Audley, *Canada's Cultural Industries*, 86–7.
75 Lorimer, 'Book Publishing,' 21.
76 Robert Wright, approaching the situation from a broader perspective, offers a deft summary of how Canadian authors benefited from 'the maturation into adulthood of the baby boom and the massive institutional growth this demographic trend occasioned (most notably in higher education), the significant improvement in the national literacy rate, the emergence of a highly visible (and literate) youth counter-culture, the igniting of latent anti-Americanism (centred on a broadly based "left-nationalist" critique of US foreign policy and the "imperialistic" practices of multinational corporations) and the dramatic expansion of state regulation and subsidy in the realm of cultural production.' See Wright, *Hip and Trivial*, 17–18.
77 Paul Audley, Canadian Institute for Economic Policy, SCoCC, Minutes, 23 March 1983, 24.
78 Stephen S. LaRue in *Time* (Canada), 8 March 1976, 7.

79 Audley, *Canada's Cultural Industries*, 61.
80 The authors were Kenneth Bagnell, Fred Bodsworth, Bruce Hutchinson, Gordon Green, Harold Horwood, Sidney Katz, Adrian Waller, and David MacDonald. See section from the letter reprinted in Sutherland, *The Monthly Epic*, 210.
81 Canada, Department of the Secretary of State, *Annual Report*, 1982–3, 32–4.
82 LAC, RG 97, vol. 282, Consultant's Papers – Symons, T.H.B. Symons, 'Directions in Canadian Culture: Education,' 20 Oct. 1979, 6.
83 Vickers, 'Liberating Theory in Canadian Studies,' 352–3.
84 The numbers are taken from Gibson, 'Waiting for Blondin,' 31, and CRTC, *Special Report on Broadcasting in Canada*, 1968–1978, 74.

9. From Citizens to Consumers

 1 Faulkner, SCoBFA, Minutes, 13 March 1975, 9:17.
 2 Francis Fox, Secretary of State and Minister of Communication, SCoCC, Minutes, 10 July 1980, 9.
 3 Pierre Trudeau at the Juno Awards, 31 March 1979; quoted in Canadian Conference of the Arts, *A Strategy for Culture*, 4.
 4 Canada, Special Senate Committee on the Mass Media, *Report*, 11.
 5 Ibid., 95.
 6 CRTC, 'CBC Television,' 34.
 7 Lyttle, *A Chartology of Canadian Popular Music*, 7.
 8 LAC, RG 97, vol. 296, file 6400–7, pt.1, Jack Shapiro, chair, Canadian Publications Committee of the Periodical Distributors of Canada; quoted in *Quill & Quire*, May 1973, 2.
 9 SCoBFA, Minutes, 13 May 1973, 4.
10 Juneau, SCoBFA, Minutes, 6 May 1970, 30, 31.
11 Don Brinton, CAB vice-chair television, CAB, 'Canadian Content Review,' oral remarks, CRTC, Public Hearing, 1 Dec. 1981, Hull, Quebec, 11.
12 Faulkner, 'On Publishing Policy,' 34, 35.
13 Canada, Department of the Secretary of State, *Annual Report*, 1979, 39.
14 CFDC, *Annual Report*, 1970–1, 6.
15 Canada, Department of the Secretary of State, *Annual Report*, 1973, 6.
16 ACTRA, 'A Policy for the Seventies,' 25; CFDC, *Annual Report*, 1973–4, 4.
17 CFDC, *Annual Report*, 1974–5, 7.
18 CFDC, *Annual Report*, 1975–6, 8.
19 CFDC, *Annual Report*, 1977–8, 7.
20 CFDC, *Annual Report*, 1979–80, 8.
21 King, '"The Coffee-Boy Syndrome,"' 88.

22 Ibid.
23 Canadian Conference of the Arts, *A Strategy for Culture*, 77, 118.
24 Canada Council, 'Submission to the Federal Cultural Policy Review Committee,' 20.
25 Canada, Federal Cultural Policy Review Committee, *Report*, 95, 96.
26 Ibid., 95.
27 Canada, Task Force on the National Arts Centre, *Accent on Access*, 71. Chapter 4 is dedicated to marketing strategies.
28 Canada, Department of Communications, *Annual Report*, 1980–1, 7.
29 Marcel Masse, minister of Communications, SCoCC, Minutes, 30 April 1985, 7.
30 Nash, *The Microphone Wars*, 440.
31 Ibid.
32 'Despite Cuts and Deficits, Creatively the Arts Are in Excellent Shape,' *Financial Post*, 29 Dec. 1984.
33 'Is Arm's-Length Principle in Jeopardy?' *Globe and Mail*, 8 Dec. 1984.
34 'Will Culture Suffer at Tories' Hands?' *Globe and Mail*, 15 Nov. 1984.
35 Fox, House of Commons, *Debates*, 27 Oct. 1983, 28385.
36 Canada, Department of Communications, *Vital Links*, 7. Interestingly, *Vital Links*, concluded by invoking St Augustine's declaration 'A nation is an association of reasonable beings united in a peaceful sharing of the things they cherish,' the same line that the Massey Commission had used at the start of its report thirty-five years earlier.
37 Poll reported in Ritchie, *Wrestling with the Elephant*, 217.
38 *Toronto Star*, 5 Aug. 1986, quoted in Hutcheson, 'Culture and Free Trade,' 115.
39 Hart, *Decision at Midnight*, 112, 113.
40 Ibid., 110, 264.
41 Doern, *Faith and Fear*, 97.
42 Carr, 'Trade Liberalization and the Political Economy of Culture,' 14, 15.
43 See Berlin, *The American Trojan Horse*.
44 Department of Communications, *Annual Report*, 1986–7, 16.
45 Barbara Fairbairn has argued that broadcasting would feel little impact and that the cable industry would primarily be affected. See Fairbairn, 'Implications of Free Trade for Television Broadcasting in Canada.'
46 Thompson, 'Canada's Quest for "Cultural Sovereignty,"' 195.
47 Arnott and Tanner, 'Hard Art / Soft Art,' 113.

10. Canadianization in a Time of Globalization

1 Robert Fulford, 'Sheila Copps and the Marketing of Culture,' *National Post*, 1 Dec. 2001.

2 Metcalf, *What Is a Canadian Literature?* 97.

3 McBride, *Paradigm Shift,* 21.

4 The policy included $312 million towards the arts, including $75 million for the Canada Council, $80 million for infrastructure, $63 million for management and financial growth, $57 million to improve access among youths to artistic experiences, and $24 million towards heritage site development. As for the cultural industries, they were to receive $196 million, with $108 million going towards 'new media,' $28 million each for the book-publishing and sound-recording industries, and $32 million to develop export opportunities. See Canada, Department of Canadian Heritage, 'Canadian Arts and Culture.'

5 Ibid., 'Speaking notes for the Honourable Sheila Copps, Minister of Canadian Heritage.'

6 Canada, Department of Canadian Heritage, 'Strategic Framework,' See also Department of Canadian Heritage Act.

7 *National Post,* 1 Dec. 2001.

8 National Arts Centre, *Annual Report,* 2002–3, 1.

9 Canada Council, *Annual Report,* 2002–3, 7.

10 'FACTOR Releases Its First Financial Statement on Record Production Aid,' *Canadian Composer,* March 1983, 30, 32.

11 This has been an international phenomenon. See, for example, Breen, 'The End of the World as We Know It.'

12 Nicholas Jennings, 'Domestic Bands Win Acclaim,' *Maclean's,* 27 Jan. 1992, 52.

13 Levine, 'I Never Heard Them Call It "Show Art,"' 94.

14 See, for example, 'Hollywood Strikes Back over Canada's Subsidies,' *National Post,* 21 Aug. 1999, and 'U.S. Celebrities' Refrain: Blame Canada,' *Globe and Mail,* 15 Sept. 2001.

15 See Tate and Allen, 'Integrating Distinctively Canadian Elements into Television Drama.'

16 Magder, 'Film and Video Production,' 160–2.

17 Maule, 'Overview of Culture and Trade,' 7.

18 'Tiny Bubbles, Huge Furor,' *Edmonton Sun,* 18 June 1999.

19 Canada, Department of Canadian Heritage, *Report of the Feature Film Advisory Committee,* iii.

20 Canada, Department of Canadian Heritage, *The Government of Canada's Response to the Report of the Standing Committee on Canadian Heritage,* 2, 3.

21 Magder, 'Film and Video Production,' 174.

22 Ritchie, *Wrestling with the Elephant,* 218.

23 Canada, Industry Canada, Information Highway Advisory Council, Canadian Content and Culture Working Group, *Report,* 2.

24 CRTC, Telecom, Public Notice, CRTC 98–20, 31 July 1998.

25 CRTC, News Release, 'CRTC Won't Regulate the Internet,' 17 May 1999.

26 'Brave New World at CRTC,' *Toronto Star*, 19 May 1999.

27 CRTC, *Information*, 17 May 1999: 'Some 1998/1999 Statistics on New Media in Canada,' '71% of all web sites are American; 5% of content on the Internet is Canadian; 5% of Internet content is French.' Document includes the following note: '(These statistics are part of the record of a public process on new media (public hearing 23 November 1998 to 4 December 1998 – oral final argument 8 to 12 February 1999) and some of this information may already be outdated.)'

28 Tariff Item 9958, noted in Department of Canadian Heritage, News Release, 'Ottawa and Washington Agree on Access to the Canadian Advertising Services Market,' 26 May 1999.

29 Canada, Task Force on the Canadian Magazine Industry, *Report*, 49.

30 Vipond, *The Mass Media in Canada*, 178.

31 See Green, 'The Great Cultural Divide.'

32 Canada, Department of Canadian Heritage, Periodical Publishing Policy and Programs, *Annual Report*, 2003–4, 10.

33 Association for the Export of Canadian Books, *Annual Report*, 2002–3, 7.

34 Ibid., 1.

35 Canada, Department of Canadian Heritage, Book Publishing Industry Development Program, Support for Publishers, *Application Guide 2004–2005*, n.p.

36 Ibid., n.p.

37 Bélanger, 'Globalization, Culture, and Foreign Policy,' 165–6.

38 Maule, 'Overview of Culture and Trade,' 1.

39 Canada, Department of Canadian Heritage, 'Canadian Arts and Culture,' Fact Sheet IX.

40 Canada, Department of Canadian Heritage, *Trade Routes*, 1.

41 Schroder, 'Can Denmark Be Canadianized?' 124.

42 Collins, *Culture, Communication, and National Identity*, ix.

43 Canada. Department of Canadian Heritage, *Canadian Content in the 21st Century in Film and Television Productions*, 50.

44 Ibid., 81.

Conclusion

1 Canada, Department of Canadian Heritage, *Culture and Heritage*, 2.

2 Ibid., 3.

3 Smith, *Nationalism and Modernism*, 3.

Bibliography

Archival and Library Collections

Library and Archives Canada, Ottawa
MG 28–I187, Canadian Sociology and Anthropology Association Fonds
MG 28–I189, Canadian Conference of the Arts Fonds
MG 28–I278, Arts in Canada Clippings Collection (assembled by the Canada Council)
MG 30–D111, James Edward Hervey (J.E.H.) MacDonald Fonds
MG 30–D304, J.T. Allard Fonds
MG 30–D401, Peter Varley – Frederick Horsman Varley Collection
MG 30–E481, J. Alphonse Ouimet Fonds
MG 31–D73, Abraham Rotstein Fonds
MG 31–D166, Hugh Armstrong Fonds
MG 31–D190, Robin Mathews Fonds
MG 32–B44, Walter Gordon Fonds
R-738–0–7–E, Sydney Newman Fonds
RG 6, Department of the Secretary of State for the Provinces Fonds
RG 33–28, Royal Commission on National Development in the Arts, Letters and Sciences Fonds
RG 33–47, Royal Commission on Publications Fonds
RG 41, Canadian Broadcasting Corporation Fonds
RG 63, Canada Council Fonds
RG 97, Department of Communications Fonds
RG 100, Canadian Radio-television and Telecommunications Commission Fonds

National Film Board of Canada Archives, Montreal

General Archives

University of Toronto Library, Toronto

Collection of speeches by Pierre Juneau; call number HE 8699 .C2J85 SCC 12, box titled 'Speeches about Canadian Broadcasting: March 9, 1971 through May 6, 1974.' Includes 'The 25 Hour Week,' Juneau to the Canadian Club, Ottawa Ontario, 9 March 1971; 'Pierre Juneau to the Chamber of Commerce of Victoria, British Columbia,' 13 March 1972; 'Broadcasting: A Perspective for Management,' Juneau to the 57th Annual Advertising Seminar of the Association of Canadian Advertisers, Toronto, 1 May 1972; 'Local Cablecasting – A New Balance,' Juneau to the Canadian Cable Association, 15th Annual Convention and Trade Show, 6 July 1972.

Minutes and Hearings

Board of Broadcast Governors. Public hearings.
Canada. Parliament. House of Commons. Special Committee on Broadcasting. Minutes.
– Special Committee on Radio Broadcasting. Minutes.
– Standing Committee on Broadcasting, Film, and Assistance to the Arts. Minutes.
– Standing Committee on Culture and Communications. Minutes.
Canada. Parliament. Senate. Standing Senate Committee on Transport and Communications. Minutes.

Publications of Government Departments and Agencies

Canada. *Domestic Control of the National Economic Environment: The Problems of Foreign Ownership and Control.* Ottawa: Information Canada, 1972.
Canada. Advisory Committee on Broadcasting. *Report.* Ottawa: Queen's Printer, 1965.
Canada. Board of Broadcast Governors. *Annual Report.* Ottawa. Various years.
– 'Comment by the Canadian Association of Broadcasters in Connection with the Board of Broadcast Governors Statement of November 16, 1960 on Possible Regulatory Modifications.' Ottawa: Board of Broadcast Governors, 1960.
– *Report of the Consultative Committee on Program Policy 1967–68, Book 1: The Immediate Problems.* Ottawa: Board of Broadcast Governors, 1968.

Canada. Committee on Broadcasting. *Report of the Committee on Broadcasting.*
Ottawa: Queen's Printer, 1965.

Canada. Department of Canadian Heritage. Book Publishing Industry Development Program. Support for Publishers. *Application Guide 2004–2005.*
Gatineau: Minister of Public Works and Government Services Canada, 2004.

– 'Canadian Arts and Culture: Tomorrow Starts Today.' Backgrounder and
Fact Sheets, 2 May 2001: Fact Sheet II, 'National Arts Training Contribution
Program,' 25 May 2001; Fact Sheet III, 'Cultural Spaces Canada Program,'
25 May 2001; Fact Sheet IX, 'Cultural Export Development: Accessing a
World of Opportunity,' 2 May 2001; 'Speaking Notes for the Honourable
Sheila Copps, Minister of Canadian Heritage, on the Occasion of the Announcement of a Major Investment in Canadian Culture,' Toronto, 2 May
2001. Available at http://www.pch.gc.ca/special/tomorrowstartstoday/
en-speeches.html.

– *Canadian Content in the 21st Century in Film and Television Productions: A Matter of
Cultural Identity.* Prepared by François Macerola. Gatineau: Minister of Public
Works and Government Services Canada, 2003.

– *Culture and Heritage: Connecting Canadians through Canada's Stories, 2003.*
Gatineau: Minister of Public Works and Government Services Canada, 2003.

– *The Government of Canada's Response to the Report of the Standing Committee on
Canadian Heritage, Our Cultural Sovereignty: The Second Century of Canadian
Broadcasting.* Gatineau: Department of Canadian Heritage, 2003.

– *A Guide to Federal Programs for the Film and Video Sector.* Gatineau: Minister of
Public Works and Government Services Canada, 2003.

– *News Releases.* Various dates.

– Periodical Publishing Policy and Programs. *Annual Report.* Gatineau. Various
years.

– *Report of the Feature Film Advisory Committee: The Road to Success.* Gatineau: Minister of Public Works and Government Services Canada, 1999.

– *Report on Plans and Priorities 2004–05: Fiches on Foundations.* Gatineau: Minister
of Public Works and Government Services Canada, 2005.

– 'Strategic Framework.' Gatineau: Department of Canadian Heritage, 2002.

– *Trade Routes: Opening Doors for Canadian Arts and Cultural Exports.* Gatineau:
Minister of Public Works and Government Services Canada, 2003.

Canada. Department of Communications. *Annual Report.* Various years.

– *Vital Links: Canadian Cultural Industries.* Ottawa: Department of Communications, 1987.

Canada. Department of External Affairs. *Annual Review.* Various years.

Canada. Department of the Secretary of State. *Annual Report.* Ottawa. Various
years.

– *The Film Industry in Canada*. Ottawa: Supply and Services, 1977.

– *The Publishing Industry in Canada*. Ottawa: Supply and Services, 1977.

Canada. Federal Cultural Policy Review Committee. *Report of the Federal Cultural Policy Review Committee*. Ottawa: Supply and Services, 1982.

Canada. Industry Canada. Information Highway Advisory Council. Canadian Content and Culture Working Group. *Report of the Canadian Content and Culture Working Group: Ensuring a Strong Canadian Presence on the Information Highway*. Ottawa: Industry Canada, 1995.

Canada. Parliament. House of Commons. *Debates*. Various years.

Canada. Royal Commission on Broadcasting. *Report*. Ottawa: Queen's Printer, 1957.

Canada. Royal Commission on National Development in the Arts, Letters and Sciences (Massey Commission). *Report of the Royal Commission on Development in the Arts, Letters and Sciences in Canada*. Ottawa: Printer to the King's Most Excellent Majesty, 1951.

Canada. Royal Commission on Publications. *Report of the Royal Commission on Publications*. Ottawa: Queen's Printer, 1961.

Canada. Royal Commission on Radio Broadcasting. *Report*. Ottawa: Printer to the King's Most Excellent Majesty, 1929.

Canada. Special Senate Committee on the Mass Media. *Report of the Special Committee on the Mass Media*. Ottawa: Information Canada, 1970.

Canada. Task Force on Broadcasting Policy. *Report of the Task Force on Broadcasting Policy*. Ottawa: Supply and Services, 1986.

Canada. Task Force on the Canadian Magazine Industry. *Report of the Task Force on the Canadian Magazine Industry: A Question of Balance*. Ottawa: Minister of Supply and Services Canada, 1994.

Canada. Task Force on the National Arts Centre. *Accent on Access: Report of the Task Force on the National Arts Centre*. Ottawa: Supply and Services, 1986.

Canada Council for the Arts. *Annual Report*. Various years.

– *Opening Proceedings*. Ottawa, 1957.

– 'Submission to the Federal Cultural Policy Review Committee.' March 1981.

Canadian Co-operation Project. *Annual Report*. Various years.

Canadian Film and Television Production Agency. *Profile 2003: An Economic Report on the Canadian Film and Television Production Industry*. Ottawa: Canadian Film and Television Production Agency, 2003.

Canadian Film Development Corporation. *Annual Report*. Various years.

Canadian Radio and Television Commission. *Canadian Ownership in Broadcasting: A Report on the Foreign Divestiture Process*. Ottawa: Canadian Radio and Television Commission, 1974.

– *FM Radio in Canada: A Policy to Ensure a Varied and Comprehensive Radio Service*. Ottawa: Canadian Radio and Television Commission, 1975.

– 'Proposed Amendments to the Radio (TV) Broadcasting Regulations.' 12 February 1970.

Canadian Radio-television and Telecommunications Commission. 'CBC Television: Programming and Audiences, the English Language Service, Committee of Inquiry into the National Broadcasting Service: Background Research Paper.' Ottawa: Canadian Radio-television and Telecommunications Commission, 1977.

– 'A Content Analysis, the Canadian Broadcasting Corporation: Similarities and Differences of French and English News, Committee of Inquiry into the National Broadcasting Service: Background Research Paper.' Ottawa: Canadian Radio-television and Telecommunications Commission, 1977.

– *Information.* Various dates.

– *News Releases.* Various dates.

– *Special Report on Broadcasting in Canada, 1968–78.* Vol. 1. Ottawa: Canadian Radio-television and Telecommunications Commission, 1978.

– *Symposium on Television Violence.* Ottawa: Canadian Radio-television and Telecommunications Commission, 1976.

National Arts Centre. *Annual Report.* Various years.

National Film Board of Canada. *Annual Report.* Various years.

Ontario. Royal Commission on Book Publishing. *Canadian Publishers & Canadian Publishing.* Toronto: Queen's Printer and Publisher, 1972.

Ontario. Select Committee on Economic and Cultural Nationalism. *Interim Report of the Select Committee on Economic and Cultural Nationalism, Colleges and Universities in Ontario.* Toronto: Select Committee on Economic and Cultural Nationalism of the Legislative Assembly of Ontario, 1973.

Quebec. *A Cultural Development Policy for Quebec.* Vol. 2. *The Three Aspects of the Policy: Ways of Life, Creative Activity, Education.* Quebec: Éditeur officiel du Québec, 1978.

Telefilm Canada. *Annual Report.* Various years.

Other Sources

Abu-Laban, Yasmeen, and Christina Gabriel. *Selling Diversity: Immigration, Multiculturalism, Employment Equity, and Globalization.* Peterborough: Broadview Press, 2002.

Acheson, Keith, and Christopher Maule. 'It Seemed Like a Good Idea at the Time.' *Canadian Journal of Communication* 16 (1991): 263–6.

Ackroyd, Peter H. *Anniversary Compulsion: Canada's Centennial Celebration, a Model Mega-anniversary.* Toronto: Dundurn Press, 1992.

Anderson, Benedict. *Imagined Communities: Reflections on the Origin and Spread of Nationalism.* London: Verso, 1991.

– 'Staging Antimodernism in the Age of High Capitalist Nationalism.' In *Anti-modernism and Artistic Experience: Policing the Boundaries of Modernism,* ed. Lynda Jessup, 97–103. Toronto: University of Toronto Press, 2001.

Apostle, Alisa. 'The Display of a Tourist Nation: Canada in Government Film, 1945–1959.' *Journal of the Canadian Historical Association* 12 (2001): 177–97.

Arnott, Brian, and Sonja Tanner. 'Hard Art / Soft Art.' In *Love and Money: The Politics of Culture,* ed. David Helwig, 100–27. Ottawa: Oberon Press, 1980.

Association for the Export of Canadian Books. *Annual Report.* Ottawa. Various years.

Association of Canadian Television and Radio Artists. 'A Policy for the Seventies.' ACTRA, 1973.

Atwood, Margaret. *Survival: A Thematic Guide to Canadian Literature.* Toronto: House of Anansi, 1972.

– 'Survival Then and Now.' *Canadian Distinctiveness into the 21st Century,* ed. Chad Gaffield and Karen L. Gould, 29–46. Ottawa: University of Ottawa Press, 2003.

Audley, Paul. *Canada's Cultural Industries: Broadcasting, Publishing, Records and Film.* Toronto: J. Lorimer, in association with the Canadian Institute for Economic Policy, 1983.

– 'A Very Grave Prognosis.' *Journal of Canadian Studies* 10, no. 2 (May 1975): 3–7.

Azzi, Stephen. *Walter Gordon and the Rise of Canadian Nationalism.* Montreal: McGill-Queen's University Press, 1999.

Babe, Robert. *Canadian Television Broadcasting Structure, Performance and Regulation.* Ottawa: Economic Council of Canada, 1979.

Baldwin, Bob. 'An Analysis of U.S. Imperialism.' Paper delivered at the 32nd Congress of the Canadian Union of Students, University of Guelph, 28 August–4 September 1968.

Barney, Robert Knight. 'Whose National Pastime? Baseball in Canadian Popular Culture.' In *The Beaver Bites Back? American Popular Culture in Canada,* ed. David H. Flaherty and Frank E. Manning, 152–62. Montreal: McGill-Queen's University Press, 1993.

Baudrillard, Jean. *The Consumer Society: Myths and Structures.* London: Sage Publications, 1998.

Bélanger, Louis. 'Globalization, Culture, and Foreign Policy: The Failure of "Third Pillarization" in Canada.' *International Journal of Canadian Studies* 22 (fall 2000): 163–95.

Berger, Carl. *The Sense of Power: Studies in the Ideas of Canadian Imperialism, 1867–1914.* Toronto: University of Toronto Press, 1970.

– 'True North Strong and Free.' In *Canadian Culture: An Introductory Reader,* ed. Elspeth Cameron, 83–102. Toronto: Canadian Scholars' Press, 1997.

Berlin, Barry. *The American Trojan Horse: U.S. Television Confronts Canadian Economic and Cultural Nationalism.* New York: Greenwood Press, 1990.

Berman, Marshall. *All That Is Solid Melts into Air: The Experience of Modernity.* New York: Viking Penguin, 1988.

Berton, Pierre. *Hollywood's Canada: The Americanization of Our National Image.* Toronto: McClelland & Stewart, 1975.

Bertrand, Ina. '"National Identity" / "National History" / "National Film": The Australian Experience.' *Historical Journal of Film, Radio and Television* 4, no. 2 (1984): 179–88.

Bhabha, Homi. *The Location of Culture.* London: Routledge, 1994.

– *Nations and Narration.* New York: Routledge, 1990.

Breen, Marcus. "The End of the World as We Know It: Popular Music's Cultural Mobility." *Cultural Studies* 9, no. 3 (1995): 486–504.

Brison, Jeffery D. 'Cultural Interventions: American Corporate Philanthropy and the Construction of the Arts and Letters in Canada, 1900–1957.' PhD thesis, Queen's University, 1998.

– 'The Kingston Conference, the Carnegie Corporation and a New Deal for the Arts in Canada.' *American Review of Canadian Studies* 23 (winter 1993): 503–22.

Bullen, John. 'The Ontario Waffle and the Struggle for an Independent Socialist Canada: Conflict within the NDP.' *Canadian Historical Review* 64, no. 2. (1983): 188–215.

Cameron, Elspeth. 'Heritage Minutes: Culture and Myth.' In *Canadian Studies at Home and Abroad,* ed. James de Finney, Gregory Kealey, John Lennox, and Tamara Palmer Seiler, 13–24. Montreal: Association for Canadian Studies, 1995.

Cameron, Ross. '"Our Ideal of an Artist": Tom Thomson, the Ideal of Manhood and the Creation of a National Icon (1917–1947).' MA thesis, Queen's University, 1998.

– 'Tom Thomson, Antimodernism, and the Ideal of Manhood.' *Journal of the Canadian Historical Association* 10 (1999): 185–208.

Campbell, Sandra. 'From Romantic History to Communications Theory: Lorne Pierce as Publisher of C.W. Jefferys and Harold Innis.' *Journal of Canadian Studies* 30, no. 3 (fall 1995): 91–116.

Canadian Broadcasting Corporation. *Annual Report.* Various years.

– *Broadcasting in Canada, History and Development of the National System.* Toronto: CBC, 1962.

– *Submission to the Royal Commission on Development in the Arts, Letters and Sciences.* [Ottawa]: Canadian Broadcasting Corporation, 1949.

Canadian Conference of the Arts. *A Strategy for Culture.* Ottawa: Canadian Conference of the Arts, 1980.

Canadian Institute of Public Opinion. *Gallup Report.* 14 October 1970.

Canadian Sociology and Anthropology Association. *Annual Report.* Various years.

Carr, Graham. '"All We North Americans": Literary Culture and the Continentalist Ideal, 1919–1939.' *American Review of Canadian Studies* 17, no. 2 (1987): 145–57.

– 'Design as Content: Foreign Influences and the Identity of English-Canadian Intellectual Magazines, 1919–1939.' *American Review of Canadian Studies* 18, no. 2 (1988): 181–93.

– 'Imperialism and Nationalism in Revisionist Historiography: A Critique of Elspeth Cameron, "Heritage Minutes: Culture and Myth."' In *Canadian Studies at Home and Abroad,* ed. James de Finney, Gregory Kealey, John Lennox, and Tamara Palmer Seiler, 91–9. Montreal: Association for Canadian Studies, 1995.

– 'Trade Liberalization and the Political Economy of Culture: An International Perspective on FTA.' *Canadian-American Public Policy,* no. 6 (June 1991).

Charland, Maurice. 'Technological Nationalism.' *Canadian Journal of Political and Social Theory* 10, no. 1–2 (1986): 196–220.

Chatterjee, Partha. *The Nation and Its Fragments: Colonial and Postcolonial Histories.* Princeton: Princeton University Press, 1993.

Christian, William. *George Grant: A Biography.* Toronto: University of Toronto Press, 1993.

Collins, Richard. *Culture, Communication, and National Identity: The Case of Canadian Television.* Toronto: University of Toronto Press, 1990.

Commission on Canadian Studies. *To Know Ourselves: The Report of the Commission on Canadian Studies.* 3 vols. in 2. Vols. 1–2 by T.H.B. Symons; vol. 3, titled *Some Questions of Balance: Human Resources, Higher Education and Canadian Studies,* by T.H.B. Symons and James E. Page. Ottawa: Association of Canadian Universities and Colleges, 1975–84.

Committee for an Independent Canada. (Tom Hendry). 'Theatre in Canada: A Reluctant Citizen.' Policy paper prepared for the Edmonton Policy Conference, September 1972.

– (Gary Lax). 'Cable Television and the Canadian Broadcasting System.' Policy paper prepared for the Edmonton Policy Conference, September 1972.

– (Charles Pachter). 'The Visual Arts in Canada, Needed: Change from Within.' Policy paper prepared for the Edmonton Policy Conference, September 1972.

– (Robert Page). 'Faculty Citizenship in Canadian Universities and Colleges.' Policy paper prepared for the Edmonton Policy Conference, September 1972.

– (Research and Policy Staff). 'Book Publishing in Canada: Independence and Identity.' Policy paper prepared for the Edmonton Policy Conference, September 1972.

Connors, Tom. *Stompin' Tom and the Connors Tone.* Toronto: Viking, 2000.

– *Stompin' Tom before the Fame.* Toronto: Viking, 1995.

Cook, Ramsay. *Canada and the French-Canadian Question.* Toronto: Macmillan, 1966.

– *Canada, Quebec, and the Uses of Nationalism.* Toronto: McClelland & Stewart, 1986.

– *French-Canadian Nationalism: An Anthology.* Toronto: Macmillan, 1969.

– *The Maple Leaf Forever: Essays on Nationalism and Politics in Canada.* Toronto: Macmillan, 1971.

– 'Nationalism in Canada or *Portnoy's Complaint* Revisited.' *South Atlantic Quarterly* 59 (1970): 1–19.

Cormier, Jeffrey. *The Canadianization Movement: Emergence, Survival, and Success.* Toronto: University of Toronto Press, 2004.

Crean, Susan M. *Who's Afraid of Canadian Culture?* Don Mills, ON: General, 1976.

Cupido, Robert. 'The Medium, the Message and the Modern: The Jubilee Broadcast of 1927.' *International Journal of Canadian Studies* 26 (fall 2002): 101–23.

– 'Sixty Years of Canadian Progress: The Diamond Jubilee and the Politics of Commemoration.' In *Canadian Identity: Region, Country, Nation,* ed. Caroline Andrew, Will Straw, and J.-Yvon Thériault, 19–33. Montreal: Association for Canadian Studies, 1988.

Davis, Ann. 'A Study in Modernism: The Group of Seven as an Unexpectedly Typical Case.' *Journal of Canadian Studies* 33, no. 1 (spring 1998): 108–20.

Dickinson, Margaret, and Sarah Street. *Cinema and State: The Film Industry and the Government, 1927–84.* London: British Film Institute, 1985.

Doern, G. Bruce. *Faith and Fear: The Free Trade Story.* Toronto: Stoddart, 1992.

Edwardson, Ryan. 'A Canadian Modernism: The Pre-Group of Seven "Algonquin School," 1912–1917.' *British Journal of Canadian Studies* 17, no. 1. (2004): 81–92.

– '"Kicking Uncle Sam Out of the Peaceable Kingdom": English-Canadian "New Nationalism" and Americanization.' *Journal of Canadian Studies* 37, no. 4 (winter 2002/3): 131–50.

– 'The Many Lives of Captain Canuck: Nationalism, Culture, and the Creation of a Canadian Comic Book Superhero.' *Journal of Popular Culture* 37, no. 2 (November 2003): 184–201.

– '"Narrating a Canadian Identity": Arthur R.M. Lower's *Colony to Nation* and the Nationalization of History.' *International Journal of Canadian Studies* 23 (fall 2002): 59–75.

– '"Of War Machines and Ghetto Scenes": English-Canadian Nationalism and The Guess Who's "American Woman."' *American Review of Canadian Studies* 33 (autumn 2003): 339–56.

– 'Other Canadian Voices: The Development of Ethnic Broadcasting in
   Canada.' In *Racism, Eh? A Critical Inter-Disciplinary Anthology of Race and Racism
   in Canada*, ed. Camille A. Nelson and Charmaine A. Nelson, 316–25.
   Concord, ON.: Captus Press, 2004.

Evans, Gary. *In the National Interest: A Chronicle of the National Film Board of Canada
   from 1949 to 1989*. Toronto: University of Toronto Press, 1991.

Fairbairn, Barbara. 'Implications of Free Trade for Television Broadcasting in
   Canada.' In *Practising the Arts in Canada*, ed. Fernand Harvey, Norman A. Best,
   and Joy Cohnstaedt, 73–82. Montreal: Association for Canadian Studies, 1990.

Faulkner, James Hugh. 'On Publishing Policy.' *Journal of Canadian Studies* 10,
   no. 2 (May 1975): 32–42.

Finkel, Alvin. *Our Lives: Canada after 1945*. Toronto: J. Lorimer, 1997.

Finlay, Karen A. *The Force of Culture: Vincent Massey and Canadian Sovereignty*.
   Toronto: University of Toronto Press, 2004.

Foster, Frank. *Broadcasting Policy Development*. Ottawa: Franfost Communications,
   1982.

Francis, Daniel. *National Dreams: Myth, Memory, and Canadian History*. Vancouver:
   Arsenal Pulp Press, 1997.

Frith, Simon. 'Towards an Aesthetic of Popular Music.' In *Music and Society: The
   Politics of Composition, Performance and Reception*, ed. Richard Leppert and
   Susan McClary, 133–49. Cambridge: Cambridge University Press, 1987.

Fulford, Robert, David Godfrey, and Abraham Rotstein, eds. *Read Canadian: A
   Book about Canadian Books*. Toronto: James Lewis and Samuel, 1972.

Gellner, Ernest. *Thought and Change*. London: Weidenfeld and Nicolson, 1964.

Gibson, Graeme. 'Waiting for Blondin.' *Journal of Canadian Studies* 10, no. 2
   (May 1975): 30–2.

Gittins, Susan. *CTV: The Television Wars*. Toronto: Stoddart, 1999.

Godfrey, Dave. *Gordon to Watkins to You: The Battle for Control of Our Economy*.
   Toronto: New Press, 1970.

Gordon, Walter. *A Choice for Canada*. Toronto: McClelland & Stewart, 1966.

– *Storm Signals: New Economic Policies for Canada*. Toronto: McClelland & Stewart,
   1975.

Gorman, Paul R. *Left Intellectuals and Popular Culture in Twentieth-Century America*.
   Chapel Hill: University of North Carolina Press, 1996.

Gramsci, Antonio. *Prison Notebooks*. New York: Columbia University Press, 1991.

Granatstein, J.L. *Canada, 1957–1967: The Years of Uncertainty and Innovation*.
   Toronto: McClelland & Stewart, 1986.

– *Yankee Go Home? Canadians and Anti-Americanism*. Toronto: HarperCollins,
   1996.

Grant, George. *Lament for a Nation*. Toronto: McClelland & Stewart, 1970 [1965].

– *Technology and Empire: Perspectives on North America*. Toronto: House of Anansi, 1969.

Grant, Peter Stuart (P.S.). 'The Regulation of Program Content in Canadian Television: An Introduction.' *Canadian Public Administration* 11 (1968): 322–60.

Grazia, Victoria de. 'Mass Culture and Sovereignty: The American Challenge to European Cinemas, 1920–1960.' *Journal of Modern History* 61 (March 1989): 53–87.

Green, Christina F. 'The Great Cultural Divide: Split-Run Magazines in the 1990s.' MA thesis, Queen's University, 1999.

Grossberg, Lawrence. 'Identity and Cultural Studies: Is That All There Is?' In *Questions of Cultural Identity*, ed. Stuart Hall, 87–107. London: Sage, 1996.

Hall, Ron. *The CHUM Chart Book, 1957–1983: A Complete Listing of Every Charted Record*. Toronto: Stardust Production, 1984.

Hardin, Herschel. *Closed Circuits: The Sellout of Canadian Television*. Vancouver: Douglas & McIntyre, 1985.

– 'Pushing Public Broadcasting Forward: Advances and Evasions.' In *Communication Canada: Issues in Broadcasting and New Technologies*, ed. Rowland Lorimer and D. Wilson, 214–31. Toronto: Kagan and Woo, 1988.

Hart, Michael. *Decision at Midnight: Inside the Canada–US Free Trade Negotiations*. Vancouver: UBC Press, 1994.

Harvey, Jean, and Roger Proulx. 'Sport and the State in Canada.' In *Not Just a Game: Essays in Canadian Sport Sociology*, ed. Jean Harvey and Hart Cantelon, 93–119. Ottawa: University of Ottawa Press, 1988.

Helwig, David, ed. *Love and Money: The Politics of Culture*. Ottawa: Oberon Press, 1980.

High, Steven. '"I'll Wrap the F*#@ Canadian Flag around Me": A Nationalist Response to Plant Shutdowns, 1969–1984.' *Journal of the Canadian Historical Association* 12 (2001): 199–225.

Hill, Charles. *The Group of Seven: Art for a Nation*. Toronto: McClelland & Stewart, 1995.

Hobsbawm, Eric. *The Invention of Tradition*. Cambridge: Cambridge University Press, 1983.

– *Nations and Nationalism since 1780: Programme, Myth, Reality*. Cambridge: Cambridge University Press, 1990.

Housser, F.B. *A Canadian Art Movement: The Story of the Group of Seven*. Toronto: Macmillan, 1974.

Hurtig, Mel. 'On Publishing and Perishing.' *Journal of Canadian Studies* 10, no. 2 (May 1975): 20–4.

Hutcheson, John. 'Culture and Free Trade.' In *The Future on the Table: Canada and the Free Trade Issue*, ed. Michael D. Henderson, 101–19. North York, ON: Masterpress, 1987.

Innis, Harold. *Bias of Communication*. Toronto: University of Toronto Press, 1951.
– *Empire and Communication*. Oxford: Clarendon Press, 1950.
– *The Strategy of Culture*. Toronto: University of Toronto Press, 1952.
James, C. Rodney. *Film as a National Art: NFB of Canada and the Film Board Idea*. New York: Arno Press, 1977.
Jeffrey, Liss. 'Private Television and Cable.' In *The Cultural Industries in Canada*, ed. Michael Dorland, 203–56. Toronto: J. Lorimer & Co., 1996.
Jennings, Nicholas. *Before the Gold Rush: Flashbacks to the Dawn of the Canadian Sound*. Toronto: Penguin Books, 1998.
Jessup, Lynda. 'The Group of Seven and the Tourist Landscape in Western Canada, or The More Things Change … ' *Journal of Canadian Studies* 37, no. 1 (spring 2002): 144–79.
– 'Prospectors, Bushwhackers, Painters: Antimodernism and the Group of Seven.' *International Journal of Canadian Studies* 17 (spring 1998): 193–214.
Jhally, Sut. *The Codes of Advertising: Fetishism and the Political Economy of Meaning in the Consumer Society*. New York: St. Martin's Press, 1987.
Johnston, Denis William. *Up the Mainstream: The Rise of Toronto's Alternative Theatres*. Toronto: University of Toronto Press, 1991.
Johnston, Russell. 'The Emergence of Broadcast Advertising in Canada, 1919–1932.' *Historical Journal of Film, Radio and Television* 17, no. 1 (1997): 29–47.
– *Selling Themselves: The Emergence of Canadian Advertising*. Toronto: University of Toronto Press, 2001.
Kedourie, Elie. *Nationalism*. New York: Praeger, 1960.
Kilbourn, William. *Canada: A Guide to the Peaceable Kingdom*. Toronto: Macmillan, 1970.
King, Allan. '"The Coffee-Boy Syndrome" and Other Observations on the State of the Canadian Film Industry.' *Journal of Canadian Studies* 16, no. 1 (spring 1981): 82–9.
Knelman, Martin. *A Stratford Tempest*. Toronto: McClelland & Stewart, 1982.
– *This Is Where We Came In: The Career and Character of Canadian Film*. Toronto: McClelland & Stewart, 1977.
Knowles, Richard Paul. 'The Stratford Festival, Free Trade, and the Discourses of Intercultural Tourism.' *Theatre Journal* 47 (1995): 19–41.
Kokotailo, Philip. 'Creating *The Peaceable Kingdom*: Edward Hicks, Northrop Frye, and Joe Clark.' In *Creating the Peaceable Kingdom and Other Essays on Canada*, ed. Victor Howard, 3–11. East Lansing: Michigan State University Press, 1998.
Korinek, Valerie J. *Roughing It in the Suburbs: Reading Chatelaine Magazine in the Fifties and Sixties*. Toronto: University of Toronto Press, 2000.
Kostash, Myrna. *Long Way from Home: The Story of the Sixties Generation in Canada*. Toronto: J. Lorimer & Co., 1980.

Kristmanson, Mark. *Plateaus of Freedom: Nationality, Culture and State Security in Canada, 1940–1960.* Don Mills, ON: Oxford University Press, 2003.

Kuffert, L.B. *A Great Duty: Canadian Responses to Modern Life and Mass Culture in Canada, 1939–1967.* Montreal: McGill-Queen's University Press, 2003.

LaMarsh, Judy. *Memoirs of a Bird in a Gilded Cage.* Toronto: McClelland & Stewart, 1970.

Lazarevich, Gordana. 'Aspects of Early Arts Patronage in Canada: From Rockefeller to Massey.' In *Taking a Stand: Essays in Honour of John Beckwith,* ed. Timothy J. McGee, 259–72. Toronto: University of Toronto Press, 1995.

Lears, T.J. Jackson. *No Place of Grace: Antimodernism and the Transformation of American Culture, 1880–1920.* Chicago: University of Chicago Press, 1994.

Lecker, Robert. *Making It Real: The Canonization of English-Canadian Literature.* Don Mills, ON: House of Anansi, 1995.

– 'The New Canadian Library: A Classic Deal.' *American Review of Canadian Studies* 24 (1994): 197–216.

Lee, Martyn J. *Consumer Culture Reborn: The Cultural Politics of Consumption.* New York: Routledge, 1993.

Lévesque, René. *An Option for Quebec.* Toronto: McClelland & Stewart, 1968.

Levine, Michael A. 'I Never Heard Them Call It "Show-Art": The Business Side of Film Production in Canada.' *Journal of Canadian Studies* 16, no. 1. (spring 1981): 90–7.

Levitt, Kari. *Silent Surrender: The Multinational Corporation in Canada.* Toronto: Macmillan of Canada, 1970.

Lewis, David, and F.R. Scott. *Make This Your Canada: A Review of C.C.F. History and Policy.* Toronto: Central Canada Publishing Co., 1943.

Litt, Paul. 'The Massey Commission as Intellectual History: Matthew Arnold Meets Jack Kent Cooke.' In *Practising the Arts in Canada,* ed. Fernand Harvey, Norman A. Best, and Joy Cohnstaedt, 23–34. Montreal: Association for Canadian Studies, 1990.

– *The Muses, the Masses, and the Massey Commission.* Toronto: University of Toronto Press, 1992.

Litvak, Keith, and Christopher Maule. *Cultural Sovereignty: The Time and Reader's Digest Case in Canada.* New York: Praeger, 1974.

Lorimer, Rowland. 'Book Publishing.' In *The Cultural Industries in Canada: Problems, Policies and Prospects,* ed. Michael Dorland, 3–34. Toronto: J. Lorimer & Co., 1996.

– 'Book Publishing in English Canada in the Context of Free Trade.' *Canadian Journal of Communication* 16, no. 1 (1991): 58–72.

Lower, Arthur R.M. *Colony to Nation: A History of Canada.* Toronto: Longmans, 1946.

Lyttle, Brendan J. *A Chartology of Canadian Popular Music, January 1965 to Decem-ber 1976.* Toronto: RPM Music Publications, 1978.

Macklem, Michael. 'Seed Money.' In *Love and Money: The Politics of Culture,* ed. David Helwig, 32–43. Ottawa: Oberon Press, 1980.

Magder, Ted. *Canada's Hollywood: The Canadian State and Feature Films.* Toronto: University of Toronto Press, 1993.

– 'Film and Video Production.' In *The Cultural Industries in Canada,* ed. Michael Dorland, 145–77. Toronto: J. Lormier & Co., 1996.

Massey, Vincent. *On Being Canadian.* Toronto: J.M. Dent & Sons, 1948.

Massolin, Philip. *Canadian Intellectuals, the Tory Tradition, and the Challenge of Modernity, 1939–1970.* Toronto: University of Toronto Press, 2001.

Mathews, Robin. 'Centennial Song.' In *The New Romans: Candid Canadian Opin-ions of the U.S..,* ed. Al Purdy, 74. Edmonton: M.G. Hurtig, 1968.

– *Treason of the Intellectuals: English Canada in the Post-Modern Period.* Prescott, ON: Voyageur Publishing, 1995.

Mathews, Robin, and James Steele, *The Struggle for Canadian Universities.* Toronto: New Press, 1969.

– 'The Universities: Takeover of the Mind.' In *Close the 49th Parallel, Etc: The Americanization of Canada,* ed. Ian Lumsden, 169–78. Toronto: University of Toronto Press, 1970.

Maule, Christopher. 'Overview of Culture and Trade.' *Canadian Foreign Policy* 9, no. 2 (winter 2002): 1–14.

McBride, Stephen. *Paradigm Shift: Globalization and the Canadian State.* Halifax: Fernwood Publishing, 2001.

McGinnis, Janice Dickin. 'Heritage Minutes: Myth and History.' In *Canadian Studies at Home and Abroad,* ed. James de Finney, Gregory Kealey, John Len-nox, and Tamara Palmer Seiler, 25–36. Montreal: Association for Canadian Studies, 1995.

McKay, Ian. 'Historians, Anthropology, and the Concept of Culture.' *Labour/Le Travailleur* 8/9 (autumn/September 1981/2): 185–241.

– 'The Liberal Order Framework: A Prospectus for a Reconnaissance of Cana-dian History.' *Canadian Historical Review* 81, no. 4 (2000): 616–25.

– *The Quest of the Folk: Antimodernism and Cultural Selection in Twentieth-Century Nova Scotia.* Montreal: McGill-Queen's University Press, 1994.

Meisel, John. 'Escaping Extinction: Cultural Defence of an Undefended Bor-der.' *Canadian Journal of Political and Social Theory* 10, no. 1–2 (1986): 260.

'Fanning the Air: The Canadian State and Broadcasting.' *Transactions of the Royal Society of Canada,* ser. 5, vol. 4 (1989): 191–204.

Metcalf, John. *What Is a Canadian Literature?* Guelph, ON: Red Kite Press, 1988.

Miller, Robert. 'The Canadian Film Development Corporation: Promoting the Feature Film Industry in Canada.' PhD thesis, University of Southern California, 1980.

Milligan, Frank. 'The Ambiguities of the Canada Council.' In *Love and Money: The Politics of Culture*, ed. David Helwig, 60–89. Ottawa: Oberon Press, 1980.

Morris, Peter. 'After Grierson: The National Film Board 1945–1953.' *Journal of Canadian Studies* 16, no. 1 (spring 1981): 3–12.

– *Embattled Shadows: A History of Canadian Cinema 1895–1939*. Montreal: McGill-Queen's Press, 1978.

– ed. *Canadian Feature Films 1913–1969*. Vol. 2. *1941–1969*. Ottawa: Canadian Film Institute, 1976.

Mowat, Farley. 'Letter to My Son.' In *The New Romans: Candid Canadian Opinions of the U.S.*, ed. Al Purdy, 1–6. Edmonton: M.G. Hurtig, 1968.

– *My Discovery of America*. Toronto: McClelland & Stewart, 1986.

Nash, Knowlton. *Cue the Elephant! Backstage Tales at the CBC*. Toronto: McClelland & Stewart, 1996.

– *The Microphone Wars: A History of Triumph and Betrayal at the CBC*. Toronto: McClelland & Stewart, 1994.

– *Swashbucklers: The Story of Canada's Battling Broadcasters*. Toronto: McClelland & Stewart, 2001.

Nelson, Joyce. *The Colonized Eye: Rethinking the Grierson Legend*. Toronto: Between the Lines, 1988.

Nolan, Michael. *CTV: The Network That Means Business*. Edmonton: University of Alberta Press, 2001.

Ostry, Bernard. *Cultural Connection: An Essay on Culture and Government Policy in Canada*. Toronto: McClelland & Stewart, 1978.

Owram, Doug. *Born at the Right Time: A History of the Baby-Boom Generation*. Toronto: University of Toronto Press, 1996.

Pallister, Janis L. *The Cinema of Quebec: Masters in Their Own House*. London: Associated University Presses, 1995.

Peers, Frank. 'The Nationalist Dilemma in Canadian Broadcasting.' In *Nationalism in Canada*, ed. Peter Russell, 252–67. Toronto: McGraw-Hill Ryerson, 1966.

– *The Politics of Canadian Broadcasting, 1920–1951*. Toronto: University of Toronto Press, 1969.

Pells, Richard. *Not Like Us: How Europeans Have Loved, Hated, and Transformed American Culture since World War II*. New York: Basic Books, 1997.

Pendakur, Manjunath. *Canadian Dreams and American Control: The Political Economy of the Canadian Film Industry*. Toronto: Garamond Press, 1991.

Peterman, Michael A., and Janet B. Friskney. '"Booming" the Canuck Book: Edward Caswell and the Promotion of Canadian Writing.' *Journal of Canadian Studies* 30, no. 3 (fall 1995): 60–90.

Pettigrew, John, and Jamie Portman. *Stratford: The First Thirty Years*. Vol. 2. *1968– 1982*. Toronto: Macmillan of Canada, 1985.

Pevere, Geoff, and Grieg Dymond. *Mondo Canuck: A Canadian Pop Culture Odyssey*. Scarborough, ON: Prentice-Hall, 1996.

Potter, Greg. *Hand Me Down World: The Canadian Pop-Rock Paradox*. Toronto: Macmillan, 1999.

Raboy, Marc. *Missed Opportunities: The Story of Canada's Broadcasting Policy*. Montreal: McGill-Queen's University Press, 1990.

– *Movement and Messages: Media and Radical Politics in Quebec*. Toronto: Between the Lines, 1984.

Repo, Marjaleena. *Who Needs the PhD? A Case Study of 190 PhD-Level Job Seekers at University of Toronto*. Toronto: Graduate Students' Union, University of Toronto, 1970.

Resnick, Philip. *Land of Cain: Class and Nationalism in English Canada, 1945– 1975*. Vancouver: New Star Books, 1977.

– *Thinking English Canada*. Toronto: Stoddart, 1994.

Richler, Mordecai. *Barney's Version*. Toronto: Alfred A. Knopf Canada, 1997.

Ritchie, Gordon. *Wrestling with the Elephant: The Inside Story of the Canada–US Trade Wars*. Toronto: Macfarlane Walter & Ross, 1997.

Rodger, Andrew. 'Some Factors Contributing to the Formation of the National Film Board of Canada.' *Historical Journal of Film, Radio, and Television* 9, no. 3 (1989): 259–68.

Rotstein, Abraham. 'Is There an English-Canadian Nationalism?' In *The Walter L. Gordon Lecture Series, 1977–78*, vol. 2: 7–22. Toronto: Omnigraphics, 1978.

Rotstein, Abraham, and Gary Lax. *Getting It Back: A Program for Canadian Independence*. Toronto: Clarke, Irwin, 1974.

Rubin, Don. *Creeping toward a Culture: The Theatre in English Canada since 1945*. Guelph, ON: Alive Press, 1974.

Rutherford, Paul. *The Making of the Canadian Media*. Toronto: McGraw-Hill Ryerson, 1978.

– *The New Icons? The Art of Television Advertising*. Toronto: University of Toronto Press, 1994.

– *When Television Was Young: Primetime Canada, 1952–1967*. Toronto: University of Toronto Press, 1990.

Schou, Soren. 'The Charisma of the Liberators: The Americanization of Postwar Denmark.' In *Small Nations, Big Neighbour: Denmark and Quebec/Canada*

Compare Notes on American Popular Culture, ed. Roger de la Garde, William Gilsdorf, and Ilja Wechselmann, 65–79. London: John Libbey & Co., 1993.

Schroder, Kim Christian. 'Can Denmark Be Canadianized? On the Cultural Role of American TV-Serials in Denmark.' In *Small Nations, Big Neighbour: Denmark and Quebec/Canada Compare Notes on American Popular Culture*, ed. Roger de la Garde, William Gilsdorf, and Ilja Wechselmann, 123–32. London: John Libbey & Co., 1993.

Simons, Roger. *Gramsci's Political Thought: An Introduction.* London: Lawrence & Wishart, 1991.

Sirluck, Ernest. 'An Opportunity to Achieve Emergent-Nation Status in Higher Education.' *Varsity Graduate* 11, no. 3 (1966): 15.

Smith, Anthony D. *The Ethnic Origins of Nations.* New York: B. Blackwell, 1986.

– *Nationalism and Modernism: A Critical Survey of Recent Theories of Nations and Nationalism.* London, New York: Routledge, 1998.

Stamps, Judith. *Unthinking Modernity: Innis, McLuhan, and the Frankfurt School.* Montreal: McGill-Queen's University Press, 1995.

Stebbins, Robert A. 'Ambivalence at the Fifty-five-Yard Line: Transformation and Resistance in Canadian Football.' In *The Beaver Bites Back? American Popular Culture in Canada*, ed. David H. Flaherty and Frank E. Manning, 163–74. Montreal: McGill-Queen's University Press, 1993.

Stewart, Andrew, and William H.N. Hull. *Canadian Television Policy and the Board of Broadcast Governors, 1958–1968.* Edmonton: University of Alberta Press, 1994.

Stewart, Sandy. *From Coast to Coast: A Personal History of Radio in Canada.* Toronto: CBC Enterprises, 1985.

Storey, John. '"Rockin" Hegemony: West Coast Rock and Amerika's War in Vietnam.' In *Tell Me Lies about Vietnam: Cultural Battles for the Meaning of the War*, ed. Alf Louvre and Jeffrey Walsh, 225–35. Philadelphia: Open University Press, 1998.

Strange, Carolyn, and Tina Loo. *True North, True Crime: The Golden Age of Canadian Pulp Magazines.* Vancouver: Raincoast Books, 2004.

Straw, Will. 'Dilemmas of Definition.' In *Slippery Pastimes: Reading the Popular in Canadian Culture*, ed. Joan Nicks and Jeanette Sloniowski, 95–108. Waterloo, ON: Wilfrid Laurier University Press, 1992.

Sutherland, Fraser. *The Monthly Epic: A History of Canadian Magazines, 1789–1989.* Markham, ON: Fitzhenry & Whiteside, 1989.

Tate, Marsha A., and Valerie Allen. 'Integrating Distinctively Canadian Elements into Television Drama: The *Due South* Experience.' *Canadian Journal of Communication* 28, no. 1 (2003): 67–83.

Taylor, Charles. *Radical Tories: The Conservative Tradition in Canada.* Toronto: House of Anansi, 1982.

Testa, Bart, and Jim Shedden. 'In the Great Midwestern Hardware Store: The Seventies Triumph in English-Canadian Rock Music.' In *Slippery Pastimes: Reading the Popular in Canadian Culture,* ed. Joan Nicks and Jeannette Sloniowski, 177–216. Waterloo, ON: Wilfrid Laurier University Press, 2002.

Thompson, John Herd. 'Canada's Quest for "Cultural Sovereignty": Protection, Promotion, and Popular Culture.' In *Seeing Ourselves: Media Power and Policy in Canada,* ed. Helen Holmes and David Taras, 188–98. Toronto: Harcourt Brace Jovanovich, 1992.

Thompson, John Herd, and Stephen J. Randall. *Canada and the United States: Ambivalent Allies.* Montreal: McGill-Queen's University Press, 1994.

Tippett, Maria. *Making Culture: English-Canadian Institutions and the Arts before the Massey Commission.* Toronto: University of Toronto Press, 1990.

Trudeau, Pierre Elliott. *Federalism and the French Canadians.* Toronto: Macmillan of Canada, 1968.

Ulff-Møller, Jens. 'The Origins of the French Film Quota Policy Controlling the Import of American Films.' *Historical Journal of Film, Radio and Television* 18, no. 2 (1998): 167–82.

Usmiani, Renate. *Second Stage: The Alternative Theatre Movement in Canada.* Vancouver: University of British Columbia Press, 1983.

Versuh, Ron. *Underground Times: Canada's Flower-Child Revolutionaries.* Toronto: Deneau, 1989.

Vickers, Jill. 'Liberating Theory in Canadian Studies.' In *Canada: Theoretical Discourse,* ed. Terry Goldie, Carmen Lambert, and Rowland Lorimer, 351–71. Montreal: Association for Canadian Studies, 1994.

Vipond, Mary. 'Best Sellers in English Canada, 1899–1918: An Overview.' *Journal of Canadian Fiction* 24 (1979): 96–119.

– 'Canadian Nationalism and the Plight of Canadian Magazines in the 1920s.' *Canadian Historical Review* 58, no 1. (1977): 43–63.

– *Listening In: The First Decade of Canadian Broadcasting, 1922–1932.* Montreal: McGill-Queen's University Press, 1992.

– *The Mass Media in Canada.* Toronto: James Lorimer & Co., 1989.

– 'The Nationalist Network: English Canada's Intellectuals and Artists in the 1920s.' *Canadian Review of Studies in Nationalism* 7 (spring 1980): 32–52.

Walden, Keith. *Becoming Modern in Toronto: The Industrial Exhibition and the Shaping of a Late Victorian Culture.* Toronto: University of Toronto Press, 1997.

Wallace, W. Stewart. *The Growth of Canadian National Feeling.* Toronto: Macmillan, 1927.

Walz, Eugene P. *Canada's Best Features: Critical Essays on 15 Canadian Films*. New York: Rodopi, 2002.

Williams, Raymond. *Culture and Society 1780–1950*. New York: Columbia University Press, 1983 [1958].

– *Keywords*. Glasgow: William Collins Sons, 1976.

Wolf-Devine, Celia. *Diversity and Community in the Academy: Affirmative Action in Faculty Appointments*. Lanham, MD: Rowman & Littlefield, 1997.

Wolfe, Morris. *Jolts: The TV Wasteland and the Canadian Oasis*. Toronto: J. Lorimer, 1985.

Woodcock, George. *Strange Bedfellows: The State and the Arts in Canada*. Vancouver: Douglas and McIntyre, 1985.

Wright, Robert A. '"Dream, Comfort, Memory, Despair": Canadian Popular Musicians and the Dilemma of Nationalism, 1968–1972.' *Journal of Canadian Studies* 22 (winter 1987–8): 27–43.

– *Hip and Trivial: Youth Culture, Book Publishing, and the Greying of Canadian Nationalism*. Toronto: Canadian Scholars' Press, 2001.

– *Virtual Sovereignty: Nationalism, Culture and the Canadian Question*. Toronto: Canadian Scholars' Press, 2004.

Year Book of the Canadian Motion Picture Industry. Toronto: Film Publications of Canada. Various years.

Yorke, Ritchie. *Axes, Chops and Hot Licks: The Canadian Rock Music Scene*. Edmonton: M.G. Hurtig, 1971.

Young, David. 'The Macmillan Company of Canada in the 1930s.' *Journal of Canadian Studies* 30, no. 3 (fall 1995): 117–33.

Index